COMPLETE
MICROWAVE
COOKERY

COMPLETE
MICROWAVE
COOKERY

COMPILED BY
CAROL BOWEN

OCTOPUS BOOKS

4

LEMON MERINGUE PIE (p.251)

Contents

A Ridgmount book

This edition first published 1985 by
Octopus Books Ltd
59 Grosvenor Street
London W1

Reprinted 1987

© Ridgmount Books Ltd 1985

ISBN 0 7064 2552 9

Printed in Portugal by
Oficinas Gráficas ASA

Microwave Know-how

WHAT IS MICROWAVE ENERGY?

Microwave energy is a type of high frequency radio wave positioned at the top end of the radio band. The electromagnetic waves are of very short length and high frequency – hence the name 'microwaves'.

Inside the microwave oven is the magnetron vacuum tube – the so-called 'heart' of the cooker. This converts ordinary household electrical energy into high-frequency microwaves. These are passed, via a wave guide, into the stirrer fan, which distributes the microwaves evenly in the oven.

Once produced and inside the oven the microwaves can then do three things:

- They can pass through a substance without changing it. Glass, pottery, china and most plastics are substances that allow microwaves to pass through them and therefore make ideal cooking utensils.
- They can be reflected from a surface. Metals reflect microwaves, which is why they are safely contained within the metal cavity of the oven, and why cooking utensils must be non-metallic.
- They can be absorbed by a substance. Microwaves are absorbed by the moisture molecules in food, causing them to vibrate rapidly, producing heat to cook the food. The rate at which these molecules vibrate is many thousands of times per second; this accounts for the very fast speed of microwave cooking.

THE MICROWAVE OVEN

All ovens consist of a basic unit comprising a door, a magnetron, wave guide, wave stirrer, power supply, power cord and controls. Some have additional features, but the basics upon which they work remain the same.

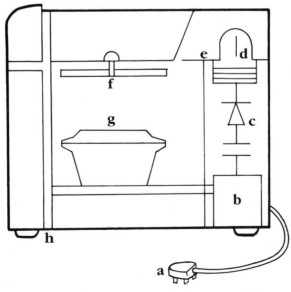

Cross-section diagram of a microwave oven

The plug (a) is inserted into the socket and the electricity flows to the power transformer (b) which increases the ordinary household voltage. This passes into a high-voltage rectifier and capacitor (c) which changes the high alternating voltage to indirectional voltage. The indirectional voltage is applied to the magnetron (d) which converts the electrical energy into electromagnetic or microwave energy.

This energy is then passed through to the wave guide (e) which directs the microwave energy into the oven cavity. As the microwaves enter the oven the wave stirrer (f) turns slowly to distribute the microwaves in an even pattern around the oven.

The oven cavity (g), made of metal, contains the microwaves safely and deflects the waves from the walls and base of the oven to be absorbed by the food.

The oven door and the door frame (h) are fitted with special seals to ensure that the microwaves are kept safely within the oven. Usually at least one cut-out device is incorporated so that the microwave energy is automatically switched off when the door is open.

TYPES OF MICROWAVE OVEN

Portable

Most microwave ovens currently available are portable. All they require is a 13- or 15-amp power supply and a stable surface upon which to sit. Most are light enough to be moved from room to room, especially if placed on a trolley. The microwave oven is therefore very useful for a family on the move, since, provided the power supply is correct, it may be used on the patio, or in the garden, caravan or holiday chalet.

Double oven

Several microwave ovens are available incorporated into the conventional oven set-up. In most cases, the microwave acts as the second oven but is still separate from the conventional oven.

Combination cookers

These are the very latest and most luxurious of microwave ovens, allowing food to be cooked conventionally, by microwave or by a combination of both methods in one oven. Some models also have the facility to cook by microwave and grill, by microwave and fan-assisted cooking and by microwave and conventional methods in tandem. Such ovens combine and effectively use the efficiency and speed of the microwave with the benefits of conventional cooking.

Most models of portable, double oven and combination microwave ovens are electric but a gas model has recently become available combining gas conventional cooking and electric microwave cooking. This gas model is not portable.

FEATURES OF MICROWAVE OVENS

The features and controls on modern microwave ovens are numerous and, with increasing sophistication, becoming more tailored to individual needs.

The very simplest controls on a microwave oven are likely to be a timer and a 'cook' button or switch. To operate them, you simply put the food in the oven, close the door, set the timer for the cooking time required and start the microwave energy by depressing the 'cook' control. The microwave will cook with microwave energy until the timer moves to the 'off' position when it will automatically stop the microwave energy.

Exactly the same would happen if the door were opened during the cooking period. Restarting can take place only when the door is closed and the 'cook' button depressed again.

Timer Control: Most microwave ovens have at least one timer, which generally is for up to 30 minutes. Graduations of a second are usually incorporated at the lower end of the scale for short cooking times where timing is very critical, whereas half-minute – and sometimes minute – graduations are given at the higher end of the scale. Often the control is in the form of a sliding device, rather than a dial, and care should be taken to set the timer accurately.

Cook Control: This is sometimes called the start control since it simply switches on the microwave power whether you are thawing, reheating or prime cooking.

On/Off Control: As well as beginning the cooking operation, in many types of microwave oven the on/off control also switches on the cooling fan and the interior oven light. Some ovens have a delay of about ten seconds after being switched on, to allow the power source to warm up. An oven without an on/off control will be operated automatically when it is switched on at the power supply. (If the door has inadvertently been left open, the oven will not switch on.)

Power Control Dial: This is discussed in greater detail below, but, very simply, it enables you to decrease the microwave energy, introducing a 'slower' cooking rate for items that require it. Basic microwave ovens with on/off controls operate the power on a constant full or high power, whereas variable control microwave ovens have a control that enables the power to be reduced to low, medium or high, graduated in numbers from, say, 1-6, or expressed verbally as 'simmer', 'roast', 'reheat', and so on.

Indicator Lights: These are very useful as a reminder that a cooking operation has been set, is in progress or has finished.

Audible Reminders: Usually in the form of a bell or buzzer, audible reminders tell you that a cooking operation is complete.

Cooking Guide: A panel incorporated into the front of the oven giving basic cooking information and times needed for various cooking operations (not on all ovens).

Thermometers: These may only be used if the manufacturer specifically states that it is possible. Some manufacturers supply integral thermometers specially designed for use in their ovens in conjunction with a control for cooking meats and roasts.

Turntable: Some ovens incorporate a turntable instead of, or as an extra to, the wave stirrer; the turntable's purpose is to distribute the microwaves evenly through the food. The revolving turntable can often be removed but, if it can't, then the size and shape of dishes that can be used in that microwave are restricted.

'Off' Indicator: This tells you when cooking time is complete.

Interior Oven Light: This generally lights up as soon as the oven is turned on.

Splash Guard: Sometimes the wave stirrer has a special protective guard to protect it from food splashing.

Removable Floor or Base: Made of special glass or plastic, a removable floor or base acts as a spillage plate and positions the food to best advantage in the oven.

Other features which may be found in microwave ovens include:

Automatic Defrost: Foods may be defrosted in the microwave oven by giving them short bursts of energy followed by rest periods until the food is evenly thawed. (For timings see p.17.) An automatic defrost button will automatically turn the energy on and off at regular intervals.

Browning Element: Rather like an electric grill, this is sometimes incorporated into the top of the microwave oven and can be used to pre-brown food, or to brown it after or during microwave cooking.

Slow Cook Control: This enables the microwave output to be reduced or the power to be 'pulsed', thereby slowing down the cooking time.

Keep Warm/Stay Hot Control: Based on a very low power pulse, this enables you to keep food warm for up to one hour without its continuing to cook.

Two Power-level Cooking: A recent innovation, in which the microwaves enter from the sides rather than from the top of the oven. This means two cooking levels or more may be used simultaneously with different power ratings.

OVEN CONTROL SETTINGS

The simplest form of microwave oven has an on/off control whereby energy is either switched on or off. The energy that is turned on operates on FULL POWER.

Greater control over energy has now been made possible with the introduction of the variable or multiple controls described previously. The variable control dial 'pulses' the energy into the microwave cavity, thereby allowing different speeds of microwave cooking. The pulse control turns the microwave power on and off automatically every so many seconds so that the food receives a quick burst of energy with rests in between to enable the heat to distribute itself evenly. This is especially useful when defrosting foods and cooking dishes that need slower cooking, such as less tender cuts of meat and delicate dishes like egg custards.

Use of Power Control Dial

Note: It is important to use the power control settings outlined here in conjunction with the chart on p. 10, showing comparable descriptions of variable control power settings for popular microwave ovens and giving a guide to adjusting the cooking time.

Low (1, Keep Warm, Low or 2): Energy on for about 25 per cent of the time. Use for keeping foods warm for up to half an hour, softening butter, cream cheese and chocolate, proving yeast mixtures, and for very gentle cooking.

Defrost (3, Stew, Medium/Low or 4): Energy on for about 40 per cent of the time. Use for defrosting meat, poultry and fish, finishing off slow-cooking casseroles and stews or for cooking delicate egg dishes.
Medium (4, Defrost, Medium or 5): Energy on for about 50 per cent of the time.

Use for roasting meats and poultry, cooking fish, yeast doughs, pâtés, rice and pasta.
Full (7, Full/High or 10): Energy on 100 per cent of the time. The only setting on basic on/off models. Use for most prime cooking, quick reheating of shallow dishes of food and fast-speed dishes.

GUIDE TO COMPARATIVE MICROWAVE OVEN CONTROL SETTINGS

Descriptions of settings used in this book	LOW		DEFROST	MEDIUM			FULL
Descriptions of settings available on popular microwave ovens	1 keep warm low 2	2 simmer 3	3 stew medium/low 4	4 defrost medium 5	5 bake medium 6	6 roast high 7-8	7 full/high normal 10
Approximate % power input	25%	30%	40%	50%	60%	75%	100%
Approximate power output in watts	150W	200W	250W	300W	400W	550-550W	650-700W
Cooking time in minutes (for times greater than 10 minutes simply add the figures in the appropriate columns)	4 8 12 16 20 24 28 32 36 40	3¼ 6¾ 10 13¼ 16¾ 20 23¼ 26¾ 30 33¼	2½ 5 7½ 10 12½ 15 17½ 20 22½ 25	2 4 6 8 10 12 14 16 18 20	1¾ 3¼ 5 6¾ 8¼ 10 12 13¼ 15 16½	1¼ 2¾ 4 5¼ 6¾ 8 9¼ 10¾ 12 13¼	1 2 3 4 5 6 7 8 9 10

FACTORS AFFECTING COOKING

Starting Temperature of Food
The colder the temperature of a food the longer it will take to cook, so you should adjust the times in the recipes according to whether your ingredients are at room temperature, chilled or frozen. *All the times given in the recipes in this book refer to foods cooked from room temperature unless otherwise stated.*

For best results, defrost frozen foods first, then cook them, rather than thaw and cook in one operation, to ensure that the food has been thoroughly defrosted.

Density of Food
The denser the food, the longer it will take

to cook. A fairly small but dense piece of steak may be similar in size to a hamburger but the looser texture of the hamburger means it will cook faster in the microwave. Defrosting and reheating times will also be longer for denser foods like meat than for light, porous foods like breads or cakes.

Remember that when cooking both a dense and a light porous substance together, you should take care to apply more energy to the denser mass of food. In most cases this can be done by arranging the denser food to the outside of the dish where it receives more energy. Where this is not possible, such as when cooking a pie, insert a rolled-up piece of brown paper about 2.5 cm (1 inch) in length into the centre of the pie to direct the energy and encourage microwaves to the dense filling rather than the light crust.

Shape of Food

In both conventional and microwave cooking, thin areas of food cook faster than thick areas. To compensate for this in microwave cooking, thicker pieces of food should be placed to the outer edges of the dish where they receive most energy, and thinner pieces kept to the centre.

Wherever possible try to secure foods into regular shapes – bone and roll a rib of beef, for example.

When cooking unstuffed poultry or game birds in a microwave oven, tuck the wings, legs and any tail end into the body shape of the bird to prevent overheating and dehydration in these areas. Alternatively these parts of the bird may be wrapped in lightweight aluminium foil which can be removed for the last 10-15 minutes cooking time. Protecting small areas of a food is the only time when foil may be used in the microwave.

Size of Food

Larger pieces of food take longer to cook than smaller pieces because microwaves only penetrate to a depth of about 5 cm (2 inches), the heat penetrating right to the centre by induction. For best results, cook portions similar in size and shape together.

Quantity of Food

Timings in the microwave oven are directly related to the quantity of food being cooked. For example, two jacket potatoes will take almost twice as long to cook as a single jacket potato.

As a general guideline, if you double the amount of food being cooked in the microwave you should increase the cooking time by 50-75 per cent. Err on the side of safety by increasing at the lower end of this percentage scale to begin with.

Composition of Food

Fats and sugars absorb microwave energy at a greater rate than liquids and other components. Therefore foods like bacon and jams will cook faster than foods like vegetables and meats.

Foods with a low water content like breads and cakes will also cook faster than those with a high water content like soups and vegetables.

Height of Food in the Oven

Any food that is positioned near to the energy source will cook faster than food further away, whether cooked conventionally or in the microwave oven. In some microwave ovens the energy source may be near the roof of the oven, in others it may be near the base; check your instruction manual for details and advice.

For best results, turn over, rearrange or stir foods during cooking to take into account this action.

Bones in Meat

Bone conducts heat into a food. Wherever possible, for even cooking, remove the bone and roll the meat into an even shape.

If you do not choose to do this then remember the meat next to the bone will cook faster, and you should shield this area with a little foil to prevent overcooking for about half of the overall cooking time.

MICROWAVE COOKING TECHNIQUES

Most of the techniques used in microwave cooking are the same as those employed in conventional cooking but, because of the speed at which foods cook, they have to be followed carefully and employed at regular intervals for good cooking results. Most of the following techniques either quicken the cooking process or promote even heating.

Turning Over: We turn foods over in conventional cooking and this is also important in microwave cooking to ensure even results. Turning is often used with the three techniques of stirring, rotating and rearranging.

Stirring: This helps to distribute the heat evenly through the food throughout the cooking time. Always stir from the outside of the dish where the food cooks first.

11

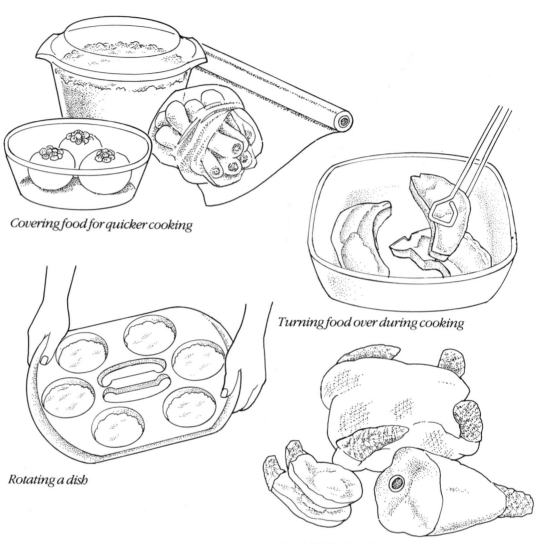

Covering food for quicker cooking

Turning food over during cooking

Rotating a dish

Food shielded with small pieces of foil

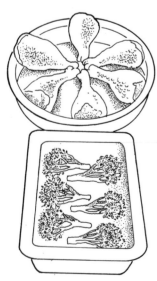

Foods carefully arranged for even cooking

Rotating: When the food cannot be stirred or turned over the dish should be rotated in the oven. This is necessary when the microwave oven does not have a turntable and is particularly important when cooking cakes and large items such as meat roasts.

Rearranging: To ensure even cooking, foods can be rearranged in the dish during cooking or defrosting. In most cases this is generally only necessary once during the cooking or defrosting time.

Covering Foods: Covering foods during cooking can speed up the cooking and retain the moisture. A loose cover will also prevent spattering on the oven walls, especially from fatty foods like bacon, sausages and chops.

A tight-fitting lid on a dish, cling film, greaseproof paper, roasting bags without the metal ties (use an elastic band or a piece of string to secure), absorbent kitchen paper, or an inverted plate all make suitable covers in the oven.

Arranging Foods: Careful arranging of foods in the microwave oven can help them to cook evenly. If you are cooking several items of the same food, arrange them in a ring shape, leaving the centre empty for even heating. The centre of a dish receives less microwave energy while the sides receive equal amounts.

Unevenly shaped foods like chicken pieces, whole fish, chops and many vegetables should be placed with the thinner parts to the centre where they will receive less energy.

Shielding: This means to protect vulnerable parts of the food from overcooking. This is the only time when small pieces of foil should be used in the microwave oven. Make sure that the area uncovered is greater than the area covered with foil or

Drying herbs

Pricking an egg to release steam pressure

Removing excess juices

does not produce dry and crisp results. Absorbent kitchen paper is one of the most useful materials that you can use to overcome this. Place jacket potatoes on a double-thickness of absorbent kitchen paper and they will cook dry and crisp. Bacon, covered with or placed between two sheets of absorbent kitchen paper, will also cook crisp rather than greasy and soggy. The same technique can also be used to dry herbs or flowers in the microwave. Place the herbs or flowers between two sheets of absorbent kitchen paper and cook until they are dry enough to crumble; this should take about five minutes on FULL POWER, but do check constantly.

Removing Excess Cooking Juices: Any juices that are produced during microwave cooking will continue to attract microwave energy and can, in effect, slow down the cooking process. Remove any juices with a bulb baster at regular intervals during cooking. If the food starts to dry out the juices can always be re-introduced later.

Observing Standing times: Foods cooked in the microwave will continue to cook after the microwave energy has been turned off because of the conduction of heat within the food. You should take account of this to make the best use of the microwave energy by ensuring that you do not cook the foods too much, otherwise the foods may overcook while standing.

the microwaves may arc (see p. 24). The foil will reflect the microwaves from sensitive areas including the wings and tips of poultry and game, the head and tails of fish, the breast bone of poultry and the bone ends of chops.

Releasing Pressure in Foods: Any foods that have a tight-fitting skin or membrane must be pricked prior to cooking in the microwave. If you do not do this they will burst or explode as the pressure from the production of steam mounts during cooking. Such foods include sausages and jacket potatoes. The same procedure must be used with cook-in bags, boil-in-the-bag pouches and roasting bags. Always prick cling film or pierce it in a couple of places if it is being used as a cover for a dish.

The yolk of an egg must also be pricked since microwave energy is attracted to the fats in the yolk, causing it to cook faster and risk exploding. Pricking the yolk carefully with a cocktail stick or the tip of a knife so it does not run will prevent this happening.

Drying Techniques: In many ways the microwave simulates a steam cabinet and

You should usually allow between five and twenty minutes for standing time. For most foods five minutes is sufficient, but for larger or denser pieces, like meat and roasts, fifteen to twenty minutes is usually recommended.

For foods that need to be served hot this standing time is best carried out under foil. The foil traps the heat inside the food, so it can be served without reheating.

ADVANTAGES OF MICROWAVE COOKING

Ask an experienced microwave user the advantages of microwave cooking and you'll get a very lengthy answer, since users discover more and more with time and use. Here are some of the more obvious ones:

Speed: It is possible to save up to three-quarters of normal cooking times, although during most cooking operations you'll

generally save between one-half and two-thirds. Times and savings will depend upon size, quantity, starting temperature, shape and density of the food being cooked.

Economy: Since microwave ovens cook faster, are on for a shorter period of time and use less power than conventional ovens they are more economical to run. There are also no lengthy and costly preheating periods required, no heavy installation costs and, with wise use, savings to be made by observing standing times (see above).

Efficiency: Heat is generated instantly into the food being cooked so microwave cooking is very efficient. There is little or no heat loss into the kitchen and the food receives all the energy, making for greater speed of cooking and efficiency of fuel.

Cooler Cooking: The microwave and its utensils – except the special browning dish (see p. 16) – stay cool during the cooking operation. The kitchen itself also stays cool – a boon during the summer months – and there is less risk of accidentally receiving a nasty burn.

Smells and Cooking Odours: These are dramatically reduced because of the shorter cooking times and because they are contained within the oven cavity. Fish cookery particularly benefits here.

Saves Washing Up: Since it is possible to freeze, defrost, cook and serve in the same container, wash loads may be greatly reduced after cooking. Food is also less likely to bake-on to dishes so they are easy to clean.

Easy Cleaning: The microwave, with its easy-to-wipe surfaces, often just needs a quick wipe to keep in pristine condition. There are fewer boil-over spillages and baked-on spatterings to deal with.

Nutritional Value and Flavour: If you follow cooking times precisely, it is unlikely that you will over-cook foods and thereby reduce their vitamin or mineral nutritional value. Colours stay bright, flavours are retained and textures stay naturally crisp. Many foods can also be cooked with just the minimum oil or butter, or even without any at all, making it the perfect cooking appliance for those on low-fat diets.

Defrosting: The microwave eliminates the need to plan the defrosting of foods hours ahead of the time they are required. Foods may be defrosted and cooked in one operation but they do taste better if they are defrosted and allowed to stand before cooking, when you will also be sure they have been fully defrosted.

Reheating: Dried-up, baked-to-a-frazzle or over-cooked dishes should become a thing of the past. Foods may be reheated in minutes or even seconds, retaining their freshness (see pp. 23-24). Leftovers for late-comers need not taste like leftovers.

Safety in Use: Microwave ovens are very simple to use and since they stay cool, and most dishes used in them stay cool enough to handle, they may be safely used by the young, elderly and disabled. (See p. 24.)

Versatility: The microwave with its basic operations of cooking, defrosting and re-heating is unbeatable. Use it to cope with those niggly chores in food preparation like melting chocolate, dissolving gelatine and softening butter.

Mobility: Look upon your microwave as a portable cooking friend. Provided you have a stable surface and a 13-amp or 15-amp plug, you can use your microwave in the dining room, patio, garden, or caravan, or on a trolley to be wheeled from room to room as required.

Among the limitations to cooking in a microwave are:

Browning: Since there is no applied surface heat, food does not brown readily in the microwave with short cooking times. See next page for some helpful hints.

Metals: These cannot be used in the microwave oven as they may cause arcing (see p. 24).

Some Foods Cannot be Cooked in a Microwave: *Eggs in shells* are liable to explode due to the build-up of pressure within the shell. *Popcorn* is too dry to attract microwave energy. *Batter* items like Yorkshire puddings, soufflés, pancakes and crêpes need conventional cooking to become crisp or firm. *Conventional meringues* should be cooked in the conventional oven. *Deep fat frying* is not recommended; since it requires prolonged heating, it is difficult to control the fat temperature and food may burn.

Liquids in Bottles: Check that bottles do not have too narrow necks or the pressure built up inside may cause them to shatter.

Very Large Food Loads: Any time advantage over the conventional cooker may be quickly eroded if you try to cook very large loads of food. Calculate the microwave cooking times and compare them for efficiency with conventional cooking.

Tips on browning

The most obvious disadvantage of microwave cooking is the lack of browning. Since there is no applied surface heat, food does not brown readily on the outside when cooking times are short. A large turkey cooked in the microwave will brown without any special treatment because of its long cooking time, but steaks, chops and small roasts may well look unappetizingly grey.

There are, though, numerous ways you may overcome this problem.

MEAT, POULTRY AND FISH

- Manufactures have now produced microwave models with integral browning elements or grills incorporated in the roof of the oven. These can be used in some cases prior to cooking, after cooking, or, in special cases, during cooking, depending upon the type. You should check the individual manufacturer's instructions. The same effect can be achieved by using a conventional grill, after cooking.
- There are several microwave browning dishes on the market which all assist with prebrowning meat, poultry and fish prior to microwave cooking (see p. 16). The same browning dish can also be used to brown and 'fry' sandwiches and eggs.
- Some manufacturers have introduced special browning agents and mixes to coat meat, fish and poultry prior to cooking. These are usually dark-coloured

marinade-type sauces which you brush on the food; there are also dark-coloured spicy mixtures to coat the food.
- Home-made browning agents that work very well include coating foods with browned breadcrumbs, dusting with ground paprika pepper, coating with a colourful dry soup mix, brushing with tomato or brown sauce, coating with crushed crisps or brushing with soy sauce.

CAKES, BISCUITS AND BREADS

Choosing a dark coloured mixture, like chocolate, ginger, coffee or spice, helps but if you wish to have a plain cake or biscuit mixture then the following tips to overcome the pale appearance may prove useful:

- Try sprinkling cakes and biscuits with chopped nuts, a mixture of cinnamon and sugar, mixed chopped glacé fruits, toasted coconut, hundreds and thousands or chocolate vermicelli before cooking.
- A colourful frosting or icing on a cake after cooking will quickly hide any pale, uncooked-looking crust.
- Quickly brown a microwave-baked bread under a preheated hot grill after cooking.
- Try sprinkling bread loaves and rolls with poppy seeds, cracked wheat, buckwheat, grated cheese, toasted sesame seeds, chopped nuts, caraway seeds or dried herbs prior to cooking, as these all give an interesting crust to the bread.

MICROWAVE COOKING UTENSILS

The range of cooking utensils that can be used in the microwave is greater than the range that can be used in the conventional oven since, as well as materials like plastic and glass, paper, basketware and linen may all be used in the microwave.

The following basic household equipment is ideal for use since microwaves pass through it, rather than acting as a barrier, enabling quick cooking, defrosting and reheating.

Glass, Pottery and China: Oven-proof and plain glass, pottery and china are all suitable for use in the microwave oven. They must not have any metallic trim,

screws or handles and pottery must be non-porous.

Paper: For low heat and short cooking times, such as thawing, reheating or very short prime cooking, and for foods with a low fat, sugar or water content, paper is excellent in the microwave oven. Napkins, paper towels, cups, cartons, paper freeze wrap and paper pulp board often used for meat packaging are all suitable. Paper towels are especially useful for cooking fatty foods since they absorb excess fats and oils and can be used to prevent splattering on the walls of the oven.

Wax-coated paper cups and plates should be avoided since the high tempera-

Temperature probe (left)
Meat thermometer (right)

ture of the food will cause the wax to melt; they can, however, be used for defrosting cold items like frozen cakes and desserts.

Plastics: The 'Dishwasher Safe' label is a useful indicator as to whether or not a plastic is suitable for use in the microwave. Plastic dishes and containers, unless made of a thermoplastic material, should not be used for cooking food with a high fat or sugar content, since the heat of the food may cause them to melt or lose their shape.

Plastic film and products like boil-in-the-bags work well in the microwave. Pierce the film or bag before cooking to allow the steam to escape.

Do not attempt to cook in thin plastic storage bags as they will not withstand the heat of the food. Thicker storage bags are acceptable. Use elastic bands, string or non-metal ties to secure the bags loosely before cooking.

Melamine is not recommended for microwave cooking since it absorbs enough microwave energy to char.

Cotton and Linen: Napkins can be used for short reheating purposes, such as re-heating bread rolls, but the material should be 100 per cent cotton or linen and should not contain any synthetic fibres.

Wooden Bowls and Basketware: These are only suitable for short reheating purposes, since the wood or wicker tends to char, dry out or crack if in the oven too long.

Roasting Bags: These provide a clean, convenient way of cooking many foods. This is particularly true of meats, since browning takes place more readily within them than in other plastic bags. However, the metal ties must be replaced with elastic bands or string. Snip a couple of holes in the bag to help the steam escape.

Microwave Containers: Several ranges of cookware manufactured from polythene, polystyrene and thermoplastic specially for microwave ovens are now widely available in a comprehensive range of shapes and sizes.

Thermometers: Ones made specially for microwave ovens are available, but these may be used in an oven only when specified by that oven's manufacturer. To take the temperature reading with a standard meat thermometer, remove the food from the oven, insert the thermometer into the thickest portion of food and let it stand for about 10 minutes to register the internal temperature. If more cooking is needed, remove the thermometer and return the meat to the oven.

Some newer ovens have an automatic cooking control, a temperature sensing probe, that can be inserted into a roast or other food while in the oven. When the food reaches a pre-set temperature, the oven turns itself off automatically.

Browning Dishes: These help the oven duplicate the conventional browning and searing processes of conventional cooking. Especially useful for pre-browning meat, poultry and fish, they can also be used for 'frying' eggs and sandwiches, and browning vegetables.

The browning dish, made of a glass-ceramic substance with a special coating that absorbs microwave energy, is pre-heated in the microwave until the base coating changes colour. The food is then placed on the dish to brown. Preheating times and browning or searing times differ according to the food being cooked and the power output of the oven. Always follow the manufacturer's instructions.

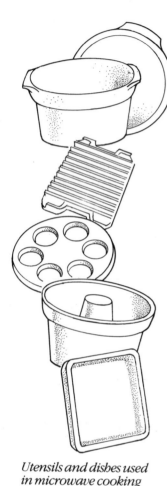

Utensils and dishes used in microwave cooking

CARE AND CLEANING

Guidelines common to caring for all microwave ovens are:

- Always disconnect the oven from the electrical supply before cleaning.
- Even though there is little chance of food baking on to the oven walls (since they stay cool), wipe up spills as they occur. If you don't, they will continue to absorb energy, effectively slowing down the cooking time.

- Wipe the oven surfaces with a damp soapy sponge or proprietary cleaner daily to avoid stale smells and build-up of moisture.
- For thorough cleaning, take out and clean removable bases, oven shelves and turntables on a regular basis.
- Do not clean surfaces with harsh abrasives. Any scratches may serve to distort the microwave pattern in the oven.

- To remove any cooking smells which may linger, place a bowl containing three parts water to one part lemon juice in the oven and cook for five-ten minutes. Wipe the oven dry after this time.
- Keep the door seals free from food, dust or grease.
- Replace or remove and clean any air filters or stirrer fan guards regularly.
- Do not splash water over the exterior vents when cleaning the outer casing of the oven.
- Have your microwave checked or serviced by a qualified engineer every 12 months. It is also worth asking whether your retailer operates an insurance scheme, so that you could insure against replacement parts and labour should they prove necessary after the guarantee period expires.

THE MICROWAVE AND FREEZER

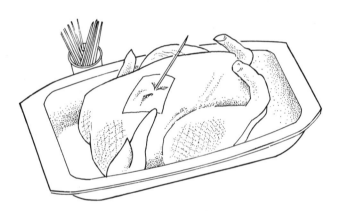

Shielding food during defrosting

The microwave has often been given the title 'the unfreezer' since it efficiently and safely defrosts foods in a fraction of the time it normally takes at room temperature. Most microwave ovens have a DEFROST POWER facility on the control dial. If your oven does not have a DEFROST POWER button then you can simulate this by turning the oven on and off at regular intervals – one minute on FULL POWER followed by ten minutes' resting, repeated as necessary – until the frozen food is defrosted. The DEFROST POWER facility automates this switching on and off.

When defrosting foods, refer to the times in the charts on pp. 18-23. Err on the side of safety by under- rather than over-timing until you can judge the cooking or defrosting speeds of your microwave.

The following hints will also ensure good even defrosting:
- Pierce any skins, membranes or pouches before defrosting.
- Remove any metal containers, ties or dishes before defrosting.
- Turn foods over during defrosting.
- If turning foods over is not possible, rotate the dish to ensure even heating.
- Flex any pouches that cannot be broken up or stirred during the defrosting time and rotate on a regular basis.
- Place any foods like cakes, bread rolls, sausage rolls and pastry items on a double sheet of absorbent kitchen paper when defrosting to absorb any excess moisture.
- Any blocks of frozen food should be broken up with a fork during defrosting so that the microwave energy can concentrate on the unfrozen block.
- Separate any blocks of frozen meats like hamburgers, sausages and steaks as they defrost.
- Remove any giblets from the cavity of chickens and other game or poultry meats as they defrost.
- Open all cartons and remove any lids before defrosting.
- Remove any thaw juices or drips from frozen foods during the defrosting time with a bulb baster as these will continue to attract microwave energy, leaving less to defrost the main food.
- With items like meat joints, whole poultry, game birds and whole fish, defrost until they appear 'frosty' then leave to defrost completely at room temperature.
- If any parts of the food start to defrost at too fast a rate or even start to cook or become warm, then shield or protect these areas with small strips of foil. These can be attached with wooden cocktail sticks where necessary.
- Always observe a standing time action as foods will continue to thaw with the heat produced via conduction.

BASIC FOOD DEFROSTING CHART

Food	Quantity	Power Setting	Time in Minutes	Instructions
Meat				
Beef – joints	per 450 g/1 lb	DEFROST	9	Turn over at least once. Leave to stand for 10-15 minutes.
– steaks (large)	per 450 g/1 lb	DEFROST	8	Leave to stand for 10-15 minutes.
– steaks (small)	per 450 g/1 lb	DEFROST	4	Leave to stand for 10-15 minutes.
– minced beef	per 450 g/1 lb	DEFROST	10	Break up with a fork during defrosting time. Leave to stand for 10-15 minutes.
– burgers	2 × 100 g/4 oz	DEFROST	2-3	Leave to stand for 2 minutes.
	4 × 100 g/4 oz	DEFROST	5	Leave to stand for 5 minutes.
Lamb – joints	per 450 g/1 lb	DEFROST	10	Turn over at least once. Leave to stand for 10-15 minutes.
– chops	per 450 g/1 lb	DEFROST	5	Turn and re-arrange halfway through defrosting time. Leave to stand for 5 minutes.
Pork – joints	per 450 g/1 lb	DEFROST	8½	Turn over at least once. Leave to stand for 10-15 minutes.
– chops	per 450 g/1 lb	DEFROST	5	Turn and re-arrange halfway through defrosting time. Leave to stand for 5 minutes.
Veal – joints	per 450 g/1 lb	DEFROST	9	Turn over at least once. Leave to stand for 10-15 minutes.
– chops	per 450 g/1 lb	DEFROST	5	Turn and re-arrange halfway through defrosting time. Stand for 5 minutes.
Kidney	per 450 g/1 lb	DEFROST	4	Turn over at least once. Leave to stand for 5 minutes.
Liver	per 450 g/1 lb	DEFROST	4	Trun over at least once. Leave to stand for 5 minutes.
Bacon – joint	450 g/1 lb	DEFROST	8	Turn over at least once. Leave to stand for 20-30 minutes.
– rashers	1 × 225 g/8 oz pkt.	DEFROST	2-3	Turn over halfway through defrosting time. Leave to stand 5 minutes.
Sausages – thin	450 g/1 lb	DEFROST	5	Turn over and re-arrange halfway through defrosting time. Leave to stand for 5 minutes.
– thick	450 g/1 lb	DEFROST	5-6	Turn over and re-arrange halfway through defrosting time. Leave to stand for 5 minutes.
Sausagemeat	per 450 g/1 lb	DEFROST	6-7	Break up with a fork during defrosting time. Leave to stand for 10-15 minutes.
Stewing or braising meat – cubed	675 g/1½ lb	DEFROST	12	Separate pieces of meat during defrosting time. Stand for 10-15 minutes.

Made-up meat products – casserole with vegetables	4 portions	FULL	14-16	Stir twice during cooking. To defrost *and reheat.*
– shepherd's pie	1 × 400 g/14 oz	FULL	5+6	Allow to stand 2 minutes between cooking times. To thaw *and reheat.*
– roast meat and gravy	350 g/12 oz	FULL	3+3½	Allow to stand 3 minutes between cooking times. To thaw *and reheat.*
Poultry and Game Chicken – whole	per 450 g/1 lb	DEFROST	6	Shield the wing tips with foil. Give the dish a quarter-turn occasionally. Leave to stand 10-15 minutes, then remove giblets.
– pieces	per 450 g/1 lb	DEFROST	5	Place the meatiest part of the chicken pieces to the outside of the dish. Turn over halfway through defrosting time. Leave to stand 5-10 minutes.
Turkey – whole	per 450 g/1 lb	DEFROST	10-12	Shield the tips of the wings and legs with foil. Turn over twice during the defrosting time and give the dish a quarter-turn occasionally. Shield any warm spots with foil during defrosting time. Leave to stand 15-20 minutes, then remove giblets.
Duck – whole	per 450 g/1 lb	DEFROST	4-6	Shield the wings, tail-end and legs with foil. Give the dish a quarter-turn occasionally. Leave to stand 10-15 minutes, then remove giblets.
Grouse, Guinea fowl, Partridge, Pheasant, Pigeon, Poussin, Quail and Woodcock	per 450 g/1 lb	DEFROST	5-6	Shield the tips of the wings and legs with foil. Turn over halfway through the defrosting time and give the dish a quarter-turn occasionally. Leave to stand 10 minutes.
Poultry stew or braising meat – cubed	675 g/1½ lb	DEFROST	9-10	Separate pieces of poultry during defrosting time. Leave to stand for 10-15 minutes.
Poultry casserole with vegetables	4 portions	FULL	12-14	Stir twice during cooking. To defrost *and reheat.*
Fish and Shellfish Fish fillets (cod, haddock, coley and plaice for example)	per 450 g/1 lb	DEFROST	7-8	Arrange thinner tail ends to centre of dish. Leave to stand for 5-10 minutes.
Fish steaks (cod, salmon and coley for example)	1 × 175 g/6 oz 2 × 175 g/6 oz	DEFROST DEFROST	2 3-4	Leave to stand for 10 minutes. Leave to stand for 10 minutes.
Whole fish (herrings, trout and mackerel for example)	1 × 225-275 g/8-10 oz 2 × 225-275 g/8-10 oz 1 × 1.5-1.75 kg/3-4 lb	DEFROST DEFROST DEFROST	4-6 10-12 20-22	Turn over halfway through defrosting time.

BASIC FOOD DEFROSTING CHART (continued)

Food	Quantity	Power Setting	Time in Minutes	Instructions
Crabmeat	per 450 g/1 lb	DEFROST	14-16	Break up with a fork during defrosting time. Leave to stand for 5-10 minutes.
Lobster – whole	1 × 450 g/1 lb 1 × 675 g/1½ lb	DEFROST DEFROST	12	Turn over halfway through defrosting time. Leave to stand 10 minutes.
Prawns, Scampi and Shrimps	per 450 g/1 lb	DEFROST	7-8	Separate pieces during defrosting time. Leave to stand for 5-10 minutes.
Scallops	per 450 g/1 lb	DEFROST	8-10	Separate pieces during defrosting time. Leave to stand for 5-10 minutes.
Kippers – fillets	per 450 g/1 lb	DEFROST	5-7	Arrange thinner tail ends to centre of dish. Leave to stand for 3 minutes.
Fish cakes	2 × 50 g/2 oz	FULL	2½ + 1	Allow to stand 3 minutes between cooking times.
Rice and Pasta Cooked long-grain rice	per 225 g/8 oz	DEFROST	5	Stir twice. Leave to stand for 2 minutes.
Cooked brown rice	per 225 g/8 oz	DEFROST	7	Stir twice. Leave to stand for 2 minutes.
Cooked egg noodles	per 225 g/8 oz	DEFROST	6	Stir twice. Leave to stand for 2 minutes.
Cooked spaghetti	per 225 g/8 oz	DEFROST	6½	Stir twice. Leave to stand for 2 minutes.
Cooked pasta shells	per 225 g/8 oz	DEFROST	7	Stir twice. Leave to stand for 2 minutes.
Cooked macaroni	per 225 g/8 oz	DEFROST	7	Stir twice. Leave to stand for 2 minutes.
Cooked lasagne	per 225 g/8 oz	DEFROST	6	Turn over once. Leave to stand for 3 minutes.
Sauces	per 300 ml/½ pint	FULL	5-6	Stir twice and whisk at end of cooking time. To defrost *and reheat*.
Stock	per 300 ml/½ pint	FULL	2½-3	Break down frozen block during defrosting time. Stand for 5 minutes.
Fruit Fruit dry-packed with sugar	per 450 g/1 lb	FULL	4-8	Gently shake or stir twice during defrosting time. Leave to stand for 5-10 minutes.
Fruit packed with sugar syrup	per 450 g/1 lb	FULL	8-12	Gently shake or stir twice during defrosting time. Stand for 5-10 minutes.

Open frozen or free-flow fruit	per 450 g/1 lb	DEFROST	4-8	Gently shake or stir twice during defrosting time. Leave to stand for 5-10 minutes.
Butter	1×250 g/9 oz	DEFROST	2-3	Turn once and leave to stand for 5 minutes.
Eggs – white only	2	DEFROST	1½-2	Leave to stand for 5 minutes.
Yogurt	1×150 ml/5 fl oz carton	FULL	1	Remove lid. Stir for 1 minute after cooking to mix.

CONVENIENCE FOOD DEFROSTING AND COOKING CHART

Food	Quantity	Power Setting	Time in Minutes	Instructions
Meat and Meat Products				
Shepherd's pie	1×400 g/14 oz	FULL	5+6	Allow to stand for 2 minutes between cooking times.
Beefburgers	4	FULL	3-4	Place on absorbent kitchen paper. Turn over once.
Meat pie	1×100 g/4 oz	DEFROST then FULL	1½/2+2	Allow to stand for 2 minutes between all defrosting and cooking times.
	1×450 g/1 lb	DEFROST then FULL	12/3+4	Allow to stand for 10 minutes after defrosting and 4 minutes between and after cooking times.
Lasagne	1×450 g/1 lb	DEFROST then FULL	8+4/9	Cover to cook. Allow to stand for 6 minutes between defrosting times.
Steak and kidney pudding	1×125 g/4 oz	DEFROST then FULL	2+3/2½	Allow to stand for 5 minutes between defrosting times and for 2 minutes after cooking.
Individual 'boil-in-bag' ready meals	1×170 g/6 oz	DEFROST then FULL	4+3/2½	Pierce bag. Allow to stand for 6 minutes between defrosting times.
Fish and Fish Products				
Fish steak in sauce	1×170 g/6 oz	FULL	7-8	Pierce bags and turn once or twice during cooking.
	2×170 g/6 oz	FULL	12-13	
	4×170 g/6 oz	FULL	16-17	
Cook-in-bag smoked haddock or buttered kipper fillets	1×198 g/7 oz	FULL	6	Pierce bag and turn once during cooking.
Fish fingers	10	DEFROST then FULL	6/1½+1	Place in a circle on a plate and dot with butter. Allow to stand for 4 minutes between defrosting times. Turn over halfway through cooking times.

CONVENIENCE FOOD DEFROSTING AND COOKING CHART (continued)

Food	Quantity	Power Setting	Time in Minutes	Instructions
Soups	300 ml/½ pint	FULL	3	Break down solid block during cooking.
	600 ml/1 pint	FULL	6	
Savoury Snacks				
Pâté	1 × 198 g/7 oz pack	DEFROST	3-4	Allow to stand for 15 minutes.
Pizza	1 individual	FULL	1½-2	Place on absorbent kitchen paper.
	1 family size	FULL	3-4	
Pancakes	8 stacked	DEFROST	6	Re-arrange twice. Allow to stand for 5 minutes.
Filled flan or quiche	1 family size	FULL	4-5	Turn once. Allow to stand for 3 minutes.
Bread	1 large unsliced loaf	DEFROST	7-8	Turn twice. Allow to stand for 5-10 minutes.
	1 small unsliced loaf	DEFROST	6	Turn twice. Allow to stand for 10 minutes.
	1 large sliced loaf.	DEFROST	10-12	Turn several times. Allow to stand for 10-15 minutes.
	1 slice bread	DEFROST	½-1	Check constantly.
	2 bread rolls	DEFROST	½-1	Place on absorbent kitchen paper. Allow to stand for 2-3 minutes.
	4 bread rolls	DEFROST	1½-2	Place on absorbent kitchen paper.
	2 pitta breads	DEFROST	1½-2	Place on absorbent kitchen paper.
	2 croissants	DEFROST	½-1	Place on absorbent kitchen paper.
	2 crumpets	FULL	½-¾	Place on absorbent kitchen paper.
	2 teacakes	FULL	¾	Place on absorbent kitchen paper.
	450 g/1 lb bread dough	DEFROST	5-3	Place on absorbent kitchen paper. Allow to stand for 8 minutes between defrosting times and for 5 minutes after defrosting. To *defrost only*.
Cakes and Biscuits				
Biscuits	225 g/8 oz	DEFROST	1	Turn once and allow to stand for 5 minutes.
Small light fruit cake	1	DEFROST	5	Turn once. Allow to stand for 10 minutes.
Buns/Rock cakes	2	DEFROST	1-1½	Allow to stand for 5 minutes.
Small cream-filled sponge	1	FULL	¾	Allow to stand for 10-15 minutes.
Small jam-filled sponge	1	DEFROST	3	Allow to stand for 5 minutes.
Cheese cake – fruit topped	Family size	DEFROST	5-6	Turn twice.
	Individual	DEFROST	1-1½	Allow to stand for 5 minutes.
Jam doughnuts	2	DEFROST	1½-2	Allow to stand for 3 minutes.
Cream doughnuts	2	DEFROST	1-1½	Allow to stand for 3 minutes.
Eclairs	2	DEFROST	¾-1	Allow to stand for 5-10 minutes.
Black Forest Gâteau	1 small	DEFROST	4-6	Allow to stand for 30 minutes.
Scones	2	DEFROST	1-1½	Place on absorbent kitchen paper.

Pastries					
Unfilled cooked flan case	1×18 cm/7 inch	DEFROST	1-1½	Allow to stand for 3 minutes.	
Danish pastry	1	DEFROST	¾	Allow to stand for 5 minutes.	
Mince pies	1	DEFROST then FULL	¾-1½-1	Place on absorbent kitchen paper.	
	1	DEFROST then FULL	1-1¼/¾-1	Place on absorbent kitchen paper.	
Raw shortcrust and	225 g/8 oz	DEFROST	1	Allow to stand for 15-20 minutes.	
Puff pastry	395 g/14 oz	DEFROST	2	Allow to stand for 20-30 minutes.	
Miscellaneous					
Jelly tablet	135 g/4¾ oz	FULL	½-1	Break cubes into a jug to melt.	
Chocolate	100 g/4 oz	FULL	1	Break pieces into a bowl. Beat well after cooking to melt.	
Dairy Produce					
Cream	300 ml/½ pint	DEFROST	1-2	Allow to stand for 10-15 minutes.	
Cream cheese	75 g/3 oz	DEFROST	1-1½	Allow to stand for 10-15 minutes.	

TIPS ON REHEATING FOOD

Dried-up meals should become a thing of the past with the use of your microwave oven. Dishes can quickly be reheated to just-cooked freshness without fear of their drying out. For the best results follow the guidelines below and the chart on page 24:

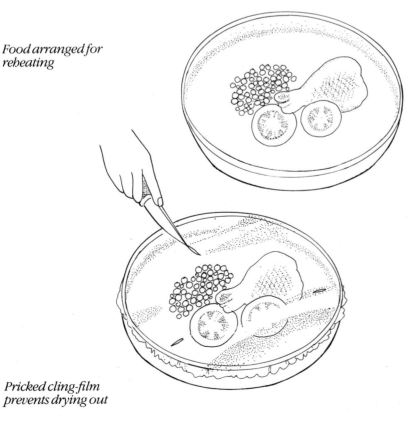

Food arranged for reheating

Pricked cling-film prevents drying out

- Arrange foods for reheating on the plate so that the thicker, denser and meatier portions are to the outer edge of the dish, where they will receive the maximum amount of energy, and the thinner areas to the centre where they will get less.
- When plating up meals for reheating, try to ensure that the food is arranged in an even layer.
- Cover foods when reheating with a layer of pricked cling film to retain moisture.
- When reheating, observe the standing time recommended in cooking procedures (see p. 13) to make maximum use of the microwave energy and to prevent over-cooking of the reheated dish.
- The times in the reheating chart refer to foods at room temperature. Allow extra time if the food is chilled.
- When reheating potatoes in their jackets, breads, pastries or moist foods, place them on a sheet of absorbent kitchen paper so that it may absorb the moisture during the reheating time.
- If you are in any doubt about a food losing moisture during reheating, wrap it in a tight skin of cling film, piercing the cling film in a couple of places.
- Stir foods regularly during the reheating process. If stirring is not possible then rotate the food or dish or re-arrange during the reheating time.

GUIDE TO REHEATING

Food	Quantity or weight	Reheating time in minutes	Power setting
Meats			
Main dishes with sauce	1 serving	3	FULL POWER
	2 servings	6	FULL POWER
	4 servings	10	FULL POWER
Plated meals – meat and two vegetables	1 serving	6	FULL POWER
Hamburgers	1 serving	1	FULL POWER
	2 servings	1½-2	FULL POWER
	4 servings	2½-3	FULL POWER
Hot dogs and frankfurters	1 serving	½	FULL POWER
	2 servings	1	FULL POWER
	4 servings	1½	FULL POWER
Sliced chicken or meat	1 serving	1½-2	MEDIUM POWER
	2 servings	2½-3½	MEDIUM POWER
Soups			
	1 serving	2	FULL POWER
	2 servings	3-4	FULL POWER
Fish			
Fish in sauce	1 serving	2	FULL POWER
	2 servings	3-3½	FULL POWER

Food	Quantity or weight	Reheating time in minutes	Power setting
Vegetables			
	1 serving	1	FULL POWER
	2 servings	2	FULL POWER
	4 servings	4	FULL POWER
Stewed Fruit			
	1 serving	1	FULL POWER
	2 servings	1½-2	FULL POWER
	4 servings	3-4	FULL POWER
Puddings and Desserts			
Sponge pudding	1 serving	½	FULL POWER
Milk pudding	1 serving	1	FULL POWER
Fruit pie	1 serving	½	FULL POWER
Miscellaneous			
Rice and pasta	1 serving	½-1	FULL POWER
	2 servings	1-2	FULL POWER
Porridge	1 serving	1-2	FULL POWER
	2 servings	2-3	FULL POWER
Baked beans	1 serving	1½-2	FULL POWER
	2 servings	2½-3	FULL POWER
Sauces	300 ml/ ½ pint	2-3	FULL POWER

SAFETY

Microwave ovens have been carefully designed to be totally safe in use. To ensure complete safety, follow these guidelines:

- Keep the door seals free from food, dust or grease. A good seal is important for safety.
- Do not use or operate the oven if it has been damaged in any way, or if the door catch seems loose. Contact a service engineer at once.
- Do not operate the oven when it is empty. For safety, place a cup of water in the oven when it is not in use. If the oven is accidentally switched on the water will absorb the energy and there is then negligible risk of damaging the magnetron.

Arcing

The most noticeable problem that could occur in your oven is arcing, when you will see sparks inside the oven cavity. It is a sign that the microwave patterns have been disturbed, usually because a large amount of metal has inadvertently been introduced into the oven, perhaps in the form of a metal trim, decoration or base on a dish, or as excessive foil covering on poultry or meat bones. Foil may also be touching the oven sides.

If arcing occurs, you should switch off the oven immediately and remove the dish or foil. Prolonged arcing could damage the dish and the oven's magnetron.

ADAPTING RECIPES

Many recipes can be converted for use in the microwave simply by adjusting, and often shortening, the recipe cooking time. Check that all the foods included in the recipe microwave well and rely upon procedures and times from other standard recipes as a good clue to times.

The following checklist is a guideline:

- In general terms, microwave foods cook in about one-quarter to one-third of the time they take conventionally. Do, however, allow for standing times (see p. 13).

- Check the cooking process regularly. Stir and re-arrange foods if necessary.
- Use less liquid when cooking stews, casseroles, soups and vegetables.
- Foods tend to rise higher during microwave cooking so, in general, choose larger containers for cooking.
- Reduce flavourings like herbs and spices by about one-third since these seem to concentrate with microwave cooking.
- Wherever possible cut food into small, uniform pieces for quick cooking.

RECIPE GUIDELINES BEFORE YOU BEGIN

All the recipes in this book were created and tested using microwave ovens with a power output of 650-700 watts on FULL POWER. The ovens also had variable power ranging from 150-700 watts for greater flexibility. If your microwave has a power output higher than 700 watts, reduce the cooking time accordingly; if your microwave has a power output lower than 700 watts then you should increase the cooking time accordingly. A few simple trial-and-error cooking tests will tell you by how much to adjust the recipe times.

Checking if Food is Cooked

Since appearances differ between microwave cooked food and conventionally cooked food, the usual procedures for checking if a food is cooked are not always appropriate. Here are a few guidelines for beginners:

Cakes and Sponge Puddings: These will often appear wet on the surface when cooked but will dry out with the residual heat during standing time. The best check is with a wooden cocktail stick at the minimum time. The cake or pudding is cooked if the stick when inserted comes out clean.

Jacket Potatoes: These often appear firm at the end of the cooking time. Check that they give a little under thumb pressure then wrap in foil and leave to stand for five minutes.

Meat: This should be fork-tender when cooked and be easy to carve after standing.

Use a thermometer where the temperature will indicate how ready the meat is.

Chicken: Juices should run clear when pricked and the flesh should be soft to the pinch when cooked. Once removed from the oven, wrap in foil and leave to stand for the recommended time (see p. 13).

Fish: The flesh will flake easily when cooked but at first may appear translucent, especially in the centre; this disappears upon standing.

Vegetables: These should be only fork-tender, not soft, when cooked. Soft vegetables, with further residual heat cooking, would become mushy upon standing.

Reheated Meals: These are generally hot enough when the base of the plate feels warm to the touch.

Custards, Quiches and Egg-based Fillings: These may appear soft or wet in the centre but will cook upon standing. The best test is to insert a knife about halfway between the centre and outer edge; if it comes out clean the dish is cooked.

Pastries: When cooked, the base of pastries should be dry and opaque.

Measurements

Metric measurements may vary from one recipe to another within this book and it is essential to follow either metric or imperial measures. The recipes have been specially balanced to get the very best results whether using metric or imperial so it is important not to interchange the measures when following a recipe.

Appetizers and Snacks

If you're hungry between meals, late for a family dinner and settling for supper, too short on time for a full-blown meal or looking for a few ideas to serve with pre-dinner drinks, then here are some quick and easy, yet nourishing, recipes to solve the problem.
Though convenient, they do not rely heavily upon convenience-style foods: with a microwave oven, a quick soup of stock, vegetables and seasonings can be made just as quickly as opening and reheating a bought can of similar soup.

AUBERGINE DIP

1 × 225 g (8 oz) aubergine
3 tablespoons soured
    cream
1 garlic clove, peeled and
    crushed
1 teaspoon salt
¼ teaspoon freshly ground
    black pepper
2 tablespoons lemon juice
1 small onion, peeled and
    chopped
1 tablespoon chopped
    parsley
3 tablespoons olive oil

Wash the aubergine, score around the middle with a sharp knife and cook for 5 minutes, turning over once.

Cut in half, scoop out the flesh and place in a blender. Add the soured cream, garlic, salt, pepper, lemon juice, onion and parsley. Purée until smooth.

Gradually blend in the olive oil and pour into a serving dish. Chill thoroughly.

Serve chilled with chunks of wholemeal bread.

Serves: 4
Power setting: FULL
Preparation time: 10 minutes, plus chilling
Cooking time: 5 minutes

DEVIL'S DIP

25 g/1 oz butter
3 tablespoons plain flour
½ teaspoon curry powder
    (medium strength)
300 ml/½ pint milk
1 green pepper, cored,
    seeded and chopped
50 g/2 oz walnuts,
    chopped
50 g/2 oz raisins
2 tablespoons wine
    vinegar
1 tablespoon lemon juice
pinch of cayenne pepper
150 ml/¼ pint double
    cream

Place the butter in a bowl and cook for 1 minute. Add the flour and curry powder, blending well. Gradually add the milk and cook for 3 minutes, stirring every 1 minute until smooth and thickened.

Add the pepper, walnuts, raisins, wine vinegar, lemon juice and cayenne pepper, blending well. Finally add the double cream and stir well to blend.

Serve hot or chilled with crisps, crackers or salad crudités.

Serves: 4
Power setting: FULL
Preparation time: 10-15 minutes
Cooking time: 4 minutes

SPICY ALMONDS

25 g/1 oz butter
1½ teaspoons chilli
   powder
1 teaspoon celery salt
pinch of cayenne pepper
½ teaspoon salt
225 g/8 oz whole
   blanched almonds

Place the butter in a large shallow dish and cook for ½ minute to melt.
   Stir in the chilli powder, celery salt, cayenne, salt and almonds, blending well.
   Cook for 6 minutes, stirring twice. Drain and allow to cool on absorbent kitchen paper.
   Store in an airtight jar until required.

Makes: 225 g/8 oz
Power setting: FULL
Preparation time: 5 minutes, plus cooling
Cooking time: 6½ minutes

ROQUEFORT CANAPÉS

100 g/4 oz curd cheese
2 tablespoons Roquefort
   cheese
1 tablespoon ground
   hazelnuts
¼ teaspoon made mustard
½ teaspoon
   Worcestershire sauce
1 teaspoon chutney
freshly ground black
   pepper
20 crisp crackers

Mix the cheeses, hazelnuts, mustard, Worcestershire sauce, chutney and pepper to taste, blending well.
   Cook for ½ minute then spread on to the crackers liberally. Serve at once.

Makes: 20
Power setting: FULL
Preparation time: 10-15 minutes
Cooking time: ½ minute

BRUNCH

1 onion, peeled and finely
   chopped
100 g/4 oz streaky bacon,
   rinded and chopped
225 g/8 oz cooked
   potatoes, sliced
4 eggs, beaten
150 ml/¼ pint milk
salt and freshly ground
   black pepper

Place the onion and bacon in a serving dish. Cover and cook on FULL POWER for 3 minutes, stirring once.
   Add the potatoes, blending well. Mix the eggs with the milk and salt and pepper to taste. Pour over the bacon mixture. Cover and cook on MEDIUM POWER for 10 minutes, turning the potatoes over twice.
   Serve at once straight from the dish.

Serves: 2
Power settings: FULL, MEDIUM
Preparation time: 10 minutes
Cooking time: 13 minutes

WELSH RAREBIT

100 g/4 oz Cheddar,
   Gouda or Gruyère
   cheese, finely grated
1 teaspoon mustard
   powder
1 egg, lightly beaten
2 teaspoons tomato
   ketchup
4 slices white or brown
   bread

Preheat a browning dish on FULL POWER for 3 minutes (or according to the manu-facturer's instructions).
   Mix the cheese with the mustard, egg and tomato ketchup, blending well. Spoon evenly on to the bread slices.
   Place on the browning dish and cook on MEDIUM POWER for 4 minutes or until the cheese starts to bubble.
   Serve at once.

Serves: 4
Power settings: FULL, MEDIUM
Preparation time: 10 minutes
Cooking time: 7 minutes

SARDINE AND RICE SNACK

1 large tomato
1 × 120 g (4¼ oz) can
  sardines, drained
1 small egg (size 4 or 5)
4 tablespoons milk
salt and freshly ground
  black pepper
25 g/1 oz cheese, grated
250 g/9 oz cooked long-
  grain rice
15 g/½ oz butter

Pierce the tomato skin with a sharp knife and place on a plate. Cook for 1 minute then peel away the skin from the tomato. Cut into thin slices.

Arrange the tomato and sardines in one half of a two-section microwave dish. Mix the egg with the milk, salt and pepper to taste and cheese, blending well. Pour over the sardines and cook for 1 minute.

Place the rice in the other half of the dish and dot with the butter. Cover the whole dish and cook for 1½ minutes. Serve hot.

Serves: 2
Power setting: FULL
Preparation time: 10 minutes
Cooking time: 3½ minutes

MUFFIN PIZZAS

1 × 227 g (8 oz) can
  tomatoes, drained and
  chopped
1 small garlic clove,
  peeled and crushed
½ teaspoon dried
  oregano
salt and freshly ground
  black pepper
2 muffins, split and
  toasted on one side
50 g/2 oz mature
  Cheddar cheese, grated
50 g/2 oz salami, sliced
2 tablespoons grated
  Parmesan cheese

Place the tomatoes, garlic, oregano and salt and pepper to taste in a bowl. Cover and cook for 2½ minutes, stirring once.

Preheat a small browning dish for 6 minutes (or according to the manufacturer's instructions).

Spread the tomato mixture evenly over the muffins, then top with the Cheddar cheese and salami. Sprinkle with the Parmesan cheese, place in the browning dish and cook for 2-3 minutes until the cheese has just melted.

Serve at once with a green salad if liked.

Serves: 2
Power setting: FULL
Preparation time: 10-15 minutes
Cooking time: 10½-11½ minutes

SCRAMBLED FISH 'N' EGG

1 × 175 g (6 oz) fillet
  smoked fish
2 tablespoons water
4 eggs, beaten
salt and freshly ground
  black pepper
25 g/1 oz butter
2 tablespoons single
  cream
2 tablespoons
  mayonnaise
snipped chives to garnish

Place the fish in a shallow dish with the water. Cover and cook for 2½-3 minutes until cooked or the flesh flakes easily. Allow to cool slightly then flake, discarding any skin and bones.

Beat the eggs with salt and pepper to taste. Place the butter in a bowl and cook for ½ minute to melt. Add the eggs and cook for 3¾-4 minutes, stirring three times until lightly scrambled.

Fold in the fish, cream and mayonnaise, blending well. Cook for ½ minute to re-heat.

Serve at once, sprinkled with chives and accompanied by hot buttered toast.

Serves: 2
Power setting: FULL
Preparation time: 5-10 minutes
Cooking time: 7¼-8 minutes

SPANISH BAKED EGGS

50 g/2 oz butter
1 garlic clove, peeled and crushed
100 g/4 oz sliced chorizo sausage or salami
1 green pepper, cored, seeded and finely chopped
4 eggs
salt and freshly ground black pepper
4 tablespoons single cream

Place the butter in a shallow dish and cook on FULL POWER for 1 minute to melt. Add the garlic, chorizo or salami and pepper, blending well. Cover and cook on FULL POWER for 4 minutes, stirring once.

Carefully break the eggs around the edge of the dish and quickly prick the yolks with the pointed end of a knife. Season with salt and pepper to taste and spoon over the cream. Cover and cook on MEDIUM POWER for 4-6 minutes or until the eggs are just lightly set.

Leave to stand, covered, for 3 minutes before serving.

Serves: 2
Power settings: FULL, MEDIUM
Preparation time: 10 minutes
Cooking time: 12-14 minutes

HOT DOGS

25 g/1 oz butter
1 onion, peeled and chopped
4 frankfurter sausages
4 soft finger bread rolls
relish to serve (optional)

Place the butter and onion in a bowl. Cover and cook for 3 minutes, stirring once.

Place the frankfurters on a plate and cook for 1 minute to reheat.

Slit the rolls and fill with the onion mixture. Top each with a frankfurter and a little relish if liked. Serve at once in paper napkins.

Serves: 4
Power setting: FULL
Preparation time: 5 minutes
Cooking time: 3 minutes

SAUSAGE GOULASH

15 g/½ oz butter
1 onion, peeled and chopped
1 green pepper, cored, seeded and chopped
1 tablespoon plain flour
225 g/8 oz tomatoes, peeled, seeded and chopped
1 tablespoon ground paprika
1 × 300 g (10½ oz) can condensed tomato soup
150 ml/¼ pint milk
450 g/1 lb potatoes, peeled and cubed
450 g/1 lb sausages, cooked and chopped
2 tablespoons plain yogurt
green pepper rings

Place the butter, onion and pepper in a medium casserole. Cover and cook for 4 minutes, stirring once.

Add the flour, blending well. Add the tomatoes, paprika, tomato soup, milk and potatoes, blending well. Cover and cook for 10 minutes, stirring twice. Add the sausages, cover and cook for a further 5 minutes.

Stir in the yogurt and garnish with green pepper rings to serve.

Serves: 4
Power setting: FULL
Preparation time: 20 minutes
Cooking time: 19 minutes

SMOKED HAM FLAN

350 g/12 oz curd cheese
2 eggs, beaten
150 ml/¼ pint milk
salt and freshly ground
    black pepper
100 g/4 oz cooked
    smoked ham, chopped
1 × 23 cm (9 inch) baked
    wholemeal flan shell
lemon slices to garnish

Preheat a microwave crisper griddle in the microwave on FULL POWER for 7 minutes.

Meanwhile, beat the cheese with the eggs, milk and salt and pepper to taste. Fold in half of the ham and spoon into the flan shell.

Place in the crisper griddle and cook on MEDIUM POWER for 12 minutes, turning the griddle twice. Leave to cool at room temperature.

Serve garnished with the remaining ham and lemon slices. Cut into wedges to serve.

Serves: 6-8
Power settings: FULL, MEDIUM
Preparation time: 20-30 minutes
Cooking time: 19 minutes

DEVILLED MUSHROOMS

225 g/8 oz button
    mushrooms, wiped
25 g/1 oz butter
100 ml/4 fl oz double
    cream
1 tablespoon
    Worcestershire sauce
1 tablespoon tomato
    ketchup
½ teaspoon mustard
    powder
1 teaspoon vinegar
salt and freshly ground
    black pepper
pinch of ground nutmeg

Place the mushrooms in a dish with the butter. Cook on FULL POWER for 3 minutes, stirring once.

Blend the cream with the Worcestershire sauce, tomato ketchup, mustard, vinegar, salt and pepper to taste and nutmeg. Stir into the mushrooms, blending well.

Carefully divide between 4 ramekin dishes. Cover and cook on DEFROST power for 3 minutes, re-arranging once.

Stir each ramekin and serve with hot toast fingers.

Serves: 4
Power settings: FULL, DEFROST
Preparation time: 10 minutes
Cooking time: 6 minutes

HERB, CHEESE AND GARLIC BREAD

1 Vienna loaf, about
    30 cm (12 inches) long
1 × 125 g (4 oz) roll
    savoury butter with
    herbs and garlic
75 g/3 oz Double
    Gloucester cheese,
    grated

Check that the loaf will fit inside the microwave and turn freely. If not, cut in half to prepare.

Make diagonal slits in the loaf almost to the base of the loaf but not quite through, about 4 cm (1½ inches) apart.

Slice the savoury butter into rounds and place a round in each slit with some of the cheese.

Loosely wrap the loaf in a piece of absorbent kitchen paper and place, cut side uppermost, in the microwave. Cook for 1½ minutes or until the butter has melted and the bread is warm.

Serve at once, perhaps as an accompaniment to soups or vegetable starters.

Serves: 4
Power setting: FULL
Preparation time: 5 minutes
Cooking time: 1½ minutes

Illustrated on p.37

CAULIFLOWER SOUP WITH CROÛTES

350 g/12 oz cauliflower
  florets
25 g/1 oz savoury butter
  with black pepper
1 large onion, peeled and
  finely chopped
600 ml/1 pint hot chicken
  stock
150 ml/¼ pint milk
2 teaspoons lemon juice
½ teaspoon ground
  nutmeg
½ teaspoon salt
75 g/3 oz savoury butter
  with herbs and garlic
6 slices French bread

Place the cauliflower florets, savoury butter and onion in a large bowl. Cover and cook for 10 minutes, stirring once.

Stir in the stock, cover loosely with cling film and cook for 10 minutes, stirring once.

Allow to cool slightly then purée in a blender or pass through a fine sieve.

Return to the bowl and add the milk, lemon juice, nutmeg and salt, blending well. Re-cover and cook for 5 minutes. Leave to stand, covered, while preparing the croûtes.

Place the savoury butter with herbs and garlic in a round shallow dish. Cook for 1 minute until hot and bubbly. Add the slices of French bread, turning them over in the savoury butter and cook for 2 minutes, turning over once. Drain on absorbent kitchen paper.

Ladle the soup into warmed soup bowls and float a croûte in each to serve.

Serves: 6
Power setting: FULL
Preparation time: 15-20 minutes
Cooking time: 28 minutes

COUNTRY-STYLE TERRINE

450 g/1 lb streaky bacon,
  rinded
225 g/8 oz pork fillet,
  minced
100 g/4 oz belly of pork,
  minced
100 g/4 oz lamb's or pig's
  liver, minced
1 small onion, peeled and
  grated
50 ml/2 fl oz brandy
50 ml/2 fl oz dry red wine
salt and freshly ground
  black pepper
1 teaspoon ground
  nutmeg
1 teaspoon dried mixed
  herbs
1 garlic clove, peeled and
  crushed
50 g/2 oz fresh white
  breadcrumbs
2 bay leaves
2 cloves

Line a 900 g (2 lb) glass loaf dish or a glazed pottery terrine dish with about three-quarters of the bacon.

Mix the pork fillet with the belly of pork, liver, onion, brandy, wine, salt and pepper to taste, nutmeg, herbs, garlic and bread-crumbs, blending well.

Spoon into the bacon-lined dish, press-ing down well. Cover with the remaining bacon slices and top with the bay leaves and cloves.

Place in a dish with warm water, so that the water comes half way up the sides of the pâté loaf dish. Cook for 40 minutes or until the pâté is cooked.

Drain off any excess fat and cover with greaseproof paper. Weight to press and chill overnight or at least for about 6-8 hours.

To serve, remove and discard the bay leaves and cloves. Turn out on to a serving dish and serve with toast, crackers or French bread.

To freeze
Cool quickly, cover, seal, label and freeze for up to 2 months.

Serves: 8-10
Power setting: FULL
Preparation time: 30-40 minutes, plus chilling
Cooking time: 40 minutes
Suitable for freezing

CHICKEN RISOTTO

400 g/14 oz cooked
   chicken, cut into bite-
   sized pieces
225 g/8 oz long-grain
   rice
1 large onion, peeled and
   chopped
2 garlic cloves, peeled and
   crushed
50 g/2 oz butter
450 ml/¾ pint boiling
   chicken stock
½ green pepper, cored,
   seeded and chopped
1 teaspoon dried mixed
   herbs
50 g/2 oz mushrooms,
   wiped and sliced
salt and freshly ground
   black pepper

Place the chicken, rice, onion, garlic and butter in a large bowl. Cook for 5 minutes, stirring once.

Add the stock, pepper and herbs, blending well. Cover and cook for 15 minutes, stirring three times.

Add the mushrooms and salt and pepper to taste, blending well. Cover and leave to stand for 5 minutes before serving.

To freeze
Cool quickly and place in a rigid container. Cover, seal, label and freeze for up to 3 months.

Serves: 4
Power setting: FULL
Preparation time: 15 minutes
Cooking time: 25 minutes
Suitable for freezing

CREAMED MUSHROOMS

25 g/1 oz butter
1 onion, peeled and finely
   chopped
450 g/1 lb button
   mushrooms, wiped
1 teaspoon plain flour
150 ml/¼ pint double
   cream
½ teaspoon ground
   nutmeg
1-2 teaspoons lemon
   juice
dash of Tabasco sauce
salt and black pepper

Place the butter and onion in a dish. Cover and cook for 2 minutes.

Add the mushrooms, blending well. Cover and cook for 8 minutes, stirring twice.

Add the flour, cream, nutmeg, lemon juice, Tabasco and salt and pepper to taste, blending well. Cook for 3 minutes, stirring once.

Serve at once with toast if liked.

Serves: 4
Power setting: FULL
Preparation time: 10 minutes
Cooking time: 13 minutes

POTTED TURKEY

50 g/2 oz savoury butter
   with black pepper
1 onion, peeled and finely
   chopped
350 g/12 oz cooked
   turkey, finely chopped
75 g/3 oz cooked ham,
   finely chopped
2 tablespoons sherry
75 g/3 oz butter

Place the savoury butter and onion in a bowl. Cover and cook for 4 minutes, stirring once.

Add the turkey, ham and sherry, blending well. Spoon into a small terrine or serving dish and press down well.

Dice the butter and place in a small bowl. Cook for 1½ minutes or until melted. Pour over the potted turkey and chill to set. Serve chilled with fingers of warm toast.

Serves: 4-6
Power setting: FULL
Preparation time: 15 minutes, plus chilling
Cooking time: 5½ minutes

STUFFED JACKET POTATOES

4 medium potatoes,
  scrubbed
25 g/1 oz savoury butter
  with black pepper
175 g/6 oz Cheddar
  cheese, grated
100 g/4 oz cooked ham,
  chopped

Dry the potatoes, prick the skins with a fork and arrange in a circle on a piece of absorbent kitchen paper. Cook for 6 minutes.

Turn the potatoes over and cook for a further 6 minutes or until soft.

Cut the potatoes in half lengthways. Scoop out the flesh into a bowl and mash well with a fork.

Add the butter, cheese and ham, blending well. Spoon the mixture back into the potato shells. Place on a fresh piece of absorbent kitchen paper and cook for 4 minutes. Serve hot.

Serves: 4
Power setting: FULL
Preparation time: 10-15 minutes
Cooking time: 16 minutes

ORIENTAL CHICKEN SOUP

25 g/1 oz butter
175 g/6 oz chicken breast,
  skinned and cut into
  thin strips
50 g/2 oz raw ham, cut
  into thin strips
50 g/2 oz mushrooms,
  wiped and sliced
1.2 litres/2 pints hot
  chicken stock
100 g/4 oz beansprouts
1 bouquet garni
1 teaspoon soy sauce
salt and freshly ground
  black pepper

Place the butter in a large casserole dish. Cook for 2 minutes.

Add the chicken, cover and cook for 5 minutes, stirring once.

Add the ham, mushrooms, stock, beansprouts, bouquet garni, soy sauce and salt and pepper to taste, blending well.

Cover and cook for 10 minutes, stirring twice.

Remove and discard the bouquet garni before serving.

Serves: 4
Power setting: FULL
Preparation time: 15 minutes
Cooking time: 17 minutes

EXOTIC KIPPER PÂTÉ

2 kippers
juice of ½ lemon
225 g/8 oz cream cheese
50 g/2 oz canned
  pineapple chunks
pinch of ground mace
pineapple juice to flavour
salt and freshly ground
  black pepper

Place the kippers in a shallow dish and sprinkle with a little of the lemon juice. Cover and cook for 5 minutes.

Allow to cool slightly then flake into a blender goblet, removing any skin and as many bones as possible.

Add the cream cheese, remaining lemon juice, pineapple chunks, mace, a little pineapple juice to flavour and salt and pepper to taste. Purée until smooth.

Spoon into a serving dish and chill until firm.

To freeze
Cover, seal, label and freeze for up to 1 month.

Serves: 4
Power setting: FULL
Preparation time: 10-15 minutes
Cooking time: 5 minutes
Suitable for freezing

Soups and Starters

Whether you choose a piping hot soup, cut-and come-again pâté or lightly tossed creamy pasta dish as a starter to a meal, the microwave will ensure that it is cooked, and reheated, if necessary, to mouth-watering perfection. For speed, heat and serve soups in their serving bowls; this will cut down on washing up, too. Serve with hot bread rolls, flavoursome garlic or herb bread or warm crackers – all welcome and speedy accompaniments.

TOMATO SOUP

1 tablespoon oil
1 onion, peeled and
    chopped
450 g/1 lb tomatoes,
    peeled and sliced
1 tablespoon tomato
    purée
1 tablespoon
    Worcestershire sauce
salt and freshly ground
    black pepper
pinch of ground paprika
1 tablespoon cornflour
750 ml/1¼ pint beef stock

Preheat a small browning dish for 3 minutes (or according to the manufacturer's instructions). Add the oil and cook for a further 1 minute. Add the onion and cook for 1½ minutes.

Transfer the onion to a large bowl. Add the tomatoes, tomato purée, Worcestershire sauce, salt and pepper to taste and paprika. Mix the cornflour with a little of the stock then stir, with the remaining stock, into the tomato mixture, blending well.

Cover and cook for 15 minutes, stirring three times. Serve hot.

To freeze
Cool quickly and pack into a rigid container. Cover, seal, label and freeze for up to 3 months.

Serves: 4
Power setting: FULL
Preparation time: 10 minutes
Cooking time: 20½ minutes
Suitable for freezing

Illustrated on p. 37

CREAM OF CORN SOUP

3 rashers streaky bacon,
    rinded and chopped
225 g/8 oz frozen corn
    kernels
150 ml/¼ pint water
25 g/1 oz butter
½ onion, peeled and
    finely chopped
25 g/1 oz plain flour
600 ml/1 pint milk
salt and freshly ground
    black pepper

Place the bacon in a bowl and cook for 3½ minutes or until crisp. Drain on absorbent kitchen towel.

Place the corn and water in a bowl. Cover and cook for 7 minutes, stirring once.

Place the butter in a bowl and cook for 1 minute. Add the onion, cover and cook for 3 minutes. Add the flour, blending well. Cook for 2 minutes, stirring once.

Place the milk in a jug. Cook for 3 minutes. Gradually add the milk to the onion mixture, blending well. Add the corn and water mixture and salt and pepper to taste and mix well to blend. Cook for 9 minutes, stirring twice.

Serve at once sprinkled with the cooked bacon.

To freeze
Cool quickly and place in a rigid container. Cover, seal, label and freeze for up to 3 months.

Serves: 4
Power setting: FULL
Preparation time: 10 minutes
Cooking time: 28½ minutes
Suitable for freezing

VICHYSSOISE

25 g/1 oz butter

3 medium leeks, trimmed, washed and coarsely sliced

1 onion, peeled and chopped

2 large potatoes, peeled and chopped

900 ml/1½ pints chicken stock

150 ml/¼ pint double cream

salt and freshly ground white pepper

snipped chives to garnish

Place the butter in a large bowl and cook for ½ minute to melt. Add the leeks and onion. Cover and cook for 3 minutes, stirring once.

Add the potatoes and chicken stock. Cover and cook for 15-18 minutes or until the potatoes are tender, stirring twice.

Purée in a blender or pass through a fine sieve.

Return to the bowl and stir in the cream and salt and pepper to taste. Cover and cook for 4 minutes, stirring once.

Serve hot or chilled sprinkled with snipped chives.

Serves: 4-6
Power setting: FULL
Preparation time: 20 minutes
Cooking time: 22½-25½ minutes

Illustrated on p. 40

PRAWN AND WATERCRESS SOUP

25 g/1 oz butter

1 large bunch watercress, washed and sorted

1 onion, peeled and thinly sliced

225 g/8 oz fresh or frozen peas

600 ml/1 pint milk

salt and freshly ground black pepper

150 ml/¼ pint single cream

100 g/4 oz shelled prawns, chopped

To garnish:

watercress sprigs

4 whole prawns

Place the butter in a large casserole dish and cook for ½ minute to melt. Stir in the watercress and onion. Cook for 2½ minutes, stirring once.

Add the peas and half of the milk. Cover and cook for 10 minutes, stirring once.

Purée in a blender until smooth with the remaining milk. Season to taste with salt and pepper. Chill thoroughly.

Whisk the cream into the soup mixture and stir in the prawns. Serve chilled, garnished with watercress sprigs and whole prawns.

Serves: 4
Power setting: FULL
Preparation time: 15 minutes, plus chilling
Cooking time: 13 minutes

BORTSCH

550-675 g/1¼-1½ lb raw beetroot, peeled and coarsely grated

900 ml/1½ pints water

1½ teaspoons salt

¼ teaspoon freshly ground black pepper

25 g/1 oz sugar

4½ tablespoons lemon juice

150 ml/¼ pint soured cream

Place the beetroot, water, salt, pepper, sugar and lemon juice in a large bowl. Cook, uncovered, for 12 minutes, stirring twice, or until the beetroot is tender.

Cover and leave to cool then chill for 4-6 hours or overnight.

Spoon into serving bowls and top with a swirl of the soured cream. Serve cold.

Serves: 6-8
Power setting: FULL
Preparation time: 20 minutes plus chilling
Cooking time: 12 minutes

MAKING STOCK

A good home-made stock can prove the vital ingredient in a soup, sauce or hot pot.

If you're in a hurry then a good commercial cube can be used, but the microwave can upstage the commercial alternative by producing traditional stock from bones in minutes.

To make a veal, lamb or beef stock:
Place bones in a large bowl and cover with boiling water. Add a selection of flavouring vegetables, a bouquet garni and salt and pepper to taste. Cover and cook on FULL POWER for 40 minutes, checking the stock level every 10 minutes and topping up if necessary to keep bones just covered.

Strain and cool completely. Skim and store in the refrigerator for up to 48 hours, or freeze for up to 6 months.

To make a poultry or game stock:
Place carcass in a large bowl and cover with boiling water. Add a selection of flavouring vegetables, a bouquet garni and salt and pepper to taste. Cover and cook on FULL POWER for 20 minutes, checking the stock level every 5 minutes and topping up if necessary to keep carcass just covered.

Strain and cool completely. Skim and store in the refrigerator for up to 48 hours, or freeze for up to 6 months.

To make a fish stock:
Place bones, head, tail and fish trimmings in a large bowl and cover with boiling water. Add a selection of flavouring vegetables, a bouquet garni and salt and pepper to taste. Cover and cook on FULL POWER for 10 minutes, checking the stock level once and topping up if necessary to keep ingredients just covered.

Strain and cool completely. Skim and store for up to 24 hours in the refrigerator. Do not freeze fish stock.

MUSSEL CHOWDER

100 g/4 oz green streaky bacon, rinded and chopped
1 onion, peeled and chopped
1 stick celery, scrubbed and chopped
1 small green pepper, cored, seeded and chopped
2 small potatoes, peeled and chopped
450 ml/¾ pint boiling water
1 bay leaf
salt and freshly ground black pepper
40 g/1½ oz plain flour
600 ml/1 pint milk
1 × 283 g (10 oz) can mussels, drained
chopped fresh parsley to garnish

Place the bacon in a large bowl. Cook for 2 minutes. Add the onion, celery and green pepper and cook for 3 minutes, stirring once.

Add the potatoes, water, bay leaf and salt and pepper to taste. Cook for 6 minutes, stirring once. Remove and discard the bay leaf.

Blend the flour with a little of the milk, then add the remaining milk. Whisk this mixture into the soup.

Cook for 10 minutes, whisking every 2 minutes. Add the mussels, blending well and cook for a further 3 minutes, stirring once.

Serve hot sprinkled with chopped parsley to garnish.

Serves: 4-6
Power setting: FULL
Preparation time: 20 minutes
Cooking time: 24 minutes

TOMATO SOUP (p.34) AND HERB, CHEESE AND GARLIC BREAD (p.30)

KIPPER PÂTÉ (p.43)

PÂTÉ MAISON (p.43)

VICHYSSOISE SOUP (p.35) AND CREAM OF MUSHROOM SOUP (opposite)

CREAM OF MUSHROOM SOUP

25 g/1 oz butter
1 tablespoon cornflour
600 ml/1 pint rich chicken
  stock
300 ml/½ pint milk
100 g/4 oz button
  mushrooms, sliced
salt and freshly ground
  black pepper
150 ml/¼ pint single
  cream
1 tablespoon lemon juice
1 tablespoon chopped
  fresh parsley

Place the butter, cornflour dissolved in a little stock, remaining stock, milk, mushrooms and salt and pepper to taste in a large bowl. Cook on FULL POWER for 5 minutes, stirring twice.

Cook on MEDIUM POWER for a further 12 minutes, stirring twice.

Purée in a blender until smooth and return to the bowl. Cook on FULL POWER for 2 minutes.

Stir in the cream, blending well. Cook on FULL POWER for a further 2 minutes.

Stir in the lemon juice and parsley, blending well. Serve at once.

Serves: 4
Power settings: FULL, MEDIUM
Preparation time: 15 minutes
Cooking time: 21 minutes

Illustrated on p. 40

'PHILLY' ONION SOUP

450 g/1 lb onions, peeled
  and finely chopped
2 potatoes (approx 250
  g/10 oz), peeled and
  chopped
900 ml/1½ pints boiling
  chicken stock
salt and freshly ground
  black pepper
125 g/5 oz Philadelphia
  soft cheese

Place the onions in a large bowl with the potatoes, stock and salt and pepper to taste. Cover and cook for 10 minutes, stirring once. Purée until smooth in a blender or pass through a fine sieve.

Cream the cheese with a little of the soup, beating well to prevent lumps. Return to the rest of the soup. Cook for 10 minutes, stirring once.

Serve hot with French bread.

To freeze
Cool quickly and pack in a rigid container. Cover, seal, label and freeze for up to 2 months.

Serves: 4
Power setting: FULL
Preparation time: 15 minutes
Cooking time: 20 minutes
Suitable for freezing

GOLDEN CARROT SOUP

25 g/ oz butter
1 onion, peeled and
  chopped
1 × 225 g (8 oz) packet
  frozen diced carrots
600 ml/1 pint chicken
  stock
salt and freshly ground
  black pepper
1 teaspoon sugar
To garnish:
4 tablespoons single
  cream
1 tablespoon chopped
  fresh parsley

Place the butter in a bowl and cook for ½ minute, to melt. Add the onion, cover and cook for 3 minutes.

Stir in the carrots, stock, salt and pepper to taste and sugar, blending well. Cover and cook for 10 minutes, stirring once. Leave to stand for 5 minutes.

Purée in a blender or pass through a fine sieve. Pour into a serving bowl and cook for 2 minutes to reheat.

Serve garnished with a swirl of the cream and sprinkled with the parsley.

To freeze
Cool quickly and pack in a rigid container. Cover, seal, label and freeze for up to 3 months.

Serves: 2
Power setting: FULL
Preparation time: 10 minutes
Cooking time: 20½ minutes
Suitable for freezing

MULLIGATAWNY SOUP

25 g/1 oz butter
1 onion, peeled and
　chopped
1 carrot, peeled and
　chopped
2 sticks celery, chopped
½ green pepper, cored,
　seeded and chopped
225 g/8 oz tomatoes,
　peeled and chopped
1 apple, peeled, cored and
　chopped
900 ml/1½ pints boiling
　stock
1 tablespoon curry
　powder
2 cloves
1 tablespoon chopped
　fresh parsley
1 tablespoon sugar
salt and freshly ground
　black pepper
2 tablespoons cornflour
150 ml/¼ pint milk
75-100 g/3-4 oz cooked
　lamb, beef or chicken,
　finely chopped
25 g/1 oz long-grain rice

Place the butter in a large bowl and cook for ½ minute to melt. Add the onion, carrot, celery and pepper and cook for 3 minutes.

Add the tomatoes and apple, blending well. Cook for a further 2 minutes.

Add the stock, curry powder, cloves, parsley, sugar and salt and pepper to taste, blending well. Cook for 10 minutes, stirring once.

Blend the cornflour with a little of the milk then stir in the remaining milk. Stir the milk mixture into the soup with the meat and rice. Stir well to blend.

Cook for 5 minutes, stirring twice. Cover and leave to stand for 5 minutes or until the rice is cooked.

Reheat by cooking for 2 minutes. Serve hot.

To freeze
Cool quickly and pack in a rigid container. Cover, seal, label and freeze for up to 1 month.

Serves: 4-6
Power setting: FULL
Preparation time: 25 minutes
Cooking time: 17½ minutes
Suitable for freezing

CHICKEN GALANTINE

25 g/1 oz butter
25 g/1 oz chopped onion
100 g/4 oz fresh brown
　breadcrumbs
finely grated rind and
　juice of 1 lemon
50 g/2 oz walnuts,
　chopped
salt and freshly ground
　black pepper
1 × 1.5 kg (3½ lb)
　chicken, boned
4 slices cooked shoulder
　ham
6 tablespoons chopped
　parsley
450 g/1 lb sausagemeat
175 g/6 oz streaky bacon,
　rinded
soy sauce　　　　(cont.)

Place the butter in a bowl and cook on FULLPOWER for ½ minute to melt. Add the onion and cook on FULL POWER for 2 minutes. Add the breadcrumbs, lemon rind, lemon juice, walnuts and salt and pepper to taste, blending well. Shape into a roll about 20 cm/8 inches long.

Place the chicken, skin-side down, on a board and spread out flat. Arrange the ham in a single layer over the top and sprinkle with the parsley. Break up the sausagemeat and spread evenly over the parsley. Lay the bacon slices in a single layer on top. Finally place the prepared stuffing roll along the length of the chicken.

Ease both hands flat under the sides of the chicken and lift up to reshape over the stuffing, trussing the legs and wings with string to hold in position. Place on a roasting rack set in a shallow dish or on a micro-

wave bacon rack, upside down. Brush with soy sauce to coat and cover lightly with greaseproof paper. Cook on MEDIUM POWER for 20 minutes.

Turn the chicken over, brush with the soy sauce, re-cover and cook on MEDIUM POWER for 10 minutes. Uncover and cook on FULL POWER for 25 minutes. Leave to cool, cover with cling film and chill overnight.

To serve, cut off the wings and legs and carve off the meat. Carve the stuffed chicken across the breasts to give slices of chicken meat surrounding the stuffing.

For a special finish, about 1 hour before serving, glaze the chicken on a serving plate with lemon aspic. To prepare, sprinkle the gelatine over the water in a small bowl. Leave to stand for 5 minutes. Stir in the lemon juice, wine vinegar, sugar and a

Lemon aspic:
2 teaspoons powdered
    gelatine
150 ml/¼ pint cold water
1 tablespoon lemon juice
1 tablespoon white wine
    vinegar
1 tablespoon caster sugar
salt

pinch of salt. Cook on FULL POWER for ½ minute to dissolve. Cool until the mixture starts to thicken then spoon evenly over the chicken. Chill to set.

Serves: 6-8
Power settings: FULL, MEDIUM
Preparation time: 1 hour, plus cooling and chilling
Cooking time: 1 hour, 3 minutes

PÂTÉ MAISON

100 g/4 oz streaky bacon,
    rinded and stretched
175 g/6 oz chicken livers,
    trimmed
1 egg, beaten
1 garlic clove, peeled and
    crushed
1 onion, peeled and
    chopped
2 tablespoons brandy
2 tablespoons chopped
    fresh thyme or
    marjoram
½ teaspoon ground
    mixed spice
pinch of ground nutmeg
freshly ground black
    pepper
225 g/8 oz lean pork,
    minced
175 g/6 oz pork fat,
    minced
100 g/4 oz ham or
    tongue, minced
2 tablespoons red wine

Line a 13×23 cm (5×9 inch) glass loaf dish or earthenware pâté dish with the bacon rashers, allowing them to hang over the edge by about 2.5 cm/1 inch.

Mix the chicken livers with the egg, garlic, onion, brandy, thyme or marjoram, mixed spice, nutmeg and pepper to taste, blending well.

In a separate bowl mix the pork with the pork fat, ham or tongue and red wine, blending well. Spoon a quarter of this mixture into the base of the prepared loaf dish. Top with the chicken liver mixture. Cover with the remaining pork mixture. Fold the bacon ends over the top of the pâté.

Pour 450 ml/¾ pint water into a large dish. Stand the pâté in this dish, cover and cook for 30 minutes, turning the dish twice.

Remove from the waterbath. Weight the pâté and chill to set.

Invert on to a serving plate and slice to serve.

To freeze
Cover, seal, label and freeze for up to 1 month.

Serves: 8
Power setting: FULL
Preparation time: 30-40 minutes
Cooking time: 30 minutes
Suitable for freezing

Illustrated on p. 39

KIPPER PÂTÉ

1×198 g (7 oz) packet
    frozen kipper fillets
75 g/3 oz butter
1×85 g (3 oz) packet
    Philadelphia soft cheese
1 teaspoon Worcestershire
    sauce
salt and freshly ground
    black pepper
lemon slices to garnish

Pierce the bag of kipper fillets and place on a plate. Cook for 6 minutes, turning over once. Allow to cool slightly then flake the fillets into a blender or food processor.

Place the butter in a bowl and cook for 1 minute to melt. Add two-thirds of the butter to the kippers with the cheese, Worcester-shire sauce and salt and pepper to taste. Blend until smooth then turn into a small terrine or serving dish.

Pour the remaining butter over the pâté and chill to set. Garnish with lemon slices and serve with hot buttered toast.

To freeze
Cover with foil, label and freeze for up to 2 months.

Serves: 4
Power setting: FULL
Preparation time: 10 minutes
Cooking time: 7 minutes
Suitable for freezing

Illustrated on p. 38

CHICKEN LIVER PÂTÉ

25 g/1 oz butter
1 onion, peeled and
  chopped
1 garlic clove, peeled and
  crushed
2 tablespoons chicken
  stock
225 g/8 oz chicken livers,
  trimmed
1 egg, beaten
1 tablespoon cornflour
4 tablespoons double
  cream
1 tablespoon sherry
salt and freshly ground
  black pepper
50 g/2 oz butter

Place the butter, onion, garlic and stock in a cooking dish. Cover and cook for 5 minutes, stirring once.

Add the chicken livers, blending well. Cover and cook for 4 minutes, stirring once.

Purée in a blender, mince or pass through a fine sieve.

Mix the egg with the cornflour and stir into the liver mixture, blending well. Add the cream, sherry and salt and pepper to taste.

Spoon into a 600 ml (1 pint) serving dish. Cover and cook for 5-5½ minutes, turning the dish twice.

Place the butter in a bowl and cook for 1 minute to melt.

Pour over the pâté and chill to set. Serve with toast fingers or crusty bread.

To freeze
Cover, seal, label and freeze for up to 2 months.

Serves: 4-6
Power setting: FULL
Preparation time: 25-30 minutes, plus chilling
Cooking time: 15-15½ minutes
Suitable for freezing

HIGHLAND PRAWNS

50 g/2 oz butter
1 small onion, peeled and
  chopped
350 g/12 oz peeled
  prawns
4 tablespoons double
  cream
2 tablespoons whisky or
  brandy
100 g/4 oz Cheddar
  cheese, grated
salt and freshly ground
  black pepper

Place the butter in a bowl and cook for 1 minute to melt. Add the onion, cover and cook for 3 minutes.

Add the prawns, blending well, Cover and cook for 2 minutes. Divide the mixture between four small ramekin dishes.

Place the cream and whisky or brandy in a bowl, cook for ½ minute. Season with salt and pepper to taste. Stir well and spoon evenly over the prawns.

Sprinkle with the cheese. Brown under a preheated hot grill.

Serve hot with toast fingers.

Serves: 4
Power setting: FULL
Preparation time: 10 minutes
Cooking time: 6½ minutes

SAVOURY SPINACH, HAM AND TOMATO

1 × 225 g (8) oz block
  frozen chopped
  spinach
7 g/¼ oz butter
1 tablespoon plain flour
¼ teaspoon ground
  nutmeg
2 tablespoons milk
salt and freshly ground
  black pepper
50 g/2 oz cooked ham,
  cut into strips
2 tomatoes, sliced and
  halved

Place the spinach in a 450 ml/¾ pint shallow glass oval dish. Cook on DEFROST POWER for 10 minutes or until defrosted.

Increase the power setting and cook on FULL POWER for 3 minutes, stirring once. Stir in the butter, blending well.

Mix the flour, nutmeg and milk in a jug and pour into the spinach. Season with salt and pepper to taste, blending well.

Cook on FULL POWER for 2 minutes, stirring once. Stir in the ham and top with the halved tomato slices. Cook on FULL POWER for 1 minute.

Serve hot with crusty French bread.

Serves: 2
Power settings: DEFROST, FULL
Preparation time: 5 minutes
Cooking time: 16 minutes

MARINATED MUSHROOMS

25 g/1 oz butter
1 small onion, peeled and
 finely chopped
1 garlic clove, peeled and
 crushed
450 g/1 lb button
 mushrooms, trimmed
 and wiped
½ teaspoon dried mixed
 herbs
150 ml/¼ pint dry white
 wine
1 bay leaf
1 teaspoon chopped fresh
 parsley
salt and freshly ground
 black pepper

Place the butter in a bowl and cook on FULL POWER for ½ minute. Add the onion and garlic. Cover and cook on FULL POWER for 1 minute.

Add the mushrooms, blending well. Cover and cook on FULL POWER for 3 minutes.

Stir in the herbs, wine, bay leaf, parsley and salt and pepper to taste. Cook on DEFROST POWER for 8 minutes, stirring once.

Leave to cool then chill lightly. Remove and discard the bay leaf. Serve chilled with French bread.

Serves: 4
Power settings: FULL, DEFROST
Preparation time: 10 minutes, plus chilling
Cooking time: 12½ minutes

HOT SPICY GRAPEFRUIT

2 grapefruit
25 g/1 oz demerara sugar
pinch of ground
 cinnamon
pinch of ground mixed
 spice
4 maraschino or glacé
 cherries

Cut the grapefruit in half and, using a grapefruit knife, separate the segments.

Mix the sugar with the cinnamon and mixed spice. Sprinkle evenly over the grapefruit halves.

Place a cherry in the centre of each grapefruit half and place in a cooking dish.

Cook, uncovered, for 3 minutes, turning the dish once.

Serve at once.

Serves: 4
Power setting: FULL
Preparation time: 5 minutes
Cooking time: 3 minutes

CRAB GRATINÉE DIABLE

25 g/1 oz butter
350 g/12 oz canned or
 frozen crabmeat,
 thawed
25 g/1 oz cheese, grated
2 tablespoons fresh white
 breadcrumbs
1 tablespoon single cream
pinch of mustard powder
pinch of cayenne pepper
salt and freshly ground
 black pepper
dash of anchovy essence
1 firm banana
lemon juice
1 tablespoon chopped
 fresh parsley

Place the butter in a bowl and cook for ½ minute to melt. Add the crabmeat, cheese, breadcrumbs, cream, mustard, cayenne, salt and pepper to taste and anchovy essence, blending well. Spoon into a small serving dish.

Cook for 2 minutes. Leave to stand for 5 minutes. Turn the dish and cook for a further 2 minutes.

Peel and slice banana and toss in the lemon juice to prevent it turning brown. Place around the edge of the crab dish. Cook for 1 minute.

Sprinkle with the chopped parsley and serve at once with toast fingers or crisp dry crackers.

Serves: 4
Power setting: FULL
Preparation time: 10-15 minutes
Cooking time: 10½ minutes

Fish and Shellfish

Simply steamed or soused, exotically stir-fried or stuffed, beautifully baked, braised or poached, fish is a perfect food for cooking in the microwave. Whether it be a budget-stretching mid-week family meal for four or an elegant dinner party main course for eight, the microwave will cook fish and shellfish excellently. Timings will be fast, so don't be tempted to cook for longer than suggested. Times given here ensure that all seafood is cooked to retain its delicate flaky texture, moistness and distinctive, delicate flavour.
If the exact fish specified in a recipe is not available for reasons of locality or season, you may substitute another of the same type.

DEVONSHIRE COD

2 × 225 g (8 oz) cod steaks
150 ml/¼ pint dry cider
salt and freshly ground
　black pepper
1 tomato, peeled and
　sliced
25 g/1 oz mushrooms,
　wiped and chopped
25 g/1 oz butter
15 g/½ oz cornflour
50 g/2 oz cheese, grated
450 g/1 lb creamed
　potatoes (see p.106)

Place the cod in a casserole dish. Pour over the cider and season with salt and pepper to taste. Top with the tomato and mushrooms and dot with half of the butter. Cover and cook for 5 minutes, turning the dish once.

Carefully strain the juices from the fish and make up to 150 ml/¼ pint with extra cider if necessary.

Place the remaining butter in a jug and cook for ½ minute to melt. Gradually add the cornflour and reserved juices, blending well. Cook for 3 minutes, stiring twice. Pour over the fish and sprinkle with the cheese.

Pipe the potatoes in a decorative border around the fish. Cook for 2 minutes, turning the dish once. Serve hot.

To freeze
Cool quickly, cover, seal, label and freeze for up to 2 months.

Serves: 2
Power setting: FULL
Preparation time: 20-25 minutes
Cooking time: 10½ minutes
Suitable for freezing

CRAB MOUSSE

25 g/1 oz butter
25 g/1 oz flour
300 ml/½ pint light
　chicken stock
5 tablespoons white wine
3 teaspoons powdered
　gelatine
300 ml/½ pint
　mayonnaise
450 g/1 lb cooked
　crabmeat, flaked
150 ml/¼ pint double
　cream, whipped
salt and freshly ground
　black pepper
cucumber slices to
　garnish

Place the butter in a bowl and cook for ½ minute to melt. Add the flour, blending well. Gradually add the stock, blending well. Cook for 4½-5 minutes, stirring every 1 minute until smooth and thickened.

Place the wine in a bowl and cook for ½ minute. Stir in the gelatine, stirring well to dissolve.

Stir the gelatine mixture into the sauce with the mayonnaise, blending well. Fold in the crabmeat, cream and salt and pepper to taste.

Spoon into individual ramekins or a large serving dish and chill to set.

Serve lightly chilled, garnished with cucumber slices. Serve with thin slices of brown bread and butter.

To freeze
Cover, seal, label and freeze for up to 1 month.

Serves: 6-8
Power setting: FULL
Preparation time: 25 minutes, plus chilling
Cooking time: 5½ minutes
Suitable for freezing

Illustrated on p. 57

FISH PIE

450 g/1 lb cod or haddock
  fillets
2 tablespoons water
25 g/1 oz butter
25 g/1 oz plain flour
300 ml/½ pint hot milk
2 hard-boiled eggs, shelled
  and chopped
100 g/4 oz cooked peas
celery salt and freshly
  ground white pepper
450 g/1 lb creamed
  potatoes (see p.106)

Place the fish in a shallow cooking dish with the water. Cover and cook for 4 minutes, turning the dish once. Drain and flake the fish, discarding any skin and bones.

Place the butter in a bowl and cook for 1 minute. Stir in the flour, blending well. Gradually add the milk and cook for 2 minutes, stirring twice.

Add the eggs, flaked fish, peas and celery salt and pepper to taste, blending well.

Line a serving dish with the creamed potatoes. Spoon the fish mixture into the centre. Cook for 5 minutes, turning the dish once. Brown under a preheated hot grill if liked. Serve hot.

To freeze
Cool quickly, cover, seal, label and freeze for up to 2 months.

Serves: 4
Power setting: FULL
Preparation time: 20-25 minutes
Cooking time: 12 minutes
Suitable for freezing

PLAICE AND ASPARAGUS

4 plaice fillets, skinned
salt and freshly ground
  black pepper
about 20 canned
  asparagus spears,
  drained or frozen ones,
  thawed
150 ml/¼ pint dry white
  wine
150 ml/¼ pint water
1 tablespoon lemon juice
25 g/1 oz butter
25 g/1 oz plain flour
1 bunch watercress,
  sorted, washed and
  dried
whole prawns to garnish

Season the fish fillets with salt and pepper to taste. Wrap each fillet around about 5 asparagus spears. Arrange 'spoke' fashion in a cooking dish. Add the wine, water and lemon juice. Cover and cook for 5 minutes, turning the dish once.

Drain the fish with a slotted spoon and place on a warmed serving plate. Keep warm. Reserve the stock.

Place the butter in a bowl and cook for ½ minute to melt. Add the flour, blending well. Gradually add the reserved stock. Cook for 3-4 minutes, stirring every 1 minute until smooth and thickened.

Pour the sauce into a blender and add half of the watercress. Process until finely chopped. Pour over the fish. Garnish with the whole prawns and remaining watercress. Serve at once.

Serves: 2
Power setting: FULL
Preparation time: 10 minutes
Cooking time: 8½-9½ minutes

Illustrated on p.75

COD GEORGETTE

4 small frozen cod steaks,
  thawed
2 large potatoes,
  scrubbed, pricked and
  baked (see p.102)
1 large egg (sizes 1, 2)
  beaten
salt and freshly ground
  black pepper
½ recipe Cheese Sauce
  (see p.140)
25 g/1 oz cheese, grated

Place the cod steaks in a cooking dish. Cover and cook for 4 minutes, turning the dish once.

Cut the potatoes in half, scoop out the soft flesh and mix with the egg and salt and pepper to taste, blending well until smooth.

Place a cod steak in each potato half and cover with the sauce. Spoon the potato mixture into a piping bag fitted with a large star nozzle and pipe around the edge of the potato skin. Sprinkle with the cheese.

Cook for 2-3 minutes to reheat.

Serves: 2-4
Power setting: FULL
Preparation time: 15-20 minutes
Cooking time: 6-7 minutes

GUIDE TO COOKING FISH

Fish		Quantity	Cooking time in minutes on FULL POWER	Preparation
Bass	whole	450 g/1 lb	5-7	Shield the head and tail with foil. Cut the skin in two or three places to prevent it from bursting.
Cod	fillets	450 g/1 lb	5-7	Place the fillet tails in the centre of the dish or shield with foil. Cut the skin in two or three places to prevent it from bursting.
	steaks	450 g/1 lb	4-5	Cover with greaseproof paper before cooking.
Haddock	fillets	450 g/1 lb	5-7	Place the fillet tails to the centre of the dish or shield with foil. Cut the skin in two or three places to prevent it from bursting.
	steaks	450 g/1 lb	4-5	Cover with greaseproof paper before cooking.
Halibut	steaks	450 g/1 lb	4-5	Cover with greaseproof paper before cooking.
Kippers	whole	1	1-2	Cover with cling film and snip two holes in the top to allow the steam to escape.
Red mullet and red snapper	whole	450 g/1 lb	5-7	Shield the head and tail with foil. Cut the skin in two or three places to prevent it from bursting.
Salmon	steaks	450 g/1 lb	4-5	Cover with greaseproof paper before cooking.
Salmon trout	whole	450 g/1 lb	7-8	Shield the head and tail with foil. Cut the skin in two or three places to prevent it from bursting.
Scallops		450 g/1 lb	5-7	Cover with dampened absorbent kitchen paper.
Smoked haddock	whole	450 g/1 lb	4-5	Cover with cling film, snipping two holes in the top to allow the steam to escape.
Trout	whole	450 g/1 lb	8-9	Shield the head and tail with foil, cut the skin in two or three places to prevent it from bursting.

PRAWN AND PASTA CREOLE

100 g/4 oz short cut
    macaroni
450 ml/¾ pint boiling
    water
2 tablespoons oil
salt and freshly ground

Place the macaroni in a deep bowl with the water, 1 tablespoon of the oil and a pinch of salt. Cover and cook for 10 minutes. Leave to stand, covered, while preparing the sauce.

Place the remaining oil in a bowl with the onion, celery, pepper and garlic. Cover and cook for 5 minutes, stirring once. Add the tomatoes with their juice, wine, tomato purée and salt and pepper to taste, blending well. Cover and cook for 6 minutes, stirring once.

black pepper
1 onion, peeled and finely
    chopped
3 sticks celery, scrubbed
    and finely chopped
1 green pepper, cored,
    seeded and sliced
1 garlic clove, peeled and
    crushed
1 × 397 g (14 oz) can
    peeled tomatoes
300 ml/½ pint dry white
    wine
2 tablespoons tomato
    purée
225 g/8 oz peeled prawns

Drain the macaroni and add to the tomato mixture with the prawns, blending well. Cover and cook for 1 minute.

Serve at once.

To freeze
Cool quickly and place in a rigid container. Cover, seal, label and freeze for up to 1 month.

Serves: 4
Power setting: FULL
Preparation time: 15-20 minutes
Cooking time: 22 minutes
Suitable for freezing

GUIDE TO REHEATING BOILED SHELLFISH

Shellfish	Quantity	Cooking time in minutes on FULL POWER	Preparation
Lobster – tails – whole	450 g/1 lb 450 g/1 lb	5-6 6-8	Turn tails over halfway through the cooking time. Allow to stand for 5 minutes before serving. Turn over halfway through the cooking time.
Prawns and scampi	450 g/1 lb	5-6	Arrange the peeled shellfish in a ring in a shallow dish and cover with cling film, snipping two holes in the top to allow the steam to escape.
Shrimps	450 g/1 lb	5-6	Arrange the peeled shrimps in a ring in a shallow dish and cover with cling film, snipping two holes in the top to allow the steam to escape.

HADDOCK WITH DILL SAUCE

800 g/1¾ lb haddock fillet
juice of 1 lemon
salt and freshly ground
    black pepper
3 rashers streaky bacon,
    rinded
water
25 g/1 oz butter
1 rounded tablespoon
    plain flour
1 teaspoon dried dill
150 ml/¼ pint double
    cream

Season the haddock fillet with the lemon juice and salt and pepper to taste. Place in a greased cooking dish. Lay the bacon rashers on top. Cover and cook for 12-14 minutes, turning the dish once.

Remove the fish and bacon with a slotted spoon and arrange on a warmed serving plate. Keep warm.

Strain the cooking juices into a measuring jug and make up to 300 ml/½ pint with water. Add the butter, flour and dill, blending well. Cook for 5 minutes, stirring 3 times.

Add the cream, blending well. Check and adjust the seasoning if necessary. Pour over the fish to serve.

Serves: 4
Power setting: FULL
Preparation time: 20 minutes
Cooking time: 17-19 minutes

HADDOCK WITH PRAWNS

675 g/1½ lb haddock
   fillets
300 ml/½ pint water
25 g/1 oz butter
1 onion, peeled and
   chopped
2 tablespoons plain flour
100 g/4 oz mushrooms,
   wiped and sliced
1 red pepper, cored,
   seeded and cut into
   strips
175 g/6 oz peeled prawns
parsley sprigs to garnish

Skin the haddock fillets. Place the skin in a bowl with the water. Cover and cook for 5 minutes. Leave to stand while preparing the sauce.

Place the butter in a bowl and cook for ½ minute to melt. Add the onion, cover and cook for 3 minutes, stirring once. Stir in the flour, blending well. Cook for a further 1 minute.

Remove and discard the fish skin from the stock. Gradually add the stock to the flour mixture, blending well. Stir in the mushrooms and pepper. Spoon into a cooking dish and top with the haddock fillets. Cover and cook for 5 minutes, turning the dish once.

Add the prawns, cover and cook for 2 minutes, turning the dish once.

Serve hot garnished with parsley sprigs.

Serves: 4
Power setting: FULL
Preparation time: 15 minutes
Cooking time: 16½ minutes

ST CLEMENT'S PLAICE

3 oranges
6 plaice fillets, skinned
juice of 1 lemon
salt and freshly ground
   white pepper

Peel, remove the pith and coarsely chop the flesh of 2 of the oranges, reserving any juice. Thickly slice the remaining orange.

Spoon the chopped flesh over the plaice fillets and roll up to enclose. Place in a cooking dish. Spoon over any reserved orange juice and the lemon juice. Season with salt and pepper to taste.

Cover and cook for 4 minutes, turning the dish twice.

Serve hot garnished with the orange slices.

Serves: 3-4
Power setting: FULL
Preparation time: 10-15 minutes
Cooking time: 4 minutes

HADDOCK FLAMENCO

1 tablespoon oil
1 onion, peeled and sliced
1 small green pepper,
   cored, seeded and
   sliced
225 g/8 oz courgettes,
   sliced
2 tomatoes, peeled and
   cut into wedges
salt and freshly ground
   black pepper
675 g/1½ lb smoked
   haddock fillets

Place the oil in a bowl with the onion and pepper. Cover and cook for 4 minutes, stirring once.

Add the courgettes, tomatoes and salt and pepper to taste, blending well. Cover and cook for 4 minutes, stirring once. Leave to stand, covered, while cooking the fish.

Place the fish in a cooking dish. Cover and cook for 5-6 minutes. Spoon over the courgette mixture. Cover and cook for 1-2 minutes.

Serve hot with creamy mashed potatoes (see p.106).

Serves: 4
Power setting: FULL
Preparation time: 10-15 minutes
Cooking time: 14-16 minutes

FISHY BACON BAKE

4 × 175 g (6 oz) cod steaks
salt and freshly ground
    black pepper
25 g/1 oz butter
1 tablespoon chopped
    fresh tarragon or
    parsley
8 rashers back bacon,
    rinded
4 tomatoes, washed and
    quartered

Season the cod steaks with salt and pepper to taste. Dot with the butter and sprinkle with the tarragon or parsley. Wrap in the bacon rashers and place in a cooking dish.

Cover and cook for 6 minutes, turning the dish once. Place the tomatoes around the fish. Cover and cook for 2-3 minutes. Leave to stand, covered, for 5 minutes before serving.

Serves: 4
Power setting: FULL
Preparation time: 10-15 minutes
Cooking time: 13-14 minutes

HADDOCK BUNWICH

1 × 175 g (6 oz) packet
    frozen buttered
    smoked haddock
1 small cottage loaf
2 tablespoons
    mayonnaise
2 tablespoons double
    cream
3 tomatoes, peeled, seeded
    and chopped
1 small onion, peeled and
    finely chopped
salt and freshly ground
    black pepper

Pierce the smoked haddock bag and place on a plate. Cook for 6 minutes, turning the bag over halfway through the cooking time. Cool, skin and flake the haddock into bite-sized pieces.

Cut a slice from the top of the loaf and scoop out the soft centre (use for bread-crumbs for another dish). Wrap the loaf loosely in cling film and cook for ½ minute to warm through.

Meanwhile mix the haddock with the mayonnaise, cream, tomatoes, onion and salt and pepper to taste. Spoon back into the loaf and replace the top.

Serve while still warm cut into wedges or slices.

Serves: 4-6
Power setting: FULL
Preparation time: 15 minutes plus
cooling
Cooking time: 6½ minutes

RICE-STUFFED TROUT

50 g/2 oz butter
100 g/4 oz streaky bacon,
    rinded and finely
    chopped
1 small onion, peeled and
    chopped
350 g/12 oz cooked long-
    grain rice
4 × 225 g (8 oz) trout,
    gutted and prepared
    for cooking
salt and freshly ground
    black pepper
1 tablespoon lime juice
1 tablespoon chopped
    fresh parsley to sprinkle

Place the butter in a bowl with the bacon and onion. Cover and cook for 2 minutes, stirring once, then mix into the rice.

Use some of the rice mixture to stuff the trout. Place the remainder in the base of a shallow cooking dish. Top with the trout and season to taste with salt and pepper.

Pour over the lime juice and sprinkle with the parsley. Cover and cook for 10-12 minutes, turning the dish twice, until tender.

Serve with a green salad.

Serves: 4
Power setting: FULL
Preparation time: 20 minutes
Cooking time: 12-14 minutes

CRISPY WHITING

4 whiting fillets
25 g/1 oz butter
salt and freshly ground
  black pepper
4 rashers back bacon,
  rinded and chopped
1 small packet cheese and
  onion crisps
50 g/2 oz cheese, grated

Place the whiting fillets in a shallow cooking dish and dot with the butter. Sprinkle with pepper to taste and scatter over the bacon. Cover and cook for 4 minutes, turning the dish once.

Meanwhile, mix the crisps with the cheese. Spoon over the fish fillets. Cook, uncovered, for 2 minutes.

Sprinkle with salt to taste. Serve with vegetables in season.

Serves: 2-4
Power setting: FULL
Preparation time: 15 minutes
Cooking time: 6 minutes

HERRINGS WITH MUSTARD

25 g/1 oz butter
1 onion, peeled and
  chopped
50 g/2 oz fresh
  breadcrumbs
2 tablespoons chopped
  fresh parsley
1 teaspoon tomato purée
2 teaspoons mustard
  powder
salt and freshly ground
  black pepper
2 large herrings, filleted
2 tablespoons malt
  vinegar
1 teaspoon granulated
  sugar

Place the butter in a bowl and cook for ½ minute to melt. Add the onion, cover and cook for 3 minutes, stirring once.

Add the breadcrumbs, parsley, tomato purée, half of the mustard and salt and pepper to taste, blending well.

Spoon the filling into each of the herrings and lay flat in a cooking dish.

Mix the vinegar with the sugar and remaining mustard. Pour over the herrings, cover and cook for 4 minutes, turning the dish once.

Serve hot or lightly chilled.

Serves: 2—4
Power setting: FULL
Preparation time: 15 minutes
Cooking time: 7½ minutes

COLEY MEDITERRANEAN-STYLE

25 g/1 oz butter
1 onion, peeled and
  chopped
1 garlic clove, peeled and
  crushed
2 tomatoes, coarsely
  chopped
225 g/8 oz courgettes,
  sliced
675 g/1½ lb coley,
  skinned and cubed
1 tablespoon tomato
  purée
1 teaspoon dried
  marjoram
salt and freshly ground
  black pepper

Place the butter in a cooking dish and cook for ½ minute to melt. Add the onion and garlic, cover and cook for 3 minutes, stirring once.

Add the tomatoes and courgettes, blending well. Cover and cook for 3 minutes, stirring once.

Add the fish, tomato purée, marjoram and salt and pepper to taste, blending well. Cover and cook for 4 minutes, stirring once. Serve hot.

To freeze
Cool quickly and place in a rigid container. Cover, seal, label and freeze for up to 2 months.

Serves: 4
Power setting: FULL
Preparation time: 15-20 minutes
Cooking time: 10½ minutes
Suitable for freezing

SCALLOPS WITH CIDER AND CREAM

50 g/2 oz butter
2 shallots, peeled and
    finely chopped
40 g/1½ oz plain flour
5 tablespoons dry cider
5 tablespoons milk
100 g/4 oz mushrooms,
    wiped and sliced
450 g/1 lb scallops,
    prepared for cooking
salt and freshly ground
    white pepper
2 tablespoons double
    cream
25 g/1 oz cheese, grated
chopped parsley to
    garnish

Place the butter and shallots in a large cooking dish. Cover and cook for 3 minutes, stirring once. Add the flour, blending well. Cook for 1 minute, stirring once.

Gradually add the cider and milk, blending well. Stir in the mushrooms, scallops and salt and pepper to taste. Cover and cook for 5-6 minutes, stirring 3 times until the scallops are cooked and coated in a creamy sauce.

Add the cream and cheese, blending well. Cover and cook for 2-3 minutes, stirring once.

Serve hot in individual scallop shells or small dishes. Sprinkle with chopped parsley to serve.

Serves: 4
Power setting: FULL
Preparation time: 15-20 minutes
Cooking time: 11-13 minutes

STIR-FRY MONKFISH

1 tablespoon oil
675 g/1½ lb monkfish tail
    fillets, boned and thinly
    sliced
225 g/8 oz white cabbage,
    shredded
1 small red pepper, cored,
    seeded and chopped
1 small green pepper,
    cored, seeded and
    chopped
1 small onion, peeled and
    chopped
100 g/4 oz fresh
    beansprouts
1-2 tablespoons soy sauce

Preheat a browning dish for 5-7 minutes (or according to the manufacturer's instructions). Add the oil and swirl to coat. Add the fish and cook for 4-5 minutes, stirring twice. Remove the fish with a slotted spoon and set aside.

Reheat the browning dish for 3 minutes. Add the cabbage, peppers and onion, blending well. Cook for 4 minutes, stirring twice.

Add the beansprouts and monkfish, blending well. Cook for 2 minutes, stirring once.

Add soy sauce to taste. Serve at once.

Serves: 4
Power setting: FULL
Preparation time: 15-20 minutes
Cooking time: 18-21 minutes

BEDFORD PRAWNS AND SCALLOPS

4 scallops with shells
1 tablespoon oil
450 g/1 lb peeled prawns
50 g/2 oz butter
2 garlic cloves, peeled and
    crushed
3 spring onions, trimmed
    and sliced
salt and freshly ground
    black pepper

Remove the scallops from their shells and slice each into four pieces. Scrub the shells well and brush the insides with the oil.

Mix the scallop slices with the prawns and spoon evenly into the scallop shells.

Blend the butter with the garlic, spring onions and salt and pepper to taste. Dot evenly over the scallop mixture. Cover with the flat scallop shells and cook for 3-4 minutes, rearranging once.

Serve hot with brown bread and butter.

Serves: 4
Power setting: FULL
Preparation time: 15-20 minutes
Cooking time: 3-4 minutes

PLAICE CURRY

1 tablespoon oil
1 onion, peeled and
    chopped
1 teaspoon curry powder
1 tomato, peeled, seeded
    and chopped
1 apple, peeled, cored and
    chopped
1 tablespoon raisins
125 ml/4 fl oz double
    cream
salt and freshly ground
    black pepper
4 plaice fillets, skinned
    and rolled

Preheat a small browning dish for 6 minutes (or according to the manufacturer's instructions).

Add the oil and onion and cook for 1 minute. Stir in the curry powder and cook for a further 1 minute, stirring once.

Add the tomato, apple, raisins, cream and salt and pepper to taste, blending well. Cover and cook for 5 minutes, stirring once.

Add the plaice fillets, cover and cook for 4 minutes, stirring once.

Serve hot with saffron rice.

Serves: 4
Power setting: FULL
Preparation time: 10-15 minutes
Cooking time: 17 minutes

GARLIC TROUT

2 tablespoons French
    wholegrain mustard
2 tablespoons oil
2 large garlic cloves,
    peeled and crushed
2-3 tablespoons chopped
    fresh parsley
2 × 225 g (8 oz) trout,
    prepared for cooking
salt and freshly ground
    black pepper
lemon wedges to garnish

Mix the mustard with the oil, garlic and parsley, blending well.

Season the trout, inside and out, with salt and pepper to taste. Slash the skin in 2-3 places to prevent bursting and shield the head and tail with a little foil.

Spread each side of each trout with the garlic mixture and place in a cooking dish. Cook for 8-9 minutes, turning the dish twice. Leave to stand for 2 minutes.

Serve hot garnished with lemon wedges.

Serves: 2
Power setting: FULL
Preparation time: 15 minutes
Cooking time: 8-9 minutes

SEAFOOD SUPPER

4 plaice fillets, skinned
fish seasoning
lemon pepper
50 g/2 oz butter, cut into
    4 pieces
2 teaspoons cornflour
150 ml/¼ pint milk
100 g/4 oz peeled prawns
150 ml/¼ pint soured
    cream
1 teaspoon lemon juice
1 teaspoon chopped fresh
    parsley
To garnish:
lemon twists
whole prawns
parsley sprigs

Sprinkle each plaice fillet with fish seasoning and lemon pepper to taste. Wrap each fillet around a piece of the butter and place in a cooking dish.

Blend the cornflour with 2 tablespoons of the milk. Pour the remaining milk over the fish, cover and cook for 7 minutes, turning the dish twice. Drain the milk from the fish and mix with the cornflour mixture, blending well. Cook for 1 minute, stirring once.

Add the prawns, soured cream, lemon juice and parsley to the sauce, blending well. Pour over the fish to coat. Cook for 1 minute.

Serve hot garnished with lemon twists, whole prawns and parsley sprigs.

Serves: 4
Power setting: FULL
Preparation time: 15 minutes
Cooking time: 9 minutes

BOUILLABAISSE

1 onion, peeled and sliced
1 garlic clove, peeled and
   crushed
2 × 397 g (14 oz) cans
   peeled tomatoes
300 ml/½ pint fish or
   chicken stock
1 bouquet garni
salt and freshly ground
   black pepper
450 g/1 lb monkfish tail
   fillets, boned and thinly
   sliced
450 g/1 lb red fish,
   skinned and filleted
350 g/12 oz coley fillet,
   skinned and chopped
450 g/1 lb catfish fillet,
   skinned and chopped
450 g/1 lb plaice fillets,
   skinned and cut into
   strips
chopped parsley to
   garnish

Place the onion, garlic, tomatoes and their juice, stock, bouquet garni and salt and pepper to taste in a large casserole dish. Cover and cook for 3 minutes, stirring once.

Add the monkfish and red fish, blending well. Cover and cook for 2 minutes.

Add the coley and catfish, blending well. Cover and cook for 1 minute.

Add the plaice, blending well. Cover and cook for 4-6 minutes, stirring once, until the fish is tender.

Remove and discard the bouquet garni and sprinkle with chopped parsley to serve.

Serve with chunks of hot fresh crusty bread.

Serves: 8-10
Power setting: FULL
Preparation time: 25-30 minutes
Cooking time: 10-12 minutes

BARBECUE BACON TROUT

4 trout fillets
8 rashers streaky bacon,
   rinded
8 tablespoons
   tomato ketchup
4 teaspoons brown sugar
4 teaspoons French
   mustard

Place the trout fillets in a cooking dish and cover with the bacon. Cover with absorbent kitchen paper and cook for 6 minutes, turning the dish once.

Meanwhile, blend the tomato ketchup with the sugar and mustard. Spoon evenly over the trout and bacon and cook, uncovered, for 3-4 minutes.

Serve hot with oven chips and baked beans.

Serves: 4
Power setting: FULL
Preparation time: 10-15 minutes
Cooking time: 9-10 minutes

CHEESY TROUT-BURGERS

8 tablespoons grated
   strong cheese
4 tablespoons
   mayonnaise
4 trout fillets
8 tablespoons crushed
   plain flavour potato
   crisps
4 soft baps, split and
   toasted

Mix the cheese with the mayonnaise, blending well. Place the trout fillets in a cooking dish and top with the cheese mixture.

Cook for 8-9 minutes until tender, turning the dish twice. Top with the crisps and serve each trout fillet in a soft bap.

Serve at once.

Serves: 4
Power setting: FULL
Preparation time: 10-15 minutes
Cooking time: 8-9 minutes

HADDOCK WITH MUSHROOM RICE

350 g/12 oz smoked
    haddock fillets
25 g/1 oz butter
100 g/4 oz button
    mushrooms, wiped and
    sliced
225 g/8 oz long-grain
    rice
600 ml/1 pint boiling
    water
1 teaspoon salt
1 × 295 g (10½ oz) can
    condensed mushroom
    soup
150 ml/¼ pint milk
1 tablespoon chopped
    fresh parsley
salt and freshly ground
    black pepper

Place the fish in a shallow dish. Cover and cook for 2 minutes. Flake the fish, removing and discarding any skin and bones.

Place the butter, mushrooms and rice in a casserole dish. Cook for 2 minutes, stirring once. Add the water and salt, blending well. Cover and cook for 14 minutes. Leave to stand while preparing the creamed haddock.

Place the soup, milk and fish in a dish. Add the parsley and salt and pepper to taste, blending well. Cover and cook for 4 minutes, stirring once. Spoon the rice mixture on to a warmed serving dish. Top with the creamed haddock mixture. Serve at once.

Serves: 4
Power setting: FULL
Preparation time: 15-20 minutes
Cooking time: 22 minutes

POTTED SHRIMPS

175 g/6 oz butter, cut into
    small pieces
350 g/12 oz peeled
    shrimps
salt and cayenne pepper

Place the butter in a bowl and cook for 2-2½ minutes to melt.

Add the shrimps and salt and cayenne pepper to taste, blending well. Pour into a serving bowl or individual ramekin dishes and chill to set.

Serve with warm wholemeal toast and lemon wedges.

Serves: 4
Power setting: FULL
Preparation time: 5 minutes plus chilling
Cooking time: 2-2½ minutes

Illustrated on p. 75

SCAMPI PROVENÇALE

25 g/1 oz butter
1 onion, peeled and
    chopped
1 garlic clove, peeled and
    chopped
1 × 397 g (14 oz) can
    peeled tomatoes,
    drained
5 tablespoons dry white
    wine
pinch of sugar
1 tablespoon chopped
    fresh parsley
salt and freshly ground
    black pepper
225 g/8 oz frozen scampi,
    thawed

Place the butter in a bowl and cook for 2 minutes. Add the onion and garlic, blending well. Cover and cook for 4 minutes, stirring once.

Add the tomatoes, wine, sugar, parsley and salt and pepper to taste, blending well. Cover and cook for 3 minutes, stirring once.

Add the scampi, blending well. Cover and cook for 2 minutes, stirring once.

Serve hot with boiled rice and a crisp green salad.

Serves: 4
Power setting: FULL
Preparation time: 10 minutes
Cooking time: 11 minutes

CRAB MOUSSE (p.46)

CIDER-SOUSED MACKEREL (p.60)

MIXED FISH CURRY

25 g/1 oz butter
1 onion, peeled and sliced
1 teaspoon ground
    cumin
1 teaspoon chilli powder
½ teaspoon ground
    turmeric
½ teaspoon dried basil
1 garlic clove, crushed
2 tablespoons cornflour
water to mix
2 tomatoes, peeled and
    chopped
1 tablespoon creamed
    coconut
300 ml/½ pint water
pinch of sugar
juice of ½ lemon
salt and freshly ground
    black pepper
275 g/10 oz peeled
    prawns
175 g/6 oz cooked white
    fish (cod, haddock,
    coley or sole, for
    example)

Place the butter in a bowl and cook for 1 minute. Add the onion, blending well. Cover and cook for 3 minutes, stirring once.

Meanwhile, blend the cumin with the chilli powder, turmeric, basil, garlic, cornflour and a little water to make a paste.

Gradually add the paste to the onion with the tomatoes, coconut, water, sugar, lemon juice and salt and pepper to taste, blending well. Cover and cook for 3-4 minutes, stirring every 1 minute.

Add the prawns and fish and cook for 2 minutes, stirring once.

Serve hot with boiled rice.

Serves: 4
Power setting: FULL
Preparation time: 15-20 minutes
Cooking time: 9-10 minutes

SOLE BONNE FEMME

2 soles, filleted and
    skinned
2 shallots, peeled and
    finely chopped
2 sprigs parsley
1 bay leaf
salt and freshly ground
    white pepper
150 ml/¼ pint dry white
    wine
50 g/2 oz butter
25 g/1 oz plain flour
150 ml/¼ pint milk
3 tablespoons single
    cream
To garnish:
100 g/4 oz button
    mushrooms, wiped
chopped parsley

Roll the sole fillets and place in a cooking dish with the shallots, parsley, bay leaf, salt and pepper to taste and wine. Cover and cook for 4-4½ minutes, turning the dish once.

Drain, reserving the stock. Remove and discard the shallots, parsley and bay leaf. Place the fish on a warmed serving plate and keep warm.

Place half of the butter in a bowl and cook for ½ minute to melt. Add the flour, blending well. Gradually add the reserved stock and milk, blending well. Cook for 3-4 minutes, stirring every 1 minute until smooth and thickened.

Add the cream and salt and pepper to taste, blending well.

Place the remaining butter and mushrooms in a bowl. Cook for 3 minutes, stirring once.

Pour the sauce over the fish and serve garnished with mushrooms and parsley.

Serves: 4
Power setting: FULL
Preparation time: 15-20 minutes
Cooking time: 10½-12 minutes

59

CIDER-SOUSED MACKEREL

2×450g (1 lb) mackerel,
  gutted with head and
  fins removed
salt and freshly ground
  black pepper
finely pared rind of ½
  lemon
1 onion, peeled and sliced
  into rings
few sprigs fresh thyme and
  rosemary
2 large bay leaves
300 ml/½ pint dry cider
150 ml/¼ pint water
2 teaspoons arrowroot
  powder

Season the inside of each mackerel with pepper to taste. Place in a cooking dish with the lemon rind, onion and herbs. Pour over the cider and water. Cover and cook for 6-7 minutes, turning the dish once.

When cooked, drain off and reserve 300 ml/½ pint of the cooking liquid. Remove the fish, onions and herbs and arrange on a serving dish.

Blend the arrowroot with a little water and stir into the reserved hot cooking liquid. Cook for 4 minutes, stirring twice. Season to taste with salt and pepper and pour over the fish. Serve at once.

Serves: 2
Power setting: FULL
Preparation time: 10-15 minutes
Cooking time: 10-11 minutes

Illustrated on p. 58

MACKEREL DOLMADES STYLE

2×125g (4½ oz) cans
  mackerel fillets in
  brine, drained
2 tablespoons chopped
  red pepper
1 tablespoon tomato
  purée
1 teaspoon grated lemon
  rind
salt and freshly ground
  black pepper
8 large cabbage leaves,
  washed
4 tablespoons water
300 ml/½ pint fish stock
1 tablespoon cornflour

Mash the mackerel fillets and mix with the pepper, tomato purée, lemon rind and salt and pepper to taste, blending well.

Place the cabbage leaves in a bowl with the water. Cover and cook for 1-2 minutes until soft. Drain thoroughly.

Divide the mackerel mixture evenly between the cabbage leaves and fold up to enclose the filling. Place, seam-side down, in a cooking dish and pour over the stock. Cover and cook for 4 minutes, turning the dish once.

Drain the stock into a jug and blend in the cornflour. Cook for 1-2 minutes, stirring every ½ minute, until smooth and thickened. Pour over the cabbage parcels and serve at once.

Serves: 4
Power setting: FULL
Preparation time: 15-20 minutes
Cooking time: 6-8 minutes

RED MULLET WITH TOMATOES

15 g/½ oz butter
½ onion, peeled and
  chopped
2 red mullet, prepared for
  cooking
1×227g (8 oz) can
  peeled tomatoes
1 teaspoon lemon juice
garlic salt
chopped parsley to
  garnish

Place the butter in a shallow cooking dish and cook for ½ minute to melt. Add the onion, cover and cook for 2½ minutes, stirring once.

Top with the red mullet, tomatoes and their juice, lemon juice and garlic salt to taste. Cover and cook for 6-7 minutes, turning the dish once.

Serve hot or chilled garnished with chopped parsley.

Serves: 2
Power setting: FULL
Preparation time: 10-15 minutes, plus chilling (optional)
Cooking time: 9-10 minutes

KIPPER PASTA MEDLEY

100 g/4 oz shell pasta
600 ml/1 pint boiling
    water
1 tablespoon vegetable oil
salt and freshly ground
    black pepper
1 × 175 g (6 oz) packet
    frozen buttered kipper
    fillets
225 g/8 oz tomatoes,
    seeded and chopped
1 green pepper, cored,
    seeded and sliced
1 onion, peeled and sliced
    into rings
3 tablespoons olive oil
1 tablespoon wine
    vinegar

Place the pasta in a deep bowl with the water, vegetable oil and a pinch of salt. Cover and cook for 12-14 minutes. Leave to stand, covered, while cooking the kippers.

Pierce the kipper fillet bag and place on a plate. Cook for 6 minutes, turning the bag over half way through the cooking time.

Drain the pasta and cool under running water. Cool the kipper fillets, skin and flake into bite-sized pieces.

Mix the pasta with the kippers, tomatoes, pepper and onion in a serving bowl. Beat the olive oil with the wine vinegar and salt and pepper to taste. Pour over the salad and toss gently to mix. Serve lightly chilled.

Serves: 4
Power setting: FULL
Preparation time: 20 minutes plus cooling and chilling
Cooking time: 18-20 minutes

HALIBUT WITH TOMATOES AND CREAM

25 g/1 oz butter
1 large onion, peeled and
    sliced into rings
1 × 397 g (14 oz) can
    peeled tomatoes,
    coarsely chopped
1 teaspoon dried
    marjoram
salt and freshly ground
    black pepper
4 halibut steaks
225 g/8 oz button
    mushrooms, halved
150 ml/¼ pint double
    cream

Place the butter in a casserole dish and cook for 1 minute. Add the onion, blending well. Cover and cook for 5 minutes, stirring once.

Add the tomatoes and their juice, marjoram and salt and pepper to taste. Add the halibut steaks, cover and cook for 8 minutes, turning the dish twice.

Stir in the mushrooms and cream, blending well. Cover and cook for 3 minutes, stirring once. Serve at once.

Serves: 4
Power setting: FULL
Preparation time: 10-15 minutes
Cooking time: 17 minutes

SKATE WITH CAPER BUTTER

2 × 450 g (1 lb) wings of
    skate
60 g/2½ oz butter
1 tablespoon capers
5 tablespoons white wine
    vinegar
1 tablespoon chopped
    fresh parsley
salt and freshly ground
    black pepper

Cut each skate wing into 3 wedges. Place in a large shallow cooking dish. Cover and cook for 5 minutes, turning the dish once.

Place the butter in a bowl and cook for 5 minutes. Add the capers, vinegar, parsley and salt and pepper to taste, blending well. Cook for a further 2 minutes.

Skin the skate and place in a heated serving dish. Pour over the caper butter. Cover and cook for 3-4 minutes, turning the dish once. Serve at once.

Serves: 3-4
Power setting: FULL
Preparation time: 20 minutes
Cooking time: 15-16 minutes

SOUSED HERRINGS

4 herrings, each weighing
    about 225 g (8 oz)
salt
2 bay leaves
6 peppercorns
2 cloves
1 bouquet garni
½ teaspoon allspice
    berries
150 ml/¼ pint dry white
    wine
150 ml/¼ pint white wine
    vinegar
1 onion, peeled and sliced
    into rings

Clean, gut and bone the herrings. Trim the heads, tails and fins from the fish and season with salt to taste. Roll up, skin side out, from the tail ends and secure with wooden cocktail sticks. Place in a single layer in a shallow dish with the bay leaves, peppercorns, cloves, bouquet garni and allspice berries. Pour over the wine and vinegar and top with the onion rings.

Cover and cook for 6 minutes, turning the dish once. Leave the herrings to cool in their liquor then chill lightly to serve. Drain before serving.

Serves: 4
Power setting: FULL
Preparation time: 20 minutes plus chilling
Cooking time: 6 minutes

PRAWN FRIED RICE

1 tablespoon oil
2 onions, peeled and
    chopped
350 g/12 oz frozen mixed
    vegetables, thawed
225 g/8 oz cooked brown
    rice
2 tablespoons soy sauce
350 g/12 oz peeled
    prawns
75 g/3 oz salted peanuts
4 eggs, beaten
salt and freshly ground
    black pepper

Place the oil and onion in a shallow cooking dish. Cover and cook for 4 minutes, stirring once.

Add the vegetables, blending well. Cook for 2 minutes, stirring once.

Add the rice, soy sauce, prawns and peanuts. Cook for 4 minutes, stirring once.

Pour the egg over the rice mixture. Cook for 1-2 minutes until lightly set. Toss the rice mixture well with a fork to distribute the cooked egg. Season to taste with salt and pepper and serve at once.

Serves: 4
Power setting: FULL
Preparation time: 10 minutes
Cooking time: 11-12 minutes

CIDERED MUSSELS

1 tablespoon oil
1 small onion, peeled and
    chopped
1 garlic clove, peeled and
    crushed
1 tablespoon chopped
    parsley
1 tablespoon plain flour
150 ml/¼ pint dry cider
150 ml/¼ pint dry white
    wine
salt and freshly ground
    black pepper
2.25 litres/2 quarts
    mussels, scrubbed

Place the oil, onion, garlic and parsley in a large bowl. Cover and cook for 1 minute, stirring once.

Add the flour, blending well. Gradually add the cider and wine. Season to taste with salt and pepper and cook for 2 minutes, stirring 3 times.

Add half of the mussels and toss to coat in the sauce. Cover and cook for 4 minutes, stirring once. Remove with a slotted spoon and place in a warmed serving dish. Remove and discard any mussels that do not open.

Add the remaining mussels to the sauce and toss to coat. Cover and cook for 4 minutes, stirring once. Discard any unopened mussels and add rest to the cooked mussels in the serving dish. Spoon over any remaining sauce and serve at once.

Serves: 2
Power setting: FULL
Preparation time: 20-30 minutes
Cooking time: 11 minutes

SAVOURY PANCAKES

1 small onion, peeled and
   finely chopped
25 g/1 oz butter
1 × 283 g (10 oz) packet
   frozen rice, peas and
   mushrooms
75 ml/3 fl oz water
2 tablespoons wholegrain
   mustard
1 × 185 g (6½ oz) can
   tuna in brine, drained
   and flaked
150 ml/¼ pint whipping
   cream
salt and freshly ground
   black pepper
12 small (15 cm/6 inch)
   cooked pancakes (see
   p.239)
1 tablespoon chopped
   fresh parsley
3 tablespoons grated
   Cheddar cheese

Place the onion, butter, rice, peas and mushrooms and water in a small casserole dish. Cover and cook for 12 minutes, until tender. Leave to stand for 5 minutes.

Add the mustard, tuna, 2 tablespoons of the cream and salt and pepper to taste, blending well. Divide between the pancakes, roll up and arrange in a shallow cooking dish.

Stir the parsley into the remaining cream with salt and pepper to taste. Pour over the pancakes. Sprinkle with the cheese and cook for 5 minutes, turning the dish twice.

Serve hot with vegetables in season.

Serves: 4
Power setting: FULL
Preparation time: 25-30 minutes
Cooking time: 22 minutes

TROUT NIÇOISE

2 tablespoons olive oil
1 × 397 g (14 oz) can
   peeled tomatoes,
   drained and chopped
1 small onion, peeled and
   finely sliced
2 garlic cloves, peeled and
   crushed
2 tablespoons tomato
   purée
2 tablespoons dry
   vermouth
3 tablespoons chopped
   fresh parsley
sugar
salt and freshly ground
   black pepper
2 × 225 g (8 oz) trout,
   boned and prepared
   for cooking
1 × 56 g (2 oz) can
   anchovy fillets in oil,
   drained
black olives
parsley sprigs to garnish

Place the oil, tomatoes, onion, garlic, tomato purée, dry vermouth, parsley, sugar, salt and pepper to taste in a bowl. Cover and cook for 5 minutes, stirring twice.

Slash the trout in 2-3 places to prevent the skin from bursting and place in a cooking dish. Spoon over the sauce. Top with a lattice of anchovy fillets and black olives. Cook for 6 minutes, turning the dish twice. Leave to cool then chill thoroughly.

Serve lightly chilled and garnished with parsley sprigs. Serves 4 as a light starter or 2 as a main course.

Serves: 2-4
Power setting: FULL
Preparation time: 25 minutes plus cooling and chilling
Cooking time: 11 minutes

SALMON TROUT WITH CHIVE DRESSING

1 × 1.75 kg (4 lb) salmon
  trout, gutted and
  prepared for cooking
2 tablespoons lemon juice
4 tablespoons boiling
  water
Dressing;
8 tablespoons soured
  cream
8 tablespoons
  mayonnaise
3 tablespoons snipped
  chives
salt and freshly ground
  black pepper
To garnish:
watercress sprigs
cucumber slices
lemon slices

Place the salmon in a shallow cooking dish with the lemon juice and water. Prick the salmon in several places to prevent it from bursting during cooking. Cover and cook for 28 minutes, giving the dish a quarter-turn every 7 minutes. Leave to cool.

Meanwhile, blend the soured cream with the mayonnaise, chives and salt and pepper to taste. Spoon into a small serving bowl and chill lightly.

Skin the salmon and place on a serving plate. Garnish with watercress sprigs and cucumber and lemon slices. Serve with the dressing.

Serves: 8-10
Power setting: FULL
Preparation time: 20 minutes plus cooling and chilling
Cooking time: 28 minutes

MACKEREL LOAF

2 × 125 g (4½ oz) cans
  mackerel fillets in
  brine, drained
50 g/2 oz wholemeal
  breadcrumbs
25 g/1 oz gherkins,
  chopped
2 teaspoons lemon juice
1 egg, beaten
1 tablespoon chopped
  fresh parsley
2 tablespoons plain
  yogurt
salt and black pepper
To garnish:
lemon slices
cucumber slices

Mash the mackerel fillets and mix with the breadcrumbs, gherkins, lemon juice, egg, parsley, yogurt and salt and pepper to taste, blending well.

Spoon into a small glass loaf dish. Cook for 7 minutes, turning the dish twice, or until the mixture begins to shrink away from the sides of the dish.

Invert on to a warmed serving dish. Serve hot or cold, cut into slices, garnished with lemon and cucumber slices.

Serves: 4
Power setting: FULL
Preparation time: 10-15 minutes
Cooking time: 7 minutes

SEAFOOD SCALLOPS

175 g/6 oz haddock fillet,
  skinned
150 ml/¼ pint dry white
  wine
small piece of onion
2 sprigs parsley
1 bay leaf   (cont.)

Place the haddock in a cooking dish with the wine, onion, parsley and bay leaf. Cover and cook for 2-3 minutes, until tender.

Drain, reserving the stock. Remove and discard the onion, parsley and bay leaf. Flake the fish.

Place 15 g/½ oz of the butter in a bowl

with the mushrooms. Cover and cook for 2 minutes. Set aside.

Place the remaining butter in a bowl and cook for ½ minute to melt. Stir in the flour, blending well. Gradually add the reserved stock and milk, blending well. Cook for 3-4 minutes, stirring every 1 minute until

40 g/1½ oz butter
50 g/2 oz button
  mushrooms, wiped and
  sliced
3 tablespoons plain flour
200 ml/7 fl oz milk
50 g/2 oz Cheddar cheese,
  grated
50 g/2 oz potted shrimps
salt and freshly ground
  black pepper
350 g/12 oz creamed
  potatoes (see p.106)

smooth and thickened.

Add the flaked fish, mushrooms, cheese, potted shrimps and salt and pepper to taste, blending well.

Pipe creamed potatoes around the edge of 4 scallop shells. Spoon the fish mixture into the centre. Cook for 3-4 minutes, re-arranging the shells once. Brown under a preheated hot grill if liked. Serve at once.

To freeze
Cool quickly, cover, seal, label and freeze for up to 2 months.

Serves: 4
Power setting: FULL
Preparation time: 25 minutes
Cooking time: 10½-13½ minutes
Suitable for freezing

DEVILLED COD STEAKS

25 g/1 oz butter
1 tablespoon sweet
  chutney
1 tablespoon chopped
  parsley
2 tablespoons tomato
  ketchup
1 tablespoon made
  mustard
salt and black pepper
4 × 100 g (4 oz) cod steaks
25 g/1 oz potato crisps
lemon slices
parsley sprigs

Place the butter in a bowl and cook for ½ minute to melt. Add the chutney, parsley, tomato ketchup, mustard and salt and pepper to taste, blending well.

Place the cod steaks in a cooking dish and spoon over the sauce. Cover and cook for 4½-5 minutes, turning the dish twice.

Sprinkle with the crushed potato crisps. Garnish with lemon slices and parsley sprigs. Serve at once with a seasonal salad.

Serves: 4
Power setting: FULL
Preparation time: 5-10 minutes
Cooking time: 5-5½ minutes

SOLE VERONIQUE

2 soles, filleted and
  skinned
1 small onion, peeled and
  sliced
4 button mushrooms,
  wiped and sliced
3 sprigs parsley
1 bay leaf
salt and white pepper
150 ml/¼ pint dry white
  wine
25 g/1 oz butter
25 g/1 oz plain flour
150 ml/¼ pint milk
1 teaspoon lemon juice
175 g/6 oz white grapes,
  peeled, halved and pips
  removed
2 tablespoons double
  cream

Place the sole fillets in a cooking dish with the onion, mushrooms, parsley, bay leaf, salt and pepper to taste and wine. Cover and cook for 4-4½ minutes, turning the dish once.

Drain, reserving the stock. Remove and discard the onion, mushrooms, parsley and bay leaf. Place the fish on a warmed serving plate and keep warm.

Place the butter in a bowl and cook for ½ minute to melt. Add the flour, blending well. Gradually add the reserved stock and milk, blending well. Cook for 3-4 minutes, stirring every 1 minute until smooth and thickened.

Add the lemon juice, two-thirds of the grapes and the cream, blending well. Pour over the fish and cook for 2-2½ minutes, turning the dish once.

Serve garnished with remaining grapes

Serves: 4
Power setting: FULL
Preparation time: 20-25 minutes
Cooking time: 9½-11½ minutes

Meat, Poultry and Game

*Roasted, braised, sautéed, casseroled, stir-fried or topped with a pastry crust —
there is a welcome microwave meat dish to suit every occasion, from the simple
family meal to the sumptuous celebration dinner.
Microwaves can also provide a meat meal to suit all pockets, from the
splash-out steak to the economical 'purse-stretching' stew or casserole.*

BEEF OLIVES PROVENÇALE

4 slices beef topside
1 tablespoon oil
1 onion, peeled and sliced
1 green pepper, cored,
    seeded and sliced
1 × 300 g (10½ oz) can
    condensed cream of
    tomato soup
150 ml/¼ pint red wine
150 ml/¼ pint beef stock or
    water
1 teaspoon dried mixed
    herbs
10-12 black olives
Stuffing:
100 g/4 oz minced pork
50 g/2 oz fresh white or
    brown breadcrumbs
1 tablespoon chopped
    fresh parsley
2 tablespoons lemon juice

Beat the pieces of beef flat with a meat hammer or rolling pin.

Place the oil, onion and pepper in a casserole dish. Cover and cook for 3 minutes. Add the soup, wine, stock or water, herbs and olives, blending well.

Mix the stuffing ingredients together. Place one quarter of the stuffing on each piece of beef. Fold the beef around the stuffing to enclose and secure with string. Add to the wine mixture.

Cover and cook for 17 minutes, turning the beef olives once. Leave to stand for 3 minutes.

Remove and discard the string before serving.

To freeze
Cool quickly, cover, seal, label and freeze for up to 3 months

Serves: 4
Power setting: FULL
Preparation time: 25 minutes
Cooking time: 23 minutes
Suitable for freezing

STROGANOFF SUPERB

40 g/1½ oz butter
450 g/1 lb beef topside, cut
    into thin strips
1 small onion, peeled and
    chopped
100 g/4 oz mushrooms,
    sliced
¼ teaspoon mustard
    powder
salt and black pepper
150 ml/¼ pint soured
    cream
4 tablespoons milk

Place the butter in a cooking dish and cook for ½ minute to melt. Stir in the beef and cook for 10 minutes, stirring twice.

Add the onion, mushrooms, mustard and salt and pepper to taste, blending well. Cook for 4 minutes, stirring once.

Add the soured cream and milk, blending well. Cook for 4 minutes, stirring once.

Serve hot with noodles and a green salad.

Serves: 4
Power setting: FULL
Preparation time: 15 minutes
Cooking time: 18½ minutes

BEEF HOT POT WITH DUMPLINGS

450 g/1 lb beef skirt,
  cubed
1½ tablespoons seasoned
  flour
2 onions, peeled and
  sliced
225 g/8 oz carrots, peeled
  and sliced
2 sticks celery, sliced
600 ml/1 pint beef stock
Dumplings:
225 g/8 oz plain flour
1 teaspoon salt
2½ teaspoons baking
  powder
100 g/4 oz shredded suet
7 tablespoons water

Toss the beef in the flour to coat. Place in a casserole dish with the onions, carrots, celery and stock. Cover and cook for 25 minutes, stirring three times.

Meanwhile, to make the dumplings, sift the flour into a bowl with the salt and baking powder. Add the suet, blending well. Stir in the water to make a fairly stiff dough. Divide and shape into 12 dumplings.

Add the dumplings to the hot pot, cover and cook for 7 minutes, turning the dish twice. Leave to stand, covered, for 5 minutes.

Serve hot with green vegetables.

Serves: 4
Power setting: FULL
Preparation time: 25-30 minutes
Cooking time: 37 minutes

HUNGARIAN GOULASH

25 g/1 oz butter
450 g/1 lb chuck steak, cut
  into bite-sized pieces
1 large onion, peeled and
  chopped
1 garlic clove, peeled and
  crushed
3 teaspoons paprika
½ teaspoon sugar
pinch of caraway seeds
1 × 227 g (8 oz) can
  peeled tomatoes
2 tablespoons plain
  yogurt or soured cream
salt

Place the butter in a casserole dish and cook on FULL POWER for ½ minute to melt. Add the steak, onion and garlic, blending well. Cover and cook on MEDIUM POWER for 15 minutes, stirring once.

Add the paprika, sugar, caraway seeds and tomatoes with their juice, blending well. Cover and cook on MEDIUM POWER for a further 15 minutes.

Add the yogurt or soured cream and salt to taste, blending well. Leave to stand, covered, for 5 minutes before serving. Serve with noodles and a green salad.

Serves: 4
Power settings: FULL, MEDIUM
Preparation time: 15 minutes
Cooking time: 35½ minutes

CARBONNADE OF BEEF

25 g/1 oz butter
2 tablespoons oil
2 onions, peeled and
  chopped
675 g/1½ lb chuck steak,
  cut into strips
1 tablespoon plain flour
300 ml/½ pint light ale
150 ml/¼ pint water
pinch of dried thyme
1 bay leaf
salt and black pepper

Place the butter and oil in a casserole dish. Cook for 1 minute. Add the onions, cover and cook for 3 minutes, stirring once.

Add the meat, blending well. Cover and cook for 3 minutes, stirring once.

Stir in the flour and gradually add the ale and water, blending well. Stir in the thyme, bay leaf and salt and pepper to taste.

Cook for 20 minutes, stirring once. Leave to stand, covered, for 10 minutes. Remove and discard the bay leaf.

Serve hot with jacket potatoes or rice.

To freeze
Cool quickly and place in a rigid container. Cover, seal, label and freeze for up to 3 months.

Serves: 4
Power setting: FULL
Preparation time: 25 minutes
Cooking time: 37 minutes
Suitable for freezing

GUIDE TO COOKING MEAT, POULTRY AND GAME

Type and cut of meat, poultry or game		Cooking time in minutes on MEDIUM POWER per 450 g/1 lb or for quantity given	Cooking time in minutes on FULL POWER per 450 g/1 lb or for quantity given	Preparation
BEEF				
topside	rare	12	5-6	Choose a good quality joint with an even covering of fat and a neat shape. Allow to stand for 15-20 minutes, wrapped in foil, before carving.
	medium	14	6½-7½	
	well done	16	8½-9½	
sirloin	rare	12	5-6	
	medium	14	6½-7½	
	well done	16	8½-9½	
rib	rare	12-13	5½-6½	Ideally, bone and roll the joint before cooking. Allow to stand for 15-30 minutes, wrapped in foil, before cooking.
	medium	14-15	7-8	
	well done	16-17	8-10	
minced beef		14-16	10-12	
rump steak	rare		2	Preheat a browning dish according to the manufacturer's instructions. Add the meat and brown. Turn over and cook for the recommended time.
	medium		3-4	
	well done		4	
fillet steak	rare		2	
	medium		2-3	
	well done		3	
braising steak		16-17	10	Ideally, cook on MEDIUM POWER. If using FULL POWER, leave to rest for 10 minutes halfway through the cooking time.
hamburgers	1 (100-g/4-oz)		2-3	Preheat a browning dish according to the manufacturer's instructions. Add the hamburgers and cook for the recommended time, turning the 100-g/4-oz burgers over halfway through the cooking time, and turning 225-g/8-oz burgers over twice during the cooking time.
	2 (100-g/4-oz)		3-4	
	3 (100-g/4-oz)		4-5	
	4 (100-g/4-oz)		5-6	
	1 (225-g/8-oz)		2½-3½	
	2 (225-g/8-oz)		6-7	
LAMB				
leg	on bone	11-13	8-10	Choose a good quality joint. Roll the meat into a neat shape if it is off the bone. Cover the pointed end with foil to protect it if on the bone. Allow to stand for 25-30 minutes, wrapped in foil, before carving.
	off bone	12-13	9-10	
breast		14-16	12	Roll and stuff, if liked, before cooking. Allow to stand for 30 minutes, wrapped in foil, before cooking.
crown roast			5	Cover tips of bone with foil during cooking.
loin of lamb		11-13	8-10	Choose a good quality joint. Roll into a neat shape if off the bone. Allow to stand for 25-30 minutes, wrapped in foil, before carving.
chops	loin or 2 chump		6-7	Preheat the browning dish according to the manufacturer's instructions. Add the chops and cook for the recommended time, turning over halfway through cooking time.
	4		7-9	
	6		15-17	

PORK leg		13-15	10	Choose a good quality joint. Cover the pointed end with foil to protect from over cooking. Score fat with a sharp knife and sprinkle liberally with salt to get a crisp crackling. Allow to stand for 20 minutes, wrapped in foil, before carving. Brown under a hot grill if liked.
loin		14-16	10-13	Roll into a neat shape before cooking. Allow to stand for 20 minutes, wrapped in foil, before carving.
fillet			7	
chops	loin or 2 chump 3 4 6	14-18 19-24 26-32 33-37		Preheat the browning dish according to the manufacturer's instructions. Add the chops and cook for the recommended time, turning over halfway through cooking time.
Bacon or Gammon joint gammon steaks (each)		11-12 14		Cook in a browning dish if liked (observing preheating times) or cover with cling film. Turn halfway through the cooking time.
Bacon	4 slices 450 g/1 lb		3½-4 12-14	Place on a plate or bacon rack and cover with absorbent kitchen paper. Turn rashers over halfway through cooking.
Liver Kidney Sausages	 2 4		5-6 7-8 1½-2 3-3½	Prick thoroughly and arrange on a rack or plate. Cover with absorbent kitchen paper and turn halfway through the cooking time.
CHICKEN	whole	9-10	6-8	Shield the tips of the wings and legs with foil. Place in a roasting bag in a dish with 2-3 tablespoons stock. Give the dish a half turn halfway through the cooking time. Place the meatiest part of the chicken piece to the outside of the dish. Cover with greaseproof paper. Give the dish a half turn halfway through the cooking time.
	pieces 1 2 3 4 5 6		2-4 4-6 5-7 6½-10 7½-12 8-14	
DUCK	whole	9-11	7-8	Shield the tips of the wings, tail end and legs with foil. Prick the skin thoroughly to help release the fat. Place in a dish in a roasting bag on a trivet or upturned saucer and turn over halfway through the cooking time.
Grouse, guinea fowl, partridge, pheasant, quail, pigeon, poussin and woodcock		9-11	6-8	Shield the tips of the wings and legs with foil. Smear the breast with a little butter and place in a roasting bag in a dish. Turn the dish halfway through the cooking time.
TURKEY		11-13	9-11	Shield wing tips and legs with foil. Put in roasting bag in a dish with 2-3 tablespoons stock. Turn over at least once during cooking, give the dish a quarter turn every 15 minutes.

STEAK AND KIDNEY PUDDING

5 teaspoons flour
1 beef stock cube
salt and black pepper
350 g/12 oz braising
 steak, cut into 1 cm/½
 inch cubes
100 g/4 oz kidney,
 skinned, cored and
 sliced
1 onion, peeled and
 thinly sliced
75 ml/3 fl oz water
225 g/8 oz suet pastry

Mix the flour with the crumbled stock cube and salt and pepper to taste. Toss the beef and kidney in the flour mixture to coat. Add the onion, blending well. Spoon into a 1.2 litre/2 pint pudding basin. Pour over the water.

Cook on FULL POWER for 5 minutes. Stir well to blend. Cover and cook on DEFROST POWER for 20 minutes, stirring twice.

Roll out the pastry on a lightly floured surface to a round large enough to cover the basin. Place on top of the meat.

Cook on DEFROST POWER for 13 minutes, turning the dish three times.

Cover with foil, shiny side inside, and leave to stand for 10 minutes before serving.

Serves: 4
Power settings: FULL, DEFROST
Preparation time: 30 minutes
Cooking time: 48 minutes

MEATLOAF WITH MUSHROOM TOPPING

450 g/1 lb minced beef
75 g/3 oz fresh wholemeal
 breadcrumbs
1 onion, peeled and finely
 chopped
1 teaspoon dried parsley
1 beef stock cube
1 tablespoon tomato
 purée
1 egg, lightly beaten
Topping:
25 g/1 oz butter
75 g/3 oz mushrooms,
 sliced
2 spring onions, trimmed
 and chopped
3 tablespoons double
 cream
1 tablespoon lemon juice

Mix the beef with the breadcrumbs, onion, parsley, crumbled stock cube, tomato purée and egg, blending well. Place in a microwave loaf dish and cook for 7 minutes, turning the dish twice.

Cover with foil, shiny side inside and leave to stand for 5 minutes.

Meanwhile, to make the topping, place the butter in a bowl. Cook for ½ minute to melt. Add the mushrooms and spring onions. Cover and cook for 3 minutes.

Stir in the cream and lemon juice and cook for ½-1 minute until hot and thickened.

To serve, invert the meatloaf on to a warmed serving dish and spoon over the mushroom topping. Cut into slices to serve.

Serves: 4
Power setting: FULL
Preparation time: 15 minutes
Cooking time: 16-17 minutes

BEEF AND APRICOT CURRY

25 g/1 oz butter
1 large onion, peeled and
 chopped
1 garlic clove, peeled and
 crushed
1 tablespoon plain flour
2 tablespoons curry
 powder
1 × 411 g (14½ oz) can
 stewed steak in gravy
1 × 285 (10 oz) can
 apricots in their juice

Place the butter in a casserole dish and cook for ½ minute to melt. Add the onion and garlic, cover and cook for 2 minutes.

Stir in the flour and curry powder and cook for ½ minute. Add the stewed steak and juice from the apricots, blending well. Cover and cook for 3½ minutes, stirring once.

Add the apricots, blending well. Cover and cook for a further ½ minute. Serve hot with boiled rice.

To freeze
Cool quickly, cover, seal, label and freeze for up to 1 month.

Serves: 4
Power setting: FULL
Preparation time: 5 minutes
Cooking time: 7 minutes
Suitable for freezing

STEAK AU POIVRE

2 × 225 g (8 oz) thick
    sirloin steaks
20 g/¾ oz butter
1 tablespoon crushed
    black peppercorns
1 tablespoon brandy
2 tablespoons double
    cream
salt

Preheat a small browning dish for 6 minutes (or according to the manufacturer's instructions).

Dry the steaks with absorbent kitchen paper and smear with the butter. Press the peppercorns into the steaks on both sides.

Add the steaks to the browning dish, pressing down well. Cook for 1 minute for a rare to medium steak or 2 minutes for a medium to well-done steak. Turn over and cook for a further 1 minute for a rare to medium steak or 2 minutes for a medium to

well-done steak. Remove from the dish and place on warmed serving plates.

Add the brandy to the dish and cook for ½ minute. Stir in the cream and salt to taste, blending well. Cook for ¾ minute.

Pour over the steaks to serve. Serve at once.

Serves: 2
Power setting: FULL
Preparation time: 5 minutes
Cooking time: 9¼-11¼ minutes

PORK AND BEANSPROUT STIR-FRY

450 g/1 lb pork fillet
½ garlic clove, peeled
salt and freshly ground
    black pepper
2 tablespoons oil
2 sticks celery, finely sliced
1 onion, peeled and finely
    chopped
1 tablespoon cornflour
½ teaspoon ground
    ginger
3 tablespoons soy sauce
1 tablespoon sweet sherry
4 tablespoons water
175 g/6 oz beansprouts

Rub the pork fillet with the cut side of the garlic and season with salt and pepper to taste. Cut into thin strips.

Preheat a lidded browning dish for 7 minutes (or according to the manufacturer's instructions), add the oil and pork and stir well. Cook for 3 minutes.

Add the celery and onion, cover and cook for 3 minutes, stirring occasionally.

Blend the cornflour with the ginger, soy sauce, sherry and water. Stir into the pork, cover and cook for 3 minutes, stirring twice.

Stir the beansprouts into the pork mixture with salt to taste. Cook, uncovered, for a further 2 minutes. Serve with boiled rice.

Serves: 4
Power setting: FULL
Preparation time: 10-15 minutes
Cooking time: 18 minutes

ORANGE-STUFFED LOIN OF PORK

25 g/1 oz butter
1 small onion, peeled and
    chopped
175 g/6 oz cooked long-
    grain rice
1 tablespoon chopped
    fresh sage
grated rind and juice of
    ½ orange
salt and freshly ground
    black pepper
1 egg, beaten
1 × 1.5 kg (3½ lb) loin of
    pork, boned
To garnish:
orange wedges
sprigs of fresh sage

Place the butter in a bowl with the onion. Cover and cook on FULL POWER for 3 minutes. Stir in the rice, sage, orange rind, orange juice, salt and pepper to taste and egg, blending well. Spread the stuffing over the meat, roll up to a neat shape and secure with string.

Place on a roasting rack in a shallow dish. Cover and cook on MEDIUM POWER for 48-56 minutes, turning over twice, until cooked.

Remove the pork, wrap in foil, shiny side inside, and leave to stand for 15-20 minutes.

Unwrap the pork and place on a warmed serving dish. Garnish with orange wedges and sprigs of fresh sage.

To freeze
Cool quickly, wrap in foil, seal, label and freeze for up to 2 months.

Serves: 6
Power settings: FULL, MEDIUM
Preparation time: 20 minutes
Cooking time: 1 hour 6 minutes-1 hour 19 minutes
Suitable for freezing

COUNTRY-STYLE PORK

4 sparerib pork chops
25 g/1 oz seasoned flour
2 tablespoons oil
1 onion, peeled and
    chopped
1 green pepper, cored,
    seeded and chopped
2 courgettes, sliced
1 × 397 g (14 oz) can
    peeled tomatoes
25 g/1 oz butter
50 g/2 oz fresh white
    breadcrumbs
1 cooking apple, peeled,
    cored and chopped
50 g/2 oz cheese, grated
salt and black pepper
beaten egg yolk to bind

Coat the chops in the seasoned flour. Place the oil in a casserole dish and cook for 1 minute. Add the chops and cook for 4 minutes, turning over once.

Add the onion, pepper and courgettes and cook for 3 minutes.

Place the tomatoes in a shallow heatproof serving dish. Top with the pork and vegetable mixture.

Place the butter in a bowl and cook for ½ minute to melt. Stir in the breadcrumbs, apple, cheese and salt and pepper to taste. Bind together with the beaten egg yolk. Press the mixture on top of the chops and vegetables.

Cook for 15 minutes, turning the dish twice. Brown under a preheated hot grill before serving.

Serves: 4
Power setting: FULL
Preparation time: 25 minutes
Cooking time: 23½ minutes

BARBECUED SPARERIBS

1 tablespoon oil
550 g/1¼ lb spare rib
    chops
15 g/½ oz butter
1 onion, peeled and finely
    chopped
100 ml/4 fl oz tomato
    ketchup
25 ml/1 fl oz cider
    vinegar
25 ml/1 fl oz hot pepper
    sauce
4 tablespoons soft brown
    sugar
1 teaspoon made
    mustard
pinch of cayenne pepper
salt

Preheat a browning dish on FULL POWER for 10 minutes (or according to the manufacturer's instructions). Add the oil and cook on FULL POWER for 1 minute. Add the chops and turn quickly on all sides to brown and seal evenly. Remove from the dish and set aside.

Place the butter and onion in a large shallow dish. Cook on FULL POWER for 2 minutes, stirring once. Add the tomato ketchup, vinegar, hot pepper sauce, sugar, mustard, cayenne pepper and salt to taste, blending well. Add the chops and turn in the sauce to coat evenly. Cook, uncovered, on FULL POWER for 5 minutes, stirring once.

Reduce the power setting and cook on DEFROST POWER for 20 minutes, stirring the dish twice.

Serve hot with boiled rice and a seasonal salad.

Serves: 4
Power settings: FULL, DEFROST
Preparation time: 10 minutes
Cooking time: 38 minutes

COUNTRY RABBIT CASSEROLE

1 rabbit, cut into about 6
    pieces
1 large onion, peeled and
    sliced
1 garlic clove, peeled and
    crushed
4 rashers bacon, rinded
    and chopped   (cont.)

Place the rabbit, onion, garlic, bacon, carrots, celery, milk, stock, herbs and bay leaf in a large casserole dish. Cover and cook for 12 minutes, stirring once. Leave to stand, covered, for 10 minutes. Cook for a further 6 minutes.

Remove and discard the bay leaf. Strain the liquid from the casserole into a jug.

Place the butter in a bowl and cook for ½ minute to melt. Stir in the flour and cook for 1 minute. Gradually add the strained liquid and salt and pepper to taste, blending well. Cook for 3 minutes, stirring every 1 minute.

Pour over the rabbit mixture. Cook for a further 2 minutes.

3 carrots, peeled and
    sliced
1 stick celery, sliced
150 ml/¼ pint milk
150 ml/¼ pint light stock
¼ teaspoon dried mixed
    herbs
1 bay leaf
25 g/1 oz butter
25 g/1 oz plain flour
salt and black pepper

To freeze
Cool quickly and place in a rigid container. Cover, seal, label and freeze for up to 3 months.

Serves: 4-6
Power setting: FULL
Preparation time: 25 minutes
Cooking time: 34½ minutes
Suitable for freezing

RICE-STUFFED BREAST OF LAMB

25 g/1 oz butter
350 g/12 oz cooked long-
    grain rice
50 g/2 oz raisins
grated rind and juice of 1
    orange
25 g/1 oz walnuts,
    chopped
salt and freshly ground
    black pepper
1 egg, beaten
1 breast of lamb, boned
1 garlic clove, peeled and
    cut into slivers

Place the butter in a bowl and cook for 1 minute. Add the rice, raisins, orange rind and juice, walnuts and salt and pepper to taste, blending well. Bind together with the beaten egg.

Lay the breast of lamb flat, skin side down, on a board and spread the stuffing over the flesh, reserving any extra. Roll up and secure neatly with string. Make deep incisions into the meat with a sharp knife and insert the garlic slivers.

Place on a roasting rack in a shallow dish, cover and cook for 28 minutes, turning the dish four times during cooking.

Spoon any reserved rice mixture on to a serving dish and top with the stuffed breast of lamb. Cook for a further 2 minutes to serve.

Brown under a preheated hot grill before serving if liked.

Serves: 4
Power setting: FULL
Preparation time: 20 minutes
Cooking time: 31 minutes

MOUSSAKA

25 g/1 oz butter
2 onions, peeled and
    finely chopped
450 g/1 lb minced lamb
    or beef
225 g/8 oz tomatoes,
    peeled and chopped
2 tablespoons tomato
    purée
2 tablespoons meat stock
1 teaspoon salt
675 g/1½ lb aubergines,
    sliced, sprinkled with
    salt and left to drain
2 tablespoons water
4 tablespoons dry white
    wine
1 egg, beaten
4 tablespoons grated
    Parmesan cheese
300 ml/½ pint White
    sauce (see p. 140)

Place the butter in a dish and cook for ½ minute to melt. Add the onions and cook, uncovered, for 2 minutes.

Add the meat, blending well. Cook, uncovered for 3-4 minutes, stirring once.

Stir in the tomatoes, tomato purée, stock and salt, blending well.

Rinse the aubergines and pat dry with absorbent kitchen towel, then place in a dish with the water. Cover and cook for 12-15 minutes, stirring once, until cooked. Drain thoroughly.

Layer the aubergines and meat mixture in a cooking dish and sprinkle with the wine.

Add the egg and half of the cheese to the sauce, blending well. Pour over the moussaka to coat. Sprinkle with the remaining cheese.

Cook, uncovered, for 20-25 minutes, turning the dish after 10 minutes.

Serve hot with a green salad.

To freeze
Cool quickly, cover, seal, label and freeze for up to 3 months.

Serves: 4
Power setting: FULL
Preparation time: 20-25 minutes
Cooking time: 37½-46½ minutes
Suitable for freezing

STUFFED SHOULDER OF LAMB VALENCIA

Stuffing:

1 tablespoon oil

1 onion, peeled and
    chopped

175 g/6 oz cooked long-
    grain rice

2 tablespoons chopped
    fresh parsley

100 g/4 oz seedless raisins

grated rind and juice of 1
    lemon

25 g/1 oz walnuts,
    chopped

salt and black pepper

1 egg, beaten

1 × 1.5 kg (3½ lb)
    shoulder of lamb,
    boned

1 garlic clove, peeled and
    cut into slivers

2 tablespoons plain flour

300 ml/½ pint meat stock

2 tablespoons single
    cream

1 tablespoon chopped
    fresh parsley

lemon wedges to garnish

Place the oil and onion in a bowl. Cover and cook on FULL POWER for 2 minutes. Add the rice, parsley, raisins, lemon rind and juice, walnuts and salt and pepper to taste, blending well. Bind together with the beaten egg.

Stuff the shoulder of lamb with the rice mixture and sew up the opening with fine string. Using a small, sharp knife, make inscisions in the flesh of the lamb and insert the galric slivers. Place on a roasting rack in a shallow dish. Cover and cook on MEDIUM POWER for 40-44 minutes, turning the dish every 10 minutes, until cooked. Remove from the dish, wrap in foil, shiny side inside and leave to stand for 15-20 minutes.

Remove and discard any excess fat from the cooking juices until just 1 tablespoon remains. Place in a bowl with the flour and cook on FULL POWER for ¾ minute. Gradually add the stock, blending well. Cook on FULL POWER for 3½ minutes, stirring twice. Stir in the cream, parsley and salt and pepper to taste.

Place the meat on a warmed serving dish and garnish with lemon wedges. Serve the sauce separately.

To freeze

Cool quickly. Wrap lamb in foil and place rice in a rigid container. Seal, label and freeze for up to 2 months.

Serves: 6
Power settings: FULL, MEDIUM
Preparation time: 25 minutes
*Cooking time: 1 hour 1¼ minutes-1 hour
10¼ minutes*
Suitable for freezing

LAMB FRICASSÉE

1 × 1.5-2 kg (3½-4 lb) leg
    of lamb, boned and cut
    into 2.5 cm/1 inch
    cubes

2 tablespoons oil

1 large onion, peeled and
    finely sliced

2 tablespoons plain flour

200 ml/7 fl oz boiling
    lamb or light stock

200 ml/7 fl oz dry
    vermouth

1 × 454 g (1 lb) packet
    frozen baby carrots

salt and black pepper

2 egg yolks

2 tablespoons lemon juice

finely grated rind of ½
    lemon

2 tablespoons chopped
    fresh parsley

Place the lamb, oil and onion in a large casserole dish. Cook for 5 minutes, stirring once.

Add the flour, blending well. Gradually add the stock and vermouth, mixing well to blend. Stir in the carrots and salt and pepper to taste, cover and cook for 25-30 minutes, stirring twice, until the lamb is cooked.

Beat the egg yolks with the lemon juice, lemon rind, parsley and 5 tablespoons of the cooking juices. Stir into the casserole, blending well.

Cover and cook for 5 minutes, stirring once, until just beginning to thicken. Leave to stand for 5 minutes before serving with noodles, rice or baby new potatoes.

Serves: 6
Power setting: FULL
Preparation time: 20 minutes
Cooking time: 40-45 minutes

POTTED SHRIMPS (p.56) AND PLAICE AND ASPARAGUS WITH WATERCRESS SAUCE (p.47)   75

CHILLI CON CARNE (p.80)

PHEASANT WITH WALNUTS AND GRAPES (p.91)

ORIENTAL LIVER (p.82)

MEAT BROWNING AIDS

There are many browning agents and aids which can be used to add colour and flavour to those foods which do not brown readily in the microwave oven:

Browning agent	Food	Preparation
Soy sauce	Beef, lamb, pork, poultry and game	Brush on to meat or rub into poultry and game.
Tomato ketchup/ Brown sauce	Beef, hamburgers, poultry	Brush on to meat and poultry.
Crushed crisps	Poultry joints	Roll in the crisps to coat.
Colourful dry soup mix	Poultry and game	Sprinkle on or roll in the soup mix to coat.
Melted butter and ground paprika	Poultry and game	Brush on butter and sprinkle with paprika.
Worcestershire sauce	Hamburgers, beef, lamb or pork	Brush on item.
Toasted breadcrumbs	Poultry	Brush with butter and roll in crumbs to coat.
Jams, jellies, glazes	Poultry, ham and game	Glaze for last 10 minutes of cooking time.
Microwave seasoning	All meats, poultry and game.	Sprinkle on item.
Browning dish	All meats, poultry and game	Preheat according to manufacturer's instructions. Turn item quickly on all sides to brown.

BACON-WRAPPED CHIPOLATAS

8 pork chipolata sausages
8 long rashers streaky
    bacon, rinded

Prick the sausages with a fork. Wrap a rasher of bacon around each sausage and secure with a wooden cocktail stick.

Place on a roasting rack and cook for 8-10 minutes, turning over once and re-arranging once. Serve hot.

Serves: 8
Power setting: FULL
Preparation time: 10 minutes
Cooking time: 8-10 minutes

LAMB PILAF

50 g/2 oz butter
225 g/8 oz long-grain
    rice
1 onion, peeled and
    chopped
1 garlic clove, peeled and
    crushed
350 g/12 oz cooked lamb,
    cubed
50 g/2 oz sultanas
1 small courgette, sliced
1 canned pimiento, sliced
juice of 1 lemon
600 ml/1 pint boiling light
    meat stock
salt and black pepper
To garnish:
25 g/1 oz flaked almonds
thin strips of lemon rind
1 lemon, sliced

Place the butter, rice, onion and garlic in a large casserole dish. Cook, uncovered, for 3 minutes until the onion is almost tender.

Add the lamb, sultanas, courgette, pimiento, lemon juice, stock and salt and pepper to taste. Cover and cook for 14 minutes. Leave to stand for 5 minutes.

Serve hot garnished with the almonds, lemon rind and lemon slices.

To freeze
Cool quickly and place in a rigid container. Cover, seal, label and freeze for up to 3 months.

Serves: 4
Power setting: FULL
Preparation time: 15 minutes
Cooking time: 22 minutes
Suitable for freezing

CHILLI CON CARNE

1 tablespoon oil
1 onion, peeled and
   chopped
1 garlic clove, peeled and
   chopped
450 g/1 lb minced
   shoulder of lamb
1 teaspoon chilli powder
1 tablespoon tomato
   purée
1 tablespoon ground
   paprika
1 × 227 g (8 oz) can
   peeled tomatoes
1 teaspoon sugar
salt and freshly ground
   black pepper
1 × 227 g (8 oz) can red
   kidney beans, drained

Place the oil in a cooking dish with the onion and garlic. Cover and cook for 4 minutes.

Add the lamb and cook for 4 minutes, stirring twice.

Add the chilli powder, tomato purée, paprika, tomatoes with their juice, sugar and salt and pepper to taste. Cover and cook for 6 minutes, stirring twice.

Add the kidney beans, blending well. Cover and cook for a further 3-4 minutes, stirring once.

Serve hot with boiled rice and a green salad.

To freeze
Cool quickly, cover, seal, label and freeze for up to 1 month.

Serves: 4
Power setting: FULL
Preparation time: 10 minutes
Cooking time: 17-18 minutes
Suitable for freezing

Illustrated on p. 76

CALF'S LIVER HELVETIA

25 g/oz butter
1 onion, peeled and finely
   chopped
450 g/1 lb calf's liver, cut
   into thin strips
150 ml/¼ pint beef stock
3 tablespoons soured
   cream
3 tablespoons red wine
1 teaspoon chopped fresh
   basil
1-2 teaspoons plain flour
1-2 tablespoons cold
   water
salt and freshly ground
   black pepper

Place the butter in a small casserole dish and cook for ½ minute to melt. Add the onion, cover and cook for 3 minutes.

Add the liver, blending well. Cover and cook for 5-6 minutes, stirring twice.

Add the stock, soured cream, wine and basil, blending well.

Mix the flour with the water to a smooth paste and stir into the liver mixture with salt and pepper to taste. Cook for 2-3 minutes, stirring twice, until smooth and thickened.

Serve at once with noodles or creamed potatoes.

Serves: 4
Power setting: FULL
Preparation time: 10-15 minutes
Cooking time: 10½-12½ minutes

SPICY SAUSAGES

450 g/1 lb pork sausages
100 g/4 oz mushrooms,
   wiped and sliced
2 slices fresh or canned
   pineapple, halved
1 teaspoon mustard
   powder
¼ teaspoon ground
   nutmeg   (cont.)

Prick the sausages and place in a cooking dish. Top with the mushrooms and pineapple.

Blend the mustard with the nutmeg, cinnamon, cornflour and sugar. Gradually add the cider, vinegar and Worcestershire sauce. Spoon the sauce mixture over the sausages. Cover and cook on MEDIUM POWER for 15 minutes, turning over once

and stirring twice.

Leave to stand, covered, for 10 minutes. Serve garnished with chopped parsley.

¼ teaspoon ground
  cinnamon
2 teaspoons cornflour
1 tablespoon demerara
  sugar
150 ml/¼ pint dry cider
1 teaspoon vinegar
few drops of
  Worcestershire sauce
chopped parsley to
  garnish

To freeze
Cool quickly and place in a rigid container. Cover, seal, label and freeze for up to 2 months.

Serves: 4
Power setting: MEDIUM
Preparation time: 10 minutes
Cooking time: 25 minutes
Suitable for freezing

DEVILLED KIDNEY AND SAUSAGE ON RICE

225 g/8 oz long-grain
  rice
600 ml/1 pint boiling
  water
1 teaspoon salt
50 g/2 oz butter
1 onion, peeled and
  chopped
8 pork chipolatas
8 lambs' kidneys, skinned,
  cored and halved
2 tablespoons dry sherry
2 tablespoons
  Worcestershire sauce
1 teaspoon mustard
  powder
1 tablespoon chopped
  fresh parsley
salt and freshly ground
  black pepper

Place the rice in a bowl with the boiling water and salt. Cover and cook for 12 minutes, stirring twice. Leave to stand while preparing the kidney and sausage mixture.

Place the butter in a bowl and cook for 1 minute to melt. Add the onion, cover and cook for 2 minutes.

Twist each chipolata into two pieces and cut. Add the kidney and sausage pieces to the onion mixture, blending well. Cover and cook for 4 minutes, stirring once. Add the sherry, Worcestershire sauce, mustard, parsley and salt and pepper to taste, blending well. Cover and cook for 3 minutes.

To serve, spoon the rice into a warmed serving dish and top with the devilled kidney and sausage mixture.

Serves: 4
Power setting: FULL
Preparation time: 15-20 minutes
Cooking time: 22 minutes
Suitable for freezing

GAMMON STEAKS HAWAIIAN

2 × 175 g (6 oz) gammon
  steaks
freshly ground black
  pepper
100 g/4 oz button
  mushrooms, trimmed
  and wiped
15 g/½ oz butter
2 fresh or canned
  pineapple rings
To garnish:
tomato wedges
watercress sprigs

Snip the rinds of the gammon steaks at 2.5 cm/1 inch intervals to prevent curling. Place on a flat dish. Season with pepper to taste and cover with absorbent kitchen towel. Cook for 5-6 minutes, turning the dish twice. Leave to stand while cooking the mushrooms and pineapple.

Place the mushrooms in a bowl with the butter. Cover and cook for 1½ minutes, stirring once.

Place the pineapple slices on a plate. Cook for 1 minute until hot.

Serve each gammon steak topped with a pineapple slice. Garnish with the mushrooms, tomato wedges and watercress sprigs. Serve at once.

Serves: 2
Power setting: FULL
Preparation time: 10 minutes
Cooking time: 7½-8½ minutes

ORIENTAL LIVER

350 g/12 oz liver, sliced
50 g/2 oz seasoned
    wholemeal flour
25 g/1 oz butter
2 onions, peeled and
    sliced
1 red or green pepper,
    cored, seeded and
    chopped
2 teaspoons chilli powder
2 tablespoons soy sauce
1 tablespoon tomato
    purée
2 tomatoes, peeled, seeded
    and chopped
salt and freshly ground
    black pepper
250 ml/8 fl oz milk
watercress sprigs to
    garnish

Coat the liver in the seasoned flour. Preheat a large lidded browning dish for 10 minutes (or according to the manufacturer's instructions). Add the butter and swirl quickly to coat.

Add the liver and turn quickly on both sides to brown evenly. Cook for 4 minutes, turning once. Set aside.

Place the onion, pepper and chilli powder in a bowl. Cover and cook for 6 minutes, stirring once. Add the soy sauce, tomato purée, tomatoes and salt and pepper to taste, blending well.

Stir into the liver with the milk, blending well. Cover and cook for 3-4 minutes, stirring twice.

Serve hot garnished with watercress sprigs.

Serves: 4
Power setting: FULL
Preparation time: 15 minutes
Cooking time: 23-24 minutes

Illustrated on p. 78

CHICKEN BREASTS WITH ASPARAGUS SAUCE

4 chicken breasts, skinned
5 tablespoons white wine
1 tablespoon dry sherry
1 × 295 g (10½ oz) can
    condensed asparagus
    soup
25 g/1 oz split almonds,
    toasted
3-4 tablespoons soured
    cream

Place the chicken breasts in a shallow cooking dish with the wine and sherry. Cover and cook for 10 minutes, turning the chicken over once.

Remove the chicken from the cooking juices with a slotted spoon and place on a warmed serving dish. Cover with foil, shiny side inside.

Add the soup and almonds to the cooking juices, blending well. Cook for 5 minutes, stirring twice.

Stir in the soured cream and spoon over the chicken breasts to serve.

Serves: 4
Power setting: FULL
Preparation time: 5 minutes
Cooking time: 15 minutes

GLAZED HAM WITH APRICOT RICE

1 × 2 kg (4 lb) ham joint
Glaze:
6 tablespoons made
    mustard
6 tablespoons clear honey
1 tablespoon dark brown
    sugar
½ teaspoon ground
    cloves
Apricot Rice:
2 tablespoons oil   (cont.)

Shield the ham shank with a little foil and place, flat side down, on a roasting rack in a shallow dish. Cover and cook on MEDIUM POWER for 22 minutes.

Remove the foil, turn the ham flat side up, cover and cook on MEDIUM POWER for a further 7 minutes.

Using a sharp knife, remove the rind and most of the outer layer of fat from the ham. Cover and cook on MEDIUM POWER for a further 10 minutes.

Meanwhile, blend the mustard with the honey, sugar and cloves.

Baste the ham evenly with the glaze, cover and cook on MEDIUM POWER for a further 5-9 minutes, until cooked. Remove the ham, wrap in foil, shiny side inside, and leave to stand while preparing the apricot rice.

Place the oil in a bowl with the onion and rice. Cook on FULL POWER for 2 minutes. Add the apricots, lemon juice and

1 large onion, peeled
   and chopped
350 g/12 oz long-grain
   rice
100 g/4 oz dried apricots,
   chopped
1 tablespoon lemon juice
1.2 litres/2 pints boiling
   light stock

stock, blending well. Cover and cook on FULL POWER for 12 minutes. Leave to stand for 3 minutes.

Place the ham on a warmed serving dish and serve with the apricot rice.

Serves: 6
Power settings: FULL, MEDIUM
Preparation time: 10 minutes
Cooking time: 1 hour 3 minutes-1 hour 7 minutes

Illustrated on p. 97

ROAST VEAL WITH MANDARIN ORANGES

1 × 1.5 kg (3½ lb) veal
   roast
½ teaspoon dried
   oregano
½ teaspoon dried basil
1 teaspoon ground
   paprika
salt and freshly ground
   black pepper
5 tablespoons dry white
   wine
Sauce:
150 ml/¼ pint chicken
   stock
1 × 200 g (7 oz) can
   mandarin oranges
2 teaspoons plain flour
3 tablespoons single
   cream
3 tablespoons dry white
   wine

Season the veal with the oregano, basil, paprika and salt and pepper to taste. Place in a shallow cooking dish with the wine. Cook on MEDIUM POWER for 18 minutes.

Turn the veal roast over and cook on MEDIUM POWER for a further 18-24 minutes until cooked. Remove from the dish with a slotted spoon. Wrap in foil, shiny side inside, and leave to stand for 20 minutes.

Meanwhile, stir the chicken stock and mandarin juice into the meat juices, blending well.

Blend the flour with the cream to a smooth paste and stir into the sauce mixture with the wine, blending well.

Cook on FULL POWER for 3-5 minutes, stirring three times, until smooth and thickened.

Stir in the mandarins. Cook on FULL POWER for a further 1 minute.

Place the veal on a warmed serving plate and serve with the hot mandarin sauce.

Serves: 6
Power settings: MEDIUM, FULL
Preparation time: 10 minutes
Cooking time: 56 minutes-1 hour 2 minutes

PRAWN AND CHICKEN PIE

4 medium potatoes,
   scrubbed
25 g/1 oz butter
2 egg yolks
salt and black pepper
1 × 411 g (14½ oz) can
   prawn or lobster bisque
4 tablespoons soured
   cream
2 cooked chicken legs,
   flesh sliced into thin
   strips
175 g/6 oz peeled prawns
To garnish:
1 tablespoon chopped
   fresh parsley
grated rind of ½ lemon

Prick the skins of the potatoes. Place on a double thickness sheet of absorbent kitchen towel and cook for 18 minutes, turning 2-3 times.

Halve the potatoes, scoop out the flesh and place in a bowl. Mash with the butter, egg yolks and salt and pepper to taste.

Mix the prawn or lobster bisque with the soured cream, chicken, prawns and salt and pepper to taste. Place in a shallow cooking dish, about 5 cm/2 inches deep.

Spoon or pipe the potato mixture on top to cover. Cook for 5 minutes, turning the dish once. Cook under a preheated hot grill to brown if liked.

Sprinkle with the parsley and lemon rind before serving. Serve with fresh vegetables in season.

To freeze
Cool quickly, cover, seal, label and freeze for up to 2 months.

Serves: 4-6
Power setting: FULL
Preparation time: 10 minutes
Cooking time: 23 minutes
Suitable for freezing

CHICKEN AND COCONUT CURRY

100 g/4 oz desiccated
    coconut
450 ml/¾ pint boiling
    water
2 teaspoons freshly grated
    root ginger
1½ tablespoons curry
    powder
4 chicken legs
2 tablespoons oil
1 onion, peeled and sliced
1 garlic clove, peeled and
    crushed
¼ teaspoon cumin seeds
10 cardamoms, seeded
    and crushed
3 green chillis, seeded and
    finely chopped
450 ml/¾ pint chicken
    stock
salt and freshly ground
    black pepper
To garnish:
1 tablespoon flaked
    coconut
curry powder

Place the coconut in a bowl with the water. Mix well then leave to soak for about 30 minutes.

Meanwhile rub the ginger and curry powder into the chicken legs and leave to stand until the coconut has soaked sufficiently.

Place the oil in a shallow cooking dish and cook for 1 minute. Add the chicken legs, any remaining root ginger and curry powder, onion, garlic, cumin, cardamoms and chillis. Cook for 5 minutes, turn the chicken legs over and add the chicken stock with salt and pepper to taste, blending well. Cook for a further 5 minutes.

Turn and re-arrange the chicken legs. Strain the 'coconut milk' from the bowl and add to the chicken, blending well. (The coconut is discarded.) Cook for a further 5 minutes.

Spoon the curry on to a warmed serving dish. Garnish with the flaked coconut and a sprinkling of curry powder.

To freeze
Cool quickly and place in a rigid container. Cover, seal, label and freeze for up to 1 month.

Serves: 4
Power setting: FULL
Preparation time: 10-15 minutes, plus
    soaking
Cooking time: 16 minutes
Suitable for freezing

CHICKEN CHANTILLY

15 g/½ oz butter
100 g/4 oz long-grain
    rice
150 ml/¼ pint chicken
    stock
5 tablespoons white wine
2 teaspoons lemon juice
1 small onion, peeled and
    coarsely chopped
1 bay leaf
450 g/1 lb cooked
    chicken, half chopped
    and half cut into small
    strips
150 ml/¼ pint
    mayonnaise
5 tablespoons double
    cream, whipped
salt and freshly ground
    black pepper
watercress sprigs to
    garnish

Place the butter in a bowl and cook for ½ minute to melt. Add the rice and cook for 1 minute. Add the stock, wine, lemon juice, onion and bay leaf, blending well. Cover and cook for 7 minutes.

Add the chopped chicken, blending well. Cover and cook for 7 minutes, stirring once. Leave to stand, covered, for 5 minutes. Cool quickly and remove and discard bay leaf.

Mix the mayonnaise with the cream and salt and pepper to taste.

Pack the rice mixture into an oiled ring mould, pressing down firmly. Invert on to a serving dish. Spoon about half of the mayonnaise mixture over the rice ring.

Fold the chicken strips into the remaining mayonnaise mixture and spoon into the centre of the ring.

Garnish with watercress sprigs to serve.

Serves: 4
Power setting: FULL
Preparation time: 25 minutes, plus
cooling
Cooking time: 20½ minutes

COQ AU VIN

25 g/1 oz butter
1 tablespoon oil
2 × 1 kg (2¼ lb) oven-
    ready chickens, jointed
3 tablespoons seasoned
    flour
12 baby onions, peeled
3 tablespoons brandy
1 garlic clove, peeled
1 bay leaf
1 stick celery, scrubbed
    and coarsely chopped
600 ml/1 pint red wine
salt and black pepper
225 g/8 oz mushrooms,
    wiped and thinly sliced

Preheat a large browning dish for 10 minutes (or according to the manufacturer's instructions). Add the butter and oil and swirl quickly to coat. Cook for 1 minute.

Coat the chicken in the seasoned flour and add to the browning dish with the onions. Turn quickly on all sides to brown evenly. Remove with a slotted spoon and place in a large casserole dish.

Stir the brandy into the dish juices, blending well. Pour over the casserole mixture.

Add the garlic, bay leaf, celery and wine. Cover and cook for 12 minutes, stirring twice.

Add the mushrooms, blending well. Cook, uncovered, for 8 minutes, until tender, stirring once.

Remove and discard the garlic and bay leaf. Serve hot with jacket potatoes.

To freeze
Cool quickly and place in a rigid container. Cover, seal, label and freeze for up to 3 months.

Serves: 4-6
Power setting: FULL
Preparation time: 25-30 minutes
Cooking time: 31 minutes
Suitable for freezing

CHICKEN GOULASH

2 tablespoons plain flour
1 tablespoon paprika
salt and black pepper
8 small or 4 large chicken
    drumsticks, skinned
25 g/1 oz butter
1 onion, peeled and finely
    chopped
300 ml/½ pint chicken
    stock
1 tablespoon tomato
    purée
4 tomatoes, peeled, seeded
    and chopped
3 tablespoons soured
    cream

Mix the flour with the paprika and salt and pepper to taste. Coat the chicken drumsticks in the mixture.

Place the butter in a casserole dish and cook for 1 minute. Add the coated drumsticks and cook for 2 minutes. Turn over and cook for a further 2 minutes. Remove the drumsticks with a slotted spoon and set aside.

Add the onion to the dish juices and cook for 3 minutes. Stir in any remaining flour mixture, chicken stock, tomato purée and tomatoes, blending well. Cook for 3 minutes.

Return the chicken drumsticks to the casserole. Cover and cook for a further 8 minutes, stirring once.

Quickly swirl in the soured cream and serve at once with cooked noodles or rice.

Serves: 4
Power setting: FULL
Preparation time: 10-15 minutes
Cooking time: 19 minutes

POUSSINS AU PRINTANIER

50 g/2 oz butter
225 g/8 oz baby onions,
    peeled
225 g/8 oz courgettes,
    sliced
225 g/8 oz button
    mushrooms, wiped
salt and black pepper
1 lemon, quartered
4 × 450 g (1 lb) oven-
    ready poussins
soy sauce

Place the butter in a large cooking dish. Cook for 1 minute to melt. Add the onions, courgettes, mushrooms and salt and pepper to taste, blending well.

Place a lemon quarter inside each poussin. Arrange on top of the vegetables breast side down. Brush the skins with soy sauce. Cook for 20 minutes, turning the dish twice.

Turn the poussins breast side up, brush with soy sauce and cook for a further 20 minutes, turning the dish twice. Cover and leave to stand for 5 minutes.

Serve the poussins, one per person, surrounded with the buttery vegetables.

Serves: 4
Power setting: FULL
Preparation time: 20 minutes
Cooking time: 46 minutes

CHICKEN BLANQUETTE

25 g/1 oz butter

1 onion, peeled and sliced

2-3 sticks celery, scrubbed
and sliced

100 g/4 oz streaky bacon,
rinded and chopped

1 × 295 g (10½ oz) can
condensed cream of
chicken soup

150 ml/¼ pint chicken
stock or water

salt and freshly ground
black pepper

4 chicken breasts, skinned

100 g/4 oz button
mushrooms, trimmed
and wiped

4-6 tablespoons soured or
double cream

Place the butter in a casserole dish and cook for ½ minute to melt. Add the onion, celery and bacon. Cover and cook for 5 minutes, stirring once.

Add the soup, stock or water and salt and pepper to taste, blending well. Add the chicken and cook for 17 minutes, stirring twice.

Stir in the mushrooms and cook for a further 3 minutes. Swirl in the cream and serve at once with rice or nooodles.

Serves: 4
Power setting: FULL
Preparation time: 10 minutes
Cooking time: 25½ minutes

CHILLI CON POLLO

1 onion, peeled and finely
chopped

1 red pepper, cored,
seeded and chopped

1 garlic clove, peeled and
finely chopped

2 tablespoons olive oil

450 g/1 lb minced raw
chicken

300 ml/½ pint chicken
stock

2 tablespoons tomato
purée

2 tablespoons chopped
fresh parsley

2 tablespoons raisins

2 tablespoons salted
peanuts

6 stuffed olives, sliced

salt and freshly ground
black pepper

grated rind and juice of
½ orange

1 tablespoon chilli
powder

1 × 439 g (15½ oz) can
red kidney beans

½ teaspoon chopped
dried chillies

Place the onion, pepper, garlic and oil in a shallow cooking dish. Cook on FULL POWER for 5 minutes, stirring once.

Add the chicken and cook on FULL POWER for 3 minutes. Add the chicken stock, tomato purée, parsley, raisins, peanuts, olives, salt and pepper to taste, orange rind and juice and chilli powder, blending well. Cover and cook on DEFROST POWER for 15 minutes, stirring twice.

Add the drained kidney beans and cook on DEFROST POWER for 3 minutes. Serve at once sprinkled with the chopped dried chillies. Serve with boiled rice.

To freeze
Cool quickly, cover, seal, label and freeze for up to 2 months.

Serves: 4-6
Power settings: FULL, DEFROST
Preparation time: 10-15 minutes
Cooking time: 26 minutes
Suitable for freezing

SWEET AND SOUR CHICKEN OVER RICE

1 carrot, peeled and cut
  into thin strips
½ green pepper, cored,
  seeded and sliced
1 tablespoon water
450 g/1 lb boneless
  chicken, cubed
1 tablespoon cornflour
150 ml/¼ pint
  unsweetened pineapple
  juice
150 ml/¼ pint vinegar
3 tablespoons brown
  sugar
salt and freshly ground
  black pepper
2 tablespoons tomato
  purée
225 g/8 oz fresh or
  canned pineapple
  pieces
225 g/8 oz long-grain
  rice
600 ml/1 pint boiling
  water
1 teaspoon salt

Place the carrot, pepper and 1 tablespoon water in a bowl. Cover and cook for 3 minutes. Drain and set aside.

Place the chicken in a cooking dish. Cover and cook for 3 minutes.

Mix the cornflour in a jug with the pineapple juice, vinegar, sugar and salt and pepper to taste. Blend in the tomato purée and pineapple pieces. Cook, uncovered, for 4½ minutes, stirring very 1 minute until thickened.

Place the rice, water and salt in a bowl. Cover and cook for 12-15 minutes. Leave to stand while cooking the sweet and sour chicken.

Mix the sweet and sour sauce with the carrot and green pepper mixture and chicken. Cover and cook for 6 minutes, stirring once.

Drain the rice if necessary and spoon into a warmed serving dish. Top with the sweet and sour chicken and serve at once.

To freeze
Freeze the chicken and rice separately. Cool quickly, cover, seal, label and freeze for up to 3 months.

Serves: 4
Power setting: FULL
Preparation time: 20 minutes
Cooking time: 28½-31½ minutes
Suitable for freezing

CHICKEN BOURGUIGNON

1 × 1.5 kg (3½ lb)
  chicken, prepared for
  cooking
1 bay leaf
1 sprig fresh thyme
1 garlic clove, peeled and
  crushed
salt and freshly ground
  black pepper
600 ml/1 pint full-bodied
  red wine
3 tablespoons bramble or
  redcurrant jelly
25 g/1 oz butter
1 thick slice lean bacon,
  rinded and cut into
  strips or cubes
12 button onions, peeled
  and trimmed
12 black olives
sprig fresh thyme to
  garnish

Place the chicken in a deep cooking dish with the bay leaf, thyme, garlic, salt and pepper to taste, wine and bramble or redcurrant jelly. Cook on DEFROST POWER for 35-40 minutes, turning over 2-3 times. Remove from the microwave, cover the chicken with foil, shiny side inside, and leave to stand for 20 minutes.

Meanwhile, place the butter, bacon and onions in a shallow cooking dish. Cook on FULL POWER for 5 minutes, stirring once.

To serve, place the chicken on a warmed serving dish. Surround with the cooked bacon, onions and olives. Spoon over some of the cooking juices and garnish with the thyme.

Serves: 6
Power settings: DEFROST, FULL
Preparation time: 15 minutes
Cooking time: 1 hour-1 hour 5 minutes

MEDITERRANEAN MEATBALLS

450 g/1 minced raw
    chicken
1 small onion, peeled and
    grated or finely
    chopped
1 garlic clove, peeled and
    crushed
salt and freshly ground
    black pepper
1 tablespoon chopped
    fresh thyme
25 g/1 oz butter
1 tablespoon olive oil
300 ml/½ pint red wine
1 tablespoon tomato
    purée
1 red pepper, cored,
    seeded and finely
    chopped
2 tablespoons raisins
8 black olives, stoned and
    coarsely chopped
6 tomatoes, peeled, seeded
    and chopped
1 tablespoon pine nuts

Mix the chicken with the onion, garlic, salt and pepper to taste and about three-quarters of the thyme, blending well. Divide and shape into small meatballs. Cover and chill for 30 minutes.

Place the butter and oil in a deep cooking dish and cook for 1 minute. Add the meatballs, turning quickly in the hot fat to coat. Cook for 4 minutes, turning over once.

Add the red wine, tomato purée, red pepper, raisins, olives, tomatoes and pine nuts, blending well, cover and cook for 7 minutes, turning twice.

Sprinkle with the remaining chopped fresh thyme to serve. Serve with hot crusty bread and a seasonal salad.

To freeze
Cool quickly and place in a rigid container. Cover, seal, label and freeze for up to 3 months.

Serves: 4
Power setting: FULL
Preparation time: 20 minutes plus chilling
Cooking time: 12 minutes
Suitable for freezing

CHICKEN BREASTS PARMESAN

50 g/2 oz fine dry
    breadcrumbs
75 g/3 oz grated
    Parmesan cheese
salt and freshly ground
    black pepper
550 g/1¼ lb boneless
    chicken breasts,
    skinned
1 egg, beaten
2 tablespoons oil
1 × 227 g (8 oz) can
    peeled tomatoes
25 g/1 oz plain flour
1 teaspoon dried oregano
¼ teaspoon garlic salt
7 tablespoons chicken
    stock
50 g/2 oz Cheddar cheese,
    grated
parsley sprigs to garnish

Mix the breadcrumbs with 25 g/1 oz of the Parmesan cheese and salt and pepper to taste in a shallow dish. Dip the chicken breasts in egg then in the breadcrumb mixture to coat.

Meanwhile, preheat a large browning dish for 10 minutes (or according to the manufacturer's instructions). Add the oil and cook for a further 1 minute.

Add the chicken breasts and turn quickly on both sides to brown evenly. Remove with a slotted spoon and place in a cooking dish.

Mix the tomatoes and their juice with the flour, oregano, garlic salt and stock in a bowl, blending well. Cook for 3 minutes, stirring once. Purée in a blender or pass through a fine sieve.

Spoon the tomato sauce over the chicken and sprinkle with the Cheddar cheese. Cover loosely with greaseproof paper and cook for 5-6 minutes, turning the dish twice.

Sprinkle with the remaining Parmesan cheese and cook uncovered for a further ½-1 minute or until the cheese has melted.

Serve at once garnished with parsley sprigs.

Serves: 4
Power setting: FULL
Preparation time: 25 minutes
Cooking time: 19½-21 minutes

ROAST TURKEY AND CRANBERRY STUFFING

1 × 3.5 kg (8 lb) oven-
   ready turkey
25 g/1 oz butter
Stuffing:
100 g/4 oz fresh white
   breadcrumbs
175 g/6 oz prunes, soaked
   overnight, stoned and
   chopped
2 dessert apples, peeled,
   cored and sliced
50 g/2 oz blanched
   almonds, chopped
3 tablespoons cranberry
   sauce
grated rind and juice of 1
   lemon
salt and freshly ground
   black pepper
1 egg, beaten
watercress sprigs to
   garnish

For the stuffing, mix the breadcrumbs with the prunes, apple, almonds, cranberry sauce, lemon rind, lemon juice and salt and pepper to taste, blending well. Bind together with the beaten egg. Use to stuff the neck end of the turkey, securing with wooden cocktail sticks.

Weigh the turkey with its stuffing and calculate the cooking time at 11-13 minutes per 450 g/1 lb on MEDIUM POWER or 9-11 minutes per 450 g/1 lb on FULL POWER.

Rub the turkey skin with butter and protect the turkey wings with a little foil. Place on a roasting rack in a roasting bag, sealing the end with a piece of string or an elastic band. Place in a shallow dish. Cook for the calculated time, turning the dish 3-4 times during cooking.

Wrap the turkey in foil, shiny side inside, and leave to stand for 15 minutes.

Serve hot or cold garnished with watercress sprigs.

Serves: 8
Power settings: FULL, MEDIUM
Preparation time: 20-25 minutes
Cooking time: approx. 1½ hours-1 hour 50 minutes

Illustrated on p. 95

TURKEY DIVAN

75 g/3 oz butter
2 tablespoons chopped
   fresh parsley
100 g/4 oz fresh white
   breadcrumbs
225 g/8 oz button
   mushrooms, sliced
3 tablespoons plain flour
175 ml/6 fl oz milk
salt and freshly ground
   black pepper
150 ml/¼ pint soured
   cream
675 g/1½ lb turkey fillets,
   thinly sliced
2 × 255 g (9 oz) packets
   frozen broccoli spears
grated Parmesan cheese
   to serve

Place 50 g/2 oz of the butter in a bowl and cook for ½ minute to melt. Add the parsley and breadcumbs, blending well. Cook for 2-4 minutes, stirring frequently, until crisp and golden brown. Drain on absorbent kitchen towel.

Place the remaining butter in a bowl with the mushrooms. Cook for 1 minute. Stir in the flour and milk, blending well. Cook for 4 minutes, stirring twice. Blend in the soured cream and salt and pepper to taste.

Add the turkey fillet slices to the sauce, cover and cook for 13-15 minutes, stirring twice.

Place the frozen broccoli spears in a bowl. Cover and cook for 2 minutes. Separate the spears.

Place the broccoli in a single layer in the base of a heatproof serving dish. Spoon over the turkey mixture. Spoon the browned breadcrumbs around the edge of the dish and sprinkle with Parmesan cheese in the centre. Cook, uncovered, for 5-8 minutes until hot and bubbly, turning twice.

Serve hot with noodles or rice.

Serves: 6
Power setting: FULL
Preparation time: 15 minutes
Cooking time: 27½-34½ minutes

ROASTING CHART USING MICROWAVE THERMOMETER

Meat	Remove from oven when this temperature reached	After standing, will reach this temperature for serving
Beef:		
Rare	55°C/130°F	65°C/150°F
Medium	60°C/140°F	70°C/160°F
Well-done	70°C/160°F	78°C/170°F
Pot Roasts	65°C/150°F	70°C/160°F
Meat Loaf	55°C/130°F	60°C/140°F
Veal	65°C/150°F	75°C/170°F
Lamb	70°C/160°F	82°C/180°F
Pork	75°C/170°F	85°C/185°F

DUCK WITH DAMSON SAUCE

1 × 2 kg (4½ lb) oven-
  ready duckling,
  prepared for cooking
salt and freshly ground
  black pepper
Sauce:
1 × 450 g (1 lb) can
  damsons in syrup
25 g/1 oz butter
1 onion, peeled and finely
  chopped
2 teaspoons soy sauce
½ teaspoon ground
  ginger

Prick the skin of the duck and season with salt and pepper to taste. Shield the tips of the wings, tail-end and legs of the duck with foil. Place in a roasting bag and secure loosely with a rubber band. Pierce the bag to allow any steam to escape.

Place the duckling, breast side down, on an upturned saucer in a shallow cooking dish. Cook on MEDIUM POWER for 25 minutes. Drain and discard the juices from the bag.

Lightly reseal the bag and return to the oven breast side up. Cook on MEDIUM POWER for a further 15-24 minutes, until cooked. Remove the duckling from the roasting bag, wrap in foil and leave to stand while preparing the sauce.

To prepare the sauce, sieve the damsons and their juice to remove the stones.

Place the butter in a bowl and cook on FULL POWER for 1 minute. Add the onion and cook on FULL POWER for 2 minutes. Stir in the damson purée, soy sauce and ground ginger. Cook, uncovered on FULL POWER for 5 minutes stirring once.

Crisp and brown the duckling under a preheated hot grill if liked. Serve hot with the damson sauce.

To freeze

Pack duck, covered with sauce, in a rigid container. Cool quickly, cover, seal, label and freeze for up to 2 months.
Serves: 4
Power settings: MEDIUM, FULL
Preparation time: 20 minutes
Cooking time: 48-57 minutes
Suitable for freezing

DUCK WITH APPLE SAUCE

1 × 2 kg (4½ lb) oven-
  ready duckling,
  prepared for cooking
salt and freshly ground
  black pepper
Sauce:
450 g/1 lb cooking apples,
  peeled, cored and
  sliced
2 tablespoons water
25 g/1 oz butter
2 teaspoons sugar

Prick the skin of the duck and season with salt and pepper to taste. Shield the tips of the wings, tail-end and legs of the duck with foil. Place in a roasting bag and secure loosely with a rubber band. Pierce the bag to allow any steam to ecape.

Place the duckling, breast side down, on an upturned saucer in a shallow cooking dish. Cook on MEDIUM POWER for 25 minutes. Drain and discard the juices from the bag.

Lightly reseal the bag and return to the oven breast side up. Cook on MEDIUM POWER for a further 15-24 minutes, until cooked. Remove the duckling from the roasting bag, wrap in foil and leave to stand while preparing the sauce.

To prepare the sauce, place the apples

and water in a bowl. Cover and cook on FULL POWER for 4 minutes, stirring once. Leave to stand, covered, for 4 minutes then beat in the butter and sugar.

Crisp and brown the duckling under a preheated hot grill if liked. Serve hot with the apple sauce.

To freeze

Pack duck, covered with sauce in a rigid container. Cool quickly, cover, seal, label and freeze for up to 2 months.

Serves: 4
Power settings: MEDIUM, FULL
Preparation time: 25 minutes
Cooking time: 48-57 minutes
Suitable for freezing

DUCK WITH GRAPEFRUIT

1 × 1.8 kg (4 lb) oven-
  ready duckling,
  prepared for cooking
1 tablespoon molasses
  sugar
2 apples, cored and sliced
1 garlic clove,   (cont.)

Stuff the duckling cavity with the sugar, apples, garlic, peppercorns and salt. Secure well to enclose with wooden cocktail sticks. Place in a roasting bag and secure loosely with a rubber band. Pierce the bag to allow any steam to escape

Place the duckling, breast side down, on

an upturned saucer in a shallow cooking dish. Cook on FULL POWER for 20 minutes.

Drain the juices from the bag and re-serve. Mix the honey with the soy sauce, blending well. Baste the duckling breast with the honey mixture. Lightly reseal the bag and return to the oven, breast side up.

peeled and crushed
8 peppercorns
salt
1 tablespoon clear honey
1 teaspoon soy sauce
Sauce:
2 tablespoons molasses
     sugar
1 tablespoon cornflour
150 ml/¼ pint
     grapefruit juice
1-2 tablespoons brandy
salt and black pepper
1 grapefruit, peeled and
     cut into segments

Cook on MEDIUM POWER for a further 20 minutes. Remove the duckling from the roasting bag. Wrap in foil and leave to stand while preparing the sauce.

To prepare the sauce, blend the sugar and cornflour with the grapefruit juice in a jug. Stir in 4 tablespoons of the reserved juices, blending well. Cook on FULL POWER for 2 minutes, stirring every ½ minute until smooth and thickened.

Stir in the brandy and season to taste with salt and pepper.

Place the grapefruit segments on a plate and cook on FULL POWER for 1 minute.

Crisp and brown the duckling under a preheated hot grill if liked. Serve hot, garnished with the grapefruit segments and accompanied by the grapefruit sauce.

Serves: 4
Power settings: FULL, MEDIUM
Preparation time: 20 minutes
Cooking time: 43 minutes

BRAISED PHEASANT IN CREAM SAUCE

75 g/3 oz butter
1 × 1.4 kg (3 lb) pheasant,
     prepared for cooking
1 teaspoon microwave
     browning seasoning
     (optional)
1 onion, peeled and
     thinly sliced
300 ml/½ pint double
     cream
juice of ½ lemon
salt and freshly ground
     black pepper
watercress sprigs to
     garnish

Place the butter in a roasting bag, loosely secure the end with a piece of string or an elastic band and cook for 1 minute to melt.

Place the pheasant in the roasting bag, turning in the butter to coat. Sprinkle with the seasoning if used. Add the onion to the bag, loosely secure the end as before and place on a plate. Cook for 15 minutes, turning over once.

Meanwhile, mix the cream with the lemon juice and salt and pepper to taste. Add to the pheasant, re-tie the bag and cook for a further 8 minutes, turning over once. Leave to stand for 10 minutes.

Carefully remove the pheasant from the bag and carve into serving portions. Place on a warmed serving plate and spoon over the creamy sauce.

Garnish with watercress sprigs and serve at once.

Serves: 3-4
Power setting: FULL
Preparation time: 15 minutes
Cooking time: 34 minutes

PHEASANT WITH WALNUTS AND GRAPES

1 × 900 g (2 lb) pheasant,
     prepared for cooking
salt and freshly ground
     black pepper
225 g/8 oz grapes, halved
     and deseeded
50 g/2 oz walnuts,
     chopped
25 g/1 oz butter
150 ml/¼ pint dry white
     wine
150 ml/¼ pint double
     cream
2 egg yolks
watercress sprigs to
     garnish (optional)

Preheat a lidded browning dish on FULL POWER for 6 minutes (or according to the manufacturer's instructions).

Season the pheasant with salt and pepper to taste and stuff with two-thirds of the grapes and walnuts. Secure the opening with wooden cocktail sticks.

Add the butter to the browning dish and swirl quickly to melt. Roll the pheasant in the melted butter. Cover and cook on MEDIUM POWER for 12 minutes.

Turn the pheasant over, cover and cook on MEDIUM POWER for a further 10 minutes.

Remove the pheasant with a slotted spoon and place on a warmed serving plate. Cover with foil, shiny side inside, and leave to stand for 10 minutes.

Meanwhile, add the remaining grapes and walnuts to the dish juices with the wine. Blend the cream with the egg yolks and stir into the sauce, blending well.

Cook on FULL POWER for 3-4 minutes, stirring twice, until lightly thickened.

Serve the pheasant hot and the sauce separately. Garnish with watercress sprigs if liked. Serve with game chips.

Serves: 2
Power settings: FULL, MEDIUM
Preparation time: 20-25 minutes
Cooking time: 41-42 minutes

Illustrated on p. 77

Vegetables and Salads

Light, leafy and green, creamy smooth and hearty, or crisp, crunchy and colourful – there is always a vegetable at its best and most flavoursome to choose, whatever the season.
Follow the seasons for variety, and the instructions for cooking in this section precisely, and you'll enjoy a vegetable or salad gastronomic feast that is hard to beat. For without doubt, vegetables stay crisper, retaining more colour and flavour, when cooked in the microwave than when cooked conventionally. And they retain vitamins and minerals more easily.

ASPARAGUS WITH HERBED BUTTER SAUCE

450 g/1 lb fresh asparagus
3 tablespoons water
100 g/4 oz butter
4 tablespoons finely
    chopped fresh herbs
    (chives, parsley and
    tarragon for example)

Trim the woody ends from the asparagus and thinly pare the outer tough skin from the stalk. Place in a cooking dish with half of the tips at each end. Add the water, cover and cook for 6-8 minutes, or until fork tender. Drain and place on a warmed serving dish.

Place the butter in a bowl. Cover and cook for 3 minutes, or until melted and bubbling hot. Stir in the herbs, blending well.

Spoon over the asparagus and serve at once.

Serves: 4
Power setting: FULL
Preparation time: 10-15 minutes
Cooking time: 9-11 minutes

BROAD BEANS WITH HAM AND CREAM

1 × 283 g (10 oz) packet
    frozen broad beans
2 tablespoons water
2 tablespoons single
    cream
75 g/3 oz cooked ham,
    chopped
salt and freshly ground
    black pepper

Place the beans in a cooking dish with the water. Cover and cook for 8 minutes, stirring once. Drain thoroughly.

Stir in the cream, ham and salt and pepper to taste, blending well. Cook for 1 minute. Serve at once.

Serves: 4
Power setting: FULL
Preparation time: 5 minutes
Cooking time: 9 minutes

HERBY BABY CARROTS

1 × 275 g (10 oz) packet
    frozen baby carrots
4 tablespoons water
25 g/1 oz butter
2 teaspoons demerara
    sugar
½ teaspoon chopped fresh
    tarragon

Place the carrots in a cooking dish with the water. Cover and cook for 8 minutes, stirring once. Drain thoroughly.

Stir in the butter, sugar and tarragon, blending well. Cook for 1 minute. Serve at once.

Serves: 4
Power setting: FULL
Preparation time: 5 minutes
Cooking time: 9 minutes

GLAZED BEETROOT

15 g/½ oz butter
½ teaspoon sugar
grated rind of ½ lemon
225 g/8 oz small cooked
  whole beetroot, peeled
1 teaspoon lemon juice
2 teaspoons capers
salt and freshly ground
  black pepper
chopped fresh parsley to
  garnish

Preheat a small browning dish by cooking for 4 minutes (or according to the manufacturer's instructions). Add the butter, sugar and lemon rind, blending well. Add the beetroot and toss in the butter mixture to coat.

Cook for 1 minute, stir well and cook for a further 1 minute.

Add the lemon juice, capers and salt and pepper to taste, blending well. Cook for a further 2 minutes.

Serve hot sprinkled with chopped parsley.

Serves: 2-3
Power setting: FULL
Preparation time: 10 minutes
Cooking time: 8 minutes

CHOP SUEY

1 tablespoon oil
1 onion, peeled and
  thinly sliced
2 sticks celery, cut into
  small strips
100 g/4 oz mushrooms,
  thinly sliced
¼ cucumber, cut into
  small strips
275 g/10 oz fresh
  beansprouts
150 ml/¼ pint chicken
  stock (see p.34)
salt and black pepper
2 tablespoons cornflour
2 tablespoons cold water
1 tablespoon sherry
1½ tablespoons soy sauce

Preheat a large browning dish for 7 minutes (or according to the manufacturer's instructions). Add the oil and cook for a further 1 minute.

Add the onion, celery, mushrooms, cucumber and beansprouts, blending well. Cook for 2 minutes, stirring once.

Add the stock and salt and pepper to taste. Cook for 2 minutes, stirring once. Mix the cornflour with the water and stir into the chop suey with the sherry and soy sauce, blending well. Cook for 1½-2 minutes, stirring once. Serve at once.

Serves: 4
Power setting: FULL
Preparation time: 15 minutes
Cooking time: 13½-14 minutes

GREEN BEANS IN TANGY TOMATO SAUCE

1 garlic clove, peeled and
  crushed
1 small onion, peeled and
  finely chopped
2 rashers back bacon,
  rinded and chopped
1 × 226 g (8 oz) can
  peeled tomatoes
1 teaspoon dried mixed
  herbs
pinch of sugar
1 × 238 g (10 oz) packet
  frozen whole green
  beans

Place the garlic, onion and bacon in a cooking dish. Cook for 2 minutes.

Add the tomatoes and their juice, herbs, sugar and beans, blending well. Cook for 10 minutes, stirring twice. Serve at once.

Serves: 4
Power setting: FULL
Preparation time: 10 minutes
Cooking time: 12 minutes

THAI HOT-COLD SALAD

4 large crisp lettuce
  leaves, washed
2 large navel oranges,
  peeled, pith removed
  and thinly sliced
2 tablespoons oil
1 garlic clove, peeled and
  crushed
675 g/1½ lb cooked cold
  pork, minced
2 tablespoons finely
  chopped peanuts
2 teaspoons sugar
2 tablespoons soy sauce
2 tablespoons water
salt and cayenne pepper
coriander sprigs to
  garnish

Line 4 serving plates with the lettuce. Arrange the orange slices on top and chill.

Place the oil in a large bowl and cook for 2 minutes. Add the garlic and pork, blending well. Cook for 3-4 minutes, stirring twice, until hot and bubbly.

Add the peanuts, sugar, soy sauce, water and salt and cayenne pepper to taste, blending well. Cook for a further 1 minute, stirring once.

Spoon the hot pork mixture over the oranges. Garnish with coriander sprigs. Serve at once.

Serves: 4
Power setting: FULL
Preparation time: 15-20 minutes
Cooking time: 6-7 minutes

POTATO CASSEROLE

50 g/2 oz smoked back
  bacon, rinded and
  chopped
1 onion, peeled and
  chopped
350 g/12 oz potatoes,
  peeled and thinly sliced
50 g/2 oz button
  mushrooms, sliced
50 g/2 oz cheese, cubed
1 large tomato, peeled
  and chopped
salt and freshly ground
  black pepper

Place the bacon and onion in a cooking dish. Cover and cook for 5 minutes, stirring once.

Add the potatoes, mushrooms, cheese, tomato and salt and pepper to taste, blending well.

Cover and cook for 12-14 minutes, turning the dish twice.

Brown under a preheated hot grill if liked. Serve hot as a vegetable accompaniment or double portions as a light supper dish.

Serves: 2-4
Power setting: FULL
Preparation time: 15 minutes
Cooking time: 17-19 minutes

CHEESY BAKED POTATOES

4 medium potatoes,
  scrubbed
1 × 397 g (14 oz) can
  cream of chicken soup
175 g/6 oz cheese, grated
½ teaspoon dried mixed
  herbs
salt and freshly ground
  black pepper

Prick the potatoes with a fork and place on absorbent kitchen paper. Cook for 7 minutes, turn over and cook for a further 7 minutes. Leave to stand for 5 minutes.

Halve the potatoes lengthways and scoop out most of the flesh into a bowl.

Mix the potato flesh with the soup, cheese, herbs and salt and pepper to taste. Return the mixture to the potato skins and Place on a serving dish.

Cook for 5 minutes, re-arranging once. Serve at once.

Serves: 4
Power setting: FULL
Preparation time: 10-15 minutes
Cooking time: 24 minutes

ROAST TURKEY (p.89) WITH BACON-WRAPPED CHIPOLATAS (p.79) 95

RATATOUILLE (p.99)

GREEN BEANS WITH TOMATO DRESSING (p.212) AND GLAZED HAM WITH APRICOT RICE (p.82)   97

FRENCH-STYLE GREEN PEAS (p.107)

CORN ON THE COB WITH GARLIC BUTTER

50 g/2 oz butter
1 garlic clove, peeled and
   crushed
2 frozen corn on the cobs
salt and freshly ground
   black pepper

Mix the butter with the garlic, blending well. Spread over the corn on the cobs.

Place in a shallow cooking dish and cover loosely with cling film or greaseproof paper.

Cook for 7-8 minutes, turning over halfway through the cooking time.

Season to taste with salt and pepper and serve.

Serves: 2
Power setting: FULL
Preparation time: 5 minutes
Cooking time: 7-8 minutes

STUFFED JACKET POTATOES

2 medium potatoes,
   scrubbed
25 g/1 oz butter
50 g/2 oz mushrooms,
   sliced
50 g/2 oz cooked ham,
   chopped
1 teaspoon made English
   mustard
salt and freshly ground
   black pepper
parsley sprigs to garnish

Prick the potatoes with a fork and place on absorbent kitchen paper. Cook for 4 minutes, turn over and cook for a further 4 minutes. Leave to stand for 5 minutes.

Meanwhile, place the butter in a bowl and cook for ½ minute to melt. Add the mushrooms, cover and cook for 2 minutes. Stir in the ham, mustard and salt and pepper to taste.

Halve the potatoes lengthways and scoop the flesh from the skins into a bowl. Mix with the ham and mushroom mixture.

Return to the potato skins and place on a serving dish. Cook for 2 minutes to reheat. Serve hot garnished with parsley sprigs.

Serves: 2
Power setting: FULL
Preparation time: 5 minutes
Cooking time: 17½ minutes

RATATOUILLE

4½ tablespoons olive oil
1 onion, peeled and
   thinly sliced
1 garlic clove, peeled and
   crushed
1 small green pepper,
   cored, seeded and
   thinly sliced
350 g/12 oz aubergines,
   cubed, sprinkled with
   salt and left to drain for
   half an hour
225 g/8 oz courgettes,
   sliced
2 tomatoes, cut into thin
   wedges
1 teaspoon dried basil
1 teaspoon dried
   marjoram
100 g/4 oz mushrooms,
   sliced
salt and freshly ground
   black pepper

Place the oil, onion and garlic in a large casserole dish. Cook for 4 minutes, stirring once.

Rinse the aubergines and pat dry with absorbent kitchen paper. Add to the onion with the pepper and courgettes. Cover and cook for 4 minutes, stirring once.

Add the tomatoes, basil, marjoram, mushooms and salt and pepper to taste, blending well. Cook, uncovered, for 4 minutes, stirring once.

Serve hot or cold as a starter or vegetable dish.

To freeze
Cool quickly and pack in a rigid container. Cover, seal, label and freeze for up to 3 months

Serves: 4
Power setting: FULL
Preparation time: 15 minutes
Cooking time: 12 minutes
Suitable for freezing

Illustrated on p. 96

GUIDE TO COOKING FRESH VEGETABLES

Vegetables	Quantity	Water/salt	Preparation	Cooking time in minutes on FULL POWER	Cooking notes
Artichokes, globe	1 2 4	8 tablespoons/ ½ teaspoon 8 tablespoons/ ½ teaspoon 250 ml/8 fl oz/ 1 teaspoon	Discard the tough, outer leaves. Snip the tips off the remaining leaves and cut off the stems. Cover to cook.	5-6 7-8 14-15	To test if cooked, at the minimum time, try to pull a leaf from the whole artichoke. If it comes away freely, the artichoke is cooked. Drain upside down before serving.
Asparagus	450 g/1 lb	6 tablespoons/ ½ teaspoon	Place in a dish, arranging any thicker stems to the outside of the dish and tender tips to the centre. Cover to cook.	6-7	Give the dish a half turn after 3 minutes cooking time.
Aubergines	2 medium, halved 1 whole peeled and cubed	2 tablespoons 2 tablespoons/ ¼ tablespoon	Cover to cook.	7-9 5-6	Scoop out the cooked flesh from the halved aubergines and use as required. Stir the cubed aubergine after 3 minutes cooking time.
Beans, all except thin French beans. French beans	450 g/1 lb 450 g/1 lb	8 tablespoons/ ½ teaspoon 8 tablespoons/ ½ teaspoon	Cover to cook. Cover to cook.	14-16 5-7	Stir the beans twice during cooking. Test after the minimum time to see if cooked.
Beetroot	2 medium 5 medium	8 tablespoons/ ½ teaspoon 8 tablespoons/ ½ teaspoon	Cover to cook.	12-16 22-25	Stir or rearrange halfway through the cooking time. Allow to stand for 10 minutes before peeling.
Broccoli	450 g/1 lb	8 tablespoons/ ½ teaspoon	Place in a dish with the stalks to the outside and florets in the centre. Cover to cook.	10-12	Stir or give the dish a half turn after 6 minutes.
Brussels sprouts	450 g/1 lb	4 tablespoons/ ½ teaspoon	Trim damaged or coarse leaves; cut large sprouts in half. Cover to cook.	7-9	Stir the sprouts after 4 minutes cooking time.
Cabbage, shredded	450 g/1 lb	8 tablespoons/ ½ teaspoon	Use a large dish and fit cabbage loosely. Cover to cook.	8-9	Stir or rearrange halfway through the cooking time.

Carrots, whole sliced	450 g/1 lb 1 kg/2 lb 450 g/1 lb	8 tablespoons/ ½ teaspoon 8 tablespoons/ ½ teaspoon	Cut carrots into 1-cm/½-in thick slices. Slicing diagonally reduces the cooking time by 2 minutes. Cover to cook.	12-14 18-20 12-14	Stir or rearrange halfway through the cooking time.
Cauliflower, whole florets	1 medium about 675 g/1½ lb 450 g/1 lb	8 tablespoons/ ½ teaspoon 8 tablespoons/ ½ teaspoon	Cook whole cauliflower on MEDIUM HIGH power. Cover to cook.	13-17 10-12	Turn a whole cauliflower or florets halfway through the cooking time. Allow whole cauliflower to stand for 5 minutes after cooking.
Celery, whole or sliced	450 g/1 lb	4 tablespoons/ ¼ teaspoon	Cover to cook.	14-16	Turn or stir halfway through the cooking time.
Chicory, whole	4 medium	4 tablespoons	Cover to cook and add salt after cooking.	5-8	Rearrange halfway through the cooking time.
Corn on the cob	1 2 4 6	3 tablespoons 3 tablespoons 5 tablespoons 5 tablespoons	Cover to cook.	4-5 7-8 13-15 17-20	Cook the corn in the husk, if liked, with no extra water. Rearrange halfway through the cooking time if cooking 4-6 cobs.
Courgettes, sliced whole	450 g/1 lb 6 small		Cover to cook.	5-6 7	Dot lightly with 25 g/ 1 oz butter before cooking. Stir or rearrange halfway through the cooking time.
Leeks, sliced	450 g/1 lb	4 tablespoons/ ½ teaspoon	Cover to cook.	10-12	Stir halfway through the cooking time.
Marrow, sliced	450 g/1 lb		Cover with greaseproof paper before cooking. Add salt after cooking.	8-10	Stir halfway through the cooking time.
Mushrooms, whole or sliced	225 g/8 oz 450 g/1 lb	2 tablespoons water or butter	Cover to cook. Add salt, if liked, after cooking.	2-4 4-6	Stir halfway through the cooking time.
Onions, whole or quartered	4 medium 8 medium	4 tablespoons/ ½ teaspoon	Cover to cook.	10-12 14-16	Stir halfway through the cooking time.
Parsnips, cubed	450 g/1 lb	8 tablespoons/ ½ teaspoon	Cover to cook.	8-10	Stir halfway through the cooking time.

GUIDE TO COOKING FRESH VEGETABLES (continued)

Vegetables	Quantity	Water/salt	Preparation	Cooking time in minutes on FULL POWER	Cooking notes
Peas, shelled	450 g/1 lb 1 kg/2 lb	8 tablespoons/ ½ teaspoon	Cover to cook.	9-11 12-14	Stir halfway through the cooking time. Add 15-25 g/½-1 oz butter after cooking and allow to stand for 5 minutes.
Potatoes, peeled and quartered baked in skins	450 g/1 lb 1 2 3 4	8 tablespoons/ ½ teaspoon	Cover to cook. Prick thoroughly and cook on absorbent kitchen paper.	10-14 4-6 6-8 8-12 12-16	Stir twice during cooking. Potatoes may still feel firm when cooked. Leave to stand for 3-4 minutes to soften.
Spinach	450 g/1 lb		Wash but do not dry before cooking. Place in a roasting bag and secure loosely with string or an elastic band. Add salt after cooking.	6-8	Drain if necessary before serving.
Tomatoes, halved	2	salt to taste	Add a knob of butter and a little pepper to each half before cooking. Cover to cook.	1-1½	
Turnips, cubed	450 g/1 lb (2-3 medium turnips)	8 tablespoons/ ¼ teaspoon	Cover to cook.	12-14	Stir twice during cooking.

FENNEL WITH HAM AND CHEESE SAUCE

450 g/1 lb fennel, trimmed and halved
300 ml/½ pint water
salt and freshly ground black pepper
2 tablespoons plain flour
4 tablespoons cold water
50 g/2 oz cooked ham, chopped
50 g/2 oz cheese, grated
2-3 tablespoons soured cream

Place the fennel, cut side down, in a cooking dish. Add the water and a pinch of salt. Cover and cook on FULL POWER for 5 minutes. Turn the fennel over and cook on MEDIUM POWER for a further 15-20 minutes until tender.

Remove the fennel with a slotted spoon and set aside.

Mix the flour and water to a smooth paste and stir into the fennel stock. Stir in the ham, cheese and pepper to taste, blending well. Cook on FULL POWER for 2 minutes, stirring twice.

Add the fennel and soured cream, tossing well so that the fennel is coated in the sauce. Cook on FULL POWER for 2 minutes. Serve hot.

Serves: 2-3
Power settings: FULL, MEDIUM
Preparation time: 10-15 minutes
Cooking time: 24-29 minutes

CRUNCHY GREEN BEANS

25 g/1 oz butter
1 small onion, peeled and chopped
25 g/1 oz flaked almonds
1 × 283 g (10 oz) packet frozen whole green beans
2 tablespoons water
1 tablespoon lemon juice
salt and freshly ground black pepper

Place the butter in a bowl and cook for ½ minute to melt. Add the onion and almonds and cook for 2 minutes.

Place the beans in a bowl with the water. Cover and cook for 8 minutes, stirring once. Drain thoroughly.

Mix the beans with the onion and almond mixture, lemon juice and salt and pepper to taste, blending well. Serve at once.

Serves: 2
Power setting: FULL
Preparation time: 5 minutes
Cooking time: 10½ minutes

BRUSSELS SPROUTS WITH HORSERADISH

1 × 250 g (10 oz) packet frozen Brussels sprouts
4 tablespoons water
1 tablespoon horseradish sauce
2 tablespoons single cream
salt and freshly ground black pepper

Place the sprouts in a cooking dish with the water. Cover and cook for 7 minutes, stirring once. Drain thoroughly.

Mix the horseradish sauce with the cream and stir into the sprouts. Cook for 1 minute. Season with salt and pepper to taste and serve at once.

Serves: 4
Power setting: FULL
Preparation time: 5 minutes
Cooking time: 8 minutes

PROVENÇALE VEGETABLES

3 small courgettes, trimmed and sliced
2 large carrots, peeled and cut into strips
½ red pepper, cored, seeded and cut into strips
½ green pepper, cored, seeded and cut into strips
1 onion, peeled and chopped
3 tomatoes, peeled and sliced
¼ cauliflower, broken into small florets
½ teaspoon dried basil
freshly ground black pepper
1 × 40 g (1½ oz) packet Provençal sauce mix
400 ml/14 fl oz water
chopped parsley to garnish

Layer the courgettes, carrots, peppers, onion, tomatoes and cauliflower in a cooking dish. Sprinkle with the basil and pepper to taste.

Mix the sauce mix with the water and pour over the vegetables. Cover with pierced cling film and cook for 10-14 minutes, stirring once, until tender but still crisp.

Leave to stand for 5 minutes. Sprinkle with chopped parsley to serve.

Serves: 4-6
Power setting: FULL
Preparation time: 15-20 minutes
Cooking time: 15-19 minutes

GUIDE TO COOKING FROZEN VEGETABLES

Generally, no extra water is required for cooking frozen vegetables but 2-3 tablespoons may be added if liked.

Vegetable	Quantity	Cooking time in minutes on FULL POWER
Asparagus	225 g/8 oz	6-7
	450 g/1 lb	11
Beans, broad	225 g/8 oz	8
	450 g/1 lb	10
Beans, French or runner	225 g/8 oz	7
	450 g/1 lb	10
Broccoli	225 g/8 oz	6-8
	450 g/1 lb	8-10
Cabbage	225 g/8 oz	6-7
	450 g/1 lb	10-11
Carrots	225 g/8 oz	7
	450 g/1 lb	10
Cauliflower florets	225 g/8 oz	5
	450 g/1 lb	8
Corn kernels	225 g/8 oz	4
	450 g/1 lb	7-8
Corn on the cob	1	4-5
	2	7-8
Courgettes	225 g/8 oz	4
	450 g/1 lb	7
Diced mixed vegetables	225 g/8 oz	5-6
	450 g/1 lb	7-9
Peas	225 g/8 oz	4
	450 g/1 lb	8
Spinach, chopped, or leaf	225 g/8 oz	7-8
	450 g/1 lb	10-11
Root vegetable stewpack (mixed)	225 g/8 oz	7
	450 g/1 lb	10
Swedes	225 g/8 oz	7
	450 g/1 lb	11
Turnips	225 g/8 oz	8
	450 g/1 lb	12

CAULIFLOWER WITH TOMATO SAUCE

1 × 675 g (1½ lb) whole cauliflower, trimmed
1 onion, peeled and finely chopped
300 ml/½ pint water
salt
7 g/¼ oz butter
3 tomatoes, peeled, seeded and quartered
3 tablespoons tomato purée
1 bay leaf
2 tablespoons plain flour
4 tablespoons cold water
pinch of sugar
2 tablespoons double cream
2 tablespoons cheese, grated

Place the cauliflower, stalk side up, in a cooking dish with the onion, water, salt to taste and butter. Cover and cook on FULL POWER for 10-12 minutes.

Turn the cauliflower stalk side down, cover and cook on MEDIUM POWER for 10 minutes. Remove the cauliflower with a slotted spoon and place on a serving plate.

Add the tomatoes, tomato purée and bay leaf to the cauliflower stock, blending well.

Mix the flour and water to a smooth paste and stir into the stock. Cook on FULL POWER for 4 minutes, stirring twice.

Season to taste with salt and sugar. Remove and discard the bay leaf. Purée in a blender or pass through a fine sieve. Stir the cream into the sauce with the cheese, blending well so that the cheese melts.

Pour the sauce over the cauliflower and cook on FULL POWER for 2 minutes to reheat. Serve at once.

Serves: 4
Power settings: FULL, MEDIUM
Preparation time: 15 minutes
Cooking time: 26-28 minutes

CAULIFLOWER IN STILTON SAUCE

1 × 250 g (10 oz) packet frozen cauliflower florets
4 tablespoons water
50 g/2 oz Stilton cheese
150 ml/¼ pint milk
2 tablespoons single cream
pinch of ground nutmeg
3 teaspoons cornflour
milk to mix
chopped parsley to garnish

Place the cauliflower in a cooking dish with the water. Cover and cook for 8 minutes, stirring once. Drain thoroughly.

Crumble the Stilton into a bowl. Add the milk, cream and nutmeg. Cook for 3 minutes, stirring once.

Mix the cornflour with a little milk and stir into the Stilton mixture. Cook for 1 minute, stirring once, until smooth and thickened.

Pour over the cauliflower florets and cook for 1 minute to reheat.

Serve at once sprinkled with chopped parsley.

Serves: 4
Power setting: FULL
Preparation time: 5 minutes
Cooking time: 13 minutes

POTATOES DAUPHINOIS

25 g/1 oz butter
1 bunch spring onions, trimmed and finely chopped
675 g/1½ lb potatoes, peeled and very thinly sliced
salt and freshly ground black pepper
5 tablespoons milk
5 tablespoons single cream
1 tablespoon snipped chives

Place the butter in a bowl and cook for ½ minute to melt. Add the spring onions, cover and cook for 2 minutes.

Layer the potatoes and spring onions in a shallow dish, seasoning between each layer with salt and pepper to taste.

Mix the milk and cream together and pour over the potato dish. Cover with cling film, snipping two holes in the top to allow the steam to escape. Cook for 7 minutes.

Carefully remove the cling film and cook for a further 7 minutes, turning the dish twice. Leave to stand for 5 minutes.

Brown under a preheated hot grill if liked. Serve sprinkled with snipped chives.

Serves: 4
Power setting: FULL
Preparation time: 20 minutes
Cooking time: 21½ minutes

GUIDE TO COOKING DRIED BEANS AND PEAS

Beans	Quantity	Preparation and cooking time			
Kidney, flageolet, butter or haricot beans and chick peas	350 g/12 oz	Place the beans in a large dish with a little chopped onion, celery and carrot. Add 2 teaspoons salt and pepper to taste. Cover with 1.4 litres/2½ pints cold stock and cook on FULL POWER for 20 minutes. Stir, re-cover and cook on MEDIUM POWER for 1 hour or until tender.	Split peas or lentils	225 g/8 oz	Place the split peas or lentils in a large dish with a little chopped onion, celery and 1 tablespoon lemon juice. Add a little salt and pepper to taste. Cover with 900 ml/1½ pints cold stock or water. Cover and cook on FULL POWER for 15 minutes. Stir and cook on MEDIUM POWER for 30 minutes, stirring every 10 minutes, until tender.

GUIDE TO BLANCHING VEGETABLES							
Vegetable	Quantity	Water (table-spoons)	Time in minutes on FULL POWER				
Asparagus	450 g/1 lb	3	3-4	Corn on the cob	4	3	5-6
Beans	450 g/1 lb	6	5-6	Courgettes, sliced	450 g/1 lb	3	3-3½
Broccoli	450 g/1 lb	6	5-6	Leeks, sliced	450 g/1 lb	3	5-6
Brussels sprouts	450 g/1 lb	6	5-6	Marrow, sliced or cubed	450 g/1 lb	3	4-4½
Cabbage, shredded	450 g/1 lb	3	4-4½	Onions, quartered	4 medium	6	4-4½
Carrots, sliced	450 g/1 lb	3	3-4	Parsnips, cubed	450 g/1 lb	3	3-4
whole	450 g/1 lb	3	6-7	Peas	450 g/1 lb	3	4-4½
Cauliflower florets	450 g/1 lb	6	4½-5		1 kg/2 lb	3	6-7
				Spinach	450 g/1 lb	–	3-3½
				Turnips, cubed	450 g/1 lb	3	3-4

HERBED SPROUTS

50 g/2 oz butter
1 garlic clove, peeled and crushed
1 onion, peeled and thinly sliced
3 sticks celery, scrubbed and thinly sliced
2 tablespoons chopped mixed herbs
1 × 454 g (1 lb) frozen Brussels sprouts
salt and freshly ground black pepper

Place the butter in a casserole dish and cook for ½ minute to melt.

Add the garlic, onion, celery and herbs. Cover and cook for 2 minutes.

Add the Brussels sprouts, blending well. Season with salt and pepper to taste. Cover and cook for 8-10 minutes, stirring once. Leave to stand for 2 minutes before serving.

Serves: 4-6
Power setting: FULL
Preparation time: 5 minutes
Cooking time: 12½-14½ minutes

CREAMY MASHED POTATOES

450 g/1 lb old potatoes, peeled and quartered
8 tablespoons water
salt and freshly ground black pepper
25 g/1 oz butter
about 100 ml/4 fl oz milk

Place the potatoes in a cooking dish with the water and salt to taste. Cover and cook for 10-14 minutes, shaking the dish twice.

Drain thoroughly then mash or beat to a smooth creamy purée with the butter, milk and salt and pepper to taste.

Serve at once in a warmed serving dish.

Variations
ONION MASH: Add 1-2 teaspoons onion flakes with the butter.
HERBY MASH: Stir in 1-2 tablespoons finely chopped fresh herbs (parsley, chives, tarragon or chervil for example).
SPICY MASH: Stir in ½ teaspoon ground mace

and a few drops of Worcestershire sauce. Or add ¼ teaspoon each of celery and mustard seeds and stir in with the butter.

Serves: 2
Power setting: FULL
Preparation time: 15 minutes
Cooking time: 10-14 minutes

CREAMY BROCCOLI SPEARS

1 × 225 g (9 oz) packet
    frozen broccoli spears
4 tablespoons water
3 tablespoons plain
    yogurt
1 tablespoon dry sherry
25 g/1 oz flaked almonds,
    toasted

Place the broccoli in a cooking dish with the water. Cover and cook for 8 minutes, separating and re-arranging the broccoli spears halfway through the cooking time. Drain thoroughly.

Mix the yogurt with the sherry and pour over the broccoli. Cook for 1 minute. Sprinkle with the almonds. Serve at once.

Serves: 4
Power setting: FULL
Preparation time: 5 minutes
Cooking time: 9 minutes

CHICORY WITH TOMATOES

350 g/12 oz tomatoes,
    sliced thickly
salt and black pepper
50 g/2 oz butter
450 g/1 lb chicory,
    trimmed and halved
1 teaspoon cornflour
2 tablespoons single
    cream

Place the tomatoes in a greased cooking dish. Season with salt and pepper to taste and dot with the butter.

Arrange the chicory halves on top and season with salt to taste. Cover and cook on FULL POWER for 10 minutes, turning the dish once. Reduce the power setting and cook on MEDIUM POWER for a further 5 minutes.

Mix the cornflour with the cream and stir into the vegetable mixture, blending well. Cook on FULL POWER for 2-3 minutes. Serve at once.

Serves: 4
Power settings: FULL, MEDIUM
Preparation time: 10-15 minutes
Cooking time: 17-18 minutes
Suitable for freezing

STUFFED TOMATOES

4 tomatoes
25 g/1 oz butter
1 garlic clove, peeled and
    crushed
75 g/3 oz fresh
    breadcrumbs
50 g/2 oz grated
    Parmesan cheese
3 tablespoons finely
    chopped fresh parsley
salt and freshly ground
    black pepper

Remove the tops from the tomatoes, scoop out and discard the seeds. Stand upside down on absorbent kitchen paper to drain.

Place the butter in a bowl and cook for ½ minute to melt. Add the garlic and cook for 1 minute.

Stir in the breadcrumbs, cheese, parsley and salt and pepper to taste. Spoon the mixture evenly into the tomato cases. Stand upright in a small baking dish. Cook for 2 minutes, turning the dish once, until just tender.

Serves: 4
Power setting: FULL
Preparation time: 10-15 minutes
Cooking time: 3½ minutes

FRENCH-STYLE GREEN PEAS

25 g/1 oz butter
2 rashers streaky bacon,
    rinded and chopped
6 spring onions, trimmed
    and finely chopped
8 outside lettuce leaves,
    washed and shredded
350 g/12 oz frozen peas
1 sprig fresh mint
1 teaspoon sugar
salt and black pepper

Place the butter in a cooking dish and cook for ½ minute to melt. Add the bacon and spring onions, cover and cook for ½ minute.

Add the lettuce, peas, mint, sugar if used and salt and pepper to taste, blending well. Cover and cook for 3½ minutes.

Stir well and cook, uncovered, for a further 1½-2 minutes.

Remove and discard the mint and serve at once perhaps garnished with fresh mint.

Serves: 4
Power setting: FULL
Preparation time: 10 minutes
Cooking time: 6-7½ minutes

Illustrated on p.98

CABBAGE WITH BACON

225 g/8 oz streaky bacon, rinded and chopped

1 onion, peeled and finely chopped

1 × 900 g (2 lb) cabbage, washed and shredded

300 ml/½ pint beef stock

½ teaspoon ground paprika

salt and freshly ground black pepper

225 g/8 oz tomatoes, peeled and sliced

Place the bacon and onion in a cooking dish, cover and cook on FULL POWER for 5 minutes, stirring once.

Add the cabbage and stock, blending well. Cover and cook on FULL POWER for 10 minutes, stirring once.

Stir in the paprika and salt and pepper to taste. Cover and cook on MEDIUM POWER for 15-20 minutes.

Add the tomatoes, blending well, Cover and cook on MEDIUM POWER for 5 minutes. Serve hot.

Serves: 5-6
Power settings: FULL, MEDIUM
Preparation time: 15 minutes
Cooking time: 35-40 minutes

MUSHROOMS WITH BACON

50 g/2 oz streaky bacon, rinded and chopped

1 onion, peeled and finely chopped

450 g/1 lb mushrooms, trimmed and sliced

150 ml/¼ pint soured cream

salt

1-2 teaspoons lemon juice

1 teaspoon plain flour

2 teaspoons cold water

chopped parsley to garnish

Place the bacon and onion in a cooking dish. Cover and cook for 3 minutes.

Add the mushrooms, cover and cook for 10 minutes, stirring once.

Add the soured cream, salt to taste and lemon juice, blending well.

Mix the flour and water to a smooth paste and stir into the mushroom mixture, blending well.

Cover and cook for 2-3 minutes, stirring twice.

Serve hot sprinkled with chopped parsley.

Serves: 4
Power setting: FULL
Preparation time: 10 minutes
Cooking time: 15-16 minutes

HEREFORDSHIRE RED CABBAGE

1 medium red cabbage, cored and shredded

3 tablespoons apple juice

4 medium cooking apples, peeled, cored and thinly sliced

¼ teaspoon ground cloves

50 g/2 oz butter

1 teaspoon brown sugar

2 tablespoons redcurrant jelly

Place the cabbage in a casserole dish with the apple juice and apples, blending well. Cover and cook for 12-14 minutes, stirring once.

Add the cloves, butter, sugar and redcurrant jelly, blending well. Leave to stand, covered, for 5 minutes.

Serve hot with roasts, game birds and gammon.

To freeze
Cool quickly and pack in a rigid container. Cover, seal, label and freeze for up to 3 months.

Serves: 4
Power setting: FULL
Preparation time: 10-15 minutes
Cooking time: 17-19 minutes
Suitable for freezing

PASTA SALAD ITALIENNE

100 g/4 oz pasta twists
600 ml/1 pint boiling
water
1 teaspoon oil
100 g/4 oz frozen sliced
green beans
2 tablespoons cold water
½ cucumber, chopped
5 tomatoes, peeled and
cut into wedges
50 g/2 oz salami, cut into
thin strips
6 black olives
3 tablespoons Italian
garlic or French
dressing

Place the pasta in a bowl with the boiling water and oil. Cover and cook for 10 minutes. Leave to stand while cooking the beans.

Place the beans in a bowl with the cold water. Cover and cook for 4 minutes. Drain and rinse in cold water.

Drain and rinse the pasta in cold water and place in a salad bowl with the beans, cucumber, tomatoes, salami and olives, blending well.

Pour over the dressing and toss well to mix. Serve at once.

Serves: 4
Power setting: FULL
Preparation time: 20 minutes
Cooking time: 14 minutes

MUSHROOM MACÉDOINE SALAD

1 tablespoon oil
225 g/8 oz button
mushrooms, wiped and
sliced
350 g/12 oz frozen mixed
vegetables
1 teaspoon finely chopped
onion
4 tablespoons
mayonnaise
2 tablespoons single
cream
salt and freshly ground
black pepper
watercress sprigs to
garnish

Place the oil in a bowl and cook for 1 minute. Add the mushrooms, blending well. Cover and cook for 3 minutes, stirring once. Remove with a slotted spoon and place in a salad bowl.

Place the frozen mixed vegetables in a bowl. Cover and cook for 6-7 minutes, stirring once. Add to the mushrooms, mixing well to blend. Leave to cool.

Meanwhile, blend the onion with the mayonnaise, cream and salt and pepper to taste. Fold into the cool vegetable mixture.

Serve lightly chilled, garnished with watercress sprigs.

Serves: 4
Power setting: FULL
Preparation time: 10 minutes, plus cooling and chilling
Cooking time: 10-11 minutes

SPINACH AND BACON SALAD

225 g/8 oz back bacon,
rinded and chopped
3 tablespoons vinegar
2 teaspoons sugar
pinch of dried mixed
herbs
salt and freshly ground
black pepper
450 g/1 lb fresh young
spinach leaves, washed
and trimmed

Place the bacon in a bowl. Cover and cook for 5-6 minutes, stirring twice, until crisp. Remove with a slotted spoon and place in a serving dish.

Stir the vinegar, sugar, herbs and salt and pepper to taste into the bacon fat, blending well.

Toss the bacon with the spinach. Pour over the warm dressing and toss gently to coat. Serve at once.

Serves: 4
Power setting: FULL
Preparation time: 15 minutes
Cooking time: 5-6 minutes

POTATO SALAD

450 g/1 lb potatoes,
   scrubbed and sliced
1 small onion, peeled and
   chopped
4 tablespoons water
salt and black pepper
5 tablespoons
   mayonnaise
1 tablespoon snipped
   chives

Place the potatoes, onion, water and a pinch of salt in a cooking dish. Cover and cook for 8 minutes, stirring twice. Leave to stand, covered, for 5 minutes, Drain well.

Add the mayonnaise, chives and salt and pepper to taste. Toss the potatoes lightly in the mixture to coat.

Serve hot or cold.

Serves: 4
Power setting: FULL
Preparation time: 10-15 minutes
Cooking time: 13 minutes

CUCUMBER, CHICKEN AND ORANGE SALAD

3 boneless chicken breasts
1 lettuce, washed and
   shredded
½ cucumber, thinly sliced
3 oranges, peeled, pith
   removed and sliced
juice of ½ orange
1 tablespoon oil
1 tablespoon snipped
   chives
salt and freshly ground
   black pepper
75 g/3 oz peanuts
watercress sprigs

Place the chicken breasts in a cooking dish, cover and cook for 7-9 minutes, turning once. Allow to cool then remove and discard the skin. Slice the chicken into thin strips.

Line a serving dish with the lettuce and top with alternate layers of cucumber, orange and chicken.

Beat the orange juice with the oil, chives and salt and pepper to taste, blending well. Spoon over the salad evenly.

Sprinkle peanuts down the centre of the dish and garnish with watercress sprigs. Serve at once.

Serves: 4
Power setting: FULL
Preparation time: 20 minutes
Cooking time: 7-9 minutes

VEGETABLE RICE SALAD

½ onion, peeled and
   finely chopped
1 tablespoon corn oil
1 teaspoon curry powder
½ teaspoon paprika
1 teaspoon tomato purée
150 ml/¼ pint cold water
1 teaspoon lemon juice
2 tablespoons salad oil
1 tablespoon white wine
   vinegar
225 g/8 oz long-grain
   rice
600 ml/1 pint boiling
   water
1 teaspoon salt
2 tomatoes, peeled, seeded
   and coarsely chopped
¼ cucumber, cubed
3 sticks celery, sliced

Place the onion, corn oil, curry powder and paprika in a bowl and cook for 1 minute. Add the tomato purée, cold water and lemon juice. Cover and cook for 3 minutes. Add the salad oil and vinegar and mix well to blend.

Place the rice, boiling water and salt in a bowl. Cover and cook for 15 minutes, stirring twice.

Stir in the curry dressing and leave to stand, covered, for 5 minutes. Allow to cool.

Fold the tomatoes, cucumber and celery into the curried rice mixture. Serve lightly chilled.

Serves: 4
Power setting: FULL
Preparation time: 15 minutes, plus
   cooling and chilling
Cooking time: 24 minutes

EXOTIC CUCUMBER SALAD

2 medium cucumbers,
    peeled, seeded and cut
    into 7.5 cm/3 inch strips
3 tablespoons water
2 tablespoons vinegar
salt
5 tablespoons oil
2 onions, peeled and
    sliced
1 garlic clove, peeled and
    sliced
pinch of ground turmeric
1 teaspoon sugar

Place the cucumber in a bowl with the water and 1 tablespoon of the vinegar. Cover and cook for 2 minutes or until the cucumber becomes transparent, shaking the dish once. Drain, sprinkle with a little salt and leave to cool.

Place the oil in a bowl and cook for 2 minutes. Add the onions and garlic, blending well. Cook for 5 minutes, stirring once. Remove with a slotted spoon and drain on absorbent kitchen paper.

Stir the turmeric, sugar and salt to taste into the juices and allow to cool.

Stir in the remaining vinegar, then fold in the cucumber to coat well in the dressing.

Drain the cucumber from the dressing and place in a serving dish. Sprinkle over the onion mixture and serve the salad cold or chilled.

Serves: 4
Power setting: FULL
Preparation time: 20 minutes, plus
    cooling and chilling
Cooking time: 9 minutes

STIR-FRY SALAD

225 g/8 oz long-grain
    rice
600 ml/1 pint boiling
    water
5 tablespoons oil
1 onion, peeled and
    chopped
3 sticks celery, scrubbed
    and thinly sliced
1 × 100 g (4 oz) packet
    frozen sliced green
    beans
1 × 100 g (4 oz) packet
    frozen garden peas
1 × 283 g (10 oz) packet
    frozen sweetcorn
    kernels
4 tablespoons soy sauce
½ teaspoon mustard
    powder
2 tablespoons white wine
    vinegar
2 teaspoons soft brown
    sugar
salt and freshly ground
    black pepper
2-3 tablespoons chopped
    salted peanuts

Place the rice in a casserole dish with the water. Cover and cook for 13 minutes. Leave to stand while cooking the vegetables.

Place 1 tablespoon of the oil in a casserole with the onion and celery. Cover and cook for 2 minutes. Stir in the beans, peas and sweetcorn. Cover and cook for 5 minutes, stirring once.

Meanwhile place the remaining oil, soy sauce, mustard powder, vinegar, sugar and salt and pepper to taste in a screw-topped jar and shake well to mix.

Gently fold the rice and dressing into the vegetable mixture and leave to cool at room temperature.

Chill, then serve topped with the peanuts

Serves: 6-8
Power setting: FULL
Preparation time: 10 minutes, plus
    cooling and chilling
Cooking time: 20 minutes

Egg and Cheese Dishes

Wonderfully nutritious, eggs and cheese are invaluable storecupboard standbys that can be transformed into a multitude of tasty, variable and economical snack, main meal or dessert dishes.
Timings are all-important in cooking egg and cheese dishes in the microwave oven. Err on the side of safety and cook these temperature-sensitive and delicate foods for only the minimum times to begin with and, if possible, use MEDIUM POWER.

SPANISH OMELETTE

25 g/1 oz butter
½ onion, peeled and
    chopped
1 tomato, chopped
¼ green pepper, cored,
    seeded and chopped
2 tablespoons cooked
    long-grain rice
2 eggs, beaten
salt and freshly ground
    black pepper

Place the butter in a shallow glass pie dish and cook for ½ minute to melt. Swirl to coat the dish.

Add the onion and cook for 1 minute. Add the tomato, pepper and rice, blending well. Cook for 2 minutes.

Add the eggs and salt and pepper to taste. Cover and cook for 1½ minutes. Using a fork, move the cooked egg from the edge of the dish to the centre. Re-cover and cook for a further ¾ minute.

Uncover and cook for ¼ minute. Leave to stand for ¼ minute then fold in half to serve.

Serve with a seasonal green salad.

Serves: 1
Power setting: FULL
Preparation time: 10-15 minutes
Cooking time: 6¼ minutes

EGGS WITH CUCUMBER SAUCE

40 g/1½ oz butter
½ cucumber, peeled and
    coarsely chopped
1 tablespoon plain flour
150 ml/¼ pint hot chicken
    stock (see p. 36)
½ tablespoon chopped
    fresh dill
salt and freshly ground
    black pepper
4 tablespoons double
    cream
2 hard-boiled eggs,
    cooled, shelled and
    halved

Place the butter in a bowl with the cucumber. Cover and cook for 2½-3 minutes until tender, stirring once.

Add the flour, blending well. Gradually add the stock and cook for 2-3 minutes, stirring every 1 minute until smooth and thickened. Add the dill, salt and pepper to taste and cream, blending well.

Place the egg halves on a serving plate and spoon the cucumber sauce over them. Serve hot with chunks of crusty bread.

Serves: 2
Power setting: FULL
Preparation time: 15 minutes
Cooking time: 4½-6 minutes

TAGLIATELLE WITH CHEESE AND NUTS

25 g/1 oz butter
350 g/12 oz cream cheese
50 g/2 oz grated
    Parmesan cheese
100 g/4 oz walnuts,
    chopped
1 tablespoon chopped
    parsley
450 g/1 lb tagliatelle
1.2 litres/2 pints boiling
    water
1 tablespoon oil
salt and freshly ground
    black pepper

Place the butter in a bowl and cook for ½ minute to melt. Add the cream cheese, Parmesan cheese, walnuts and parsley. Cook for 1½ minutes, stirring once. Leave to stand, covered, while cooking the tagliatelle.

Place the tagliatelle, water and oil in a bowl. Cover and cook for 6 minutes. Leave to stand, covered, for 3 minutes.

Drain the tagliatelle and place in a warmed serving dish. Cook the cheese sauce for 1 minute, stirring once. Pour over the tagliatelle and toss well to coat. Season to taste with salt and pepper and serve at once.

Serves: 6
Power setting: FULL
Preparation time: 10-15 minutes
Cooking time: 12 minutes

PIPERADE

1 tablespoon oil
1 onion, peeled and finely
    chopped
1 green or red pepper,
    cored, seeded and
    chopped
1 fresh chilli, seeded and
    chopped
1 garlic clove, peeled and
    crushed
1 × 227 g (8 oz) can
    peeled tomatoes,
    drained and chopped
4 eggs, beaten
salt and freshly ground
    black pepper

Place the oil in a cooking dish with the onion, pepper and chilli, Cover and cook for 5 minutes, stirring once.

Add the garlic and tomatoes, blending well. Cook for 3 minutes, stirring once.

Add the beaten eggs and salt and pepper to taste. Cook for a further 3½-4½ minutes or until the eggs are just lightly scrambled, stirring twice. Serve at once.

Serves: 2
Power setting: FULL
Preparation time: 10-15 minutes
Cooking time: 11½-12½ minutes

EGG AND BACON ROLLS

4 crispy bread rolls
2 rashers bacon, rinded
    and finely chopped
50 g/2 oz mushrooms,
    wiped and finely
    chopped
4 eggs
salt and freshly ground
    black pepper

Slice the tops off the rolls and scoop out the centre (use for breadcrumbs for another dish). Reserve the tops.

Place the bacon and mushrooms in a bowl and cook, uncovered, for 2½-3 minutes. Drain thoroughly then divide evenly between the bread roll shells. Break an egg into each roll, prick the yolk carefully and season with salt and pepper to taste. Cover with the bread roll tops and cook for 2½-3 minutes.

Leave to stand for 1 minute before serving.

Serves: 4
Power setting: FULL
Preparation time: 10-15 minutes
Cooking time: 6-7 minutes

Guide to Cooking Fried Eggs

Eggs	Cooking time in minutes on MEDIUM POWER	Cooking time in seconds/minutes on FULL POWER
1	¾-1	40-50 seconds
2	1½-2	1½-1¾ minutes
4	2-2½	2-2¼ minutes

To fry eggs in the microwave, cook in a flat-based microwave browning dish. Pre-heat the dish according to the manufacturer's instructions – approximately 1 minute for each egg on FULL POWER. Allow 1 teaspoon butter to each egg, place it in the dish, then break the eggs into the dish. Cover and cook for the times given in the table.

Guide to Cooking Poached Eggs

Eggs	Cooking time in minutes on FULL POWER	Cooking time in minutes on MEDIUM POWER
1	¾-1	1
2	1-1½	1¾
3	1½-2½	4
4	2½-3	3¼

Illustrated on p. 115

To poach eggs, use either small dishes or cocottes, or a large dish. If you are using small dishes, pour 6 tablespoons hot water into each with a little vinegar. Bring to the boil on FULL POWER for about 1½ minutes. Carefully break the egg into the dish and puncture the yolk quickly with the tip of a pointed knife, then cook for the times recommended in the table.

Alternatively, place 475 ml/16 fl oz hot water in a bowl and bring to the boil by cooking on FULL POWER for 5-6 minutes. Break the eggs on to a plate and quickly puncture the yolk with the tip of a pointed knife. Swirl the boiling water with a spoon and slip the eggs gently into it. Cook on MEDIUM POWER for the times given in the table. Allow to stand in the cooking water for ½-1 minute before removing with a slotted spoon.

Guide to Cooking Scrambled Eggs

Eggs	Butter	Milk	Cooking time in minutes on FULL POWER
1	1 teaspoon	1 tablespoon	¾-1
2	2 teaspoons	2 tablespoons	1¾-2
4	4 teaspoons	4 tablespoons	3¾-4
6	2 tablespoons	6 tablespoons	5½-6

To cook scrambled eggs, allow 1 teaspoon butter for each egg. Place the butter in a glass measuring jug or bowl and cook on FULL POWER until melted – about ½-1 minute, depending on the quantity. Add the beaten eggs and milk according to the quantities given in the table. Cook on FULL POWER for half the recommended cooking time. Stir the set pieces of egg from the outside to the centre, then cook for the remaining recommended cooking time, stirring twice. When cooked, the eggs should be just beginning to set. Allow to stand for 1-2 minutes to finish cooking from the residual heat until lightly set.

POACHED EGGS (opposite) WITH HOLLANDAISE SAUCE (p.141) AND BAKED EGG (p.117)   115

116

STORECUPBOARD PIZZA (p.123)

OMELETTE

4 eggs, beaten
3 tablespoons milk
½ teaspoon salt
freshly ground black
    pepper
15 g/½ oz butter

Mix the eggs with the milk, salt and pepper to taste, blending well.

Place the butter in a 25 cm (10 inch) pie plate and cook for ½ minute to melt. Swirl the butter over the plate to cover. Add the egg mixture, cover and cook for 1½ minutes.

Using a fork, move the cooked egg from the edge of the dish to the centre. Cover and cook for a further 1¼-1½ minutes. Leave to stand for 1½-2 minutes.

Loosen the omelette with a spatula, fold in half and serve at once.

Variations

CHEESE OMELETTE: Prepare as above, stirring 40-50 g/1½-2 oz finely grated cheese into the egg mixture before cooking as above.
CHICKEN OMELETTE: Prepare as above, adding 100 g/4 oz chopped cooked chicken just before folding the omelette in half.
FRENCH OMELETTE: Prepare as above and sprinkle with parsley before serving.

Serves: 1
Power setting: FULL
Preparation time: 5 minutes
Cooking time: 4¾-5½ minutes

MEDITERRANEAN OMELETTE

15 g/½ oz butter
1 onion, peeled and
    chopped
1 small red pepper, cored,
    seeded and chopped
1 garlic clove, peeled and
    crushed
50 g/2 oz mushrooms,
    wiped and sliced
2 tomatoes, peeled, seeded
    and chopped
Omelette:
4 eggs, beaten
3 tablespoons milk
1 teaspoon dried mixed
    herbs
salt and black pepper
15 g/½ oz butter
25 g/1 oz grated
    Parmesan cheese

To make the filling, place the butter, onion, pepper and garlic in a bowl. Cook for 4 minutes, stirring once. Add the mushrooms and tomatoes, blending well. Cook for 3 minutes, stirring once. Leave to stand, covered, while preparing the omelette.

To make the omelette, beat the eggs with the milk, herbs and salt and pepper to taste. Place the butter in a 25 cm (10 inch) pie plate and cook for ½ minute to melt. Swirl over the plate to coat. Pour in the egg mixture, cover and cook for 1½ minutes. Using a fork, move the cooked egg from the edge of the dish to the centre. Re-cover and cook for a further 1¼-1½ minutes, then allow to stand for 1½-2 minutes.

Loosen the omelette with a spatula. Spoon the vegetable mixture over the omelette. Fold in half and sprinkle with the Parmesan cheese. Cut into two to serve.

Serves: 2
Power setting: FULL
Preparation time: 15 minutes
Cooking time: 11¾-12½ minutes

Guide to Cooking Baked Eggs

Eggs	Cooking time in minutes on MEDIUM POWER
1	1-1¼
2	2-2¼
4	3½-4
6	5½-6

Illustrated on p. 115

To cook baked eggs, place the eggs in either a buttered microwave bun tray or buttered small glass cup, custard cup or shallow dish. Puncture the egg yolk carefully to prevent it from bursting during cooking. Cover the dish with cling film, snipping two holes in the top to allow the steam to escape. Cook on MEDIUM POWER for half the recommended cooking time, give the dish a half turn and cook for the remaining time.

SPANISH BAKED EGGS

25 g/1 oz butter
1 garlic clove, peeled and
 crushed
100 g/4 oz chorizo
 sausage or salami,
 sliced
1 green pepper, cored,
 seeded and chopped
4 eggs
salt and freshly ground
 black pepper
4 tablespoons single
 cream

Place the butter, garlic, sausage and pepper in a bowl. Cover and cook on FULL POWER for 4-5 minutes until tender, stirring twice.

Spoon equally into four large individual ramekins. Break an egg over each and carefully prick the yolks. Season to taste with salt and pepper and spoon over the cream.

Cover and cook on MEDIUM POWER for 3½-4½ minutes, re-arranging the dishes twice, until the eggs are just cooked. Serve at once.

Serves: 2-4
Power settings: FULL, MEDIUM
Preparation time: 15 minutes
Cooking time: 7½-9½ minutes

BAKED EGG CUSTARD

300 ml/½ pint milk
2 eggs
1 egg yolk
40 g/1½ oz caster sugar
½ teaspoon vanilla
 essence
ground nutmeg to dust

Place the milk in a jug and cook on FULL POWER for 1½ minutes.

Beat the eggs with the egg yolk, caster sugar and vanilla essence, blending well. Strain into a greased cooking dish. Dust the top with ground nutmeg and cook on DEFROST POWER for 18-20 minutes, turning the dish 4 times, until the custard is set.

Leave to stand, covered, for 20 minutes. Serve warm or cold.

Serves: 4
Power settings: FULL, DEFROST
Preparation time: 10 minutes
Cooking time: 39½-41½ minutes

SPICY EGG CURRY

1 tablespoon oil
1 small onion, peeled and
 finely chopped
1 garlic clove, peeled and
 crushed
1 teaspoon ground
 coriander
1 teaspoon ground
 cumin
½ teaspoon chilli powder
freshly ground black
 pepper
2 tablespoons sesame
 seeds
½ teaspoon salt
150 ml/¼ pint plain
 yogurt
1 tablespoon lemon juice
4 hard-boiled eggs,
 cooled, shelled and
 halved

Place the oil, onion and garlic in a bowl. Cook for 2 minutes, stirring once. Add the coriander, cumin, chilli powder, pepper to taste and sesame seeds. Cook for 1 minute, stirring once.

Add the salt, yogurt and lemon juice, blending well. Cook for 1½-2 minutes until hot but *not* boiling.

Add the eggs, blending well. Cook for 1-2 minutes until hot.

Serve at once with boiled rice or lentils and green salad.

Serves: 2
Power setting: FULL
Preparation time: 15 minutes
Cooking time: 5½-7 minutes

MUSHROOM AND EGG RAMEKINS

225 g/8 oz small button
  mushrooms, wiped
1 garlic clove, peeled and
  crushed
150 ml/¼ pint beef stock
  (see p. 36)
4 eggs
1 tablespoon chopped
  parsley
salt and freshly ground
  black pepper

Place the mushrooms, garlic and stock in a bowl. Cook on FULL POWER for 4 minutes, stirring once.

Meanwhile, break the eggs into each of four greased ramekins. Pierce the egg yolks carefully to prevent them bursting. Cover and cook on MEDIUM POWER for 3½-4 minutes, re-arranging once.

Stir the parsley and salt and pepper to taste into the mushroom mixture. Spoon on top of the eggs and serve at once.

Serves: 4
Power settings: FULL, MEDIUM
Preparation time: 15 minutes
Cooking time: 7½-8 minutes

CAULIFLOWER CHEESE

1 × 675 g (1½ lb)
  cauliflower, trimmed
  but left whole
8 tablespoons water
½ teaspoon salt
1 recipe Cheese Sauce (see
  p. 140)
25 g/1 oz grated cheese
ground paprika

Place the cauliflower in a deep dish with the water and salt. Cover and cook on MEDIUM POWER for 13-17 minutes, turning over once. Leave to stand, covered, for 5 minutes. Drain thoroughly.

Place the cauliflower in a serving dish and pour over the cheese sauce. Sprinkle with the cheese and ground paprika to taste. Cook on FULL POWER for 3 minutes or until the cheese melts. Brown under a preheated hot grill if liked. Serve hot.

Serves: 4
Power settings: MEDIUM, FULL
Preparation time: 10 minutes
Cooking time: 21-25 minutes

VEGETABLE CHEESE CRUMBLE

Crumble topping:
150 g/5 oz plain flour
salt and freshly ground
  black pepper
50 g/2 oz butter
75 g/3 oz cheese, grated
Filling:
50 g/2 oz butter
2 onions, peeled and
  sliced
2 sticks celery, scrubbed
  and chopped
3 carrots, peeled and
  sliced
25 g/1 oz plain flour
450 ml/¾ pint hot light
  stock
225 g/8 oz cabbage,
  cored and shredded
225 g/8 oz tomatoes,
  peeled, seeded and
  chopped

Sift the flour into a bowl with salt and pepper to taste. Rub in the butter until the mixture resembles fine breadcrumbs. Stir in the cheese, blending well.

To make the filling, place the butter in a bowl and cook for 1 minute to melt. Add the onions, celery and carrots, cover and cook for 6 minutes, stirring once. Stir in the flour, blending well. Gradually add the stock and cook for 5 minutes, stirring three times. Add the cabbage and tomatoes, blending well.

Carefully spoon the crumble mixture over the vegetables, cook for 11-13 minutes, giving the dish a turn every 3 minutes. Leave to stand for 5 minutes.

Brown under a preheated hot grill if liked. Serve at once.

To freeze
Cool quickly, cover, seal, label and freeze for up to 3 months.

Serves: 4
Power setting: FULL
Preparation time: 35-40 minutes
Cooking time: 28-30 minutes
Suitable for freezing

EGGS SWEET AND SOUR

25 g/1 oz butter
½ green pepper, cored,
    seeded and chopped
1 onion, peeled and sliced
2 sticks celery, scrubbed
    and chopped
1 × 210 g (7½ oz) can
    pineapple pieces
1 tablespoon tomato
    purée
1 teaspoon cornflour
1 tablespoon ground
    paprika
2 teaspoons vinegar
1 teaspoon soy sauce
salt and freshly ground
    black pepper
4 hard-boiled eggs, shelled
    and halved
chopped parsley to
    garnish

Place the butter in a bowl and cook for ½ minute to melt. Add the pepper, onion and celery, blending well. Cover and cook for 5 minutes, stirring once.

Drain the juice from the pineapple and mix with the tomato purée, cornflour, paprika, vinegar, soy sauce and salt and pepper to taste. Add to the onion mixture, blending well. Cook for 3-5 minutes, stirring every 1 minute, until smooth and thickened.

Add the pineapple pieces and eggs. Cover and cook for 3-4 minutes until hot and bubbly. Serve at once sprinkled with chopped parsley, and accompanied by boiled rice.

Serves: 2
Power setting: FULL
Preparation time: 15-20 minutes
Cooking time: 11½-14½ minutes

CHEESE PUDDING

225 g/8 oz brown bread,
    crusts removed and cut
    into 1 cm (½ inch)
    cubes
150 g/5 oz cheese, grated
3 eggs, beaten
600 ml/1 pint milk
salt and freshly ground
    black pepper

Layer the bread cubes and cheese in a shallow cooking dish. Mix the eggs with the milk and salt and pepper to taste. Pour over the bread and cheese mixture.

Cover and cook for 15 minutes, turning the dish twice. Leave to stand, covered, for 5 minutes before serving.

Serves: 4
Power setting: DEFROST
Preparation time: 10-15 minutes
Cooking time: 20 minutes

CHEESY MUSHROOMS AND PRAWNS

50 g/2 oz savoury butter
    with black pepper
1 small onion, peeled and
    chopped
100 g/4 oz button
    mushrooms, wiped and
    sliced
225 g/8 oz peeled prawns
150 ml/¼ pint double
    cream
50 g/2 oz Cheddar cheese,
    grated
1 tablespoon chopped
    parsley

Place the savoury butter, onion and mushrooms in a bowl. Cover and cook for 3 minutes, stirring once.

Add the prawns, blending well. Cover and cook for 3 minutes, stirring once.

Add the double cream, blending well. Spoon equally into four ramekin dishes and sprinkle with the cheese. Cook for 2 minutes.

Brown under a preheated hot grill if liked. Sprinkle with the chopped parsley and serve with brown bread and butter.

Serves: 4
Power setting: FULL
Preparation time: 10 minutes
Cooking time: 8 minutes

SPICED EGGS AND CAULIFLOWER

2 tablespoons corn oil
1 teaspoon ground
 ginger
1 teaspoon ground
 coriander
1 teaspoon ground
 turmeric
1 small cauliflower,
 broken into florets
2 carrots, peeled and
 sliced
2 sticks celery, scrubbed
 and chopped
1 onion, peeled and sliced
100 ml/4 fl oz light stock
4 hard-boiled eggs, shelled
 and halved
1 tablespoon chopped
 parsley
225 g/8 oz long-grain
 rice
600 ml/1 pint boiling
 water
1 teaspoon salt
150 ml/¼ pint plain
 yogurt

Place the oil in a large bowl and cook for 1 minute. Add the ginger, coriander and turmeric, blending well. Cook for 1 minute, stirring once.

Add the cauliflower, carrots, celery, onion and stock, blending well. Cover and cook for 10 minutes, stirring once.

Add the eggs and parsley, cover and leave to stand while cooking the rice.

Place the rice, water and salt in a bowl. Cover and cook for 12 minutes. Leave to stand covered, for 5 minutes.

Reheat the spiced cauliflower and egg mixture by cooking for 2 minutes. Stir in the yogurt, blending well.

Spoon the rice on to a warmed serving dish and top with the spiced cauliflower and egg mixture. Serve at once.

Serves: 4
Power setting: FULL
Preparation time: 20 minutes
Cooking time: 31 minutes

MEATLOAF WITH CHEESE

450 g/1 lb minced beef
 and pork mixed
100 g/4 oz fresh white
 breadcrumbs
1 onion, peeled and finely
 chopped
1 egg, separated
2 tablespoons tomato
 purée
1 small green pepper,
 cored, seeded and
 chopped
100 g/4 oz Gouda cheese,
 grated
1 small garlic clove,
 peeled and crushed
pinch of dried thyme
pinch of ground nutmeg
salt and freshly ground
 black pepper
ground paprika to
 sprinkle

Mix the meat with the breadcrumbs, onion, egg yolk, half the egg white, tomato purée, green pepper, cheese, garlic, thyme, nutmeg and salt and pepper to taste, blending well. Place in a glass loaf dish and brush with the reserved egg white. Sprinkle with the paprika.

Cook for 17 minutes, turning the dish three times. Serve hot cut into slices.

Serves: 4
Power setting: FULL
Preparation time: 15-20 minutes
Cooking time: 17 minutes

PIPERANDA

50 g/2 oz butter
1 small onion, peeled and
    finely chopped
1 small green pepper,
    cored, seeded and
    finely chopped
75 g/3 oz tomatoes,
    chopped
75 g/3 oz cooked ham,
    chopped
4 eggs, beaten
salt and black pepper

Place the butter, onion and pepper in a bowl. Cover and cook on FULL POWER for 3 minutes, stirring once.

Add the tomatoes, ham, eggs and salt and pepper to taste, blending well. Cover and cook on MEDIUM POWER for 12-15 minutes, stirring 3 times.

Leave to stand, covered, for 2 minutes, before serving.

Serves: 4
Power settings: FULL, MEDIUM
Preparation time: 15 minutes
Cooking time: 17-20 minutes

GARDEN CASSEROLE

40 g/1½ oz butter
1 onion, peeled and
    thinly sliced
3 tablespoons plain flour
1 teaspoon ground
    nutmeg
300 ml/½ pint milk
300 ml/½ pint hot
    chicken stock (see p. 36)
175 g/6 oz Cheddar
    cheese with ham and
    mustard, grated
salt and freshly ground
    black pepper
450 g/1 lb peeled and
    thinly sliced potatoes
2 × 283 g (10 oz) packets
    frozen sweetcorn, peas
    and carrots
sliced tomatoes (optional)

Place the butter in a large bowl. Cook for ½ minutes to melt. Add the onion and cook for 2 minutes, stirring once.

Add the flour and nutmeg, blending well. Gradually add the milk and stock and cook for 4 minutes, stirring every 1 minute until smooth and thickened. Add the cheese and salt and pepper to taste, blending well.

Layer one-third of the potatoes, vegetables and sauce in a cooking dish. Repeat twice, finishing with a layer of sauce. Top with the tomato slices, if liked. Cook for 30 minutes, turning the dish twice. Serve hot.

To freeze
Cool quickly, cover, seal, label and freeze for up to 3 months.

Serves: 4
Power setting: FULL
Preparation time: 20 minutes
Cooking time: 36½ minutes
Suitable for freezing

SPICY CHEDDAR RAREBIT

15 g/½ oz butter
250 g/9 oz Cheddar
    cheese, grated
½ teaspoon
    Worcestershire sauce
dash of hot chilli sauce
pinch of cayenne pepper
3 tablespoons double
    cream
1 egg yolk, beaten
4 slices bread, toasted and
    buttered

Place the butter and cheese in a bowl. Cook on FULL POWER for 2-3 minutes, stirring twice, until smooth and creamy.

Add the Worcestershire sauce, chilli sauce, cayenne, cream and egg yolk, blending well. Cook on MEDIUM POWER for 5-7 minutes, stirring every 1 minute until hot, smooth and thickened.

Spoon equally over the toast slices to serve.

Serves: 4
Power settings: FULL, MEDIUM
Preparation time: 10 minutes
Cooking time: 7-10 minutes

STORECUPBOARD PIZZA

Topping:
15 g/½ oz butter
1 small onion, peeled and
    finely chopped
1 teaspoon cornflour
1 × 198 g (7 oz) can
    peeled tomatoes
½ teaspoon dried
    oregano
salt and freshly ground
    black pepper
100 g/4 oz cheese, grated
4 rinded and cooked
    bacon rashers, cut into
    thin strips or
1 × 50 g (2 oz) can
    anchovy fillets, drained
    and halved lengthways
8 stuffed green olives,
    sliced into rings
Base:
100 g/4 oz plain flour
¼ teaspoon salt
7 g/¼ oz butter
5 tablespoons water
pinch of sugar
2 teaspoons dried yeast
1 tablespoon oil
extra oil for brushing

To make the topping, place the butter in a large bowl and cook for ½ minute to melt. Add the onion and cook for 3 minutes, stirring once. Stir in the cornflour, tomatoes and their juice, oregano and salt and pepper to taste, blending well. Cook for 4 minutes, stirring twice.

To make the pizza base, sift the flour and salt into a bowl. Rub in the butter. Place the water in a jug and cook for ½ minute or until warm to the touch. Add the sugar, blending well. Sprinkle over the yeast and whisk with a fork. Leave to stand for 10 minutes until well risen and frothy.

Make a well in the centre of the flour and pour in the yeast mixture and oil. Mix to form a sticky dough. Turn on to a lightly floured surface and knead until smooth and elastic. Place in a bowl, cover and leave to prove for 20 minutes (*or see* Quick Proving, p. 172). Flatten with the hand or roll out to fit a small browning plate.

Brush the browning plate with oil and preheat for 6 minutes. Quickly press the pizza base on to the hot surface with a fish slice. Turn over and cook for 2 minutes.

Spread the pizza topping over the base and cover with the grated cheese and a lattice of strips of cooked bacon or anchovy fillets. Garnish with the olives. Cook for 2 minutes. Serve at once.

Serves: 1-2
Power setting: FULL
Preparation time: 35-40 minutes
(including proving time)
Cooking time: about 18 minutes

WENSLEYDALE AND CIDER FONDUE

½ garlic clove, peeled
    and crushed
150 ml/¼ pint medium
    dry cider
1 teaspoon lemon juice
1½ tablespoons gin or
    Kirsch
400 g/14 oz Wensleydale
    cheese, grated
1 tablespoon cornflour
pinch of dried mixed
    herbs or nutmeg
freshly ground black
    pepper
cubes of French bread to
    serve

Place the garlic, cider, lemon juice and gin or Kirsch in a fondue dish or casserole. Cook on FULL POWER for 3½-4 minutes until very hot.

Toss the cheese with the cornflour, herbs or nutmeg and pepper to taste until well blended. Quickly stir or whisk the cheese into the hot liquid and cover. Cook on MEDIUM POWER for 2½-3½ minutes, stirring every 1 minute until the cheese is just melted.

Serve at once with cubes of French bread for dipping.

Serves: 4
Power settings: FULL, MEDIUM
Preparation time: 15 minutes
Cooking time: 6-7½ minutes

CHEESE AND HAM QUICHE

Pastry:
100 g/4 oz plain flour
pinch of salt
100 g/4 oz butter
100 g/4 oz rolled oats
about 3 tablespoons
    water
Filling:
1 tablespoon oil
1 large onion, peeled and
    sliced
2 eggs, beaten
150 ml/¼ pint milk
100 g/4 oz Cheddar
    cheese, grated
50 g/2 oz cooked ham,
    chopped
4 mushrooms, wiped and
    sliced
salt and freshly ground
    black pepper

Sift the flour and salt into a bowl. Rub in the butter until the mixture resembles fine breadcrumbs. Stir in the oats then add enough cold water to bind to a soft dough.

Roll out the pastry on a lightly-floured surface to a round large enough to line a 20 cm (8 inch) flan dish. Press in firmly taking care not to stretch the pastry. Cut the pastry away leaving a 5 mm (¼ inch) 'collar' above the dish (this allows for any shrinkage that may occur). Prick the base well with a fork. Line the inside, upright edge of the pastry case with a long strip of foil, about 4 cm (1½ inches) wide. (This prevents the outer edges from overcooking). Place a double thickness layer of absorbent kitchen paper over the base, easing into position around the edges to keep the foil in place. Cook on FULL POWER for 4-4½ minutes, giving the dish a quarter turn every 1 minute. Remove the paper and foil and cook on FULL POWER for a further 1-2 minutes. Allow to cool.

Meanwhile, place the oil and onion in a bowl and cook for 3-4 minutes until tender, stirring once.

Lightly beat the eggs with the milk. Add the cheese, ham, mushrooms, onion and salt and pepper to taste, blending well. Pour into the pastry case. Cook on DEFROST POWER for 14-16 minutes, giving the dish a quarter turn every 3 minutes. Leave to stand, covered, for 15-20 minutes. The quiche should set completely in this time. Serve hot or cold.

To freeze
Cool quickly and pack in a rigid container. Cover, seal, label and freeze for up to 2 months.

Serves: 4-6
Power settings: FULL, DEFROST
Preparation time: 35-40 minutes
Cooking time: 37-46½ minutes
Suitable for freezing

CHEESEBURGERS

4 × 50 g (2 oz) beefburgers
4 baps, split and buttered
4 quick-melting cheese
    slices
2 tablespoons tomato
    ketchup

Place the beefburgers in a circle on a piece of absorbent kitchen paper on a plate. Cook for 1-2 minutes. Turn over and cook for a further 1-2 minutes.

Place in the buttered baps and top with the cheese slices then the tomato ketchup.

Place the filled baps on fresh absorbent kitchen paper and cook for 1-1½ minutes until the baps are hot and the cheese has completely melted.

Leave to stand for 1 minute before serving.

Serves: 4
Power setting: FULL
Preparation time: 5 minutes
Cooking time: 4-6½ minutes

SWISS FONDUE

1 garlic clove, peeled
150 ml/¼ pint dry white
    wine
1 tablespoon lemon juice
450 g/1 lb Gruyère or
    Emmenthal cheese,
    grated
1 tablespoon cornflour
2 tablespoons Kirsch
salt and freshly ground
    white pepper

Cut the garlic clove in half and rub around the inside of a fondue or casserole dish. Add the wine and lemon juice, blending well. Cook for 1-2 minutes until very hot.

Add half the cheese and stir well to blend. Add the remaining cheese and cook for 1 minute.

Blend the cornflour with the Kirsch and stir into the fondue mixture. Add salt and pepper to taste then cook for 3-4 minutes, stirring every 1 minute until the mixture is smooth and completely melted.

Serve hot with cubes of French bread for dipping.

Serves: 4
Power setting: FULL
Preparation time: 15 minutes
Cooking time: 5-7 minutes

CHEESE AND ONION BAKE

550 g/1¼ lb peeled
    potatoes
6 tablespoons water
25 g/1 oz butter
1 large onion, peeled and
    sliced
150 g/5 oz cheese, grated
300 ml/½ pint milk
salt and freshly ground
    black pepper

Place the potatoes in a dish with the water. Cover and cook for 5 minutes. Leave to stand, covered, while cooking the onion.

Place the butter and onion in a bowl. Cook for 4 minutes, stirring once.

Drain and slice the potatoes. Layer the potatoes, onion and cheese in a cooking dish. Season the milk with salt and pepper to taste. Pour over the potato mixture. Cover and cook for 15 minutes, turning the dish twice. Leave to stand, covered, for 5 minutes.

Brown under a preheated hot grill if liked. Serve hot.

Serves: 4
Power setting: FULL
Preparation time: 15 minutes
Cooking time: 29 minutes

MACARONI CHEESE WITH BACON

225 g/8 oz quick-cook
    macaroni
600 ml/1 pint boiling
    water
salt and freshly ground
    black pepper
350 g/12 oz streaky
    bacon, rinded
50 g/2 oz butter
2 tablespoons plain flour
½ teaspoon mustard
    powder
450 ml/¾ pint milk
100 g/4 oz Double
    Gloucester cheese,
    grated

Place the macaroni in a deep bowl with the water and pinch of salt. Cover and cook for 10 minutes, stirring once. Leave to stand, covered, for 3 minutes.

Meanwhile, place the bacon on a roasting rack or plate and cover with absorbent kitchen paper. Cook for 8-10 minutes until cooked and crisp. Drain on absorbent kitchen paper and crumble.

Place the butter in a large jug and cook for 1 minute to melt. Add the flour and mustard, blending well. Gradually add the milk and cook for 4 minutes, stirring every 1 minute until smooth and thickened. Add three-quarters of the cheese and stir to melt.

Drain the macaroni and place in a serving dish. Pour over the sauce and sprinkle with the remaining cheese. Cook for 2 minutes. Serve hot sprinkled with the crumbled bacon.

To freeze
Cool quickly, cover, seal, label and freeze for up to 2 months.

Serves: 4
Power setting: FULL
Preparation time: 15-20 minutes
Cooking time: 28-30 minutes
Suitable for freezing

HAM AND CHEESE PUDDING

50 g/2 oz cooked ham,
    finely chopped
175 g/6 oz mature
    Cheddar cheese, grated
225 g/8 oz fresh brown
    breadcrumbs
1 teaspoon dried mixed
    herbs
pinch of mustard powder
salt and freshly ground
    black pepper
3 eggs, beaten
600 ml/1 pint milk
chopped parsley to
    garnish

Mix the ham with the cheese, breadcrumbs, herbs, mustard and salt and pepper to taste, blending well. Add the eggs and milk and stir well to blend.

Pour into a 1.8 litre (3 pint) soufflé dish and leave to stand for 10 minutes.

Cook, uncovered, for 12-14 minutes, stirring once. Sprinkle with the parsley and serve at once.

Serves: 4
Power setting: FULL
Preparation time: 10-15 minutes
Cooking time: 22-24 minutes

Rice, Pasta and Cereals

Fluffy separate rice, 'al dente' pasta and creamily cooked cereals are the promises delivered by cooking the microwave way.
There are no valuable time savings over conventional cooking since rice, pasta and cereals still need time in which to rehydrate. But, since you can cook and serve in the same dish, the microwave does offer the virtues of no sticky saucepans, or steamy kitchen and less washing up.
The microwave oven will, however, reheat rice, pasta and cereals faster than conventional cookers and without the danger of drying out.

KEDGEREE

225 g/8 oz long-grain rice
600 ml/1 pint boiling water
1 teaspoon salt
1 teaspoon corn oil
450 g/1 lb cooked smoked haddock, flaked
50 g/2 oz butter
2 eggs, beaten
1 tablespoon milk
cayenne pepper
chopped parsley to garnish

Place the rice, water, salt and oil in a large bowl, blending well. Cover and cook for 12 minutes, Leave to stand, covered, for 5 minutes.

Stir the fish, butter, egg and milk into the rice, blending well. Cover and cook for 3 minutes, stirring once.

Pile on to a warmed serving dish and sprinkle with cayenne pepper to taste. Garnish with chopped parsley. Serve at once.

Serves: 4
Power setting: FULL
Preparation time: 20 minutes
Cooking time: 20 minutes

ROAST BEEF WITH ONION RICE

25 g/1 oz butter
2 garlic cloves, peeled and crushed
freshly ground black pepper
1 × 1.5 kg (3½ lb) boned and rolled rib of beef
2 onions, peeled and sliced
2 tablespoons oil
350 g/12 oz long-grain rice
900 ml/1½ pints boiling beef stock

Place the butter in a bowl and cook for ½ minute to melt. Add the garlic and pepper to taste, blending well. Brush the beef with the garlic butter and place on a roasting rack set in a shallow dish. Cook for 12-13 minutes, turning the dish twice.

Turn the beef over and brush with any remaining garlic butter. Cover with grease-proof paper and cook for a further 12-14 minutes, turning the dish twice. Wrap the beef in foil, shiny side inside, and leave to stand while preparing the onion rice.

Place the onion, oil and rice in a bowl, blending well. Cook for 2-3 minutes, stirring once. Add the stock, cover and cook for 12 minutes. Leave to stand, covered, for 5 minutes.

Serve the beef carved into thin slices with the onion rice.

Serves: 6
Power setting: FULL
Preparation time: 20-25 minutes
Cooking time: 43½-47½ minutes

HERBED RICE SALAD

450 g/1 lb long-grain rice
900 ml/1½ pints boiling
    water
1 onion, peeled and
    thinly sliced
6 tablespoons chopped
    fresh herbs (basil,
    parsley and chives for
    example)
6 tablespoons French
    dressing

Place the rice in a large bowl with the water, blending well. Cover and cook for 13 minutes. Leave to stand, covered, for 10 minutes.

Stir in the onion, herbs and dressing, blending well. Leave to cool then chill until required.

Stir just before serving to blend.

Serves: 6-8
Power setting: FULL
Preparation time: 10 minutes plus cooling and chilling
Cooking time: 23 minutes

TURKEY RISOTTO

25 g/1 oz butter
1 large onion, peeled and
    sliced
175 g/6 oz long-grain
    rice
2 carrots, peeled and cut
    into thin strips
100 g/4 oz frozen peas
225 g/8 oz cooked turkey,
    skinned and chopped
3 tablespoons sage and
    onion mustard
350 ml/12 fl oz boiling
    chicken stock
salt and freshly ground
    black pepper

Place the butter in a large bowl with the onion. Cover and cook for 3 minutes, stirring once.

Add the rice, carrots, peas, turkey, mustard, stock and salt and pepper to taste, blending well. Cover and cook for 20 minutes, stirring twice. Leave to stand, covered, for 5 minutes.

Serve hot with a crisp green salad.

To freeze
Cool quickly and place in a rigid container. Cover, seal, label and freeze for up to 3 months.

Serves: 4
Power setting: FULL
Preparation time: 15-20 minutes
Cooking time: 28 minutes
Suitable for freezing

SAVOURY RICE RING

100 g/4 oz butter
1 small onion, chopped
½ green pepper, cored,
    seeded and chopped
grated rind of 1 orange
225 g/8 oz long-grain
    rice
600 ml/1 pint boiling
    stock
225 g/8 oz pork fillet,
    sliced
1 onion, sliced
juice of ½ orange
2 tablespoons sherry
2 teaspoons cornflour
2 tablespoons water
orange slices to garnish

Place half the butter in a bowl and cook for 1 minute to melt. Add the chopped onion and pepper, blending well. Cover and cook for 2 minutes. Add the orange rind, rice and stock, blending well. Cover and cook for 14 minutes. Leave to stand for 5 minutes.

Spoon the rice into a large greased glass ring mould, pressing down well.

Meanwhile, place the remaining butter in a bowl and cook for 1 minute to melt. Add the pork and sliced onion. Cover and cook for 2 minutes. Add the orange juice and sherry, blending well.

Blend the cornflour with the water and stir into the pork mixture. Cover and cook for 1 minute, stirring once.

Reheat the rice mould by cooking for 3-4 minutes. Invert on to a warmed serving plate. Fill with the pork mixture and garnish with the orange slices.

Serves: 4
Power setting: FULL
Preparation time: 15-20 minutes
Cooking time: 29-30 minutes
Suitable for freezing

127

GUIDE TO COOKING RICE

Rice	Quantity	Preparation	Cooking time in minutes on FULL POWER	Standing time
Brown rice	225 g/8 oz	Place in a deep, covered container with 600 ml/1 pint boiling salted water.	20-25	5-10
American easy-cook rice	225 g/8 oz	Place in a deep, covered container with 600 ml/1 pint boiling salted water.	12-15	5-10
Long-grain, patna rice	225 g/8 oz	Place in a deep, covered container with 600 ml/1 pint boiling salted water and 1 tablespoon oil.	10	5-10

GUIDE TO COOKING PASTA

Pasta	Quantity	Preparation	Cooking time in minutes on FULL POWER	Standing time
Egg noodles and tagliatelle	225 g/8 oz	Place in a deep, covered container with 600 ml/1 pint boiling salted water and 1 tablespoon oil.	6	3
Macaroni	225 g/8 oz	Place in a deep, covered container with 600 ml/1 pint boiling salted water and 1 tablespoon oil.	10	3
Pasta shells and shapes	225 g/8 oz	Place in a deep, covered container with 900 ml/1½ pints boiling salted water and 1 tablespoon oil.	12-14	5-10
Spaghetti	225 g/8 oz	Hold in a deep, covered container with 1 litre/1¾ pints boiling salted water to soften, then submerge or break in half and add 1 tablespoon oil.	10	5-10

VEGETABLE RISOTTO

2 tablespoons oil
1 large onion, peeled and sliced
225 g/8 oz long-grain rice
1 × 300 g (10 oz) packet frozen stir-fry vegetables
600 ml/1 pint boiling stock
1 teaspoon dried marjoram
salt and freshly ground black pepper
50 g/2 oz cheese, grated

Place the oil, onion and rice in a large casserole dish. Cook for 3 minutes, stirring once.

Add the frozen stir-fry vegetables. Cover and cook for 2 minutes.

Add the stock, marjoram and salt and pepper to taste, blending well. Cover and cook for 15 minutes, leave to stand, covered, for 5 minutes.

Spoon into a warmed serving dish and sprinkle with the grated cheese. Serve at once.

Serves: 4
Power setting: FULL
Preparation time: 10-15 minutes
Cooking time: 25 minutes

BROWN RICE SALAD

900 ml/1½ pints water
175 g/6 oz brown long-
    grain rice
salt and black pepper
½ cucumber, chopped
4 spring onions, sliced
¼ green pepper, cored,
    seeded and chopped
¼ red pepper, cored,
    seeded and chopped
50 g/2 oz green olives
450 g/1 lb cooked meat or
    fish, chopped or flaked
Dressing:
2 tablespoons salad oil
1 tablespoon lemon juice
1 teaspoon chopped fresh
    parsley
pinch of garlic salt

Boil the water and place in a bowl with the rice and a pinch of salt. Cover and cook for 25 minutes, until tender. Leave to stand, covered, for 5-10 minutes. Rinse under cold running water until cool then drain thoroughly.

Place the rice in a bowl with the cucumber, spring onions, peppers, olives and meat. Add salt and pepper to taste and mix well to blend.

Beat the oil with the lemon juice, parsley and garlic salt. Stir into the salad just before serving.

Serves: 4-6
Power setting: FULL
Preparation time: 30-40 minutes
Cooking time: 30-35 minutes

SPICY SAUSAGE RISOTTO

1 onion, peeled and sliced
½ green pepper, cored,
    seeded and sliced
2 tablespoons corn oil
225 g/8 oz long-grain
    rice
600 ml/1 pint boiling
    stock
225/8 oz salami, sliced
    and quartered
100 g/4 oz frozen peas
2 tomatoes, peeled, seeded
    and chopped
salt and black pepper
50 g/2 oz cheese, grated

Place the onion, pepper and oil in a casserole dish. Cover and cook for 3 minutes, stirring once. Add the rice and cook for 2 minutes. Pour in the stock, blending well. Cover and cook for 10 minutes.

Add the salami, peas, tomatoes and salt and pepper to taste, slending well. Cover and cook for 5 minutes, stirring once. Leave to stand for 5 minutes.

Serve hot sprinkled with the cheese.

To freeze
Cool quickly and place in a rigid container. Cover, seal, label and freeze for up to 2 months.

Serves: 4
Power setting: FULL
Preparation time: 15-20 minutes
Cooking time: 25 minutes
Suitable for freezing

CASSEROLED RICE WITH SPINACH

50 g/2 oz butter
450 g/1 lb long-grain
    Italian rice
600 ml/1 pint boiling
    chicken stock
225 g/8 oz fresh spinach,
    washed and sorted
50 g/2 oz walnuts,
    coarsely chopped
salt and black pepper

Place the butter in a casserole dish and cook for 1 minute to melt. Add the rice and stock, blending well. Cover and cook for 13 minutes. Leave to stand, covered, for 10 minutes.

Meanwhile, place the spinach in a bowl with just the water clinging to the leaves. Cover and cook for 2 minutes or until just soft.

Drain the spinach and stir into the rice with the walnuts and salt and pepper to taste. Toss lightly with two forks to mix. Serve at once as a main meal accompaniment.

Serves: 4
Power setting: FULL
Preparation time: 15-20 minutes
Cooking time: 26 minutes

QUICK SEAFOOD PAELLA

1 onion, chopped
½ red pepper, cored, seeded and chopped
1 garlic clove, peeled and crushed
2 tablespoons oil
225 g/8 oz long-grain rice
600 ml/1 pint boiling fish stock
1 teaspoon ground turmeric
1 × 198 g (7 oz) can tuna fish, drained and flaked
100 g/4 oz peeled prawns
100 g/4 oz cooked or canned mussels

Place the onion, pepper, garlic and oil in a casserole dish. Cook for 2 minutes, stirring once. Add the rice, blending well. Cook for a further 2 minutes, stirring once.

Add the stock and turmeric, blending well. Cover and cook for 10 minutes.

Add the tuna, prawns and mussels, blending well. Cover and cook for a further 5 minutes, stirring once. Leave to stand covered, for 5 minutes before serving.

To freeze
Cool quickly and place in a rigid container. Cover, seal, label and freeze for up to 1 month.

Serves: 4
Power setting: FULL
Preparation time: 10-15 minutes
Cooking time: 24 minutes
Suitable for freezing

VEAL CONTINENTAL WITH RICE

675 g/1½ lb stewing veal, cubed
25 g/1 oz seasoned flour
25 g/1 oz butter
300 ml/½ pint beef stock
2 tomatoes, peeled and quartered
100 g/4 oz mushrooms, wiped and halved
1 onion, peeled and chopped
1 tablespoon tomato purée
salt and black pepper
225 g/8 oz long-grain rice
600 ml/1 pint boiling water
1 teaspoon salt

Preheat a browning dish on FULL POWER for 5 minutes (or according to the manufacturer's instructions).

Toss the veal in the flour to coat. Add the butter to the browning dish and swirl to coat. Add the veal and cook on FULL POWER for 2 minutes, stirring once. Add any remaining flour and cook on FULL POWER for a further 1 minute. Gradually add the stock, blending well. Cover and cook on FULL POWER for 10 minutes, stirring once.

Add the tomatoes, mushrooms, onion, tomato purée and salt and pepper to taste, blending well, Cover and cook on FULL POWER for 10 minutes, stirring once.

Reduce the power setting and cook on MEDIUM POWER for 25 minutes, stirring twice, or until the veal is tender. Leave to stand, covered, while cooking the rice.

Place the rice, water and salt in a bowl. Cover and cook on FULL POWER for 12 minutes. Leave to stand for 5 minutes.

Spoon the rice on to a warmed serving dish and top with the veal continental. Serve at once.

Serves: 4
Power settings: FULL, MEDIUM
Preparation time: 20 minutes
Cooking time: 1 hour

FESTIVE CHICKEN WITH RICE

4 chicken breasts, skinned
25 g/1 oz seasoned flour
75 g/3 oz butter
2 tablespoons corn oil
1 × 175 (6 oz) jar cranberry sauce (cont.)

Preheat a browning dish for 5 minutes (or according to the manufacturer's instructions). Dip the chicken in the seasoned flour to coat.

Add the butter and oil to the browning dish and swirl to coat. Add the chicken and

cook for 2 minutes, turning over once.

Place the cranberry sauce in a casserole dish. Cook for 1-2 minutes, stirring once until hot, smooth and bubbly. Add the sugar, onion, orange rind, orange juice, cinnamon and ginger, blending well. Add

25 g/1 oz sugar
1 onion, peeled and sliced
grated rind and juice of 1
   orange
½ teaspoon ground
   cinnamon
½ teaspoon ground
   ginger
225 g/8 oz long-grain
   rice
600 ml/1 pint boiling
   water
1 teaspoon salt

the chicken and toss well to coat in the sauce. Cover and cook for 10 minutes, stirring once. Leave to stand while cooking the rice.

Place the rice, water and salt in a bowl. Cover and cook for 12 minutes. Leave to stand, covered, for 5 minutes.

Spoon the rice on to a warmed serving dish and top with the festive chicken.

Serves: 4
Power setting: FULL
Preparation time: 10-15 minutes
Cooking time: 35-36 minutes

CHILLI MACARONI BEEF

1 onion, peeled and
   chopped
75 g/3 oz frozen chopped
   peppers
225 g/8 oz minced beef
100 g/4 oz quick-cooking
   macaroni
1 × 397 g (14 oz) can
   peeled tomatoes
300 ml/½ pint beef stock
3 tablespoons tomato
   purée
1-2 teaspoons chilli
   powder
salt and freshly ground
   black pepper

Place the onion, peppers and beef in a casserole dish. Cover and cook on FULL POWER for 5 minutes, stirring and breaking up the meat once.

Add the macaroni, tomatoes and their juice, stock, tomato purée, chilli powder and salt and pepper to taste, blending well, Cover and cook on FULL POWER for 6 minutes, stirring once.

Reduce the power setting and cook on DEFROST POWER for 30 minutes, stirring once. Leave to stand for 5 minutes before serving.

Serves: 3
Power settings: FULL, DEFROST
Preparation time: 10-15 minutes
Cooking time: 46 minutes

NOODLES WITH PEA AND BACON SAUCE

225 g/8 oz smoked back
   bacon, rinded and
   chopped
1 onion, peeled and
   chopped
1 tablespoon chopped
   mixed fresh herbs
450 g/1 lb frozen peas
100 ml/4 fl oz rich
   chicken stock
225 g/8 oz dried egg
   noodles
600 ml/1 pint boiling
   water
1 tablespoon oil
salt and black pepper
150 ml/¼ pint single
   cream

Place the bacon in a casserole dish. Cover and cook for 7 minutes, stirring once. Remove the bacon with a slotted spoon and drain on absorbent kitchen paper.

Stir the onion and herbs into the cooking juices, blending well. Cover and cook for 3 minutes, stirring once. Add the peas and stock, blending well. Cover and cook for 10 minutes, stirring once.

Place the noodles in a bowl with the water, oil and a pinch of salt. Cover and cook for 6 minutes. Leave to stand while preparing the sauce.

Purée the pea mixture in a blender or pass through a fine sieve. Add the cream and salt and pepper to taste, blending well. Cook for 1-2 minutes to reheat.

Drain the noodles and place on a warmed serving dish. Spoon over the sauce and sprinkle with the bacon to serve.

Serves: 4
Power setting: FULL
Preparation time: 20 minutes
Cooking time: 27-28 minutes

SEAFOOD LASAGNE

175 g/6 oz dried green
lasagne
900 ml/1½ pints boiling
water
1 teaspoon oil
salt and freshly ground
black pepper
50 g/2 oz butter
50 g/2 oz plain flour
300 ml/½ pint milk
150 ml/¼ pint dry cider
100 g/4 oz pint fish or
chicken stock
100 g/4 oz peeled prawns
100 g/4 oz cooked
smoked haddock,
flaked
2 tablespoons chopped
parsley
50 g/2 oz Cheddar cheese,
grated

Place the lasagne in a deep rectangular casserole with the water, oil and a pinch of salt. Cover and cook for 9 minutes. Leave to stand while preparing the sauce then drain thoroughly.

Place the butter in a bowl and cook for 1 minute to melt. Add the flour, blending well. Gradually add the milk, cider and stock. Cook for 6-7 minutes, stirring 3 times until smooth and thickened. Add the prawns, haddock, parsley and salt and pepper to taste, blending well.

Layer the lasagne and seafood mixture in the casserole, finishing with a layer of sauce.

Sprinkle with the cheese and cook for 2-4 minutes until heated through. Brown under a preheated hot grill if liked.

To freeze
Cool quickly, cover, seal, label and freeze for up to 2 months.

Serves: 4-6
Power setting: FULL
Preparation time: 15-20 minutes
Cooking time: 18-21 minutes
Suitable for freezing

SEAFOOD PASTA SALAD

225 g/8 oz dried pasta
shells
1.2 litres/2 pints boiling
water
450 g/1 lb firm white fish
(cod or haddock, for
example)
2 tablespoons cold water
100 g/4 oz peeled shrimps
1 red or green pepper,
cored, seeded and
chopped
Green Onion Dressing:
5 tablespoons oil
2 tablespoons lemon juice
1 garlic clove, peeled and
crushed
2 tablespoons chopped
fresh parsley
3 spring onions, trimmed
and sliced
3 tablespoons grated
Parmesan cheese
salt and freshly ground
black pepper
few radishes, washed and
sliced, to garnish

Place the pasta shells and boiling water in a bowl, blending well. Cover and cook for 6 minutes. Leave to stand while cooking the fish.

Place the fish in a cooking dish with the cold water. Cover and cook for 4 minutes, turning the dish once. Drain, remove any skin and bones and flake into bite-sized chunks.

Mix the pasta with the fish, shrimps and pepper, blending well. Leave to cool.

Meanwhile place the oil, lemon juice, garlic, parsley, spring onions, Parmesan cheese and salt and pepper to taste in a blender or food processor and blend until thoroughly combined.

Pour the dressing over the pasta salad and toss to coat. Chill lightly before serving garnished with sliced radishes.

Serves: 4-6
Power setting: FULL
Preparation time: 20-25 minutes plus
cooling and chilling
Cooking time: 10 minutes

ITALIAN PASTA DISHES, INCLUDING (centre) SPAGHETTI WITH NEAPOLITAN SAUCE (p.229)

134   HOLLANDAISE SAUCE (p.141) ON ASPARAGUS; MOUSSELINE (top right) IS HOLLANDAISE WITH CREAM

SPAGHETTI MILANESE

25 g/1 oz butter
1 onion, peeled and
  chopped
25 g/1 oz plain flour
300 ml/½ pint water
1 × 56 g (2 oz) can tomato
  purée
pinch of dried mixed
  herbs
175 g/6 oz cooked ham,
  chopped
100 g/4 oz mushrooms,
  wiped, trimmed and
  sliced
salt and freshly ground
  black pepper
450 g/1 lb cooked
  spaghetti

Place the butter in a large bowl. Cook for ½ minute to melt. Add the onion, cover and cook for 4 minutes, stirring once.

Add the flour, blending well. Cook for a further 1 minute. Gradually add the water, tomato purée and herbs, blending well. Cook for 6 minutes, stirring every 2 minutes, until smooth and thickened.

Add the ham, mushrooms and salt and pepper to taste, blending well. Cover and cook for 4 minutes, stirring once.

Add the cooked spaghetti and toss gently to coat in the sauce. Cook for 2 minutes. Serve at once.

Serves: 4
Power setting: FULL
Preparation time: 15-20 minutes
Cooking time: 17½ minutes

SPAGHETTI BOLOGNESE

225 g/8 oz dried spaghetti
1 litre/1¾ pints boiling
  water
1 tablespoon oil
pinch of salt
Sauce:
50 g/2 oz streaky bacon,
  rinded and chopped
1 onion, peeled and
  chopped
1 carrot, peeled and
  chopped
1 garlic clove, peeled and
  crushed
1 stick celery, scrubbed
  and chopped
450 g/1 lb minced beef
1 × 398 g (14 oz) can
  crushed tomatoes
2 tablespoons tomato
  purée
pinch of ground nutmeg
2 teaspoons dried
  oregano
2 tablespoons red wine
salt and freshly ground
  black pepper
2 tablespoons double
  cream

Hold the spaghetti in a deep bowl with the water to soften then submerge. Add the oil and a pinch of salt. Cover and cook for 12 minutes, stirring once. Leave to stand, covered, while preparing the sauce.

Place the bacon, onion, carrot, garlic, celery and beef in a bowl. Cook for 7 minutes, stirring and breaking up twice. Add the tomatoes, tomato purée, nutmeg, oregano, wine and salt and pepper to taste, blending well. Cover and cook for 12-15 minutes, stirring twice.

Add the cream to the sauce, blending well. Drain the spaghetti and place in a warmed serving dish. Pour over the sauce and serve at once.

To freeze
Cool quickly and pack pasta and sauce separately in rigid containers. Cover, seal, label and freeze for up to 2 months.

Serves: 4
Power setting: FULL
Preparation time: 15-20 minutes
Cooking time: 31-34 minutes
Suitable for freezing

Illustrated on p. 133

135

MACARONI CHEESE

225 g/8 oz macaroni
600 ml/1 pint boiling
water
1 tablespoon oil
salt and freshly ground
black pepper
600 ml/1 pint hot Cheese
sauce (see p. 140,
variation 2)
ground paprika

Place the macaroni in a large bowl with the water, oil and a pinch of salt. Cover and cook for 10 minutes. Leave to stand, covered, for 3 minutes.

Drain the macaroni and mix with the cheese sauce and salt and pepper to taste, blending well. Spoon into a serving dish and cook for 5-7 minutes or until heated through.

Serve sprinkled with ground paprika. Brown under a preheated hot grill if liked.

To freeze
Cool quickly, cover, seal, label and freeze for up to 3 months.

Serves: 4
Power setting: FULL
Preparation time: 15-20 minutes
Cooking time: 18-20 minutes
Suitable for freezing

NOODLE AND HAM BAKE

225 g/8 oz cooked ham,
chopped
1 onion, peeled and finely
chopped
3 tablespoons chopped
fresh parsley
225 g/8 oz cooked
noodles
300 ml/½ pint milk
2 eggs, beaten
½ teaspoon salt
pinch of ground nutmeg
50 g/2 oz Cheddar cheese,
grated
25 g/1 oz butter
1 teaspoon ground
paprika

Place the ham, onion and parsley in a dish. Cover and cook on FULL POWER for 5 minutes, stirring once.

Place half of the noodles in a greased cooking dish. Top with the ham mixture then the remaining noodles.

Mix the milk with the eggs, salt and nutmeg, blending well. Pour over the noodles. Sprinkle with the cheese and dot with the butter. Sprinkle with paprika and cook on FULL POWER for 10 minutes, turning the dish once.

Reduce the power setting and cook on MEDIUM POWER for 18-20 minutes, turning the dish twice. Leave to stand for 5-10 minutes before serving.

To freeze
Cool quickly, cover, seal, label and freeze for up to 3 months.

Serves: 4
Power settings: FULL, MEDIUM
Preparation time: 15-20 minutes
Cooking time: 38-45 minutes
Suitable for freezing

TROPICAL-STYLE MACARONI

1 small red pepper, cored,
seeded and chopped
1 small green pepper,
cored, seeded and
chopped
100 g/4 oz streaky bacon,
rinded and chopped
1 × 225 g (8 oz) can
pineapple pieces,
drained and chopped
450 g/1 lb cooked
macaroni
75 g/3 oz cheese, grated
1 tablespoon snipped
chives
salt and black pepper

Place the peppers, bacon and pineapple in a bowl. Cover and cook for 2 minutes, stirring once.

Add the macaroni, blending well. Cover and cook for 2 minutes, stirring once.

Add the cheese, chives and salt and pepper to taste, blending well. Cook for 2 minutes, stirring once.

Serve at once as a main meal dish.

Serves: 4
Power setting: FULL
Preparation time: 15-20 minutes
Cooking time: 6 minutes

SPAGHETTI WITH GORGONZOLA

175 g/6 oz spaghetti
900 ml/1½ pints boiling
  water
1 tablespoon oil
pinch of salt
Sauce:
100 ml/4 fl oz single
  cream
100 g/4 oz Gorgonzola
  cheese, crumbled
salt and freshly ground
  black pepper
25 g/1 oz butter
ground nutmeg
2 spring onions, trimmed
  and finely chopped
25 g/1 oz grated
  Parmesan cheese
snipped chives to garnish

Hold the spaghetti in a deep bowl with the water, oil and a pinch of salt to soften, then submerge. Cover and cook for 10 minutes. Leave to stand, covered, while preparing the sauce.

Place the cream and Gorgonzola in a bowl. Cook for 2-3 minutes, stirring twice until smooth and melted. Add salt and pepper to taste, blending well.

Drain the spaghetti and toss with the butter, nutmeg, spring onions and Parmesan cheese. Place in a warmed serving dish and pour over the Gorgonzola sauce. Sprinkle with chives and serve at once with a tomato and basil salad.

Serves: 2
Power setting: FULL
Preparation time: 15-20 minutes
Cooking time: 12-13 minutes

TORTELLINI IN CREAMY PESTO SAUCE

175 g/6 oz tortellini
900 ml/1½ pints boiling
  water
1 tablespoon oil
salt and freshly ground
  black pepper
150 ml/¼ pint single
  cream
1 tablespoon canned or
  bottled Pesto sauce
grated Parmesan cheese

Place the tortellini in a bowl with the water, oil and a pinch of salt. Cover and cook for 12-14 minutes. Leave to stand, covered, while preparing the sauce.

Place the cream in a bowl and cook for 1½ minutes. Add the Pesto sauce and pepper to taste, blending well.

Drain the tortellini and add to the sauce. Toss well to mix. Sprinkle with Parmesan cheese and serve with a crisp green salad.

Serves: 2
Power setting: FULL
Preparation time: 10 minutes
Cooking time: 13½-15½ minutes

PIQUANT PASTA

175 g/6 oz fettucine
  (narrow ribbon
  noodles)
600 ml/1 pint boiling
  water
3 tablespoons olive oil
salt and freshly ground
  black pepper
2 garlic cloves, peeled and
  crushed
1 small chilli, seeded and
  chopped
2 tablespoons chopped
  fresh parsley

Place the fettucine in a bowl with the water, 1 tablespoon oil and a pinch of salt. Cover and cook for 6 minutes. Leave to stand, covered, while preparing the garlic mixture.

Place the remaining oil, garlic and chilli in a bowl. Cover and cook for 3 minutes.

Drain the fettucine and place in a warmed serving bowl. Pour over the hot oil with the garlic and chilli, add the parsley and salt and pepper to taste and toss well to mix. Serve at once.

Serves: 2
Power setting: FULL
Preparation time: 10 minutes
Cooking time: 9 minutes

BEAN AND PRAWN CHOW MEIN

350 g/12 oz dried egg or
  green noodles
900 ml/1½ pints boiling
  water
2 tablespoons oil
salt and freshly ground
  black pepper
1 onion, peeled and finely
  chopped
1 garlic clove, peeled and
  crushed
2 sticks celery, scrubbed
  and finely chopped
1 green pepper, cored,
  seeded and finely
  chopped
2 × 225 g (8 oz) cans
  curried beans with
  sultanas
150 ml/¼ pint chicken
  stock
4 canned water chestnuts,
  thinly sliced
½ teaspoon crushed fresh
  root ginger
225 g/8 oz peeled prawns
2 tablespoons chopped
  fresh parsley

Place the noodles in a bowl with the water, 1 tablespoon of the oil and a pinch of salt. Cover and cook for 6 minutes. Leave to stand while preparing the sauce.

Place the rest of the oil and the onion in a bowl. Cover and cook for 3 minutes, stirring once. Add the garlic, celery and pepper, blending well. Cover and cook for 2 minutes.

Add the beans, stock, water chestnuts and ginger, blending well. Cover and cook for 3 minutes, stirring once.

Stir in the prawns and chopped parsley and cook for 1 minute.

Drain the noodles thoroughly and pile on to a warmed serving dish. Top with the bean and prawn sauce. Serve at once.

Serves: 4
Power setting: FULL
Preparation time: 15-20 minutes
Cooking time: 15 minutes

CURRIED CHICKEN PASTA SALAD

175 g/6 oz dried pasta
  shells
900 ml/1½ pints boiling
  water
1 tablespoon oil
salt and freshly ground
  black pepper
150 ml/¼ pint
  mayonnaise
2 tablespoons single
  cream
2 teaspoons mild curry
  powder
225 g/8 oz cooked
  chicken, skinned and
  chopped into bite-size
  pieces
2 sticks celery, scrubbed
  and chopped
lettuce leaves to serve

Place the pasta in a bowl with the water, oil and a pinch of salt. Cover and cook for 12-14 minutes, stirring once. Leave to stand for 5-10 minutes, until tender. Drain and cool under running water.

Meanwhile, mix the mayonnaise with the cream, curry powder and salt and pepper to taste, blending well.

Add the chicken, celery and cool, drained pasta shells to the dressing and toss gently to coat.

Line a serving dish with lettuce leaves. Top with the curried chicken pasta salad to serve.

Serves: 4
Power setting: FULL
Preparation time: 20 minutes
Cooking time: 17-24 minutes

TAGLIATELLE WITH MUSHROOM SAUCE

50 g/2 oz butter
225 g/8 oz bacon, rinded and chopped
100 g/4 oz mushrooms, wiped and sliced
25 g/1 oz plain flour
300 ml/½ pint milk
salt and freshly ground black pepper
350 g/12 oz green tagliatelle
600 ml/1 pint boiling water
1 tablespoon oil

Place half the butter in a bowl and cook for ½ minute to melt. Add the bacon, cover and cook for 6 minutes, stirring once. Remove with a slotted spoon and drain on absorbent kitchen paper.

Add the mushrooms to the bacon juices, blending well. Cover and cook for 2 minutes.

Place the remaining butter in a bowl and cook for ½ minute to melt. Add the flour, blending well. Gradually add the milk and cook for 3½-4 minutes, stirring every 1 minute until smooth and thickened. Stir in the bacon, mushrooms with their juice and salt and pepper to taste, blending well.

Place the tagliatelle in a bowl with the water and oil. Cover and cook for 6 minutes. Leave to stand, covered, for 3 minutes.

Drain thoroughly and place in a heated serving dish.

Meanwhile, reheat the sauce for 2 minutes, stirring once. Spoon over the tagliatelle and serve at once.

Serves: 4
Power setting: FULL
Preparation time: 15-20 minutes
Cooking time: 21½-22 minutes

MUESLI

1 tablespoon safflower oil
2 tablespoons clear honey
100 g/4 oz rolled oats
2 tablespoons wheatgerm
2 teaspoons bran
25 g/1 oz flaked almonds
25 g/1 oz hazelnuts, chopped
25 g/1 oz dried pears, chopped
25 g/1 oz dried apricots, chopped
25 g/1 oz raisins

Place the oil and honey in a large bowl and cook for ½ minute. Add the oats, wheatgerm, bran and almonds, blending well.

Spread on to a large plate or microwave baking tray and cook for 3 minutes, stirring every ½ minute so that the muesli browns evenly.

Add the hazelnuts, pears, apricots and raisins, blending well. Cover and leave to stand for 1 minute.

Serve while still warm with plain yogurt.

Serves: 6-8
Power setting: FULL
Preparation time: 10 minutes
Cooking time: 4½ minutes

PORRIDGE

Porridge oats are generally available in two varieties – the traditional type and the quick-cook type. They should both be cooked in a mixture of half milk and half water, or all water, for good results in the microwave. Recipes using all milk tend to boil over and spoil the appearance and taste of the dish. Always cook porridge in a deep bowl: a deep individual cereal bowl is ideal for cooking a single portion so that you can cook and serve in one simple operation. Cover three-quarters of the bowl with cling film as this will enable you to stir the cereal easily without removing its cover. The times given in the table are a basic guideline; for a softer porridge leave to stand, covered, for 2-3 minutes before serving.

Number of servings	Water	Salt	Cereal	Cooking time in minutes on FULL POWER	Cooking time in minutes on LOW POWER
Traditional oatmeal/slow-cook oatmeal					
1	175 ml/6 fl oz	¼ teaspoon	30 g/1¼ oz	3-5	10
2	350 ml/12 fl oz	½ teaspoon	65 g/2½ oz	6-7	10
4	750 ml/1¼ pints	¾ teaspoon	125 g/4½ oz	8-9	12
Quick-cook oatmeal					
1	175 ml/6 fl oz	¼ teaspoon	30 g/1¼ oz	1-2	5
2	350 ml/12 fl oz	½ teaspoon	65 g/2½ oz	2-3	5
4	750 ml/1¼ pints	¾ teaspoon	125 g/4½ oz	5-6	7-8

Sauces and Stuffings

Without doubt, a sauce or stuffing can lift the humblest cut of meat, piece of fish or variety of vegetable from the pauper to the luxury class.
Often considered the time-extravagant area of cookery, sauces and stuffings will quickly become regular features on the menus of microwave cooks because they are so simple and quick to prepare.
An instant savoury sauce in a jug in just 4-6 minutes, a hot bubbly ready-to-pour dessert topping in under 3 minutes and a satisfying stuffing ready to use in under 5 minutes are all possible when cooked in the microwave oven.

BASIC WHITE POURING SAUCE

25 g/1 oz butter
25 g/1 oz plain flour
300 ml/½ pint milk
salt and freshly ground
    black or white pepper

Place the butter in a large heatproof jug and cook for ½ minute to melt. Add the flour, blending well. Gradually add the milk and salt and pepper to taste.

Cook for 3½-4 minutes, stirring every 1 minute until smooth and thickened. Use as required.

Variations
BASIC WHITE COATING SAUCE: Prepare as above but use 50 g/2 oz butter, 50 g/2 oz plain flour.
CHEESE SAUCE: Prepare as above but stir 75 g/3 oz grated cheese and 1 teaspoon made mustard into the finished sauce.
MUSHROOM SAUCE: Prepare as above but stir 50-100 g/2-4 oz lightly cooked and thinly sliced mushrooms into the finished sauce.
PARSLEY SAUCE: Prepare as above but stir 1-2 tablespoons chopped fresh parsley into the finished sauce.
ONION SAUCE: Prepare as above but stir 1 large chopped and cooked onion into the finished sauce.
SWEET WHITE SAUCE: Prepare as above but omit the salt and pepper. Stir sugar to taste into the finished sauce.

To freeze
Cool quickly and place in a rigid container. Cover, seal, label and freeze for up to 3 months.

Makes: 300 ml/½ pint
Power setting: FULL
Preparation time: 5 minutes
Cooking time: 4-4½ minutes
Suitable for freezing

BREAD SAUCE

1 onion, peeled and
    studded with 4 cloves
300 ml/½ pint milk
½ small bay leaf
6 white peppercorns
1 small blade of mace or
    pinch of ground
    nutmeg
65 g/2½ oz fresh white
    breadcrumbs
15 g/½ oz butter
2 tablespoons single
    cream
salt and black pepper

Place the onion, milk, bay leaf, peppercorns, mace or nutmeg in a bowl. Cook, uncovered, for 4 minutes. Cover and leave to stand for 10 minutes.

Strain the milk into a bowl and stir in the breadcrumbs. Cook, uncovered, for 2 minutes.

Add the butter, cream and salt and pepper to taste, blending well. Cook for 1 minute, stirring once.

Serve hot with poultry or game.

Makes: 450 ml/¾ pint
Power setting: FULL
Preparation time: 10 minutes
Cooking time: 17 minutes

BÉCHAMEL SAUCE

1 small onion, peeled
1 carrot, peeled and sliced
1 bay leaf
blade of mace
12 peppercorns
few sprigs of parsley
300 ml/½ pint milk
25 g/1 oz butter
25 g/1 oz plain flour
salt and freshly ground
    black pepper

Place the onion, carrot, bay leaf, mace, peppercorns, parsley and milk in a large jug. Cook on DEFROST POWER for 10-11 minutes until hot. Strain and discard flavourings.

Place the butter in another jug and cook on FULL POWER for 1 minute to melt. Stir in the flour and salt and pepper to taste.

Gradually add the strained milk, blending well. Cook on FULL POWER for 1½-2 minutes until smooth and thickened, stirring once. Use as required.

Variations

MORNAY SAUCE: Prepare and cook as above but add 1 egg yolk mixed with 2 tablespoons double cream and 50 g/2 oz grated cheese to the hot sauce. Whisk until the cheese melts and the sauce is smooth.
CHAUD-FROID SAUCE: Prepare and cook as above. Dissolve 1 tablespoon powdered gelatine in 150 ml/¼ pint hot water. Cook on FULL POWER for 1 minute then stir into the sauce, blending well. Use when cold.

To freeze
Cool quickly and pack in a rigid container. Cover, seal, label and freeze for up to 3 months.

Makes: 300 ml/½ pint
Power settings: DEFROST, FULL
Preparation time: 5 minutes
Cooking time: 12½-14 minutes
Suitable for freezing

HOLLANDAISE SAUCE

50 g/2 oz butter
50 g/2 oz savoury butter
    with black pepper
2 egg yolks
2 tablespoons wine
    vinegar or lemon juice

Place the butter and savoury butter in a bowl. Cook for 1½ minutes or until melted.

Gradually whisk in the egg yolks and vinegar or lemon juice, blending well. Cook for ½ minute, whisking 3 times to prevent curdling.

Whisk for a further ½ minute then pour into a warmed sauceboat to serve.

Serve hot with poached fish, especially salmon, globe artichokes or other cooked vegetables.

Serves: 4
Power setting: FULL
Preparation time: 5-10 minutes
Cooking time: 2 minutes

Illustrated on pp. 115 and 134

BÉARNAISE SAUCE

50 g/2 oz butter
50 g/2 oz savoury butter
    with herbs and garlic
2 egg yolks
2 tablespoons tarragon
    vinegar

Place the butter and savoury butter in a bowl. Cook for 1½ minutes or until melted.

Gradually whisk in the egg yolks and vinegar, blending well. Cook for ½ minute, whisking 3 times to prevent curdling.

Whisk for a further ½ minute then pour into a warmed sauceboat to serve.

Serve with steaks, fish, poached eggs on toast or cooked green vegetables.

Serves: 4
Power setting: FULL
Preparation time: 5-10 minutes
Cooking time: 2 minutes

CURRY SAUCE

50 g/2 oz savoury butter
  with black pepper
1 onion, peeled and
  chopped
1 apple, peeled cored and
  chopped
1 tablespoon ground
  coriander
½ teaspoon ground
  cumin
½ teaspoon ground
  ginger
25 g/1 oz sultanas
2 tablespoons plain flour
2 teaspoons curry powder
pinch of salt
450 ml/¾ pint chicken
  stock
1 teaspoon black treacle

Place the butter, onion, apple, coriander, cumin, ginger and sultanas in a bowl. Cover loosely with cling film and cook for 10 minutes, stirring once.

Add the flour, curry powder and salt, blending well. Gradually add the stock and treacle. Re-cover and cook for 10 minutes, stirring once. Use as required.

To freeze

Cool quickly and place in a rigid container. Cover, seal, label and freeze for up to 1 month.

Serves: 4
Power setting: FULL
Preparation time: 10 minutes
Cooking time: 20 minutes
Suitable for freezing

GRAVY

2 tablespoons meat juices
  or drippings
1-2 tablespoons plain
  flour
300 ml/½ pint hot beef or
  chicken stock
salt and freshly ground
  black pepper

Place the meat juices or drippings in a bowl. Stir in the flour, depending upon thickness required, blending well. Cook for 3 minutes, stirring once.

Gradually add the stock, blending well. Cook for 2-3 minutes, stirring every 1 minute until smooth and thickened. Season to taste with salt and pepper. Pour into a warmed sauceboat to serve.

Makes: 300 ml/½ pint
Power setting: FULL
Preparation time: 5 minutes
Cooking time: 5-6 minutes

TOMATO SAUCE

2 rashers streaky bacon,
  rinded and chopped
1 large carrot, peeled and
  sliced
1 large onion, peeled and
  chopped
2 sticks celery, scrubbed
  and sliced
1 × 397 g (14 oz) can
  peeled tomatoes
2 tablespoons tomato
  purée
½ teaspoon dried basil
1 tablespoon chopped
  fresh parsley
salt and black pepper

Place the bacon in a dish and cook for 2 minutes, stirring once. Add the carrot, onion and celery, blending well. Cover and cook for 6 minutes, stirring once.

Add the tomatoes and their juice, tomato purée, basil, parsley and salt and pepper to taste, blending well. Cover and cook for 6 minutes, stirring once.

Serve chunky, or purée in a blender until smooth. Use as required.

To freeze

Cool quickly and place in a rigid container. Cover, seal, label and freeze for up to 3 months.

Serves: 4
Power setting: FULL
Preparation time: 10-15 minutes
Cooking time: 14 minutes
Suitable for freezing

APPLE SAUCE

450 g/1 lb cooking apples,
  peeled, cored and
  sliced
15 g/½ oz butter
1 teaspoon lemon juice
½-1 tablespoon caster
  sugar
1 tablespoon water

Place the apples, butter, lemon juice, sugar to taste and water in a bowl. Cover and cook for 6-8 minutes until the apple is soft.

Rub through a fine nylon sieve, beat with a spoon until smooth, or purée in a blender.

Serve hot with pork, duck, goose or game birds.

To freeze
Cool quickly and place in a rigid container. Cover, seal, label and freeze for up to 6 months.

Makes: 300 ml/½ pint
Power setting: FULL
Preparation time: 10 minutes
Cooking time: 6-8 minutes
Suitable for freezing

SWEET AND SOUR SAUCE

1 × 400 g (14 oz) can
  pineapple pieces in
  natural juice
150 ml/¼ pint chicken
  stock
1½ tablespoons brown
  sugar
3 tablespoons wine
  vinegar
2 teaspoons soy sauce
1 teaspoon tomato
  ketchup
pinch of 5 spice powder
1½ tablespoons
  cornflour
50 g/2 oz spring onions,
  trimmed and chopped
1 small red pepper, cored,
  seeded and chopped
1 small green pepper,
  cored, seeded and
  chopped

Drain the juice from the pineapple into a bowl. Add the stock, sugar, vinegar, soy sauce, ketchup, 5 spice powder and cornflour, blending well. Cook for 5-7 minutes, stirring 3 times, until clear and thickened.

Add the pineapple pieces, spring onions and peppers, blending well. Cook for 2 minutes, stirring once. Cover and leave to stand for 5 minutes.

Serve hot with pork, chicken or shellfish.

Makes: 750 ml/1¼ pints
Power setting: FULL
Preparation time: 10 minutes
Cooking time: 12-14 minutes

CUMBERLAND SAUCE

1 orange
1 lemon
3 tablespoons water
4 tablespoons redcurrant
  jelly
4 tablespoons port wine
½ teaspoon mustard
  powder
½ teaspoon ground
  ginger
1 teaspoon arrowroot
  powder

Thinly pare the rinds from the orange and lemon and cut into very thin strips. Squeeze the juice from the orange and lemon and reserve.

Place the rinds in a bowl with 2 tablespoons of the water. Cover and cook for 2 minutes, then drain thoroughly.

Add the redcurrant jelly, port, mustard, ginger and orange and lemon juice, blending well. Cover and cook for 2½ minutes, stirring once.

Blend the arrowroot with the remaining water and stir into the sauce, blending well. Cook for 1 minute, stirring once.

Serve warm or cold with meats and pâtés.

Serves: 4
Power setting: FULL
Preparation time: 10-15 minutes
Cooking time: 5½ minutes

WHITE WINE SAUCE

25 g/1 oz butter
25 g/1 oz plain flour
150 ml/¼ pint white wine
150 ml/¼ pint milk
salt and freshly ground
    black pepper

Place the butter in a bowl and cook for 1 minute. Stir in the flour, blending well. Cook for 1 minute.

Gradually add the wine and milk, blending well. Season to taste with salt and pepper. Cook for 3-4 minutes, stirring every 1 minute until smooth and thickened. Use as required.

To freeze
Cool quickly and pack in a rigid container. Cover, seal, label and freeze for up to 3 months.

Makes: 300 ml/½ pint
Power setting: FULL
Preparation time: 5 minutes
Cooking time: 5-6 minutes
Suitable for freezing

CRANBERRY WINE SAUCE

450 g/1 lb fresh
    cranberries, sorted
6 tablespoons port wine
grated rind of 1 small
    orange
grated rind of ½ small
    lemon
350 g/12 oz granulated
    sugar

Place the cranberries, wine, orange rind, lemon rind and sugar in a bowl, blending well. Cover and cook for 18-20 minutes, stirring every 6 minutes, until pulpy.

Serve warm or cold with roast game or poultry.

Makes: 750-900 ml/1¼-1½ pints
Power setting: FULL
Preparation time: 5-10 minutes
Cooking time: 18-20 minutes

GREEN PEPPERCORN SAUCE

1 tablespoon juices or
    dripping from roast
    poultry or game
1 small onion, peeled and
    finely chopped
50 ml/2 fl oz
    concentrated dry white
    cooking wine
300 ml/½ pint well-
    seasoned poultry or
    game stock
1 tablespoon canned or
    bottled green
    peppercorns, drained
    and lightly crushed
1 tablespoon cornflour
1 tablespoon cold
    water
2-3 tablespoons double
    cream
salt and freshly ground
    black pepper

Place the juices or dripping in a bowl with the onion. Cover and cook for 2 minutes, stirring once.

Add the wine, stock and peppercorns, blending well. Cover and cook for 2½ minutes.

Meanwhile, blend the cornflour with the water. Stir into the peppercorn mixture, blending well. Cook for 1 minute, stirring twice until smooth and thickened.

Stir in the cream and salt and pepper to taste, blending well.

Serve hot with roast chicken, duck or game birds.

Serves: 4
Power setting: FULL
Preparation time: 5-10 minutes
Cooking time: 5½ minutes

144

PIZZAIOLA SAUCE

1 tablespoon oil
2 onions, peeled and very
    finely chopped or
    minced
2 garlic cloves, peeled and
    crushed
2 small green peppers,
    cored, seeded and
    sliced
50 g/2 oz mushrooms,
    wiped and sliced
1 × 397 g (14 oz) can
    peeled tomatoes
2 teaspoons dried
    marjoram or oregano
dash of chilli sauce
salt and freshly ground
    black pepper

Place the oil in a bowl and cook for 1 minute. Add the onion, garlic and peppers, blending well. Cover and cook for 5 minutes, stirring once.

Add the mushrooms, tomatoes and their juice, herbs, chilli sauce and salt and pepper to taste, blending well. Cover and cook for 5 minutes, stirring once.

Serve hot with hamburgers, chops and chicken pieces.

To freeze
Cool quickly and place in a rigid container. Cover, seal, label and freeze for up to 1 month.

Serves: 4
Power setting: FULL
Preparation time: 10-15 minutes
Cooking time: 10 minutes
Suitable for freezing

BUTTERSCOTCH SAUCE

250 g/9 oz light brown
    sugar
40 g/1½ oz butter
6 tablespoons evaporated
    milk

Place the sugar and butter in a large heat-proof jug. Cook for 1 minute.

Add the evaporated milk, blending well. Cook for 1¼ minutes, stirring once.

Serve at once.

Makes: 300 ml/½ pint
Power setting: FULL
Preparation time: 5 minutes
Cooking time: 2¼ minutes

HOT FUDGE SAUCE

25 g/1 oz plain chocolate
15 g/½ oz butter
2 tablespoons milk
100 g/4 oz soft brown
    sugar
1 tablespoon golden
    syrup

Break the chocolate into small pieces and place in a bowl with the butter. Cook for 1 minute, stirring once.

Add the milk, sugar and golden syrup, blending well. Cook for 3-4 minutes, stirring every 1 minute.

Serve hot over ice cream or mousse.

Serves: 2
Power setting: FULL
Preparation time: 4-5 minutes
Cooking time: 4-5 minutes

QUICK CUSTARD SAUCE

2 tablespoons custard
    powder
1-2 tablespoons sugar
600 ml/1 pint milk

Place the custard powder and sugar to taste in a bowl. Mix with about 2 tablespoons of the milk to make a smooth paste. Gradually add the rest of the milk, blending well.

Cook for 6 minutes, stirring the mixture every 2 minutes, until smooth and thickened.

Variation
BRANDY SAUCE: Prepare as above but use cornflour instead of the custard powder. When the sauce is cooked, stir in 2 tablespoons brandy, blending well.

Makes: 600 ml/1 pint
Power setting: FULL
Preparation time: 5 minutes
Cooking time: 6 minutes

CHOCOLATE MINT SAUCE

75 g/3 oz plain
   unsweetened chocolate
50 ml/2 fl oz water
200 g/7 oz sugar
150 g/5 oz golden syrup
pinch of salt
75 ml/3 fl oz single cream
   or evaporated milk
⅛ teaspoon peppermint
   essence

Place the chocolate and water in a large heatproof bowl. Cook for ¾ minute, stirring once.

Add the sugar, syrup and salt, blending well. Cook, uncovered, for 9 minutes, stirring every 1 minute, or until a preserving thermometer reaches 115°C/240°F or a small drop of the mixture forms a soft ball when dropped into a glass of cold water.

Gradually add the cream or milk and peppermint essence, blending well. Use as required.

Makes: 450 ml/¾ pint
Power setting: FULL
Preparation time: 10-15 minutes
Cooking time: 9¾ minutes

MOCK GOOSE STUFFING

15 g/½ oz butter
1 small onion, peeled and
   chopped
100 g/4 oz fresh white
   breadcrumbs
225 g/8 oz cooking
   apples, peeled, cored
   and chopped
75 g/3 oz prunes, stoned
   and sliced
¼ teaspoon ground ginger
salt and freshly ground
   black pepper
1 egg, beaten

Place the butter in a bowl with the onion. Cover and cook for 2 minutes, stirring once.

Add the breadcrumbs, apple, prunes, ginger and salt and pepper to taste, blending well. Bind together with the beaten egg. Use as required.

Makes: enough to stuff a boned leg of lamb
Power setting: FULL
Preparation time: 10-15 minutes
Cooking time: 2 minutes

CHESTNUT STUFFING

50 g/2 oz butter
1 onion, peeled and finely
   chopped
1 turkey heart, chopped
1 turkey liver, chopped
175 g/6 oz mushrooms,
   wiped and sliced
50 g/2 oz liver pâté
225 g/8 oz chestnut purée
1 stick celery, chopped
100 g/4 oz smoked
   bacon, rinded and
   chopped
1 tablespoon chopped
   fresh parsley
salt and black pepper
25-50 g/1-2 oz soft white
   breadcrumbs

Place the butter in a large bowl and cook for ½ minute to melt. Add the onion, turkey heart, turkey liver and mushrooms, blending well. Cover and cook for 3 minutes, stirring once.

Add the liver pâté, chestnut purée, celery, bacon, parsley and salt and pepper to taste, blending well. Add sufficient breadcrumbs to bind the stuffing ingredients together. Use as required.

Makes: enough to stuff a large turkey
Power setting: FULL
Preparation time: 10-15 minutes
Cooking time: 3½ minutes

FESTIVE STUFFING

450 g/1 lb sausagemeat

100 g/4 oz cooked ham, chopped

1 onion, peeled and grated

1 apple, peeled, cored and grated

1 teaspoon dried mixed herbs

25 g/1 oz white breadcrumbs

salt and freshly ground black pepper

watercress sprigs to garnish

For the stuffing, mix the sausagemeat with the ham, onion, apple, herbs, breadcrumbs and salt and pepper to taste, blending well.

Use to stuff the neck end of the turkey, securing with wooden cocktail sticks.

Makes: enough to stuff 1 × 3.5 kg (8 lb) turkey
Power settings: FULL, MEDIUM
Preparation time: 20 minutes

PEANUT STUFFING

40 g/1½ oz butter

1 small onion, peeled and finely chopped

50 g/2 oz salted peanuts, chopped

½ teaspoon dried sage

50 g/2 oz fresh white breadcrumbs

1 cooking apple, peeled, cored and sliced

2 teaspoons chopped fresh parsley

1 tablespoon water

freshly ground black pepper

lemon juice

Place the butter in a large bowl. Cook for 1 minute to melt. Add the onion and peanuts, blending well. Cook for 2½ minutes, stirring once.

Add the sage, breadcrumbs, apple, parsley and water, blending well. Cover and cook for 5 minutes, stirring once.

Season to taste with pepper and lemon juice. Use as required.

Serves: 5-6
Power setting: FULL
Preparation time: 15 minutes
Cooking time: 8½ minutes

TURKEY STUFFING

4 rashers back bacon, rinded and chopped

225 g/8 oz sausagemeat

4 tablespoons chestnut purée

25 ml/1 fl oz pear juice

6 cooked prunes, stoned and chopped

2 canned pear halves, chopped

1 teaspoon chopped fresh parsley

salt and black pepper

Place the bacon in a bowl and cook for 1½ minutes, stirring once. Drain on absorbent kitchen paper.

Mix the bacon with the sausagemeat, chestnut purée and pear juice, blending well. Carefully fold in the prunes, pear, parsley and salt and pepper to taste. Use as required.

To freeze
Place in a rigid container, cover, seal, label and freeze for up to 1 month.

Makes: enough to stuff the neck end of 1 × 3.5 kg (8 lb) turkey
Power setting: FULL
Preparation time: 10-15 minutes
Cooking time: 1½ minutes
Suitable for freezing

Puddings and Desserts

If you're sweet-toothed, a chocoholic or fruit fan then you'll be delighted and surprised at the vast array of puddings and desserts that can be cooked in the microwave.
Silky smooth mousses and ice creams, juicy baked fruits and compôtes, light and airy soufflés and fools, or mouth-watering and hearty sponge or suet puddings and crumbles all feature on the microwave menu.

APRICOT UPSIDE-DOWN PUDDING

25 g/1 oz demerara sugar
1 × 385 g (13½ oz) can apricot halves, drained
4 glacé cherries, halved
2 tablespoons frozen concentrated orange juice, thawed
100 g/4 oz soft margarine
100 g/4 oz caster sugar
2 eggs, beaten
1 teaspoon almond essence
100 g/4 oz self-raisisng flour
1 spoon baking powder
2 tablespoons milk

Line a 1.75 litre (3 pint) soufflé dish with cling film.

Sprinkle the base with demerara sugar and top with the apricot halves and cherries, arranged attractively. Carefully spoon the orange juice over the top.

Cream the margarine and sugar until light and fluffy. Beat in the eggs and almond essence. Fold in the flour and baking powder with a metal spoon and stir in the milk.

Spoon the sponge mixture over the prepared base. Loosely cover with cling film and cook for 6½-7 minutes, turning the dish every 1½ minutes.

To serve, invert the pudding on to a warmed serving dish. Serve cut into wedges with custard or single cream.

To freeze
Cool quickly, pack in a rigid container. Cover, seal, label and freeze for up to 6 months.

Serves: 6
Power setting: FULL
Preparation time: 20 minutes
Cooking time: 6½-7 minutes
Suitable for freezing

STEAMED GOLDEN SYRUP PUDDING

Sauce:
3 teaspoons custard powder
150 ml/¼ pint water
grated rind and juice of ½ lemon
4 tablespoons golden syrup
Pudding:
100 g/4 oz self-raising flour
50 g/2 oz shredded suet
25 g/1 oz caster sugar
25 g/1 oz soft brown sugar
1 teaspoon raising agent
1 egg
90 ml/3 fl oz milk
1 teaspoon vanilla essence

To make the sauce, mix the custard powder and water to a smooth paste in a 600 ml/1 pint bowl. Add the lemon rind, juice and golden syrup, blending well. Cook for 2 minutes, stirring once.

Grease a 900 ml (1½ pint) pudding basin and place half of the sauce in the base.

Mix the flour with the suet, sugars and raising agent, blending well. Beat in the egg, milk and vanilla essence. Spoon into the bowl on top of the sauce mixture.

Cover loosely with cling film and cook for 4½ minutes, turning the bowl once. Leave to stand for 2 minutes.

To serve, invert the pudding on to a warmed serving plate. Cut into wedges to serve with the remainder of the sauce.

Serves: 4
Power setting: FULL
Preparation time: 10 minutes
Cooking time: 8½ minutes

PINEAPPLE RICE PUDDING

50 g/2 oz round-grain
  pudding rice
¼ teaspoon ground
  nutmeg
7 g/¼ oz butter
900 ml/1½ pints boiling
  water
25 g/1 oz caster sugar
1 × 170 g (6 oz) can
  evaporated milk
1 × 396 g (13 oz) can
  pineapple tidbits in
  natural juice

Place the rice, nutmeg, butter and water in a 900 ml (1½ pint) oval pie dish. Stir gently to mix and half cover with cling film. Cook for 20 minutes, stirring occasionally.

Stir in the sugar and evaporated milk and cook for 9 minutes or until the pudding is creamy and the rice is tender, stirring once. Cover completely and leave to stand for 5 minutes.

Stir in the pineapple and its juice, blending well. Cook for a further 2 minutes. Serve at once.

Serves: 4
Power setting: FULL
Preparation time: 5 minutes
Cooking time: 36 minutes

MELBA CHEESECAKE PIE

Base;
50 g/2 oz butter
100 g/4 oz digestive
  biscuits, crushed
25 g/1 oz sugar
Filling:
1 × 425 g (15 oz) can
  sliced peaches, drained
225 g/8 oz cream cheese
75 g/3 oz sugar
150 ml/¼ pint soured
  cream
1 egg, beaten
½ teaspoon almond
  essence
3-4 tablespoons raspberry
  jam or raspberry pie
  filling

To make the base, place the butter in a bowl and cook on FULL POWER for 1 minute to melt. Stir in the biscuit crumbs and sugar, blending well. Press on to the bottom and sides of a 23 cm (9 inch) pie plate. Cook on FULL POWER for 1½-2 minutes.

Arrange the drained peaches on the pie crust.

Place the cream cheese in a bowl and cook on MEDIUM POWER for 1 minute. Add the sugar, soured cream, egg and almond essence, blending well. Spoon over the peaches evenly.

Cook on MEDIUM POWER for 8-10 minutes or until just set, turning the dish twice. Chill lightly to set.

Spoon or spread the jam or pie filling over the cheesecake. Serve lightly chilled.

Serves: 4-6
Power settings: FULL, MEDIUM
Preparation time: 25 minutes, plus chilling
Cooking time: 11½-14 minutes

HOT SWISS TRIFLE

1 jam Swiss roll
1 × 410 g (14 oz) can fruit
  cocktail, drained
40 g/1½ oz custard
  powder
40 g/1½ oz sugar
450 ml/¾ pint milk
1 egg, separated
50 g/2 oz caster sugar

Slice the Swiss roll and use to line a 900 ml (1½ pint) serving dish. Spoon the fruit cocktail into the base of the dish over the Swiss roll.

Mix the custard powder with the sugar and a little of the milk to a smooth paste. Add the egg yolk and remaining milk, blending well. Cook for 5 minutes, stirring three times. Pour over the fruit mixture.

Whisk the egg white until it stands in stiff peaks. Gradually whisk in the caster sugar until thick and glossy. Swirl over the trifle mixture and cook for 1½ minutes.

Brown under a preheated hot grill if liked. Serve at once.

Serves: 4
Power setting: FULL
Preparation time: 10 minutes
Cooking time: 6½ minutes

GUIDE TO COOKING FRUIT

Fruit – type and quantity	Preparation	Cooking time in minutes on FULL POWER
450 g/1 lb apricots	Stone and wash, then sprinkle with 100 g/ 4 oz sugar.	6-8
450 g/1 lb cooking apples	Peel, core and slice, then sprinkle with 100 g/ 4 oz sugar.	6-8
450 g/1 lb gooseberries	Top and tail, then sprinkle with 100 g/ 4 oz sugar.	4
4 medium-sized peaches	Stone and wash, then sprinkle with 100 g/ 4 oz sugar.	4-5
6 medium-sized pears	Peel, halve and core. Dissolve 75 g/3 oz sugar in a little water and pour over the pears.	8-10
450 g/1 lb plums, cherries, damsons or greengages	Stone and wash. Sprinkle with 100 g/ 4 oz sugar and the grated rind of ½ lemon.	4-5
450 g/1 lb soft berry fruits	Top and tail or hull. Wash and add 100 g/ 4 oz sugar.	3-5
450 g/1 lb rhubarb	Trim and cut into short lengths. Add 100 g/4 oz sugar and the grated rind of 1 lemon.	8-10

BAKED STUFFED BRAMLEYS

4 medium Bramley apples, cored, total weight about 900 g/2 lb
50 g/2 oz sultanas
50 g/2 oz chopped mixed peel
25 g/1 oz walnuts, chopped
4 tablespoons clear honey

Slit the skin around the centre of the apples and place in a cooking dish.

Mix the sultanas with the peel, walnuts and enough honey to bind. Fill the centre of the apples with this mixture and spoon the remaining honey over.

Cover loosely with buttered grease-proof paper and cook for 6-8 minutes, or until the apples are just cooked but not fallen. Leave to stand, covered, for 5 minutes.

Serve hot with cream.

Serves: 4
Power setting: FULL
Preparation time: 10 minutes
Cooking time: 11-13 minutes

FESTIVE PUDDING

4 tablespoons mincemeat
1 cooking apple, peeled, cored and chopped
40 g/1½ oz custard powder
40 g/1½ oz sugar
450 ml/¾ pint milk
1 egg, separated
50 g/2 oz caster sugar
25 g/1 oz flaked almonds

Mix the mincemeat with the apple, blending well.

Mix the custard powder with the sugar and a little of the milk. Stir in the beaten egg yolk and the remaining milk, whisking well to blend. Cook on FULL POWER for 5 minutes, stirring three times.

Layer the mincemeat mixture and custard in a 1.4 litres (2½ pint) serving dish, finishing with a layer of the custard.

Whisk the egg white until it stands in stiff peaks. Fold in the caster sugar with a metal spoon. Spread the meringue over the custard and sprinkle with the flaked almonds. Cook on MEDIUM POWER for 3 minutes.

Brown under a preheated hot grill if liked. Serve at once.

Serves: 4
Power settings: FULL, MEDIUM
Preparation time: 10 minutes
Cooking time: 8 minutes

GOOSEBERRY SOUFFLÉ (p.167) AND RASPBERRY MOUSSE (p.160)   151

PINEAPPLE STREUSEL (p.159)

FRUITY SPONGE PUDDING

100 g/4 oz soft margarine
100 g/4 oz soft light
 brown sugar
2 eggs, lightly beaten
100 g/4 oz self-raising
 flour
4 tablespoons raisins or
 sultanas

Grease a 900 ml (1½ pint) pudding basin.
 Cream the margarine and sugar until light and fluffy. Gradually beat in the eggs, adding 1 tablespoon of flour with each addition. Fold in the remaining flour and fruit with a metal spoon.
 Spoon the mixture into the prepared basin and cover loosely with cling film. Cook for 4-5 minutes, or until the pudding is dry and spongy on top. Leave to stand for 5 minutes.
 To serve, invert the pudding on to a warmed serving dish. Serve hot, cut into wedges, with cream or custard.

To freeze
Cover with foil, seal, label and freeze for up to 6 months.

Serves: 4
Power setting: FULL
Preparation time: 10 minutes
Cooking time: 9-10 minutes
Suitable for freezing

BREAD AND BUTTER PUDDING

6 large slices white or
 brown bread, crusts
 removed
75 g/3 oz butter
50 g/2 oz sultanas
3 eggs
40 g/1½ oz caster sugar
450 ml/¾ pint milk
few drops of vanilla
 essence

Generously spread the bread slices with the butter, then cut each slice in half diagonally. Arrange the bread in layers in a 900 ml (1½ pint) pie dish, sprinkling sultanas between each layer.
 Beat the eggs with the sugar. Stir in the milk and vanilla essence, blending well. Pour over the bread slices.
 Stand the pie dish in a shallow water bath in the microwave. Cook for 5 minutes. Leave to stand for 5 minutes. Turn the dish and cook for a further 5 minutes, or until the custard sets in the centre.
 Brown and crisp under a preheated hot grill if liked. Cut into wedges to serve.

Serves: 4
Power setting: FULL
Preparation time: 10 minutes
Cooking time: 15 minutes

RHUBARB AND GINGER CRUMBLE

900 g/2 lb rhubarb,
 chopped
1 cooking apple, peeled,
 cored and chopped
2 teaspoons ground
 ginger
50 g/2 oz brown sugar
25 g/1 oz crystallised
 ginger, chopped
Topping:
100 g/4 oz butter
175 g/6 oz wholemeal
 flour
60 g/2½ oz brown sugar

Mix the rhubarb with the apple, ground ginger, sugar and crystallised ginger in a cooking dish.
 Rub the butter into the flour until the mixture resembles fine breadcrumbs. Stir in the sugar, blending well. Carefully spoon on top of the fruit.
 Cook for 11-13 minutes, turning the dish three times. Brown under a preheated hot grill if liked.
 Serve hot with cream or custard.

To freeze
Cool quickly, cover, seal, label and freeze for up to 3 months.

Serves: 4
Power setting: FULL
Preparation time: 20 minutes
Cooking time: 11-13 minutes
Suitable for freezing

153

MARIE LOUISE CUPS

100 g/4 oz plain
chocolate
50 g/2 oz chocolate
sponge cake, crumbled
75 g/3 oz prepared soft
fruit (raspberries,
strawberries or cherries,
for example)
2-3 tablespoons sherry
300 ml/½ pint double
cream
chocolate curls to
decorate

Break the chocolate into pieces and place in a bowl. Cook for 1½-2 minutes, stirring twice, until melted. Use the melted chocolate to coat the insides of 7 paper baking bun cases, then turn the cases upside down so that the chocolate edges remain thicker than the base. Chill until set, about 1-2 hours.

Mix the sponge cake with the chopped or sliced fruit and enough sherry to moisten.

Carefully peel away the paper cases from the chocolate. Fill each chocolate cup with an equal quantity of the sponge mixture.

Whip the cream until it stands in soft peaks. Spoon into a piping bag fitted with a large star nozzle and pipe generously, in swirls, on top of the sponge mixture.

Decorate with chocolate curls. Serve lightly chilled.

Serves: 7
Power setting: FULL
Preparation time: 20 minutes, plus chilling
Cooking time: 1½-2 minutes

HOT BRAZIL SUNDAES

7 g/¼ oz butter
25 g/1 oz Brazil or
cashew nuts, coarsely
chopped
4 tablespoons single
cream
25 g/1 oz brown sugar
1 banana, peeled and
sliced
coffee ice cream to serve

Place the butter and nuts in a bowl. Cook for 1-1½ minutes until just golden. Add the cream and sugar, blending well. Cover and cook for ½-1 minute, until boiling, stirring twice.

Arrange the banana slices and scoops of coffee ice cream on two serving plates. Spoon over the hot sauce. Serve at once.

Serves: 2
Power setting: FULL
Preparation time: 10 minutes
Cooking time: 1½-2½ minutes

MARMALADE ROLY POLY

Pastry:
225 g/8 oz self-raising
flour
pinch of salt
100 g/4 oz shredded suet
150 ml/¼ pint cold water
Filling:
100 g/4 oz marmalade
1 teaspoon lemon juice
1 tablespoon raisins
Topping:
2 tablespoons caster
sugar
pinch of ground nutmeg
pinch of ground
cinnamon

Sift the flour and salt into a bowl. Stir in the suet, blending well. Add the cold water and mix to a soft dough. Roll out, on a lightly floured surface, to 23 cm (9 inch) square.

Mix the marmalade with the lemon juice and raisins in a small bowl. Cook for ½ minute. Spread evenly over the suet pastry square, leaving a 1 cm/½ inch border around the edge. Carefully roll up like a Swiss roll.

Place, seam side down, on a large piece of greaseproof paper and roll the greaseproof up loosely around the pastry roll, allowing plenty of space for the pudding to rise. Tie the ends of the paper with string or secure with elastic bands. Place on a large plate and loosely cover with cling film.

Cook for 8 minutes, turning the plate once, or until well risen and cooked

through. Test by inserting a skewer into the centre of the pudding – if it comes out clean of pastry dough it is cooked.

Mix the sugar with the nutmeg and cinnamon.

Remove all wrappings and place the roly poly on a warmed serving dish. Sprinkle with the sugar mixture. Serve hot with custard.

Serves: 6
Power setting: FULL
Preparation time: 20-25 minutes
Cooking time: 8½ minutes

PEPPERMINT MERINGUE WITH PEARS

275 g/10 oz icing sugar,
  sifted
1 egg white, lightly beaten
1 teaspoon peppermint
  essence
few drops of green food
  colouring (optional)
6 canned pear halves,
  well drained
300 ml/½ pint double
  cream
50 g/2 oz plain chocolate,
  melted
toasted flaked almonds to
  decorate

Mix the icing sugar with the egg white, peppermint essence and food colouring, if used, to form a soft dough. Knead lightly until smooth and shiny.

Pat the dough into a 15 cm (6 inch) circle and place on a round serving dish. Cook for 3½-4 minutes. Leave to cool.

When cool, top the meringue with the pear halves. Whip the cream until it stands in soft peaks and pipe or swirl over the meringue and pears.

Drizzle with the melted chocolate and sprinkle with the toasted almonds to decorate. Serve at once cut into wedges.

Serves: 6
Power setting: FULL
Preparation time: 25 minutes, plus cooling
Cooking time: 3½-4 minutes

MINCEMEAT TARTLETS NOËL

225 g/8 oz shortcrust
  pastry
flour to dust
275 g/10 oz mincemeat
75 g/3 oz butter
175 g/6 oz icing sugar,
  sifted
3-4 tablespoons brandy
grated lemon or orange
  rind

Roll out the pastry on a lightly floured surface until thin. Using a fluted cutter, cut into small circles, large enough to cover the base of about 16 teacups or ramekin dishes. Place a piece of greaseproof paper over the base of each inverted container, then mould the rolled-out pastry rounds over the top.

To cook, arrange in a circle on the base of the microwave, 4 at a time, and cook for 4-5 minutes. Leave to stand for 5 minutes before carefully removing the pastry from the dishes.

Place the mincemeat in a bowl and cook until hot and bubbly, about 3-4 minutes, stirring once. Spoon equal amounts of the mixture into the cooked tartlet cases. Leave until cool.

Meanwhile, cream the butter until pale and soft then gradually add the icing sugar, beating to keep smooth. Finally beat in the brandy to taste.

When the mincemeat tartlets are cool, top each with a swirl of the brandy butter and sprinkle with grated lemon or orange rind.

Serves: 16
Power setting: FULL
Preparation time: 30 minutes, plus cooling
Cooking time: 12-14 minutes

HOT COMPÔTE

450 g/1 lb mixed dried
  fruits (pineapple, pears,
  peaches for example)
250 ml/8 fl oz cold tea
200 ml/7 fl oz water
4 tablespoons clear honey
juice of ½ lemon
1 cinnamon stick
3-4 cloves
2 tablespoons brandy or
  Madeira

Mix the fruit with the tea, water, honey, lemon juice, cinnamon and cloves in a large deep dish. Leave to stand for 2 hours.

Cover loosely with cling film and cook for 12-14 minutes, or until the fruit is tender, stirring twice.

Remove and discard the cinnamon stick and cloves. Stir in the brandy or Madeira, blending well.

Serve hot or chilled with yogurt, soured cream, whipped cream or ice cream.

Serves: 4
Power setting: FULL
Preparation time: 10 minutes, plus soaking
Cooking time: 12-14 minutes

155

RUSSIAN PUDDING

450 g/1 lb cooking apples,
    peeled, cored and cut
    into chunks
75 g/3 oz demerara sugar
25 g/1 oz butter
grated rind and juice of 1
    lemon
40 g/1½ oz cornflour
600 ml/1 pint milk
25 g/1 oz sugar
1 egg, beaten
ground nutmeg to
    sprinkle

Place the apples in a pie dish with the sugar, butter, lemon rind and juice, blending well. Cover and cook on FULL POWER for 3 minutes, stirring once.

Blend the cornflour and milk in a jug. Cook on FULL POWER for 4 minutes, stirring twice. Stir in the sugar and egg, blending well. Pour over the fruit mixture. Sprinkle with ground nutmeg.

Reduce the power setting and cook on DEFROST POWER for 6 minutes, turning the dish twice. Leave to stand for 5 minutes before serving.

Serves: 4
Power settings: FULL, DEFROST
Preparation time: 10-15 minutes
Cooking time: 18 minutes

BANANAS RIO

4 ripe bananas, peeled
6 tablespoons orange
    juice
2 tablespoons lemon juice
4 tablespoons brown
    sugar
pinch of salt
25 g/1 oz butter
2 tablespoons desiccated
    coconut
whipped cream to serve

Place the bananas in a greased shallow serving dish.

Mix the orange juice with the lemon juice, sugar and salt, blending well. Spoon over the bananas.

Dot with the butter and cover loosely with greaseproof paper. Cook for 4-4½ minutes, turning the dish once.

Serve hot or warm, sprinkled with the coconut and topped with whipped cream.

Serves: 4
Power setting: FULL
Preparation time: 10 minutes
Cooking time: 4-4½ minutes

LEMON ALMOND CHEESECAKE

50 g/2 oz butter
100 g/4 oz digestive
    biscuits, crushed
50 g/2 oz flaked almonds
100 g/4 oz cream cheese
100 g/4 oz curd cheese
50 g/2 oz caster sugar
1 egg, beaten
2 teaspoons lemon juice
½ teaspoon vanilla
    essence
½ teaspoon cornflour
300 ml/½ pint double
    cream

Place the butter in a bowl and cook on FULL POWER for 1 minute to melt. Stir in the biscuit crumbs and almonds, blending well. Press the mixture evenly into the base and sides of a 21.5 cm (8½ inch) diameter shallow glass cake dish. Cook on FULL POWER for 1 minute.

To make the filling, mix the cream cheese with the curd cheese, sugar, egg, lemon juice, vanilla essence and cornflour, blending well. Pour into the crumb crust. Cook on DEFROST POWER for 8 minutes, turning the dish three times. When cooked the filling will be set around the outside of the dish but the centre will still be slightly soft. Leave to stand for 10 minutes.

Spoon 2-3 tablespoons of the cream over the surface of the cheesecake and cook on FULL POWER for 1 minute. Chill the cheesecake for 2-4 hours.

Just before serving, whip the remaining cream until it stands in soft peaks. Pipe over the top of the cheesecake in an attractive design. Cut into wedges to serve.

To freeze
Pack in a rigid container, cover, seal, label and freeze for up to 2 months.

Serves: 5-6
Power settings: FULL, DEFROST
Preparation time: 25 minutes, plus
    chilling
Cooking time: 21 minutes
Suitable for freezing

CHOCOLATE AND ORANGE FONDUE

100 g/4 oz plain dessert chocolate
250 ml/8 fl oz whipping cream
225 g/8 oz sugar
finely grated rind of 1 orange
sponge fingers, marshmallows or fruit pieces to serve

Break the chocolate into pieces and place in a fondue or casserole dish. Add the cream, blending well. Cook for 2-3 minutes or until the chocolate melts, stirring twice.

Add the sugar and orange rind, blending well. Cook for 3-4 minutes or until the sugar has completely dissolved, stirring twice.

Serve hot with sponge fingers, marshmallows or fruit pieces for dipping

Serves: 3-4
Power setting: MEDIUM
Preparation time: 15 minutes
Cooking time: 5-7 minutes

ORANGE JELLY

300 ml/½ pint water
3 tablespoons sugar
3 rounded teaspoons powdered gelatine
300 ml/½ pint orange juice

Place the water in a jug and cook for 2 minutes or until hot. Stir in the sugar, beating well. Stir in the gelatine until dissolved.

Add the orange juice and stir well to blend. Pour into a 600 ml (1 pint) mould or bowl and chill to set.

If using a mould, dip briefly into hot water and invert on to a plate to serve.

Serves: 4
Power setting: FULL
Preparation time: 5 minutes, plus chilling
Cooking time: 2 minutes

PEACH FLAKES

25 g/1 oz butter
1 tablespoon golden syrup
25 g/1 oz cornflakes
1×410 g (14 oz) can sliced peaches, drained
40 g/1½ oz custard powder
40 g/1½ oz sugar
1 egg yolk
450 ml/¾ pint milk

Place the butter in a bowl with the golden syrup. Cook for ½ minute. Stir in the cornflakes to lightly coat.

Coarsely chop the peaches and place in a 900 ml (1½ pint) serving dish.

Mix the custard powder with the sugar and egg yolk in a cooking dish. Gradually add the milk, blending well. Cook for 5 minutes, stirring three times, until smooth and thickened. Pour the custard over the peaches and sprinkle with the cornflake mixture. Serve at once.

Serves: 4
Power setting: FULL
Preparation time: 5 minutes
Cooking time: 5½ minutes

ORANGE DAIRY PUDDING

600 ml/1 pint milk
4 tablespoons semolina or ground rice
25 g/1 oz sugar
3 tablespoons orange curd

Place the milk and semolina or ground rice in a large bowl. Cook on FULL POWER for 5-6 minutes or until the milk boils, stirring twice.

Add the sugar and orange curd, blending well. Cover and cook on FULL POWER for 2 minutes.

Reduce the power setting and cook on LOW POWER for 10-15 minutes until creamy, and the grain is clear and cooked,

stirring three times. Leave to stand, covered, for 5 minutes.

Serve in individual pudding dishes with extra orange curd if liked.

Serves: 4
Power settings: FULL, LOW
Preparation time: 5 minutes
Cooking time: 22-28 minutes

BAKED ORANGES

4 large oranges, peeled,
  pith removed and
  thinly sliced
50 g/2 oz brown sugar
3 tablespoons brown rum
15 g/½ oz butter

Place the orange slices in a heatproof serving dish. Sprinkle over the sugar and pour over the rum.

Dot with the butter, cover and cook for 2-3 minutes until very hot and bubbly.

Serve warm with whipped cream or ice cream.

Serves: 4
Power setting: FULL
Preparation time: 10 minutes
Cooking time: 2-3 minutes

RASPBERRY MOUSSE CAKE

175 g/6 oz butter
175 g/6 oz caster sugar
3 eggs, beaten
finely grated rind and
  juice of 1 lemon
175 g/6 oz self-raising
  flour
1 teaspoon baking
  powder
350 g/12 oz raspberries,
  hulled
2 tablespoons icing sugar
2 tablespoons Cointreau
  liqueur
3 tablespoons orange
  juice
1½ teaspoons powdered
  gelatine
1 egg white
150 ml/¼ pint double
  cream
150 ml/¼ pint extra thick
  plain yogurt
toasted flaked almonds

Cream the butter and sugar until light and fluffy. Gradually beat in the eggs, lemon rind and lemon juice.

Sift the flour and baking powder together and fold into the cake mixture with a metal spoon. Spoon into a large microwave baking ring. Cook for 7 minutes, turning the ring twice – the top will still be moist when cooked but will dry out after standing. Leave to stand for 10 minutes then turn out to cool on a wire rack.

When cold, slice a thin layer from the top of the cake and set aside.

Return the rest of the cake to the washed ring mould. Using a grapefruit knife, cut out the cake to leave a 1 cm/½ inch thick shell. (Use the cake crumbs for another recipe, such as Poached Fruits with Crunchy Topping, p. 167.)

Purée 225 g/8 oz of the raspberries in a blender with the icing sugar and Cointreau. Sieve to remove the seeds.

Place the orange juice in a bowl and cook for ½ minute until hot. Briskly stir in the gelatine to dissolve. Stir into the fruit purée, blending well.

Whisk the egg white until it stands in stiff peaks and lightly whip the cream until it stands in soft peaks. Fold the egg white, the remaining raspberries and half of the cream into the fruit purée with a metal spoon.

Spoon into the sponge shell and cover with the reserved top slice. Cover and chill overnight or for at least 6-8 hours.

To serve, unmould the mousse cake on to a serving dish. Whisk the yogurt into the remaining cream and spoon over the cake. Sprinkle with almonds to decorate. Cut into wedges to serve.

Serves: 6-8
Power Setting: FULL
Preparation time: 45 minutes plus
cooling and chilling
Cooking time: 17½ minutes

APPLE FOOL

900 g/2 lb cooking apples,
  peeled, cored and
  sliced
100 g/4 oz sugar
300 ml/½ pint double
  cream
green food colouring

Mix the apples with the sugar in a cooking dish. Cover and cook for 13 minutes, stirring twice.

Allow to cool then purée in a blender or pass through a fine sieve.

Whip the cream until it stands in soft peaks. Fold into the apple mixture with a metal spoon.

Divide the mixture in half and colour one half with green food colouring.

Layer the plain and coloured apple fool in 4 dessert glasses. Chill lightly before serving with crisp dessert biscuits.

Serves: 5-6
Power setting: FULL
Preparation time: 20 minutes plus
chilling
Cooking time: 13 minutes

PINEAPPLE STREUSEL

Base:
75 g/3 oz plain flour
50 g/2 oz butter
25 g/1 oz caster sugar
1 × 227 g (8 oz) can
  pineapple rings in
  natural juice, drained
Topping:
50 g/2 oz plain flour
50 g/2 oz butter
50 g/2 oz caster sugar
icing sugar to dust
whipped cream to serve

To make the base, sift the flour into a bowl. Rub in the butter until the mixture resembles fine breadcrumbs. Stir in the sugar. Knead to a firm dough and press into a 20 cm (8 inch) ceramic flan dish.

Coarsely chop the pineapple and spoon over the dough base.

To make the topping, sift the flour into a bowl. Rub in the butter until the mixture resembles fine breadcrumbs. Stir in the sugar and sprinkle over the pineapple. Cook for 9 minutes, turning the dish once.

Dust with icing sugar and serve hot or cold, cut into wedges, with whipped cream.

To freeze
Cool quickly and pack into a rigid container. Cover, seal, label and freeze for up to 3 months.

Serves: 4-6
Power setting: FULL
Preparation time: 15 minutes
Cooking time: 9 minutes
Suitable for freezing

Illustrated on p. 152

PINEAPPLE ROLL

1 × 425 g (15½ oz) can
  pineapple rings in
  sugar and water
6 glacé cherries
1 tablespoon caster sugar
1 drop of green colouring
3 teaspoons powdered
  gelatine
To decorate:
whipped cream
pieces of glacé cherry

Drain the pineapple juice into a small jug. Leaving the pineapple rings in the can, stuff the centre with 5 glacé cherries.

Cook the juice for 2 minutes. Stir in the sugar and colouring. Stir in the gelatine until dissolved.

Pour the jelly over the pineapple rings. Insert two cocktail sticks to prevent the rings from floating unevenly. Place the last cherry in the centre of the top piece of pineapple. Chill to partially set. When partially set remove the cocktail sticks.

Unmould by dipping the can in hot water. Turn upside down to remove the base with a can opener. Push gently down until the jelly is on the plate.

Serve the jelly roll on its side decorated with whipped cream and pieces of glacé cherry. Slice to serve.

Serves: 4
Power setting: FULL
Preparation time: 20 minutes, plus chilling
Cooking time: 2 minutes

HUNGARIAN WITCHES FROTH

6 cooking apples, peeled,
  cored and sliced
150 ml/¼ pint lemon juice
225 g/8 oz caster sugar
1½ tablespoons brandy
3 egg whites
25 g/1 oz walnuts,
  chopped

Place the apples in a cooking dish with the lemon juice. Cover and cook for 10-12 minutes, until cooked and soft.

Stir in the sugar, blending well to dissolve. Purée in a blender or pass through a fine nylon sieve. Add the brandy and chill.

Whisk the egg whites until they stand in stiff peaks. Fold into the apple purée with a metal spoon, Spoon into individual glass dishes and sprinkle with chopped walnuts. Serve chilled.

Serves: 6
Power setting: FULL
Preparation time: 20 minutes plus chilling
Cooking time: 10-12 minutes

SEMOLINA PUDDING

1 rounded tablespoon
  custard powder
25 g/1 oz semolina
50 g/2 oz caster sugar
2 eggs, separated
600 ml/1 pint milk

Mix the custard powder with the semolina, caster sugar, egg yolks and milk in a cooking dish. Cook on FULL POWER for 8 minutes, stirring twice.

Reduce the power setting and cook on LOW POWER for 10 minutes, stirring twice.

Whisk the egg whites until they stand in stiff peaks. Fold into the hot semolina pudding with a metal spoon.

Serve hot or cold with stewed or fresh fruit.

Serves: 4
Power settings: FULL, LOW
Preparation time: 5 minutes
Cooking time: 18 minutes

BLACKCURRANT BAKED CHEESECAKE

Base:
50 g/2 oz butter
175 g/6 oz digestive
  biscuits, crushed
Filling:
50 g/2 oz butter
50 g/2 oz sugar
225 g/8 oz cream cheese
150 ml/¼ pint soured
  cream
2 eggs, separated
1 × 396 g (14 oz) can
  blackcurrant pie filling

Line a 23 cm (9 inch) round cake dish with cling film.

To make the base, place the butter in a bowl and cook for ½ minute to melt. Stir in the biscuit crumbs, stirring well to coat. Spoon into the base of the dish, pressing down well.

To make the filling, cream the butter and sugar until light and fluffy. Gradually beat in the cream cheese, soured cream and egg yolks, blending well.

Whisk the egg whites until they stand in stiff peaks. Fold into the cream mixture with a metal spoon. Spoon on top of the biscuit base. Cook for 8 minutes, turning the dish twice. Leave to stand until cool.

When cool, top the cheesecake with the pie filling. Serve lightly chilled.

To freeze
Place in a rigid container, cover, seal, label and freeze for up to 3 months.

Serves: 8
Power setting: FULL
Preparation time: 25 minutes, plus
cooling and chilling
Cooking time: 8½ minutes
Suitable for freezing

RASPBERRY MOUSSE

450 g/1 lb raspberries,
  hulled
100 g/4 oz cream cheese
50 g/2 oz caster sugar
4 tablespoons water
3 teaspoons powdered
  gelatine
2 egg whites
150 ml/¼ pint double
  cream
To decorate:
whipped cream
raspberries

Purée the raspberries. Beat the cheese with the sugar until soft and smooth. Stir in the raspberry purée and set aside.

Place the water in a small jug and cook for ½ minute. Stir in the gelatine until dissolved. Gradually stir the gelatine into the raspberry purée, blending well.

Whisk the egg whites until they stand in stiff peaks. Fold the cream into the raspberry mixture, blending well. Fold in the egg whites, with a metal spoon. Pour into a 900 ml (1½ pint) soufflé dish and chill until set.

Serve decorated with whipped cream and raspberries.

To freeze
Cover with foil, seal, label and freeze for up to 3 months.

Serves: 6
Power setting: FULL
Preparation time: 20 minutes, plus
chilling
Cooking time: ½ minute
Suitable for freezing

Illustrated on p. 151

PLUMS WITH PORT

900 g/2 lb plums, halved
  and stoned
75-100 g/3-4 oz brown
  sugar
100 ml/4 fl oz port wine

Place the plums in a cooking dish. Sprinkle over the sugar and pour over the port wine.

Cover and cook for 7-8 minutes, stirring twice, until tender.

Serve warm or lightly chilled with whipped cream.

To freeze
Cover with foil, seal, label and freeze for up to 3 months.

Serves: 4
Power setting: FULL
Preparation time: 10 minutes
Cooking time: 7-8 minutes
Suitable for freezing

TANGY BAKED BANANAS

2 large bananas, peeled
4 tablespoons frozen
  concentrated orange
  juice, thawed
1 tablespoon soft brown
  sugar
2 teaspoons lemon juice
orange slices to decorate

Slice the bananas lengthwise and then cut each slice in half.

Place in a shallow cooking dish with the orange juice, sugar and lemon juice, blending well.

Cook for 4 minutes, stirring twice. Serve hot decorated with orange slices. Serve with pouring cream if liked.

Serves: 2
Power setting: FULL
Preparation time: 5 minutes
Cooking time: 4 minutes

BAVARIAN RUM PIE

Base:
175 g/6 oz butter, cut into
  pieces
225 g/8 oz digestive
  biscuits, crushed
Rum layer:
75 ml/2½ fl oz water
2 teaspoons powdered
  gelatine
1 egg yolk
50 g/2 oz caster sugar
3 tablespoons brown rum
150 ml/¼ pint milk
150 ml/¼ pint double
  cream, whipped
Chocolate layer:
75 ml/2½ fl oz water
2 teaspoons powdered
  gelatine
75 g/3 oz plain chocolate,
  broken into pieces
25 g/1 oz caster sugar
150 ml/¼ pint milk
1 egg white
whipped cream
grated chocolate

To prepare the base, place the butter in a small bowl and cook for 1¼ minutes to melt. Add the biscuit crumbs and mix well to coat. Spread the mixture over the base of a 20 cm (8 inch) loose-bottomed cake tin. Smooth over with the back of a spoon.

To prepare the rum layer, place the water in a small jug and cook for ½ minute. Stir in the gelatine until dissolved. Allow to cool slightly.

Beat the egg yolk and sugar together. Stir in the gelatine, rum, milk and whipped cream and set aside to thicken.

When thickened, turn into the crumb base and chill to set.

To prepare the chocolate layer, place the water in a small jug and cook for ½ minute. Stir in the gelatine until dissolved. Allow to cool slightly.

Place the chocolate in a small jug. Cook for 3 minutes or until melted. Stir into the gelatine with the sugar and milk. Leave to cool until thickened.

Whisk the egg white until it stands in stiff peaks and gently fold into the chocolate mixture with a metal spoon. Pour over the rum layer and chill to set.

To serve, remove the pie from the tin by quickly immersing in hot water then by pushing the base upwards, leaving the ring over the arm.

Place on a serving plate and decorate with whipped cream and grated chocolate.

To freeze
Cover with foil, seal, label and freeze for up to 3 months.

Serves: 4-6
Power setting: FULL
Preparation time: 40 minutes, plus
  chilling
Cooking time: 5¼ minutes
Suitable for freezing

161

DISSOLVING GELATINE

Gelatine is an important ingredient in the preparation of sweet and savoury jellies, mousses, soufflés and galantines, and the microwave is a useful appliance for dissolving powdered gelatine quickly and economically

In most cases, unless the recipe specifies otherwise, simply heat the liquid until hot, but not boiling – about ½ minute on FULL POWER. Add the gelatine and stir briskly to dissolve.

Alternatively, mix the gelatine with the cold liquid and leave until spongy, about 5 minutes. Cook the mixture until clear and dissolved – about ½ minute on FULL POWER.

Allow to cool slightly then use as required.

ZABAGLIONE

1 large egg (sizes 1, 2)
2 large egg yolks (sizes 1, 2)
50 g/2 oz caster sugar
150 ml/¼ pint sweet sherry
2 teaspoons finely grated lemon rind
8 sponge finger biscuits

Place the egg and egg yolks in a large bowl and whisk until creamy. Add the sugar and whisk further until pale and thickened.

Place the sherry and lemon rind in a small jug and cook on FULL POWER for 1½ minutes until just boiling. Add to the egg mixture, whisking constantly.

Cook on LOW POWER for 1½ minutes. Remove from the oven and whisk until very thick and frothy, about 5 minutes.

Serve at once in warmed dessert glasses with the sponge fingers.

Serves: 4
Power settings: FULL, LOW
Preparation time: 10-15 minutes
Cooking time: 3 minutes

PEACHES WITH CHOCOLATE SAUCE

8 canned peach halves
4 tablespoons brandy
50 g/2 oz plain chocolate, broken into pieces
1 tablespoon sugar
2 tablespoons lemon juice
1-2 tablespoons peach juice
flaked almonds

Place 2 peach halves in each of 4 small dessert dishes. Sprinkle evenly with 2 tablespoons of the brandy.

Place the chocolate in a bowl with the sugar and cook for 2 minutes, stirring once. Add the lemon juice, peach juice and remaining brandy, blending well.

Pour over the peach halves and decorate with flaked almonds. Serve with cream.

Serves: 4
Power setting: FULL
Preparation time: 5 minutes
Cooking time: 2 minutes

RUBY PEARS

150 g/5 oz sugar
150 ml/¼ pint water
4 ripe dessert pears, peeled but keeping stalks intact
grated rind and juice of 1 lemon
4 cloves
red food colouring

Place the sugar and water in a deep cooking dish. Cook for 4 minutes, stirring twice.

Add the pears, lemon rind, lemon juice and cloves. Cook for 5 minutes, turning the dish once.

Carefully remove the pears with a slotted spoon, and set aside. Add sufficient red food colouring to the syrup to produce a bright pink colour.

Return the pears to the syrup and turn in the syrup frequently for an even colour.

Serve hot or cold with cream.

Serves: 4
Power setting: FULL
Preparation time: 20-25 minutes
Cooking time: 9 minutes

APPLE AND COCONUT CHARLOTTE

100 g/4 oz butter
225 g/8 oz fresh
  breadcrumbs
50 g/2 oz desiccated
  coconut
150 g/5 oz brown sugar
450 g/1 lb cooking apples,
  peeled, cored and
  thinly sliced
grated rind and juice of 1
  lemon

Place the butter in a bowl and cook for 1½ minutes to melt. Stir in the breadcrumbs and cook for a further 3 minutes, stirring once. Stir in the coconut and cook for a further 1 minute.

Place half of the mixture in the base of a 1.2 litre (2 pint) pudding dish, pressing down well. Sprinkle with half of the sugar.

Top with the apples and sprinkle with the remaining sugar. Spoon over the lemon juice and sprinkle with the lemon rind.

Cover with the remaining coconut mixture. Cook for 5 minutes, turning the dish once..

Brown under a preheated hot grill if liked. Serve hot with cream or custard.

Serves: 4
Power setting: FULL
Preparation time: 15 minutes
Cooking time: 10½ minutes

CHOCOLATE REFRIGERATOR CAKE

100 g/4 oz plain cooking
  chocolate, broken into
  pieces
150 g/5 oz unsalted
  butter
2 tablespoons golden
  syrup
225 g/8 oz semi-sweet
  biscuits, crushed
25 g/1 oz chopped nuts
25 g/1 oz glacé cherries,
  chopped
25 g/1 oz raisins

Place the chocolate, butter and golden syrup in a bowl. Cook for 4 minutes stirring once.

Add the biscuit crumbs, nuts, cherries and raisins, blending well.

Spoon into a greased 23 cm (9 inch) cake tin and freeze for 2-4 hours to set.

Cut into 16 pieces for serving. Top with a little whipped cream if liked. Store in the refrigerator for up to 2 weeks.

Makes: 16 pieces
Power setting: FULL
Preparation time: 15 minutes, plus freezing
Cooking time: 4 minutes

BLACKBERRY AND HONEY SORBET

900 g/2 lb blackberries,
  hulled
4 tablespoons clear honey
225 g/8 oz sugar
300 ml/½ pint water
2 egg whites

Place the blackberries, honey, sugar and water in a cooking dish. Cover and cook for 6-8 minutes until tender, stirring once.

Allow to cool then rub through a fine nylon sieve.

Spoon into a freezer tray and freeze until almost solid.

Spoon into a bowl and whisk until the ice crystals have been broken down and the mixture is smooth.

Whisk the egg whites until they stand in stiff peaks. Fold into the blackberry mixture with a metal spoon.

Return the mixture to the freezer tray and freeze until firm.

Serve scooped into dessert glasses. Serve with crisp dessert biscuits or wafers.

To freeze
Cover, seal, label and freeze for up to 1 year.

Serves: 4-6
Power setting: FULL
Preparation time: 20 minutes, plus cooling and freezing
Cooking time: 6-8 minutes
Suitable for freezing

BRAMBLE SYLLABUB

450 g/1 lb blackberries, hulled
1½ tablespoons sugar
¾ teaspoon ground mace
3 egg whites
150 g/5 oz caster sugar
2 tablespoons lemon juice
150 ml/¼ pint dry white wine
300 ml/½ pint double cream, whipped
a few whole blackberries to decorate

Place the blackberries in a cooking dish with the sugar and mace. Cook for 3-4 minutes, until soft but still whole, stirring once. Leave to cool.

When cool, spoon the fruit into the bases of 8 stemmed dessert glasses.

Whisk the egg whites until they stand in stiff peaks. Fold in the sugar, lemon juice, wine and cream with a metal spoon.

Carefully spoon over the fruit mixture. Chill for 1 hour.

Serve lightly chilled decorated with a few whole blackberries.

Serves: 8
Power setting: FULL
Preparation time: 20 minutes, plus chilling
Cooking time: 3-4 minutes

EASY CHOCOLATE MOUSSE

150 ml/¼ pint water
50 g/2 oz caster sugar
1 tablespoon cocoa powder
½ teaspoon vanilla essence
3 teaspoons powdered gelatine
2 egg whites
200 ml/7 fl oz evaporated milk, chilled
To decorate:
whipped cream
flaked chocolate

Place the water in a jug and cook for 1½ minutes. Stir in the sugar, cocoa powder and vanilla essence, beating well. Stir in the gelatine until dissolved. Set aside.

Whisk the egg whites until they stand in stiff peaks. Whisk the evaporated milk until thick and creamy. Beat the evaporated milk into the gelatine mixture then fold in the egg whites with a metal spoon, blending well.

Pour into a 900 ml (1½ pint) soufflé dish and chill until set.

Serve decorated with whipped cream and flaked chocolate.

Serves: 6
Power setting: FULL
Preparation time: 20 minutes, plus chilling
Cooking time: 1½ minutes

RASPBERRY CREAM

50 g/2 oz ground rice
600 ml/1 pint milk
grated rind of 1 lemon
25 g/1 oz sugar
1 × 213 g (7½ oz) can raspberries in natural juice, drained
1 teaspoon raspberry jam
150 ml/¼ pint double cream

Place the ground rice and milk in a large bowl. Cook on FULL POWER for 5-6 minutes, or until the milk boils, stirring twice.

Add the lemon rind and sugar, blending well. Cover and cook on FULL POWER for 2 minutes.

Reduce the power setting and cook on LOW POWER for 10-15 minutes until creamy, and the grain is clear and cooked, stirring three times. Leave to stand, covered, for 5 minutes.

Stir in the raspberries and jam, blending well.

Whip the cream until it stands in soft peaks. Fold two-thirds into the raspberry mixture with a metal spoon.

Pour into 4 small dessert glasses and chill thoroughly.

Serve lightly chilled, decorated with swirls of the remaining cream.

Serves: 4
Power settings: FULL, LOW
Preparation time: 20 minutes, plus chilling
Cooking time: 22-28 minutes

RICH CHOCOLATE CHIP ICE CREAM

*300 ml/½ pint single
  cream*
3 eggs, beaten
40 g/1½ oz caster sugar
*2 teaspoons vanilla
  essence*
*150 ml/¼ pint double
  cream*
*100 g/4 oz plain
  chocolate, grated or
  100 g/4 oz chocolate
  polka dots (chocolate
  drops)*

Mix the single cream with the eggs and sugar in a heatproof bowl. Cook for 4-6 minutes, stirring every 1 minute, until lightly thickened. Stir in the vanilla essence and allow to cool.

Pour the mixture into freezer trays and freeze until half frozen.

Meanwhile, whip the double cream until it stands in soft peaks. Whisk the half-frozen custard base until smooth. Fold in the whipped cream and chocolate with a metal spoon.

Return to the freezer trays and freeze until firm. Serve scooped into dessert glasses with wafers or crisp dessert biscuits.

To freeze
Cover, seal, label and freeze for up to 3 months.

Serves: 4-6
Power setting: FULL
*Preparation time: 15 minutes, plus
freezing*
Cooking time: 4-6 minutes
Suitable for freezing

CRÈME CARAMEL

150 ml/¼ pint cold water
150 g/5 oz sugar
2 tablespoons hot water
600 ml/1 pint milk
4 large eggs (sizes 1, 2)
*few drops of vanilla
  essence*

Place the water and 100 g/4 oz of the sugar in a heatproof cake dish. Cook on FULL POWER for 3 minutes. Stir well and cook on FULL POWER for 11-14 minutes until the syrup forms a rich golden brown. Carefully stir in the hot water, blending well.

Place the milk in a jug and cook on FULL POWER for 3 minutes.

Whisk the eggs with the remaining sugar and vanilla essence. Whisk in the milk, blending well.

Strain into the cooking dish over the caramel mixture. Cook on DEFROST POWER for 20 minutes, turning the dish three times, until just set. Leave to stand for 10 minutes. Cool quickly then chill.

To serve, invert on to a serving dish. Serve with cream if liked.

Serves: 6
Power settings: FULL, DEFROST
*Preparation time: 10 minutes, plus
chilling*
Cooking time: 47-51 minutes

CREAMY VANILLA ICE CREAM

2 eggs, beaten
450 ml/¾ pint milk
175 g/6 oz sugar
*3 teaspoons vanilla
  essence*
*300 ml/½ pint double
  cream*

Mix the eggs with the milk and sugar in a heatproof bowl. Cook for 6 minutes, stirring every 2 minutes, until lightly thickened. Allow to cool.

Add the vanilla essence and cream, blending well. Pour into a freezer tray and freeze until almost firm.

Remove from the freezer, turn into a bowl and whisk until smooth and creamy. Return to the freezer tray and freeze until firm.

About 30 minutes before serving, transfer the ice cream to the refrigerator and leave to soften slightly.

Scoop into dessert glasses to serve. Serve with crisp dessert biscuits or wafers.

To freeze
Cover, seal, label and freeze for up to 3 months.

Serves: 4-6
Power setting: FULL
*Preparation time: 10 minutes, plus
freezing*
Cooking time: 6 minutes
Suitable for freezing

CHRISTMAS PUDDING

225 g/8 oz mixed dried
    fruit
25 g/1 oz glacé cherries,
    chopped
1 small cooking apple,
    peeled, cored and
    chopped
25 g/1 oz mixed cut peel
40 g/1½ oz blanched
    almonds, chopped
grated rind of 1 lemon
grated rind and juice of 1
    small orange
50 g/2 oz plain flour
¼ teaspoon salt
¼ teaspoon ground mixed
    spice
¼ teaspoon ground
    cinnamon
¼ teaspoon ground
    nutmeg
50 g/2 oz brown sugar
25 g/1 oz fresh white or
    brown breadcrumbs
50 g/2 oz shredded suet
75 ml/3 fl oz brandy
1 tablespoon black treacle
2 eggs, beaten
milk to mix

Mix the dried fruit, glacé cherries, apple, peel, almonds, lemon rind, orange rind and juice in a bowl, blending well.

Sift the flour with the salt, mixed spice, cinnamon and nutmeg.

Add the sugar, breadcrumbs and suet to the fruit mixture, blending well. Stir in the flour mixture, brandy, treacle, eggs and sufficient milk to produce a mixture with a soft dropping consistency.

Spoon into a greased 900 ml (1½ pint) pudding basin. Cover loosely with cling film and cook for 8 minutes, turning the basin twice. Leave to stand for 10 minutes.

To serve immediately, invert on to a warmed serving plate. Cut into wedges and serve with cream, custard or brandy butter.

Alternatively, wrap the basin in foil and store. To reheat, remove foil, cover loosely with cling film and cook for 2-3 minutes.

Serves: 4
Power setting: FULL
Preparation time: 20 minutes
Cooking time: 18 minutes

GOLDEN AUTUMN PUDDING

100 g/4 oz butter
100 g/4 oz soft brown
    sugar
40 g/1½ oz raisins
15 g/½ oz walnut pieces
1 small banana, peeled
    and finely chopped
1 dessert apple, peeled,
    cored and finely
    chopped
grated rind and juice of 1
    small orange
1 egg, beaten
150 g/5 oz self-raising
    flour
1 teaspoon ground
    cinnamon
1 tablespoon milk
2 tablespoons brown rum

Place 40 g/1½ oz of the butter in a bowl and cook on FULL POWER for ½ minute to melt. Stir in 40 g/1½ oz of the sugar, the raisins, walnut pieces, banana and apple.

Cream the remaining butter with the remaining sugar and the orange rind until light and fluffy. Gradually beat in the egg.

Sift the flour with the cinnamon and fold into the creamed mixture with the orange juice. Add the milk and rum, blending well to give a mixture with a soft dropping consistency.

Spoon one-third of the apple mixture on the base of a greased pudding basin or ring mould, top with one-third of the cake mixture. Repeat twice, finishing with a layer of cake mixture.

Cook on LOW POWER for 5 minutes. Raise the power setting and cook on FULL POWER for 4 minutes, turning the dish twice. Leave to stand for 5 minutes.

To serve, invert the pudding on to a warmed serving plate. Serve hot with cream or custard.

Serves: 4
Power settings: FULL, LOW
Preparation time: 20 minutes
Cooking time: 14½ minutes

POACHED FRUITS WITH CRUNCHY TOPPING

Plums:
300 ml/½ pint sweet red vermouth
2 tablespoons sugar
675 g/1½ lb plums
Apricots:
300 ml/½ pint water
100 g/4 oz sugar
1 teaspoon almond essence
675 g/1½ lb apricots
Crunchy topping:
about 100 g/4 oz cake crumbs
4 tablespoons sugar
50 g/2 oz flaked almonds
Zabaglione Sauce:
4 egg yolks
50 g/2 oz caster sugar
100 ml/4 fl oz sweet white wine, sherry or Marsala
150 ml/¼ pint whipping cream, lightly whipped

To prepare the plums, place the vermouth and sugar in a bowl. Cook, uncovered, for 8 minutes. Add the plums, blending well. Cover and cook for 10 minutes, stirring once. Leave to cool then chill lightly.

To prepare the apricots, place the water, sugar and almond essence in a bowl. Cook, uncovered, for 8 minutes. Add the apricots, blending well. Cover and cook for 10 minutes, stirring once. Leave to cool then chill lightly.

To make the topping, place the cake crumbs, sugar and almonds on a flat dish and lightly stir together to mix. Cook for 6 minutes, stirring every 1 minute, until brown and crisp. Leave to cool then sprinkle over the poached fruits.

To make the sauce, whisk the egg yolks and sugar until pale and creamy. Whisk in the wine, blending well. Cook for 2-3 minutes, whisking every 1 minute until thickened. Remove from the microwave and continue to whisk for 3-4 minutes until very thick and creamy. Gradually whisk in

the cream then chill lightly.

Serve the poached fruits with their crispy topping, with the sauce served separately.

Serves: 6-8
Power Setting: FULL
Preparation time: 45 minutes, plus cooling and chilling
Cooking time: 44-45 minutes

LEMON SOUFFLÉ

165 g/6½ oz caster sugar
3 teaspoons powdered gelatine dissolved in 2 tablespoons water
pinch of salt
200 ml/7 fl oz water
3 eggs, separated
grated rind and juice of 1 lemon
200 ml/7 fl oz double cream
To decorate:
whipped cream
lemon butterflies

Lightly grease a 600 ml (1 pint) soufflé dish. Cut a double strip of greaseproof paper, equal in width to the height of the dish plus 5 cm/2 inches and long enough to go right round the outside of the dish. Lightly grease the top 5 cm/2 inches and tie securely with string around the outside of the dish, greased side inside.

Mix 100 g/4 oz of the sugar with the dissolved gelatine, salt, water and egg yolks in a cooking dish, blending well. Cook for 6 minutes or until the mixture *almost* reaches boiling point but *do not allow to boil*, stirring twice.

Add the lemon rind and juice, blending well. Leave to cool and thicken but not set.

Whisk the egg whites until they stand in stiff peaks. Whisk in the remaining caster sugar until firm and shiny.

Whip the cream until it stands in soft peaks. Fold into the lemon mixture with the egg mixture using a metal spoon.

Pour into the prepared soufflé dish and chill until set.

Before serving, carefully ease the greaseproof paper away from the soufflé using the back of a knife. Decorate with swirls of whipped cream and lemon butterflies.

Variation

GOOSEBERRY SOUFFLÉ: Prepare and cook as above but use 100 ml/4 fl oz unsweetened gooseberry purée instead of the lemon rind and juice. Tint the mixture pale green with food colouring if liked.

To freeze

Place in a rigid container, cover, seal, label and freeze for up to 3 months.
Serves: 4-6
Power setting: DEFROST
Preparation time: 30 minutes, plus cooling and chilling
Cooking time: 6 minutes
Suitable for freezing

Variation illustrated on p. 151

Baking

Crisp biscuits, light-as-air sponges, rich dark fruit cakes, wholesome baked bread and flaky pastries – there is a baker's dozen and more to tempt the family cook in this section.

Since baking is perhaps the most controversial area in microwave cooking, this is a section to follow carefully. You may juggle with the techniques and tips on browning, but check timings with stop-watch accuracy at first and follow recipe instructions carefully until familiarity makes the traditional baking day a 1-hour stint!

BASIC WHITE BREAD

1 teaspoon sugar
1 teaspoon dried yeast
300 ml/½ pint warm water
450 g/1 lb plain flour
½ teaspoon salt
40 g/1½ oz butter
2 teaspoons oil
1 tablespoon cracked wheat to sprinkle

Mix the sugar with the yeast and half of the water in a jug. Leave to stand in a warm place until well risen and frothy.

Sift the flour and salt into a mixing bowl and cook on FULL POWER for ½ minute or until warm. Rub in the butter, add the yeast liquid and remaining water, and mix to a pliable dough.

Knead on a lightly floured surface until smooth and elastic, about 5 minutes. Return to the bowl, cover and leave in a warm place until the dough has doubled in size. This process can be hastened by using the microwave: cook on FULL POWER for 5 seconds then leave to stand for 10-15 minutes and repeat.

Knead the dough for a further 2-3 minutes then shape and place in a greased 1 kg (2 lb) loaf dish. Leave in a warm place until doubled in size, repeating the micro-wave hastening process if liked.

Lightly brush the bread with the oil and sprinkle with the cracked wheat. Cook on FULL POWER for 1 minute, reduce the power setting and cook on LOW POWER for 7-9 minutes, giving the dish a half turn three times during the cooking time. Alternatively, the bread may be cooked on FULL POWER for 5 minutes, turning twice.

Leave to stand for 5 minutes before turning out on to a wire rack to cool.

Brown under a preheated hot grill if a crispy brown crust is liked.

Makes: 1 × 1 kg (2 lb) loaf
Power settings: FULL, LOW
Preparation time: about 45 minutes
Cooking time: 13½-15½ minutes

RICE WHOLEMEAL MUFFINS

175 g/6 oz cooked long-grain rice
250 ml/8 fl oz milk
2 eggs, beaten
75 g/3 oz butter, melted
100 g/4 oz wholemeal flour
100 g/4 oz plain white flour
½ teaspoon salt
2 tablespoons sugar
1 tablespoon baking powder

Place the rice, milk, eggs and butter in a bowl and beat briskly to mix.

Mix the flours with the salt, sugar and baking powder. Add to the rice mixture and mix well to blend.

Lightly grease a microwave bun tray and fill each cup about two-thirds full with the mixture. Cook, six cups or 1 tray at a time, for 3 minutes, turning once. Turn out to cool on a wire rack.

Repeat with the remaining mixture to make 24 muffins in total. Serve warm or cold with a butter curl.

Makes: 24
Power setting: FULL
Preparation time: 20 minutes
Cooking time: 12 minutes

VICTORIA SANDWICH (p.174)   169

CHRISTMAS CAKE (p.181)

WHOLEMEAL LOAF

1 teaspoon caster sugar
1 teaspoon dried yeast
300 ml/½ pint warm
    water
450 g/1 lb plain
    wholemeal flour
½ teaspoon salt
15 g/½ oz butter
1 tablespoon bran to
    sprinkle

Mix the sugar with the yeast and half of the water in a jug. Leave in a warm place until well risen and frothy, about 10-15 minutes.

Place the flour and salt in a bowl and cook for ½ minute to warm. Rub in the butter, add the yeast liquid and the remaining water and mix to a firm but pliable dough.

Return to the bowl, cover and leave in a warm place until doubled in size. This process may be hastened by cooking for 5 seconds then leaving to stand for 10-15 minutes. Repeat as necessary.

Knead for a further 2-3 minutes then shape and place in a greased 450 g (1 lb) loaf dish. Cover and leave to rise until the dough reaches the top of the dish. Use the microwave hastening process again if liked.

Sprinkle with the bran and cook for 6 minutes, giving the dish a quarter turn every 2 minutes. Remove from the dish and allow to cool on a wire rack.

For a crisp brown crust, place the bread under a preheated hot grill until golden.

Makes: 1 × 450 g (1 lb) loaf
Power setting: FULL
Preparation time: about 45 minutes
Cooking time: 6½ minutes

CHELSEA BUNS

450 g/1 lb white bread
    dough (see p. 168)
25 g/1 oz butter
150 g/5 oz currants
50 g/2 oz soft brown
    sugar
soft brown sugar for
    sprinkling
pinch of ground
    cinnamon
2 tablespoons sieved
    apricot jam

Lightly grease a large shallow dish.

Follow the instructions and method for the white bread dough until the end of the first proving (see p. 168).

Knead the dough on a lightly floured surface until smooth and elastic. Roll out to a rectangle measuring about 30×23 cm (12×9 inches).

Place the butter in a bowl and cook for 1 minute to melt. Brush over the dough and sprinkle with the currants and sugar. Roll up from one of the long ends like a Swiss roll.

Cut across the roll to make 8 slices and place side by side in the cooking dish. Cover and leave in a warm place until doubled in size.

Sprinkle the top with a little sugar and cinnamon. Cook for 4-5 minutes, turning the dish once. Leave to stand for 5-10 minutes before cooling on a wire rack.

Place the jam in a bowl and cook for ½ minute. Brush while still hot over the Chelsea buns.

Makes: 8
Power setting: FULL
Preparation time: about 45 minutes
Cooking time: 10½-15½ minutes

PROVING DOUGH

Making bread and yeasted pastries is a rewarding but laborious part of a cook's repertoire. Dough proving is a long, slow process where patience is a necessity!

The microwave can speed up this process by halving proving times.

Simply give the dough a short burst of energy during the rising process – about 5-15 seconds depending upon the amount of dough – then leave to stand for 5-10 minutes to allow an even distribution of heat through the dough.

Don't be tempted to cook longer, for yeast is very delicate and can easily be killed if affected by too hot a temperature.

MALT LOAF

150 ml/¼ pint water
1 teaspoon sugar
7 g/¼ oz dried yeast
225 g/8 oz plain flour
½ teaspoon salt
50 g/2 oz sultanas
1 tablespoon malt extract
2 teaspoons black treacle
15 g/½ oz butter
apricot glaze (see opposite)

Lightly grease a small round dish.

Place the water and sugar in a small jug and cook for ¼-½ minute until warm. Stir in the yeast then leave in a warm place until well risen and frothy, about 10-15 minutes.

Sift the flour and salt into a bowl and stir in the sultanas.

Meanwhile place the malt, treacle and butter in a bowl and cook for ½ minute. Add the yeast liquid and malt mixture to the flour and mix to a soft dough. Knead until smooth, shape and place in the prepared dish.

Cook for ¼ minute, leave to stand for 5 minutes then give the dish a quarter turn. Repeat 3-4 times until the dough has doubled in size.

Cook for 4-5 minutes, turning the dish once. Allow to cool slightly before turning out on to a wire rack to cool.

Brush with the apricot glaze and serve sliced with butter.

Makes: 1
Power setting: FULL
Preparation time: about 15 minutes
Cooking time: about 45 minutes

LEMON AND HERB BREAD

1 short, crusty French stick
100 g/4 oz butter
grated rind of 1 lemon
2 teaspoons chopped fresh parsley and chives

With a sharp knife, cut the bread stick into 2.5 cm (1 inch) slices, almost through to the base. Mix the butter with the lemon rind and herbs, blending well.

Spread evenly between the slices of bread and re-form the loaf into a neat shape.

Protect or shield the thin ends of the loaf with a little foil and cover the whole stick with dampened greaseproof paper.

Cook for 1½ minutes or until the butter has just melted and the bread is warm. Pull the slices of bread completely apart before serving.

Serves: 4-6
Power setting: FULL
Preparation time: 10 minutes
Cooking time: 1½ minutes

CHEESY SODA BREAD

450 g/1 lb plain
    wholemeal or white
    flour
2 teaspoons mustard
    powder
2 teaspoons bicarbonate
    of soda
2 teaspoons cream of
    tartar
1 teaspoon salt
25 g/1 oz lard
1 teaspoon dried sage
100 g/4 oz Cheddar
    cheese, grated
300 ml/½ pint milk
1 tablespoon lemon juice
25 g/1 oz porridge oats

Mix the flour with the mustard powder, bicarbonate of soda, cream of tartar and salt.

Rub in the lard until the mixture resembles fine breadcrumbs. Stir in the sage and cheese, blending well.

Mix the milk with the lemon juice and mix into the dry ingredients, blending well to make a soft dough. Knead on a lightly-floured surface until smooth and elastic then shape into a round, and sprinkle the oats over it.

Place on a large plate or microwave baking tray and mark into 4 sections with a sharp knife. Cook on MEDIUM POWER for 5 minutes, turning the dish once.

Cook on FULL POWER for a further 3 minutes. Leave to stand for 10 minutes before transferring to a wire rack to cool.

Serves: 4
Power settings: MEDIUM, FULL
Preparation time: 15 minutes
Cooking time: 18 minutes

SAVARIN

150 ml/¼ pint water
1 teaspoon sugar
15 g/½ oz dried yeast
250 g/9 oz plain flour
½ teaspoon salt
few blanched almonds
50 g/2 oz butter
2 eggs, beaten
Syrup:
100 g/4 oz caster sugar
150 ml/¼ pint water
few drops of lemon juice
few drops of rum or other
    flavouring
Apricot glaze:
4 tablespoons sieved
    apricot jam
2-3 tablespoons hot water

Place the water and sugar in a small jug and cook for ¼-½ minute until warm. Stir in the yeast then leave in a warm place until well risen and frothy, about 10-15 minutes.

Sift the flour and salt into a bowl. Stir in the yeast liquid, mixing well. Knead to a soft dough. Return the dough to the bowl, cover with cling film and cook for ¼ minute. Leave to stand for 5 minutes. Repeat 3-4 times or until the dough has doubled in size.

Meanwhile, grease a 23 cm (9 inch) microwave savarin mould and arrange a few blanched almonds in the bottom.

Place the butter in a bowl and cook for 1½-2 minutes. Gradually beat the melted butter and beaten eggs into the dough to make a rich smooth batter.

Pour the batter into the mould. Cover with pierced cling film and cook for ¼-½ minute, give a quarter turn and leave to stand for 5 minutes. Repeat this procedure until the mixture rises to the top of the mould.

Cook for 10 minutes, turning twice. Leave to stand for 2-3 minutes before turning out to cool on a wire rack.

To make the syrup, place the sugar and water in a heatproof bowl. Cook for 8 minutes until a thick syrup forms. Stir in the

lemon juice and rum or other flavouring to taste. Carefully spoon over the still warm savarin. Allow to cool completely.

Place the savarin on a large serving plate. Mix the apricot jam with the hot water and brush over the savarin.

Serve with whipped cream and fresh or canned fruits.

Serves: 6-8
Power setting: FULL
Preparation time: about 1 hour
Cooking time: about 1 hour 10 minutes

VICTORIA SANDWICH

175 g/6 oz butter
175 g/6 oz caster sugar
3 eggs, beaten
175 g/6 oz plain flour
2 teaspoons baking
   powder
pinch of salt
2 tablespoons hot water
5 tablespoons raspberry
   jam
icing sugar to dust

Line a 20 cm (8 inch) cake or soufflé dish with cling film.

Cream the butter and sugar until light and fluffy. Add the eggs, a little at a time, beating well to blend.

Sift the flour with the baking powder and salt and fold into the creamed mixture with the hot water.

Spoon into the prepared dish and level the surface carefully. Cook for 6½-7½ minutes, giving the dish a quarter turn every 2 minutes. The cake will still be slightly sticky and moist on the surface at this stage but will dry out with the residual heat in the cake. Allow to stand for 5 minutes before turning out on to a wire rack to cool.

To serve, split the cake in half and sandwich together with the jam. Dust the top with sifted icing sugar.

Serves: 6
Power setting: FULL
Preparation time: 10-15 minutes, plus cooling
Cooking time: 11½-12½ minutes

Illustrated on p. 169

GENOESE SPONGE

4 eggs
100 g/4 oz caster sugar
100 g/4 oz plain flour
pinch of salt
50 g/2 oz butter
5 tablespoons jam
150 ml/¼ pint whipped
   cream
icing sugar to dust

Line a 20 cm (8 inch) cake or soufflé dish with cling film.

Whisk the eggs and sugar together until they are very thick and pale and have trebled in volume.

Sift the flour and salt together and fold into the whisked mixture very carefully with a metal spoon.

Place the butter in a bowl and cook for 1-1½ minutes to melt. Gently fold into the whisked mixture with a metal spoon.

Pour into the prepared dish and cook for 4½-5 minutes, giving the dish a quarter-turn every 1½-2 minutes. Leave to stand for 5-10 minutes before turning out on to a wire rack to cool.

To serve, split the cake in half and sandwich together again with the jam and cream. Dust the top with icing sugar and serve cut into wedges.

Serves: 6
Power setting: FULL
Preparation time: 10-15 minutes, plus cooling
Cooking time: 10½-16½ minutes

MARBLE CAKE

175 g/6 oz butter
3 eggs
175 g/6 oz caster sugar
50 ml/2 fl oz milk
100 g/4 oz self-raising
   flour, sifted
1 teaspoon dried yeast
25 g/1 oz cocoa powder,
   sifted
icing sugar to dust

Line a 20 cm (8 inch) cake dish with buttered greaseproof paper.

Place the butter in a bowl and cook for 1 minute to melt.

Place the eggs and sugar in a bowl and whisk until very light and fluffy. Using a metal spoon, fold in the melted butter, milk, flour and yeast.

Divide the mixture into two portions and stir the cocoa powder into one of them.

Layer the plain and chocolate mixture in the prepared cake dish, finishing with a chocolate layer.

Cook for 6 minutes, turning the dish every 1½ minutes. Allow to stand for 5 minutes before turning out on to a wire rack to cool. Dust with icing sugar to serve.

Serves: 6-8
Power setting: FULL
Preparation time: 10-15 minutes
Cooking time: 12 minutes

RICH FRUIT CAKE

150 g/5 oz butter
2 eggs
150 g/5 oz soft brown sugar
2 tablespoons black treacle
1 tablespoon brandy
75 g/3 oz plain flour
75 g/3 oz self-raising flour
3 tablespoons milk
2 teaspoons ground mixed spice
25 g/1 oz chopped nuts
25 g/1 oz glacé cherries, chopped
450 g/1 lb mixed dried fruit

Place the butter in a large mixing bowl. Cook on FULL POWER for 1½ minutes.

Add the eggs, sugar, treacle and brandy, blending well.

Fold in the flours with a metal spoon. Add the milk, spice, nuts, cherries and mixed dried fruit and stir well to blend.

Spoon into a 1.5 litre (2½ pint) soufflé dish and level the surface. Cook on DEFROST POWER for 35 minutes, turning the dish twice.

Allow to stand for 30 minutes before turning out on to a wire rack to cool. Serve when cold cut into wedges.

Serves: 10
Power settings: FULL, DEFROST
Preparation time: 15 minutes, plus cooling
Cooking time: 66½ minutes

CHOCOLATE AND COFFEE CROWN CAKE

Cake:
175 g/6 oz butter
150 g/5 oz dark soft brown sugar
3 eggs, beaten
175 g/6 oz plain flour, sifted
2 teaspoons coffee and chicory essence
4 tablespoons cocoa powder
½ teaspoon baking powder
¼ teaspoon ground nutmeg
¼ teaspoon vanilla essence
1 tablespoon milk
Butter Icing:
175 g/6 oz unsalted butter
¼ teaspoon coffee and chicory essence
175 g/6 oz icing sugar, sifted

Grease a 23 cm (9 inch) ring mould and line the base with greaseproof paper.

To make the cake, beat the butter and sugar together until light and fluffy. Beat in the eggs a little at a time then fold in the flour with a metal spoon. Place one-quarter of the mixture in a small bowl and flavour with the coffee and chicory essence. Set aside.

Add the cocoa powder, baking powder and nutmeg to the remaining mixture, blending well. Stir in the vanilla essence and milk. Pour into the prepared ring mould and cook for 5 minutes, giving the dish a quarter-turn 3 times during the cooking. Leave to stand for 5 minutes then loosen with a knife and turn out on to a wire rack to cool.

Reverse the mould, grease well and line the base with greaseproof paper. Spoon in the coffee-flavoured batter mixture and cook for 2 minutes. Leave to stand for 4 minutes then loosen with a knife, turn out and leave to cool on a wire rack.

To make the butter icing, beat the butter and coffee and chicory essence together. Gradually work in the icing sugar to make a soft icing.

Generously spread the butter icing around the sides and narrower end of the coffee cake, then insert the cake, smooth side up, into the upturned chocolate ring.

Pipe butter icing in a circle on top of the cake where the two sections meet. Serve cut into wedges.

To freeze
Open freeze until firm. Wrap in foil, seal, label and freeze for up to 3 months.

Serves: 8
Power setting: FULL
Preparation time: about 45 minutes, plus cooling
Cooking time: 16 minutes
Suitable for freezing

SUBSTITUTE CONTAINERS FOR METAL BAKING TINS

Although metal containers cannot be used in the microwave oven, there is great scope for using other traditional containers.

Soufflé dishes and other round dishes with straight sides are perfect large cake containers and cups, heatproof glasses and mugs make ideal bun cases.

Cardboard shoe boxes, lined with cling film, can be used to cook square or oblong sponge cakes quickly and clay or plastic flowerpots can be used for cooking unusual bread loaves. If your microwave has a cooking shelf, this makes an ideally shaped and sized baking tray.

A quick appraisal of your glass, china or plastic cookware will tell you if you need to buy any of the special microwave bakeware available, but first juggle and improvise with what you already have. For example, a tumbler placed in a round dish becomes an 'instant' ring mould at no cost.

CHOCOLATE YOGURT CAKE

150 ml/5 fl oz vegetable oil
150 ml/5 fl oz plain yogurt
4 tablespoons golden syrup
175 g/6 oz caster sugar
3 eggs
3 tablespoons cocoa powder
½ teaspoon bicarbonate of soda
225 g/8 oz self-raising flour
pinch of salt

Grease a 20 cm (8 inch) cake or soufflé dish.

Place the oil, yogurt, golden syrup, sugar and eggs in a bowl. Beat well with a wooden spoon until well blended.

Add the cocoa powder, bicarbonate of soda, flour and salt and mix well to blend.

Spoon into the prepared dish and level the surface. Cook for 9 minutes, giving the dish a quarter-turn every 2 minutes.

Leave to stand for 6 minutes before turning out on to a wire rack to cool.

Serve plain, or top with a little melted chocolate or chocolate butter icing if liked. Cut into wedges to serve.

Serves: 10
Power setting: FULL
Preparation time: 15 minutes, plus cooling
Cooking time: 15 minutes

UPSIDE-DOWN PEACH CAKE

25 g/1 oz soft brown sugar
1 × 400 g (14 oz) can peach slices
few glacé cherries
½ × 454 g (1 lb) packet sponge mix
grated rind of 1 orange
4 tablespoons water

Sprinkle the sugar over the base of a 22 cm (8½ inch) Pyrex cake dish. Spoon over 2 tablespoons of the peach juice. Cook for 1-1½ minutes or until the sugar has melted.

Arrange the drained peach slices and cherries over the base of the dish in an attractive design.

Make up the sponge mix using the orange rind and water according to the packet instructions. Spoon over the fruit mixture and level the surface.

Cook for 7-7½ minutes or until the cake feels dry to the touch. Allow to stand for 5 minutes then turn out on to a serving dish.

Serve warm with custard or cream.

Serves: 4-6
Power setting: FULL
Preparation time: 15-20 minutes
Cooking time: 13-14 minutes

GINGER CAKE

75 g/3 oz unsalted butter
75 g/3 oz soft dark brown
  sugar
150 g/5 oz golden syrup
1 teaspoon bicarbonate
  of soda
225 g/8 oz plain flour
2 teaspoons ground
  ginger
1 egg
5 tablespoons milk

Grease a 23 cm (9 inch) ring mould.

Place the butter, sugar and golden syrup in a bowl. Beat well to blend. Cook for 2 minutes, stirring once.

Sift the bicarbonate of soda with the flour and ginger. Add to the melted butter mixture, blending well.

Beat the egg with the milk and stir into the cake mixture to make a thick batter.

Pour into the ring mould and cook for 6 minutes, giving the mould a quarter-turn every 1½ minutes. Leave the cake to stand for 10 minutes then turn out on to a wire rack to cool.

Serve plain, or split and fill with butter-cream if liked.

To freeze
Cool quickly, wrap in foil, seal, label and freeze for up to 3 months.

Serves: 10
Power setting: FULL
Preparation time: 20 minutes, plus cooling
Cooking time: 18 minutes
Suitable for freezing

GINGERBREAD

100 g/4 oz butter
100 g/4 oz soft brown
  sugar
3 tablespoons golden
  syrup
1 tablespoon black treacle
2 eggs, beaten
225 g/8 oz plain flour
1 tablespoon ground
  ginger
1 teaspoon bicarbonate
  of soda
25 g/1 oz mixed dried
  fruit

Line an 18 cm (7 inch) square cake dish with cling film or grease and base line with greaseproof paper.

Place the butter, sugar, golden syrup and treacle in a bowl and cook for 3 minutes, stirring once. Allow to cool slightly then beat in the eggs.

Sift the flour with the ginger and bicarbonate of soda. Fold into the egg mixture with the dried fruit.

Put the gingerbread mixture into the prepared cake dish and level the surface. Cook for 7-8 minutes, giving the dish a quarter turn every 2 minutes.

Turn out on to a wire rack to cool. Cut into squares to serve.

Serves: 6-8
Power setting: FULL
Preparation time: 15 minutes
Cooking time: 10-11 minutes

DRIED FRUIT AND BANANA LOAF

275 g/10 oz mixed dried
  fruit
175 ml/6 fl oz cold tea
100 g/4 oz soft dark
  brown sugar
1 banana, peeled and
  mashed
175 g/6 oz self-raising
  flour
1 large egg (sizes 1, 2),
  beaten

Lightly grease a 900 g (2 lb) loaf dish.

Place the fruit and tea in a large mixing bowl. Cook for 7 minutes then leave to stand until cool.

When cool add the sugar, banana, flour and egg. Mix well to blend.

Spoon into the prepared loaf dish and cook for 6-7 minutes, turning twice.

Leave to stand for 5 minutes before turning out on to a wire rack to cool.

To freeze
Cool quickly, wrap in foil, seal, label and freeze for up to 3 months.

Serves: 10
Power setting: FULL
Preparation time: 10 minutes, plus cooling
Cooking time: 18-19 minutes
Suitable for freezing

ORANGE TIPSY CAKE

Cake:
175 g/6 oz butter
175 g/6 oz caster sugar
175 g/6 oz self-raising
    flour
1 teaspoon baking
    powder
3 large eggs (sizes 1, 2)
finely grated rind of 2
    oranges
Tipsy Syrup:
75 g/3 oz caster sugar
juice of 2 oranges
1 teaspoon Cointreau
    liqueur
Topping:
225 g/8 oz plain
    chocolate-flavoured
    cake covering
1 teaspoon vegetable oil

Grease an 18 cm (7 inch) deep round cake dish and line the base with greaseproof paper. Using string, fix a double thickness 'collar' of greaseproof paper round the sides of the dish, protruding 2.5 cm (1 inch) above the rim.

Place the butter in a bowl and cook for 1 minute. Add the remaining cake ingredients and beat well until smooth and blended. Spoon into the prepared dish and level the surface. Cook for 6 minutes, giving the dish a half-turn once. Leave to stand for 5 minutes, then loosen the cake with a knife, remove the paper collar and turn out on to a wire rack set over a tray. Peel away any paper on the base of the cake.

To make the tipsy syrup, mix the sugar and orange juice in a bowl. Cook for 2 minutes or until boiling. Cook for a further 2 minutes or until the syrup thickens slightly. Stir in the Cointreau, blending well.

Using a sharp pointed knife, pierce deeply through the warm cake in several places. Gradually pour the syrup over the cake until it is all absorbed.

To make the topping, break up the chocolate and place in a bowl. Cook for 1-2 minutes until just beginning to melt. Stir in the oil until well blended. Pour over the top and sides of the cake. Leave until slightly set then swirl with a fork to give a raised effect.

Leave in a cool place until the chocolate is completely set. Cut into wedges to serve.

Serves: 8-10
Power setting: FULL
Preparation time: 35-40 minutes, plus cooling
Cooking time: 17-18 minutes

WALNUT CAKE

175 g/6 oz margarine
175 g/6 oz soft brown
    sugar
3 eggs, beaten
225 g/8 oz plain flour
1½ teaspoons baking
    powder
½ teaspoon salt
2 tablespoons milk
1 teaspoon vanilla
    essence
75 g/3 oz chopped
    walnuts

Grease an 18 cm (7 inch) deep round cake dish and line the base with greaseproof paper.

Cream the margarine and sugar until light and fluffy. Add the eggs, a little at a time, beating well to blend.

Sift the flour with the baking powder and salt. Fold into the creamed mixture with the milk and vanilla essence using a metal spoon. Finally, fold in the walnuts.

Spoon into the prepared dish and level the surface. Cook for 6-7 minutes, turning the dish every 1½ minutes.

Leave to stand for 5 minutes before turning out on to a wire rack to cool.

Serves: 6
Power setting: FULL
Preparation time: 10-15 minutes
Cooking time: 11-12 minutes

LIGHTNING COFFEE CAKE

50 g/2 oz soft margarine
50 g/2 oz soft brown
  sugar
75 g/3 oz self-raising
  flour
1 large egg (sizes 1, 2)
2 teaspoons instant coffee
  powder
2 teaspoons milk
whipping cream and
  demerara sugar to
  decorate

Lightly grease an 0.7 litre (1¼ pint) Pyrex soufflé dish.

Place the margarine, sugar, flour, egg and coffee powder dissolved in the milk in a bowl. Stir only enough to make a smooth, soft mixture.

Spread evenly into the prepared dish and cook for 4 minutes or until the top of the cake is dry to the touch. Allow to cool in the dish.

When cool top with whipped cream and sprinkle with demerara sugar. Serve straight from the dish while fresh.

Serves: 6-8
Power setting: FULL
Preparation time: 10 minutes, plus cooling
Cooking time: 4 minutes

CHOCOLATE-TOPPED SPONGE RING

100 g/4 oz soft margarine
100 g/4 oz caster sugar
100 g/4 oz self-raising
  flour
2 large eggs (sizes 1, 2)
50 g/2 oz chocolate,
  grated

Lightly grease a 22 cm (8½ inch) Pyrex savarin dish.

Place the margarine, sugar, flour and eggs in a bowl and stir only enough to make a smooth, soft mixture.

Spread evenly into the prepared dish and cook for 5-5½ minutes or until the top of the cake is dry to the touch. Sprinkle immediately with the chocolate and leave to cool.

Serve while fresh straight from the dish. Serve with ice cream if liked.

Serves: 10
Power setting: FULL
Preparation time: 10 minutes, plus cooling
Cooking time: 5-5½ minutes

STREUSEL CAKE

Topping:
25 g/1 oz butter
75 g/3 oz soft brown
  sugar
25 g/1 oz self-raising
  flour
50 g/2 oz walnuts,
  chopped
1 teaspoon ground
  cinnamon
Cake:
75 g/3 oz butter
175 g/6 oz caster sugar
1 egg, beaten
175 g/6 oz self-raising
  flour
pinch of salt
150 ml/¼ pint milk

Lightly grease a 19 cm (7½ inch) round deep dish and line the base with grease-proof paper.

Prepare the topping by beating the butter and sugar until light and fluffy. Add the flour, walnuts and cinnamon and mix until a light crumb mixture is obtained.

To make the cake, cream the butter and sugar until light and fluffy. Beat in the egg, blending well. Add the flour, salt and milk and beat well to blend.

Spoon into the prepared dish and level evenly. Cook for 4-5 minutes, turning the dish twice.

Sprinkle the topping over the cake and cook for another 1½ minutes.

Allow to cool slightly, then turn out on to a wire rack to cool.

Cut into wedges to serve.

Serves: 8
Power setting: FULL
Preparation time: 15-20 minutes
Cooking time: 5½-6½ minutes

IDEAS FOR TOPPING BREADS, CAKES AND PASTRIES

Although the microwave oven is excellent for cooking plain, fancy and rich breads, cakes and pastries, the speed of microwave cooking and the lack of prolonged surface heat means that baking remains pale after cooking.

As a general guide, you may add colourings such as brown sugar, cocoa powder and black treacle to the basic cooking mixture where appropriate, or give a quick dusting of icing sugar or brown foods under the grill after cooking. Here are a few other suggestions for adding colour to baking:

- Top savoury breads with colourful and interesting herbs, chopped green or red pepper, browned onions, crumbled cooked bacon or grated cheese before cooking.
- Brush teabreads and savoury pastries with a little gravy browning before cooking.
- Sprinkle sweet cakes, breads and biscuits before cooking with a colourful edible mixture like cinnamon and sugar, mixed chopped glacé fruits, toasted coconut, chocolate vermicelli, chopped nuts or coffee sugar.
- Top sweet breads, cakes and biscuits with a colourful icing, frosting or marzipan coating after cooking.
- Glaze teabreads with a fruit preserve, marmalade, dark sugar, honey or golden syrup after cooking.
- Top breads before cooking with bran, nibbed wheat, porridge oats, sesame seeds, poppy seeds, crunchy cereal or buckwheat.

SUPREME CHOCOLATE CAKE

Cake:
50 g/2 oz flaked almonds
175 g/6 oz butter, softened
175 g/6 oz dark brown sugar
3 large eggs (sizes 1, 2)
5 tablespoons clear honey
150 ml/¼ pint soured cream
175 g/6 oz self-raising flour
6 tablespoons cocoa powder
6 tablespoons ground almonds
3 tablespoons granulated sugar
3 tablespoons cold water
Sauce:
40 g/1½ oz butter
175 g/6 oz plain chocolate
6 tablespoons brown rum

Grease and line the base of a 2 litre (3½ pint) round straight-sided casserole dish.

Arrange the almonds in a single layer on a plate. Cook for 5 minutes, stirring once or twice until golden, checking frequently. Allow to cool on absorbent kitchen paper.

Cream the butter and brown sugar until pale and fluffy. Beat in the eggs, one at a time, then the honey and soured cream.

Sift the flour and cocoa together. Fold lightly into the cake mixture with a metal spoon. Finally fold in the ground almonds.

Spoon the mixture into the prepared cooking dish and cook for 10 minutes until cooked, turning the dish twice. Sprinkle at once with the flaked almonds.

Place the sugar and water in a small bowl and cook for 3-4 minutes until just beginning to caramelise. Very quickly drizzle over the almonds on the cake surface. Leave to stand for 10 minutes. Invert on to a baking sheet then on to a wire rack to cool.

The cake may be served plain at this stage or with chocolate rum sauce. To make the sauce, place the butter and chocolate in a bowl. Cook for 3 minutes, stirring twice, to melt. Whisk in the rum and serve at once. This sauce hardens quickly on cooling but can be melted again using DEFROST POWER.

Serves: 4-6
Power setting: FULL
Preparation time: about 30 minutes, plus cooling
Cooking time: 31-32 minutes

CHRISTMAS CAKE

800 g/1 lb 12 oz currants
375 g/13 oz sultanas
375 g/13 oz raisins
250 g/9 oz glacé cherries, halved
150 g/5 oz mixed cut peel
150 g/5 oz blanched almonds, coarsely chopped
1 teaspoon grated lemon rind
600 g/1 lb 5 oz plain flour
1 teaspoon ground mixed spice
1 teaspoon ground cinnamon
500 g/1 lb 2 oz butter
500 g/1 lb 2 oz soft brown sugar
9 large eggs (sizes 1, 2), beaten
3 tablespoons brandy

Line a large microwave round casserole, about 25 cm (10 inches) in diameter with cling film, smoothing out the surface well, or grease and coat with caster sugar.

Mix the currants with the sultanas, raisins, cherries, peel, almonds, lemon rind, flour and spices, blending well.

Cream the butter and sugar until light and fluffy. Add the beaten eggs, a little at a time, beating well after each addition.

Fold in half the flour and the fruit then fold in the remainder of the flour and add the brandy.

Spoon into the prepared dish, smoothing and packing down well to ensure there are no air pockets.

Cook for 2½ hours, turning the dish every 30 minutes.

Leave to cool slightly in the dish then turn out on to a wire rack to cool further. If liked, prick the cake with a fine skewer and slowly pour extra brandy into the cake before storing.

Coat with 900 g (2 lb) almond paste and 1.05 kg (2¼ lb) royal icing and decorate if liked.

Makes: 1×25 cm (10 inch) round cake
Power setting: DEFROST
Preparation time: 20-25 minutes
Cooking time: 2½ hours

Illustrated on p. 170

APPLE CRUNCH CAKE

100 g/4 oz butter
2 pkts. gingernut biscuits (approx. 150g/5 oz each), crushed
675 g/1½ lb apples, peeled, cored and sliced
juice of 1 lemon
50 g/2 oz demerara sugar
100 g/4 oz sultanas

Place the butter in a bowl and cook for 2 minutes to melt. Stir in the biscuit crumbs and mix well.

Toss the apples in the lemon juice to coat. Layer the apples, sugar, sultanas and biscuit crumbs in a serving dish, finishing with a layer of biscuit crumbs.

Cook for 10 minutes, turning the dish once. Serve hot or cold with whipped cream.

Serves: 6-8
Power setting: FULL
Preparation time: 10-15 minutes
Cooking time: 12 minutes

COFFEE ALMOND TORTE

1 recipe Genoese Sponge (see p. 174)
300 ml/½ pint whipping cream
1 tablespoon strong black coffee
2 tablespoons sifted icing sugar
100 g/4 oz flaked almonds

Prepare and cook the Genoese Sponge as on p. 174. Allow to cool then split into two layers.

Whip the cream with the coffee and sugar until it stands in soft peaks.

Sandwich the cake layers together with some of the coffee cream. Use the remainder to cover the top and sides of the cake.

Press the flaked almonds against the sides of the cake to coat.

Serve while very fresh cut into wedges.

Serves: 6
Power setting: FULL
Preparation time: 15-20 minutes, plus cooling
Cooking time: 10½-16½ minutes

CHOCOLATE LEMON CAKE

100 g/4 oz margarine
100 g/4 oz caster sugar
grated rind of 1 lemon
2 eggs, beaten
100 g/4 oz self-raising
    flour
100 g/4 oz plain or milk
    dessert chocolate

Grease a 22 cm (8½ inch) glass ring mould.
Cream the margarine and sugar until light and fluffy. Beat in the lemon rind and gradually add the eggs, blending well. Fold in the flour with a metal spoon. Spoon into the prepared ring mould and level the surface.

Cook on MEDIUM POWER for 5 minutes. Increase the power setting and cook on FULL POWER for 1 minute. Leave to stand for 5 minutes before turning out on to a wire rack to cool.

Place the chocolate in a bowl and cook on LOW POWER for 4-5 minutes until melted, stirring once. Cover and coat the cake with the melted chocolate. Leave to set and harden. Cut into wedges to serve.

Serves: 8-10
Power settings: MEDIUM, FULL, LOW
Preparation time: 20 minutes, plus cooling
Cooking time: 15-16 minutes

COFFEE ICE CREAM CAKE

2 eggs, separated
2 tablespoons coffee
    essence
50 g/2 oz icing sugar,
    sifted
150 ml/¼ pint double
    cream
1 recipe Genoese Sponge
    (see p. 174)
icing sugar to dust

Beat the egg yolks and coffee essence together. Whisk the egg whites until they stand in soft peaks, then gradually whisk in the sugar until thick and glossy. Fold the egg yolks into the egg white mixture with a metal spoon.

Whip the cream until it stands in soft peaks and fold into the coffee mixture with a metal spoon. Pour the mixture into a freezer tray and freeze until firm, about 2-4 hours.

Meanwhile prepare and cook the Genoese Sponge (see p. 174). Allow to cool.

Carefully split the cake into three layers. Sandwich together with the coffee ice cream.

Place on a serving plate and dust with icing sugar. Serve at once cut into wedges.

Serves: 4-6
Power setting: FULL
Preparation time: 20-25 minutes, plus freezing
Cooking time: 5½-6½ minutes

GINGER COCONUT CAKE

1 recipe Victoria
    Sandwich (see p. 174)
5 tablespoons raspberry
    jam
50 g/2 oz butter, softened
50 g/2 oz brown sugar
grated rind and juice of 1
    small orange
25 g/1 oz preserved
    ginger, chopped
3 tablespoons desiccated
    coconut

Prepare and cook the Victoria Sandwich as on p. 174. Allow to cool.

Spread the bottom layer of the cake with the raspberry jam.

Cream the butter with the sugar, orange rind and juice until light and fluffy. Beat in the ginger and coconut. Spread half the coconut mixture on the underside of the top layer of cake and sandwich the two cake halves together.

Spread the remaining coconut mixture over the top of the cake. Brown under a preheated hot grill until golden. Allow to cool then serve cut into wedges.

Serves: 6
Power setting: FULL
Preparation time: 30 minutes, plus cooling
Cooking time: 11½-12½ minutes

CHOCOLATE QUICKIES

100 g/4 oz butter

2 tablespoons cocoa
  powder

1 tablespoon demerara
  sugar

2 tablespoons golden
  syrup

225 g/8 oz semi-sweet
  biscuits, crushed

100 g/4 oz plain or milk
  chocolate

Grease an 18 cm (7 inch) square cake dish.

Place the butter in a bowl with the cocoa, demerara sugar and golden syrup. Cook on FULL POWER for 3-4 minutes, stirring once until boiling and bubbly.

Stir in the biscuits crumbs, blending well. Pour into the prepared cake dish and press out evenly.

Break the chocolate into pieces and place in a bowl. Cook on LOW POWER for 4-5 minutes until melted. Pour over the biscuit mixture. As the chocolate sets, mark it into swirls with a knife. Chill until set, then cut into about 12-16 squares or bars.

Makes: 12-16
Power settings: FULL, LOW
Preparation time: 15 minutes, plus cooling
Cooking time: 7-9 minutes

CHOCOLATE OATIES

100 g/4 oz plain
  chocolate

100 g/4 oz butter

175 g/6 oz brown sugar

2 eggs, beaten

100 g/4 oz plain flour

1 teaspoon salt

1 teaspoon baking
  powder

75 g/3 oz walnuts,
  chopped

175 g/6 oz rolled oats

2 teaspoons vanilla
  essence

Break the chocolate into pieces and place in a bowl. Cook for 1 minute to melt.

Meanwhile, cream the butter and sugar until light and fluffy. Beat in the eggs and cooked chocolate, blending well.

Sift the flour with the salt and baking powder. Add to the chocolate mixture with the walnuts, oats and vanilla essence. Beat well to blend.

Place in walnut-sized pieces on a lightly greased microwave baking tray, about 15 at a time. Cook for 3 minutes, turning the tray once.

Allow to cool on a wire rack.

To freeze
Cool quickly and place in a rigid container. Cover, seal, label and freeze for up to 2 months

Makes: about 60
Power setting: FULL
Preparation time: 15 minutes
Cooking time: 13 minutes
Suitable for freezing

QUICK VIENNA SPONGE

75 g/3 oz self-raising
  flour

2 teaspoons cornflour

pinch of salt

75 g/3 oz caster sugar

50 g/2 oz butter

2 teaspoons cocoa
  powder, sifted

3 eggs, beaten

Base line a 20 cm (8 inch) deep round glass dish with high sides. Do not grease the sides of the dish.

Sift the flour, cornflour and salt into a bowl. Add the sugar, blending well.

Place the butter in a bowl and cook on FULL POWER for 1-1½ minutes to melt. Add the cocoa powder, blending well.

Add to the flour mixture with the eggs and beat well to blend. Pour into the prepared dish and cook on LOW POWER for 5½-7 minutes until cooked, turning the dish twice. Leave to stand for 5 minutes before loosening with a knife and turning out on to a wire rack to cool.

Serve cut into wedges.

Serves: 6
Power settings: FULL, LOW
Preparation time: 10 minutes, plus cooling
Cooking time: 11½-13½ minutes

SHORTBREAD

175 g/6 oz plain flour
50 g/2 oz ground rice
pinch of salt
150 g/5 oz butter,
    softened
50 g/2 oz caster sugar

Line an 18 cm (7 inch) flan dish with cling film.

Sift the flour, ground rice and salt into a bowl. Rub in the butter until the mixture resembles fine breadcrumbs. Stir in half of the sugar and knead to make a dough.

Press into the prepared flan dish with the back of a metal spoon. Mark into 8 wedges with a sharp knife and prick well with a fork.

Cook for 3-4 minutes, turning the dish every 1 minute.

Sprinkle with the remaining sugar and leave to cool in the dish. Remove carefully with a palette knife to serve.

Makes: 8 pieces
Power setting: FULL
Preparation time: 10-15 minutes
Cooking time: about 3-4 minutes

FLAPJACKS

100 g/4 oz butter
25 g/1 oz caster sugar
40 g/1½ oz soft brown
    sugar
4 tablespoons golden
    syrup
pinch of salt
200 g/7 oz rolled oats
50 g/2 oz grapenuts

Lightly grease a 23 cm (9 inch) square shallow glass dish.

Place the butter and sugars in a bowl. Cook for 1½ minutes.

Add the syrup, salt, oats and grapenuts, blending well. Press the mixture evenly into the prepared dish.

Cook for 5 minutes turning the dish twice. Leave to cool in the dish.

Cut into squares to serve.

Makes: about 16 pieces
Power setting: FULL
Preparation time: 10 minutes, plus cooling
Cooking time: 6½ minutes

RASPBERRY AND RHUBARB TART

Base:
75 g/3 oz soft margarine
100 g/4 oz plain flour
50 g/2 oz dark brown
    sugar
¼ teaspoon vanilla
    essence
50 g/2 oz chopped nuts
Filling:
175 g/6 oz chopped
    frozen rhubarb
225 g/8 oz frozen
    raspberries
75-100 g/3-4 oz sugar
1 egg, lightly beaten
2 teaspoons cornflour
2 tablepoons water
whipped cream to
    decorate

Place the margarine, flour, sugar and vanilla essence in a bowl. Whisk with an electric beater until well blended. Stir in the nuts, blending well.

Place in a greased 25 cm (10 inch) pie dish and press over the base and sides to coat. Cook for 3 minutes, turning twice. Leave to cool while preparing the filling.

Place the rhubarb, raspberries, sugar to taste and egg in a bowl. Cook for 8 minutes, stirring twice.

Blend the cornflour with the water and stir into the raspberry mixture. Cook for 2 minutes, stirring twice until smooth and thickened.

Pour into the cooled tart case and chill until firm, about 2-3 hours.

Serve chilled decorated with swirls of whipped cream.

Serves: 6-8
Power setting: FULL
Preparation time: 25 minutes, plus cooling and chilling
Cooking time: 13 minutes

FLORENTINES

50 g/2 oz butter
50 g/2 oz demerara sugar
1 tablespoon golden
　syrup
50 g/2 oz glacé cherries,
　chopped
75 g/3 oz walnuts,
　chopped
25 g/1 oz sultanas
25 g/1 oz blanched
　almonds, chopped
25 g/1 oz cut mixed peel
25 g/1 oz plain flour

Place the butter, sugar and golden syrup in a bowl. Cook for 1-1½ minutes until melted.

Add the cherries, walnuts, sultanas, almonds, peel and flour. Mix well to blend.

Cook the florentines in about 3 batches by placing teaspoonfuls of the mixture, spaced well apart, on greaseproof paper. Cook each batch for 1½ minutes. Remove from the oven and shape the edges neatly with the side of a fork.

When slightly cooled, lift carefully with a palette knife on to a cooling rack. Serve plain or coat one side with melted chocolate if liked.

Makes: 12-15
Power setting: FULL
Preparation time: 15-20 minutes
Cooking time: about 5½-6 minutes

SCONES

225 g/8 oz plain flour
1 tablespoon baking
　powder
pinch of salt
50 g/2 oz butter
1 tablespoon caster sugar
150 ml/¼ pint milk
oil to brush browning dish

Sift the flour, baking powder and salt into a bowl. Rub in the butter, then stir in the sugar. Bind to a soft but not sticky dough with the milk.

Roll out the dough on a lightly floured surface to about 4 cm (1½ inches) thick and cut out 8-10 rounds using a 5 cm (2 inch) cutter.

Preheat a large browning dish for 5 minutes (or according to the manufacturer's instructions). Lightly brush the base with oil.

Add the scones and cook for 1 minute. Turn over with a spatula and cook for a further 1½-2 minutes.

Transfer to a wire rack to cool. Serve warm or cold, split and buttered.

To freeze
Cool quickly and place in a rigid container. Cover, seal, label and freeze for up to 3 months.

Makes: 8-10
Power setting: FULL
Preparation time: 10 minutes
Cooking time: 7½-8 minutes
Suitable for freezing

Illustrated on p. 187

STRAWBERRY SHORTCAKES

1 recipe scones (see
　above)
40 g/1½ oz butter
150 ml/¼ pint double
　cream, whipped
100 g/4 oz strawberries,
　hulled and sliced
icing sugar to dust

Prepare the scone dough as above. Roll out the dough on a lightly floured surface to about 2.5 cm (1 inch) thick and cut out 6 rounds using a 10 cm (4 inch) cutter.

Preheat a large browning dish for 5 minutes (or according to the manufacturer's instructions). Lightly brush the base with oil.

Add the shortcakes and cook for 1 minute. Turn over with a spatula and cook for a further 1½-2 minutes. Transfer to a wire rack to cool.

When cool, split and lightly butter each shortcake half. Sandwich together again with whipped cream and strawberries. Dust with icing sugar before serving.

Makes: 6
Power setting: FULL
Preparation time: 15 minutes, plus cooling
Cooking time: 7½-8 minutes

CHEESE AND BACON SCONES

225 g/8 oz plain flour
1 tablespoon baking
   powder
pinch of salt
50 g/2 oz butter
4 tablespoons grated
   onion
100 g/4 oz Cheddar
   cheese, grated
1½ teaspoons dried
   mixed herbs
40 g/1½ oz chopped
   cooked bacon
150 ml/¼ pint milk

Sift the flour, baking powder and salt into a bowl. Rub in the butter, then stir in the onion, cheese, herbs and bacon. Bind to a soft but not sticky dough with the milk.

Roll out on a lightly floured surface to about 4 cm (1½ inch) thick and cut out 8-10 rounds using a 5 cm (2 inch) cutter.

Preheat a large browning dish for 5 minutes (or according to the manufacturer's instructions). Lightly brush the base with oil.

Add the scones and cook for one minute. Turn over with a spatula and cook for a further 1½-2 minutes.

Transfer to a wire rack to cool. Ideally, serve the scones warm, split and buttered.

Serves: 8-10
Power setting: FULL
Preparation time: 10-15 minutes
Cooking time: 7½-8 minutes

FROSTED COCONUT CAKE

Cake:
175 g/6 oz self-raising
   flour
100 g/4 oz soft margarine
100 g/4 oz caster sugar
2 large eggs (size 2)
75 ml/3 fl oz milk
grated rind of 1 lemon
50 g/2 oz desiccated
   coconut
Topping:
1 tablespoon caster sugar
1 tablespoon lemon juice
1 tablespoon desiccated
   coconut
10 glacé cherries, halved

Grease a 23 cm (9 inch) ring mould.

Place the flour, margarine, sugar, eggs, milk and lemon rind in a bowl. Beat for 1½ minutes with an electric mixer or for about 3 minutes by hand using a wooden spoon.

Fold in the coconut with a metal spoon, place the mixture in the ring mould, level the surface and cook for 8 minutes, giving the mould a quarter-turn every 2 minutes. Leave to stand for 6 minutes then turn out on to a wire rack to cool.

To make the topping, mix the caster sugar with the lemon juice and spoon over the top of the cooled cake. Sprinkle at once with the coconut to coat evenly.

Decorate with the cherry halves. Cut into wedges to serve.

Serves: 10
Power setting: FULL
Preparation time: 20 minutes, plus cooling
Cooking time: 14 minutes

CHOCOLATE OAT CHEWS

75 g/3 oz butter
50 g/2 oz caster sugar
2 tablespoons golden
   syrup
225 g/8 oz quick-cook
   oats
3 tablespoons cocoa
   powder
1 teaspoon vanilla or
   rum essence
25 g/1 oz walnuts,
   chopped
50 g/2 oz raisins, chopped

Grease a 20 cm (8 inch) square cake dish.

Place the butter, sugar and golden syrup in a bowl. Cook for 3-4 minutes or until boiling and bubbly, stirring once.

Add the oats, cocoa powder, essence, walnuts and raisins, blending well.

Spoon into the prepared cake dish, levelling the surface. Allow to cool then chill until set.

Cut into 5 cm (2 inch) squares to serve.

Makes: 16
Power setting: FULL
Preparation time: 10 minutes, plus cooling and chilling
Cooking time: 3-4 minutes

SCONES (p.185, 186)

COCONUT ICE (p.200)

Drinks

Homely and steaming hot, soothingly warm and elegant, or sharp, cool and quenching – a wide range of beverages may be prepared quickly in the microwave oven for breakfast, mid-morning, late-afternoon or after-supper drinking.

When heating drinks in the microwave always leave room for the liquid to expand. Liquids should never be heated in narrow-necked bottles or jugs, since the pressure built up can cause them to shatter.

Check that there is no metal present, such as screws in handles, and also that glass is not of the lead crystal type.

REAL OLD-FASHIONED LEMONADE

finely grated rind of 2 lemons
juice of 4 lemons
3 tablespoons water
225 g/8 oz sugar
iced water to serve

Place the lemon rind, lemon juice, water and sugar in a large heatproof jug, blending well. Cook for 4 minutes, stirring twice. Leave to stand, covered, until cool. Chill thoroughly then dilute to taste with iced water (about 300 ml/½ pint iced water to 50 ml/2 fl oz lemonade concentrate).

Serves: 6-8
Power setting: FULL
Preparation time: 10 minutes plus cooling and chilling
Cooking time: 4 minutes

FRESH TOMATO JUICE

12 ripe tomatoes, peeled and chopped
100 ml/4 fl oz water
1 onion, peeled and sliced
2 sticks celery (with leaves), scrubbed and sliced
1 bay leaf
3 sprigs parsley
1 teaspoon Worcestershire sauce
1 teaspoon sugar
salt and freshly ground black pepper

Place the tomatoes in a bowl with the water, onion, celery, bay leaf and parsley, blending well. Cover and cook on FULL POWER for 3 minutes.

Reduce the power setting and cook on MEDIUM POWER for 4 minutes.

Strain the mixture and add the Worcestershire sauce, sugar and salt and pepper to taste, blending well. Cool and chill before serving.

Serves: 2
Power settings: FULL, MEDIUM
Preparation time: 10 minutes plus cooling and chilling
Cooking time: 7 minutes

ORANGEADE

4 oranges
1 lemon
900 ml/1½ pints cold water
75 g/3 oz sugar

Thinly pare the rind from the oranges and lemon and place in a bowl with the water. Cook for 6-7 minutes until very hot. Add the sugar and stir to dissolve. Cover and leave until cold.

Strain the mixture into a jug and add the juice from the oranges and lemon, blending well. Serve cold.

Makes: 1.2 litres/2 pints
Power setting: FULL
Preparation time: 10 minutes plus cooling
Cooking time: 6-7 minutes

RUSSIAN CHOCOLATE

300 ml/½ pint milk
5 teaspoons drinking chocolate
1 measure brandy
1 tablespoon double cream
grated chocolate

Place the milk in a heatproof mug and cook for 1¼ minutes. Stir in the drinking chocolate, blending well.

Add the brandy, blending well. Cook for ½ minute. Pour the cream on top of the chocolate mixture and sprinkle with grated chocolate. Serve at once.

Serves: 1
Power setting: FULL
Preparation time: 5 minutes
Cooking time: 1¾ minutes

HOT PEPPERMINT CHOCOLATE

4 teaspoons drinking chocolate
600 ml/1 pint milk
¼ teaspoon peppermint essence
grated chocolate

Blend the drinking chocolate with the milk in a large heatproof jug. Cook for 4-5 minutes until very hot but not boiling.

Add the peppermint essence, blending well. Pour into mugs or heatproof glass tumblers and sprinkle with grated chocolate. Serve at once.

Serves: 2
Power setting: FULL
Preparation time: 5 minutes
Cooking time: 4-5 minutes

RICH HOT CHOCOLATE

50 g/2 oz plain chocolate, broken into pieces
5 tablespoons hot water
450 ml/¾ pint milk
chocolate aerosol cream to top

Place the chocolate in a large jug. Cook for 3½ minutes or until the chocolate has melted.

Stir in the water and then the milk, blending well. Cook for 3 minutes, stirring once.

Pour into 4 warmed cups and top each with a squirt of chocolate aerosol cream. Serve at once.

Serves: 4
Power setting: FULL
Preparation time: 5 minutes
Cooking time: 6½ minutes

CREAMY COCOA

3 tablespoons cocoa powder
50 g/2 oz sugar
900 ml/1½ pints milk

Blend the cocoa, sugar and milk in a large heatproof jug. Cook for 4-5 minutes until very hot but not boiling.

Whisk well until hot, steaming and frothy. Pour into mugs and serve at once.

Serves: 4
Power setting: FULL
Preparation time: 5 minutes
Cooking time: 4-5 minutes

FOAMING MOCHA

4 teaspoons drinking chocolate
3 teaspoons instant coffee granules
1 teaspoon sugar
600 ml/1 pint milk
1 egg white
ground cinnamon

Blend the drinking chocolate, coffee, sugar and milk in a large heatproof jug. Cook for 4-5 minutes until very hot but not boiling. Pour into mugs or heatproof glass tumblers.

Whisk the egg white until it stands in stiff peaks. Spoon on top of the mocha drink and sprinkle with ground cinnamon. Serve at once.

Serves: 2
Power setting: FULL
Preparation time: 5 minutes
Cooking time: 4-5 minutes

IRISH COFFEE

175 ml/6 fl oz cold coffee
2-3 tablespoons Irish
    whiskey
1-2 teaspoons sugar
1-2 tablespoons double
    cream

Place the coffee, whiskey and sugar to taste in an Irish coffee goblet or heatproof glass. Cook for 1½-2 minutes until very hot but not boiling. Stir well to blend.

Whip the cream lightly until slightly thickened. Pour over the back of a teaspoon on to the coffee so that it forms a distinctive layer. Serve at once.

Serves: 1
Power setting: FULL
Preparation time: 5 minutes
Cooking time: 1½-2 minutes

AFTER EIGHT COFFEE

1 tablespoon crème de
    menthe liqueur
1 rounded teaspoon
    demerara sugar
175 ml/6 fl oz cold, made
    black coffee
1-2 tablespoons double
    cream

Place the crème de menthe, sugar and coffee in a stemmed, heatproof glass. Cook for 1½-2 minutes until very hot but not boiling. Stir well to dissolve the sugar completely.

Whip the cream lightly, then pour over the back of a spoon on to the coffee so that it forms a layer on the surface. Serve the coffee at once.

Serves: 1
Power setting: FULL
Preparation time: 5 minutes
Cooking time: 1½ minutes

TOM AND JERRYS

150 ml/¼ pint milk
20 g/¾ oz butter
2 eggs, separated
1 tablespoon sugar
¼ teaspoon vanilla
    essence
75 ml/3 fl oz brandy
75 ml/3 fl oz brown rum
ground nutmeg to
    sprinkle

Place the milk and butter in a large heatproof jug. Cook for 1½ minutes, stirring once.

Whisk the egg whites until they stand in stiff peaks. Add the sugar and whisk until stiff and glossy. Fold in the egg yolks and vanilla essence, blending well.

Slowly pour the milk mixture into the egg mixture, whisking constantly. Whisk in the brandy and rum. Cook for 1 minute.

Whisk the mixture until it becomes frothy. Serve at once, with a little nutmeg sprinkled on top.

Serves: 3
Power setting: FULL
Preparation time: 10 minutes
Cooking time: 2½ minutes

MULLED WINE

300 ml/½ pint water
1 cinnamon stick
3 cloves
100 ml/4 fl oz orange
    syrup
4 dessertspoons lemon
    syrup
1 × 75 cl (26.4 fl oz) bottle
    red wine
1 orange, sliced

Place the water, cinnamon stick and cloves in a bowl. Cook for 5 minutes.

Strain the liquid into a large heatproof jug. Add the orange syrup, lemon syrup and wine, blending well. Cook for 4 minutes.

Pour into 6 warmed heatproof glasses and decorate with the orange slices. Serve at once.

Serves: 6
Power setting: FULL
Preparation time: 5-10 minutes
Cooking time: 9 minutes

BITTER LEMON

4 lemons, washed and cut
  into pieces
600 ml/1 pint cold water
100 g/4 oz sugar
300 ml/½ pint soda water

Place the lemons and water in a large heat-proof jug. Cook on FULL POWER for 5 minutes.

Reduce the power setting and cook on MEDIUM POWER for 5 minutes.

Add the sugar and stir to dissolve. Leave until cool then strain.

Top up the bitter lemon mixture with soda water and serve at once.

Makes: 900 ml/1½ pints
Power settings: FULL, MEDIUM
Preparation time: 5 minutes plus
  cooling
Cooking time: 10 minutes

LEMON TEA

750 ml/1¼ pints made
  China tea
1 lemon, very finely sliced

Place the tea in a large heatproof jug. Cook for 4½-5 minutes until very hot but not boiling.

Add the finely sliced lemon, cover and leave the tea to stand for 5 minutes before serving.

Serves: 4
Power setting: FULL
Preparation time: 5 minutes
Cooking time: 9½-10 minutes

GUIDE TO HEATING COFFEE AND MILK

	Time in minutes on FULL POWER
Black coffee	
600 ml/1 pint (cold)	4½-5
1.15 litres/2 pints (cold)	7-7½
Milk	
150 ml/¼ pint (cold)	1-1½
300 ml/½ pint (cold)	2-2½
Coffee and milk together	
600 ml/1 pint coffee and 150 ml/¼ pint milk (both cold)	5-5½
1.15 litres/2 pints coffee and 300 ml/½ pint milk (both cold)	8-8½

SPICY APPLE JUICE

450 g/1 lb cooking apples,
  peeled, cored and
  sliced
2 tablespoons water
sugar to taste
150 ml/¼ pint dry white
  wine
¼ teaspoon ground
  cinnamon
300 ml/½ pint sparkling
  cider

Place the apples in a bowl with the water and sugar to taste. Cover lightly and cook for 5 minutes.

Liquidise the mixture in a blender with the wine and cinnamon. Allow to cool or keep warm. Stir in the cider and serve at once, either warm or cold.

Makes: 750 ml/1¼ pints
Power setting: FULL
Preparation time: 10-15 minutes
Cooking time: 5 minutes

JAPANESE PUNCH

300 ml/½ pint brewed tea
4 cloves
1 cinnamon stick
½ teaspoon ground
  ginger
small sprig mint
1.2 litres/2 pints
  lemonade

Place the tea, cloves, cinnamon, ginger and mint in a large heatproof bowl. Cook for 3 minutes. Leave to stand until cool.

Strain the tea mixture into a jug and top up with the lemonade. Mix well to blend. Serve lightly chilled.

Makes: 6-8 glasses
Power setting: FULL
Preparation time: 5 minutes plus
  cooling
Cooking time: 3 minutes

TIPSY TEA

600 ml/1 pint cold tea
1 bottle red wine
150 g/5 oz sugar
3 cloves
pinch of ground
    cinnamon
150 ml/¼ pint brown rum
    or Arrack
juice of 1 lemon

Place the tea, red wine, sugar, cloves and cinnamon in a large heatproof jug. Cook for 5-6 minutes until very hot.

Stir in the rum or Arrack and lemon juice, blending well. Serve at once.

Serves: 4
Power setting: FULL
Preparation time: 5 minutes
Cooking time: 5-6 minutes

HONEYED POSSET

3 egg yolks
2 rounded tablespoons
    clear honey
150 ml/¼ pint medium
    white wine
grated rind of 1 orange

Place the egg yolks and honey in a bowl and whisk well to blend.

Place the wine and orange rind in a jug and cook on FULL POWER for 1½ minutes until just boiling. Pour on to the egg mixture, whisking continuously.

Return the bowl to the microwave and cook on LOW POWER for 1½ minutes. Whisk until very thick and frothy, about 3-5 minutes.

Serve at once in warmed glasses.

Serves: 4
Power settings: FULL, LOW
Preparation time: 10 minutes
Cooking time: 3 minutes

RUM WARMER

300 ml/½ pint milk
1 egg yolk
2 teaspoons brown sugar
1 tablespoon instant
    coffee granules
2-3 tablespoons brown
    rum

Whisk the milk with the egg yolk and sugar and place in a heatproof glass. Cook, uncovered, for 2-2½ minutes or until very hot.

Add the coffee and rum to taste and stir well to blend. Serve at once.

Serves: 1
Power setting: FULL
Preparation time: 5 minutes
Cooking time: 2-2½ minutes

REHEATING A BABY'S BOTTLE

Without doubt, the microwave takes on almost 'magical' powers in the area of reheating liquids and none more so than with the baby's bottle at 3 o'clock in the morning!

Prepared ahead, covered and stored in the refrigerator for no more than 12 hours, baby milk may be reheated to the correct drinking temperature very quickly.

Do not heat with the teat in the bottle and shake well after heating to distribute the heat. The timings below refer to average quantities of chilled baby milk. Always check the temperature of the milk by shaking a few drops on the back of your hand before feeding.

200 ml/7 fl oz
        about 1 minute on FULL POWER
150 ml/5 fl oz
        about ½-¾ minute on FULL POWER
75 ml/3 fl oz
        about ¼-½ minute on FULL POWER

Preserves and Confectionery

A few shelves of really individual and fresh-flavoured jams, jellies, chutneys, pickles and sweetmeats, made at home, are a source of infinite satisfaction the whole year round. For there is nothing more beguiling or rewarding than an unusual pot of jam or marmalade at breakfast or tea, a laden jar of fruit for a pudding or pie, a home-made pickle or chutney to cheer up a cold joint or a daintily laid dish of truffles for after-dinner eating.

Made in the microwave, preserves and confectionery prove economical on energy, certainly efficient with time and safer to prepare than those cooked the conventional way, since any spillages and burns are enclosed within the oven, and the cook does not have to lean over a hot stove to stir the dishes.

MICROWAVE STRAWBERRY JAM

1.2 kg/2½ lb strawberries, hulled
juice of 1 lemon
1.4 kg/3 lb sugar
7 g/¼ oz butter
½ bottle liquid pectin (Certo, for example)

Place the strawberries in a large heatproof bowl and crush thoroughly. Add the lemon juice and sugar, blending well.

Cook for 15 minutes, stirring every 5 minutes. Add the butter and stir well to blend. Cook for a further 10 minutes, stirring twice. Remove from the oven and stir in the pectin. Allow to cool until syrupy so that the fruit does not float.

Ladle into warm sterilized jars, cover, seal and label. Store in a cool dark place until required.

Makes: about 2.25 kg/5 lb
Power setting: FULL
Preparation time: 30 minutes plus cooling
Cooking time: 25 minutes

THREE FRUIT MARMALADE

1½ lemons (medium size)
1½ oranges (medium size)
1½ grapefruit (medium size)
600 ml/1 pint boiling water
1.5 kg/3½ lb granulated or preserving sugar

Wash the fruit, cut into quarters and slice thinly. Retain the pips and tie them in a piece of muslin.

Place the fruit and the pips in a large heatproof bowl. Add 150 ml/¼ pint of the water. Leave to stand overnight.

Add the remaining water, cover and cook for 25 minutes. Remove and discard the muslin. Add the sugar and stir until dissolved. Cook, uncovered, for 20-30 minutes or until setting point is reached, stirring every 5 minutes.

Ladle into clean warmed jars, cover, seal, label and store until required.

Makes: about 2.25-2.7 kg/5-6 lb
Power setting: FULL
Preparation time: 20 minutes plus soaking
Cooking time: 45-55 minutes

194

TEST FOR SETTING

As in conventional cooking, several minutes of a good rolling boil in the microwave are often required to achieve setting point.

To test for the setting point in jams and jellies that are made without liquid pectin, place a little of the mixture on a cold saucer. Allow to cool then push the mixture with the finger.

If the surface does not wrinkle then cook the mixture for another 2-3 minutes and test again. If the surface wrinkles then setting point has been reached.

FRESH APRICOT JAM

1.4 kg/3 lb apricots, halved and stoned
7 g/¼ oz citric acid
200 ml/7 fl oz water
1.6 kg/3½ lb granulated or preserving sugar

Place the apricots in a large heatproof bowl. Mix the citric acid with the water and pour over the apricots. Cover and cook for 20 minutes or until the apricots are soft.

Stir in the sugar, blending well. Cook for 45-50 minutes or until setting point is reached, stirring every 10 minutes.

Ladle into clean warmed jars, cover, seal, label and store until required.

Makes: about 2.7 kg/6 lb
Power setting: FULL
Preparation time: 30 minutes
Cooking time: 1 hour 5 minutes-1 hour 10 minutes

RASPBERRY JAM

800 g/1¾ lb raspberries, hulled
7 g/¼ oz citric acid
625 g/22 oz preserving sugar
15 g/½ oz unsalted butter

Place the raspberries in a large heatproof bowl and sprinkle with the citric acid. Cook for 10 minutes until soft.

Add the sugar and butter, blending well. Cook for 40-45 minutes, stirring every 5 minutes, until setting point is reached.

Leave to stand for 20 minutes. Ladle into warm sterilized jars, cover, seal and label. Store in a cool dark place until required.

Makes: 900 g/2 lb
Power setting: FULL
Preparation time: 20 minutes
Cooking time: 1 hour 10 minutes-1 hour 15 minutes

LEMON CURD

100 g/4 oz butter
grated rind and juice of 3 lemons
225/8 oz granulated sugar
3 eggs
1 egg yolk

Place the butter, lemon rind and lemon juice in a large bowl and cook on FULL POWER for 3 minutes, stirring once.

Add the sugar, blending well. Cook on FULL POWER for 2 minutes, stirring once.

Beat the eggs with the egg yolk and stir into the mixture, blending well. Cook, uncovered, on LOW POWER for 12-14 minutes until the mixture has thickened and will coat the back of a wooden spoon, stirring every 3 minutes.

Pour into clean sterilized jars, cover, seal, label and store in a cool place or the refrigerator. Keep for up to 2-3 weeks.

Makes: 675 g/1½ lb
Power setting: FULL, LOW
Preparation time: 20-25 minutes
Cooking time: 17-19 minutes

ORANGE AND REDCURRANT JELLY

900 g/2 lb redcurrants, topped and tailed
5 tablespoons water
5 tablespoons unsweetened orange juice
675 g/1½ lb sugar
¼ bottle liquid pectin (Certo, for example)

Place the redcurrants in a bowl and crush with a wooden spoon. Add the water and orange juice, blending well. Cook for 10 minutes, stirring once.

Strain the mixture through a jelly bag into a bowl and, if necessary, make up to 600 ml/1 pint with water.

Add the sugar, blending well. Cook for 8 minutes, stirring twice. Cook the sugar mixture until boiling, about 2 minutes, then cook for 1 minute.

Stir in the liquid pectin, blending well. Cook for 4 minutes, stirring once.

Cool slightly then ladle into warm sterilized jars. Cover, seal, label and store until required.

Makes: 1.4 kg/3 lb
Power setting: FULL
Preparation time: 25-35 minutes
Cooking time: 25 minutes

CIDER AND SAGE JELLY

150 ml/¼ pint boiling water
4 tablespoons chopped fresh sage
900 g/2 lb sugar
450 ml/¾ pint sweet cider
150 ml/¼ pint liquid pectin (Certo, for example)

Mix the water with the sage and leave to stand for 15 minutes.

Place the sugar and cider in a large heatproof bowl. Cook for 8½ minutes, stirring once.

Strain the herbs and add the water to the syrup mixture. Cook for 6 minutes or until boiling.

Stir in the liquid pectin, blending well. Cook for 3 minutes. Stir well then leave to stand for 1 minute.

Ladle into warm sterilized jars, cover, seal, label and store until required.

Makes: about 1.25 kg/2½ lb
Power setting: FULL
Preparation time: 20-30 minutes
Cooking time: 33½ minutes

MICROWAVE MINT JELLY

50 g/2 oz fresh mint, washed
450 g/1 lb sugar
300 ml/½ pint distilled vinegar
1 bottle liquid pectin (Certo, for example)
green food colouring

Finely chop half of the mint and set aside. Place the remaining mint in a large heatproof bowl with the sugar and vinegar. Cook for 8 minutes, stirring twice.

Remove the mint with a slotted spoon. Cook the sugar mixture until boiling, about 2 minutes, then cook for 1 minute.

Strain the liquid through muslin, stir in the liquid pectin and a few drops of green food colouring, blending well. Return to the bowl and cook for 4 minutes, stirring once.

Stir in the chopped mint. Cool slightly then stir again. Ladle into warm sterilized jars, cover, seal, label and store until required.

Makes: 900 g/2 lb
Power setting: FULL
Preparation time: 20 minutes
Cooking time: 15 minutes

SWEETCORN RELISH

200 ml/8 fl oz distilled
    malt vinegar
few strands of saffron
1 red pepper, cored,
    seeded and chopped
1 green pepper, cored,
    seeded and chopped
1 stick celery, scrubbed
    and chopped
1 onion, peeled and finely
    chopped
1 garlic clove, peeled and
    chopped
225 g/8 oz sugar
675 g/1½ lb sweetcorn
    kernels
15 g/½ oz salt
pinch of mustard powder
pinch of ground mace
pinch of dried tarragon
2 tablespoons arrowroot
    powder
water

Mix the vinegar with the saffron and leave to turn yellow.

Place the peppers, celery, onion and garlic in a bowl. Strain in the vinegar, blending well. Cover and cook for 5 minutes.

Add the sugar, sweetcorn, salt, mustard, mace and tarragon, blending well. Cook for 5 minutes.

Blend the arrowroot with a little cold water and stir into the vegetable mixture, blending well. Cook for 8 minutes stirring once. Leave to stand for 5 minutes.

Ladle into warmed clean jars. Seal, label and store until required.

Makes: 1.5 kg/3 lb
Power setting: FULL
Preparation time: 20-30 minutes
Cooking time: 23 minutes

MEDITERRANEAN CHUTNEY

900 g/2 lb tomatoes,
    peeled and chopped
450 g/1 lb Spanish
    onions, peeled and
    chopped
450 g/1 lb courgettes,
    thinly sliced
1 large green pepper,
    cored, seeded and
    chopped
1 large red pepper, cored,
    seeded and chopped
225 g/8 oz aubergine,
    chopped
2 large garlic cloves,
    peeled and crushed
1 tablespoon cayenne
    pepper
1 tablespoon ground
    paprika
1 tablespoon ground
    coriander
300 ml/½ pint malt
    vinegar
350 g/12 oz sugar

Place the tomatoes in a large heatproof bowl with the onions, courgettes, peppers, aubergine, garlic, cayenne pepper, paprika and coriander. Cook, uncovered, for 15 minutes, stirring twice.

Add the vinegar and sugar, blending well. Cook for 15 minutes, stirring twice, Leave to stand for 5 minutes.

Ladle into warmed clean jars, seal, label and store until required.

Makes: 2.75 kg/6 lb
Power setting: FULL
Preparation time: 30-40 minutes
Cooking time: 35 minutes

DRYING HERBS

The spring and summer months bring an abundance of fresh herbs – so much so that it is worth drying some for winter-time use. The microwave will dry fresh herbs so that they retain a good flavour and, moreover, colour.

Herbs are best dried between two sheets of absorbent kitchen paper but must be turned or re-arranged frequently so that they do not become too dry and brittle.

Fleshy herbs like parsley, chervil, chives and mint should be chopped and cooked on FULL POWER for about 5 minutes. More brittle herbs like sage and rosemary should be stripped from their stems and cooked on FULL POWER for 2-3 minutes.

Check the herbs frequently during the cooking time for best results.

Store herbs in a cool dry place until needed.

TOMATO CHUTNEY

2.7 kg/6 lb ripe tomatoes, peeled and chopped
225 g/8 oz onions, peeled and finely chopped
4 teaspoons whole allspice, tied in a piece of muslin
½ teaspoon cayenne pepper
1 tablespoon ground black pepper
½ teaspoon ground ginger
grated rind and juice of 1 lemon
grated rind and juice of 1 orange
350 g/12 oz soft brown sugar
300 ml/½ pint vinegar

Place the tomatoes, onions, allspice, cayenne pepper, black pepper, ginger, lemon rind, lemon juice, orange rind and orange juice in a large heatproof bowl, blending well. Cook for 10 minutes, stirring twice.

Add the sugar and vinegar, blending well. Cook for 30-40 minutes until the mixture has thickened to a pulp, stirring occasionally.

Ladle into clean warmed jars, cover, seal, label and store until required.

Makes: about 3.6 kg/8 lb
Power setting: FULL
Preparation time: 30-40 minutes
Cooking time: 40-50 minutes

BLACKBERRY AND CURAÇAO JAM

450 g/1 lb caster sugar
150 ml/¼ pint hot water
675 g/1½ lb blackberries, hulled
3 tablespoons Curaçao

Place the sugar and water in a large heat-proof bowl. Cook for 3 minutes, stirring once.

Add the blackberries, blending well. Cook, uncovered, for 8-10 minutes, stirring once. Test for set. If a skin does not form then cook for a further 2-3 minutes and test again. Then stir in the Curaçao, blending well.

Ladle into warm sterilized jars, cover, seal, label and store in a cool place until required.

Makes: 900 g/2 lb
Power setting: FULL
Preparation time: 20-25 minutes
Cooking time: 11-13 minutes

ROSY PEARS

175 g/6 oz caster sugar
450 ml/¾ pint dry red or
    rosé wine
6 large pears, peeled
2 teaspoons lemon juice

Place the sugar and wine in a 1.8 kg (4 lb) preserving jar. Cook, uncovered, on FULL POWER for 4-5 minutes, stirring the mixture once.

Brush the pears with the lemon juice and add to the jar. Cover with cling film, snipping two holes in the top to allow any steam to escape. Cook on FULL POWER for 4 minutes.

Reduce the power setting and cook on MEDIUM POWER for 4 minutes.

Cover, seal, label and leave until cold. Wipe any stickiness from the jar and check that the seal is good. Store the pears until required.

Makes: 1 × 1.8 kg/ (4 lb) jar
Power settings: FULL, MEDIUM
Preparation time: 20 minutes plus cooling
Cooking time: 12-13 minutes

BOTTLED DAMSONS

450 g/1 lb caster sugar
300 ml/½ pint boiling
    water
900 g/2 lb damsons,
    halved and stoned

Place the sugar and water in a 1.8 kg (4 lb) preserving jar. Cook, uncovered, on FULL POWER for 4 minutes, stirring once.

Add the damsons to the jar, packing down well. Cover with cling film, snipping two holes in the top to allow any steam to escape. Cook on FULL POWER for 5 minutes.

Reduce the power setting and cook on MEDIUM POWER for 5 minutes.

Cover, seal, label and leave until cold. Wipe any stickiness from the jar and check that the seal is good. Store the damsons until required.

Serves: 1 × 1.8 kg (4 lb) jar
Power settings: FULL, MEDIUM
Preparation time: 20 minutes plus cooling
Cooking time: 14 minutes

ALMOND AND PEANUT BRITTLE

225 g/8 oz sugar
6 tablespoons golden
    syrup
100 g/4 oz salted peanuts
100 g/4 oz flaked
    almonds
7 g/¼ oz butter
1 teaspoon vanilla
    essence
1 teaspoon baking
    powder

Place the sugar and golden syrup in a large heatproof bowl. Cook for 4 minutes, stirring twice.

Add the peanuts and almonds, blending well. Cook for 3-5 minutes or until a rich golden colour.

Add the butter and vanilla essence, blending well. Cook for 1-2 minutes. Stir in the baking powder and stir gently until light and foamy.

Pour on to a lightly greased baking tray and leave to set.

To serve, break the brittle up into small pieces. Store it in an airtight tin until required.

Makes: 450 g/1 lb
Power setting: FULL
Preparation time: 15 minutes plus cooling
Cooking time: 8-11 minutes

COLETTES

275 g/10 oz plain
   chocolate, broken into
   pieces
150 ml/¼ pint double
   cream
1 tablespoon brandy
20 whole hazelnuts,
   skinned

Place 100 g/4 oz of the chocolate in a bowl. Cook for 1½-2 minutes, stirring once, until melted. Use to coat the inside of 20 round petit four cases, then turn the cases upside down so that the chocolate edges remain thicker than the base. Chill until set, about 1-2 hours.

Place the cream in a bowl and cook for 1-1½ minutes or until just to the boil. Add the remaining chocolate, stirring well to completely melt. Cook for 1-1½ minutes or until just to the boil. Stir in the brandy, blending well.

Allow to cool then chill until the chocolate mixture just begins to set. Spoon into a piping bag fitted with a star nozzle and pipe equal quantities of the chocolate truffle mixture into the chocolate-lined cases. Chill to set.

Carefully peel away the paper cases from the chocolate colettes and decorate each with a hazelnut. Return to new petit four cases and serve lightly chilled.

Makes: 20
Power setting: FULL
Preparation time: 40 minutes plus cooling
Cooking time: 3½-5 minutes

ALMOND AND GINGER CLUSTERS

50 g/2 oz flaked almonds
75 g/3 oz plain chocolate
25 g/1 oz crystallized
   ginger, chopped
finely chopped
   crystallized ginger to
   decorate

Place the almonds on a plate and cook for 2 minutes. Stir to rearrange and cook for a further 2 minutes until lightly browned. Leave to cool then cut into thin slivers.

Break the chocolate into pieces and place in a bowl. Cook for 1-1½ minutes, stirring once, until melted. Add the almonds and ginger, blending well.

Spoon into 12 paper sweet cases. Sprinkle with the ginger to decorate and leave to set.

Makes: 12
Power setting: FULL
Preparation time: 20 minutes plus cooling
Cooking time: 5-5½ minutes

COCONUT ICE

450 g/1 lb caster sugar
150 ml/¼ pint milk
75 g/3 oz desiccated
   coconut
pink food colouring

Lightly grease an 18×23×2.5 cm (7×9×1 inch) shallow dish or tray.

Place the sugar and milk in a large heatproof bowl. Cook for 4-5 minutes, stirring twice.

Cook further until the soft boil stage is reached or until a candy thermometer registers 115°C/240°F (about 4-6 minutes).

Add the coconut, blending well. Pour half of the mixture into the prepared tray. Colour the remainder pink with food colouring and pour over the white layer. Leave to harden and set. Cut into squares to serve.

Makes: about 550 g/1¼ lb
Power setting: FULL
Preparation time: 15 minutes plus cooling
Cooking time: 8-11 minutes

Illustrated on p. 188

TRUFFLES

75 g/3 oz plain dessert
   chocolate, broken into
   pieces
1 egg yolk
1 teaspoon single cream
7 g/¼ oz butter
1 teaspoon brown rum
40 g/1½ chocolate
   vermicelli

Place the chocolate in a bowl and cook for 1½ minutes to melt, stirring twice.

Add the egg yolk, cream, butter and rum, blending well. Beat until cool and thick, about 5-10 minutes. Chill until just setting.

Divide and shape into about 15 small balls and roll in the chocolate vermicelli. Place in small paper sweet cases to serve.

Makes: 15
Power setting: FULL
Preparation time: 20 minutes
Cooking time: 1½ minutes

CHOCOLATE CRACKLES

2 tablespoons clear honey
75 g/3 oz butter
2 teaspoons drinking
   chocolate powder
175 g/6 oz icing sugar
100 g/4 oz chocolate rice
   cereal (Coco Pops, for
   example)

Place the honey and butter in a large bowl and cook for 2-2½ minutes until melted.

Add the drinking chocolate, sugar and rice cereal, blending well.

Spoon equally into about 30 paper bun cases and leave to set.

Store in an airtight tin. Eat within 2 days of making.

Makes: 30
Power setting: FULL
Preparation time: 15 minutes plus cooling
Cooking time: 2-2½ minutes

SPEEDY FUDGE

75 g/3 oz butter, diced
1×170 g (6 oz) can
   evaporated milk
450 g/1 lb icing sugar
1 tablespoon malt
   vinegar
1 tablespoon golden
   syrup
1 teaspoon vanilla
   essence
65 ml/2½ fl oz double
   cream

Lightly grease an 18.5×22.5 cm (7½×9 inch) shallow tin.

Place the butter and evaporated milk in a large heatproof bowl. Cook for 1 minute then stir well to blend.

Add the sugar, vinegar and syrup, blending well. Cook for 10 minutes, stirring twice.

Add the vanilla essence and whisk for about 8 minutes, gradually adding the cream, until smooth and creamy.

Pour into the prepared tin and leave to set in a cool place. When cold mark then cut into squares to serve.

Makes: about 36 squares
Power setting: FULL
Preparation time: 15-20 minutes
Cooking time: 11 minutes

SOFT TREACLE TOFFEE

225 g/8 oz black treacle
100 g/4 oz butter
225 g/8 oz granulated
   sugar
2 teaspoons vinegar

Place the treacle, butter, sugar and vinegar in a large heatproof bowl. Cook for 6-7 minutes, stirring twice.

Test for setting by dropping a little in a cup of cold water. The mixture will form a hard but pliable ball when pressed between the fingers.

Pour into a small greased tin and leave to set. Just before setting mark into squares.

Makes: 450 g/1 lb
Power setting: FULL
Preparation time: 5 minutes plus cooling
Cooking time: 6-7 minutes

Slimmers' Recipes

The microwave can be a valuable aid at times when it proves necessary to trim the diet a little, for it can cook foods with little or no additional fat without sacrificing flavour.
Its speed and efficiency also mean the cook need spend little time in the kitchen – a dieter's danger area. And since foods can be frozen then quickly reheated for fresh-tasting meals there is no need to finish off leftovers – another problem time for dieters.

SMOKED SEAFOOD PÂTÉ

550 g/1¼ lb smoked haddock or cod
1 small onion, peeled and thinly sliced
4 tablespoons water
1×300 g (10 oz) packet frozen chopped spinach
2 eggs
1×150 g (5 oz) packet low-fat soft cheese
¼ teaspoon ground mace
salt and freshly ground black pepper

Place the fish, onion and water in a cooking dish. Cover and cook for 3 minutes, turning the dish once. Drain thoroughly then flake the fish, removing and discarding any skin and bones.

Place the spinach in a bowl and cook for 2-3 minutes, breaking up twice to defrost completely.

Place the fish and onion in a processor or blender goblet and purée until smooth. Add the eggs, cheese, mace and salt and pepper to taste and purée until smooth.

Add the spinach and process until just combined – the mixture should still have a flecked appearance.

Spoon into a large microwave baking ring, smooth the top and cook for 10 minutes, turning the ring twice.

Leave to stand for 5 minutes to serve hot or until cool before chilling to serve cold.

Unmould on to a serving dish to serve.

Serves: 8-10
Power setting: FULL
Preparation time: 20 minutes plus chilling (optional)
Cooking time: 20-21 minutes

Calories per portion: 150-155

COX'S TROUT

1 Cox's eating apple, cored
2 teaspoons grated onion
2 tablespoons low fat curd cheese
salt and freshly ground black pepper
1×225 g (8 oz) trout, boned and prepared for cooking
2 tablespoons unsweetened apple juice

Finely chop three-quarters of the apple and mix with the onion, cheese and salt and pepper to taste. Use to stuff the trout and place in a cooking dish.

Spoon over the apple juice and top with the remaining apple cut into thick slices. Cook for 4 minutes, turning the dish once.

Leave to stand for 2 minutes before serving. Delicious hot or cold.

Serves: 1
Power setting: FULL
Preparation time: 10 minutes
Cooking time: 6 minutes

Calories per portion: 300

PASTA SLAW

100 g/4 oz wholewheat
    spaghetti rings
450 ml/3⁄4 pint boiling
    water
salt and freshly ground
    black pepper
100 g/4 oz white cabbage,
    shredded
4 sticks celery, scrubbed
    and chopped
100 g/4 oz carrots, peeled
    and grated
1 medium onion, peeled
    and finely chopped
175 ml/6 fl oz low fat
    plain yogurt

Place the spaghetti rings in a bowl with the water and a pinch of salt. Cover and cook for 12 minutes, stirring once. Leave to stand, covered, for 5 minutes then cool under running water.

Mix the pasta with the cabbage, celery, carrots and onion, blending well. Mix the yogurt with salt and pepper to taste and pour over the salad. Toss well to mix. Chill lightly before serving.

Serves: 4
Power setting: FULL
Preparation time: 15 minutes plus cooling and chilling
Cooking time: 17 minutes

Calories per portion: 170

QUICK AND EASY PAELLA

15 g/1⁄2 oz low fat spread
1 small onion, peeled and
    chopped
75 g/3 oz cooked chicken,
    skinned and chopped
1 × 295 g (101⁄2 oz) can
    slimmer's chicken soup
50 g/2 oz brown rice
50 g/2 oz red pepper,
    cored, seeded and
    chopped
1 tomato, peeled, seeded
    and quartered
pinch of ground turmeric
salt and freshly ground
    black pepper
25 g/1 oz peeled prawns
25 g/1 oz shelled mussels
25 g/1 oz frozen peas

Place the low fat spread in a casserole dish with the onion. Cover and cook for 2 minutes, stirring once.

Add the chicken and soup, blending well. Cover and cook for 3 minutes, Stir in the rice, pepper, tomato, turmeric and salt and pepper to taste, blending well. Cover and cook for 20 minutes, stirring twice (and adding a little boiling water if the mixture starts to cook too dry).

Add the prawns, mussels and peas, blending well. Cover and leave to stand for 10 minutes.

Cook for 2 minutes to reheat. Serve at once with a green salad.

Serves: 1
Power setting: FULL
Preparation time: 15 minutes
Cooking time: 37 minutes

Calories per portion: 530 (without salad)

SLIMMER'S JACKET POTATO

1 × 225 g (8 oz) jacket
    potato, scrubbed
25 g/1 oz corned beef,
    chopped
11⁄2 tablespoons
    Worcestershire sauce
100 g/4 oz baked beans in
    tomato sauce

Prick the potato thoroughly and place on absorbent kitchen paper. Cook for 4-6 minutes. Leave to stand for 3-4 minutes then cut a cross in the top and squeeze the potato to gently open up.

Meanwhile, place the corned beef, Worsestershire sauce and beans in a bowl. Cook for 3 minutes, stirring once. Spoon into the potato and serve at once.

Serves: 1
Power setting: FULL
Preparation time: 5 minutes
Cooking time: 10-13 minutes

Calories per portion: 330

CREOLE SALAD

1 × 283 g (10 oz) packet
frozen rice, sweetcorn
and peppers
200 ml/7 fl oz boiling
water
3 tomatoes, peeled and
chopped
¼ cucumber, chopped
1 × 200 g (7 oz) can
shrimps in brine,
drained
100 g/4 oz cooked ham,
cut into strips
Dressing:
1 tablespoon white wine
vinegar
2 teaspoons hot pepper
sauce
2 teaspoons coarse grain
mustard
3 tablespoons oil
1 garlic clove, peeled and
crushed
1 teaspoon soft brown
sugar
salt and freshly ground
black pepper

Place the frozen rice, sweetcorn and peppers in a bowl with the water. Cover and cook for 12 minutes, stirring once. Leave to stand, covered, for 2 minutes. Drain if necessary.

Add the tomatoes, cucumber, shrimps and ham, blending well.

Combine all the dressing ingredients in a screw-topped jar and pour over the still warm rice mixture, tossing well to coat. Cover and chill thoroughly before serving.

Serves: 4
Power setting: FULL
Preparation time: 20 minutes, plus chilling
Cooking time: 14 minutes

Calories per portion: 330

LEANLINE MEDITERRANEAN HOT-POT

40 g/1½ oz low fat spread
1 onion, peeled and sliced
225 g/8 oz cooked
chicken, skinned and
chopped
1 × 397 g (14 oz can)
peeled tomatoes
1 red or green pepper,
cored, seeded and
sliced
225 g/8 oz frozen peas
300 ml/½ pint mussels,
scrubbed
175 g/6 oz peeled prawns
300 ml/½ pint boiling
chicken stock
1 bay leaf
½ teaspoon ground
turmeric
6 unpeeled prawns to
garnish

Place the low fat spread and onion in a large bowl. Cover and cook for 3 minutes, stirring once.

Add the chicken, tomatoes with their juice, pepper, peas, mussels, prawns, stock bay leaf and turmeric, blending well. Cover and cook for 20 minutes, stirring twice.

Leave to stand, covered, for 5 minutes. Garnish with the unpeeled prawns and serve hot, perhaps with a little plain boiled rice.

Serves: 4
Power setting: FULL
Preparation time: 30-40 minutes
Cooking time: 28 minutes

Calories per portion: 150

Illustrated opposite

LEANLINE MEDITERRANEAN HOT-POT (opposite)

FRUIT COMPÔTE (p.226), FRUIT CONDÉ (p.213) AND PEACHES AND CURAÇAO (p.226)

POTATO AND CARROT SOUP

450 g/1 lb potatoes, peeled and chopped
450 g/1 lb carrots, peeled and chopped
1 onion, peeled and chopped
1 stick celery, peeled and chopped
1.2 litres/2 pints boiling chicken stock
salt and freshly ground black pepper
1 tablespoon lemon juice
chopped parsley to garnish

Place the potatoes, carrots, onion, celery, a quarter of the stock and salt and pepper to taste in a large bowl. Cover and cook for 20 minutes, stirring twice.

Purée in a blender with the remaining stock or pass through a fine sieve and mix with the stock. Stir in the lemon juice, blending well.

Serve hot garnished with the chopped parsley.

Serves: 6
Power setting: FULL
Preparation time: 20 minutes
Cooking time: 20 minutes

Calories per portion: 95

STUFFED CABBAGE ROLLS

8 large cabbage leaves
350 g/12 oz turkey fillets, minced
100 g/4 oz button mushrooms, wiped and finely chopped
1 onion, peeled
2 tablespoons wholegrain mustard
salt and freshly ground black pepper
300 ml/½ pint hot chicken stock
2 tablespoons tomato purée

Place the cabbage leaves in a dish. Cover and cook for 2 minutes to soften.

Mix the turkey with the mushrooms, blending well. Finely chop half of the onion and slice the remainder. Add the chopped onion, mustard and salt and pepper to taste to the turkey mixture, blending well. Divide and shape the mixture into 8 rolls and wrap each in a cabbage leaf.

Place the sliced onion, stock and tomato purée in a cooking dish, blending well. Add the cabbage rolls. Cover and cook for 20 minutes, turning the dish twice. Leave to stand, covered, for 5 minutes before serving.

To freeze
Cool quickly, cover, seal, label and freeze for up to 3 months.

Serves: 4
Power setting: FULL
Preparation time: 25 minutes
Cooking time: 27 minutes
Suitable for freezing

Calories per portion: 150

SESAME JELLY

75 ml/3 fl oz cold water
15 g/½ oz powdered gelatine
300 ml/½ pint unsweetened orange juice
25 g/1 oz sesame seeds
100 g/4 oz cottage cheese
150 ml/¼ pint low fat plain yogurt

Place the water in a jug and cook for 1 minute until hot but not boiling. Add the gelatine and stir briskly to dissolve.

Add the orange juice and sesame seeds, blending well. Alllow to set slightly then divide between 4 sundae glasses and set in the refrigerator tilted at an angle.

Sieve or purée the cottage cheese in a blender and mix with the yogurt.

To serve, top the sesame jelly sundaes with the yogurt mixture. Serve lightly chilled.

Serves: 4
Power setting: FULL
Preparation time: 15 minutes, plus chilling
Cooking time: 1 minute

Calories per portion: 115

KIDNEY CASSEROLE

25 g/1 oz butter

1 onion, peeled and chopped

1 carrot, peeled and finely sliced

8 lamb's kidneys, cored and halved

50 g/2 oz cap mushrooms, wiped and sliced

50 g/2 oz frozen peas

50 g/2 oz frozen French beans

2 tablespoons chopped parsley

1 garlic clove, peeled and crushed

150 ml/¼ pint dry red wine

1 × 397 g (14 oz) can peeled tomatoes, chopped (juices retained)

salt and freshly ground black pepper

Place the butter, onion and carrot in a casserole dish. Cover and cook for 4 minutes.

Add the kidneys, mushrooms, peas, French beans, half of the parsley and the garlic, blending well. Cover and cook for 5 minutes, stirring once.

Add the wine, tomatoes and their juice and salt and pepper to taste, blending well. Cover and cook for 5 minutes, stirring once.

Leave to stand, covered, for 3 minutes before serving. Garnish with the remaining chopped parsley to serve.

Serve each portion with 50 g/2 oz cooked long-grain rice.

Serves: 4
Power setting: FULL
Preparation time: 20-25 minutes
Cooking time: 17 minutes

Calories per portion: 300

MUSHROOMS À LA GRECQUE

1 tablespoon oil

1 small garlic clove, peeled and crushed

1 small onion, peeled and chopped

100 ml/4 fl oz dry white wine

2 tablespoons tomato purée

½ teaspoon dried mixed herbs

2 tomatoes, peeled, seeded and chopped

175 g/6 oz button mushrooms, wiped and trimmed

salt and freshly ground black pepper

chopped parsley to garnish

1 × 50 g (2 oz) wholemeal bread roll to serve (as a complete meal)

Place the oil, garlic and onion in a bowl. Cover and cook for 2 minutes, stirring once. Add the wine, tomato purée, herbs and tomatoes. Cook, uncovered for 3 minutes, stirring once.

Add the mushrooms and cook for a further 3 minutes, stirring once. Leave to cool then chill lightly.

Season with salt and pepper to taste. Serve cold sprinkled with chopped parsley. Serve with the bread roll as a complete meal.

Serves: 1
Power setting: FULL
Preparation time: 10 minutes
Cooking time: 8 minutes

Calories per portion: 390 (including bread roll)

CALORIE-COUNT DIETING

Most nutritionists agree that a calorie-cutting diet has the greatest chance of success with would-be slimmers because it is a very flexible way of dieting. It fits in with family routine, social arrangements and the dieter's own whims and fancies. It also does not mean saying goodbye to favourite foods, but wisely limit them to reasonable quantities.

Generally, most women will lose weight successfully by limiting themselves to 1000 calories per day and most men 1500 calories per day. However, for women who are more than 2 stone (13 kg) overweight then 1500 calories a day is a good starting point, to be reduced later to 1000 calories.

The way in which you decide to spread your calorie allowance throughout the day will be a personal one. Try and plan the day according to your habits. You are bound to find that you have angelic and devilish days when your calorie allowance stays well within or creeps a little above the limit. Mix and match these days by all means but do remember to have a final tally at the end of the week to check whether you are staying firmly on course.

As a start, this typical day's menu indicates the kind of food that could be chosen to provide around 1000 calories per day:

	CALORIES
BREAKFAST	
½ grapefruit	40
1 boiled, poached or scrambled egg (which needs no butter or milk when cooked in a microwave oven)	100
1 slice wholemeal bread with low fat spread	100
LUNCH	
1 portion Boston Bean Bake (see below)	190
1 bran crispbread	25
1 portion Sesame Jelly (see p. 207)	115
DINNER	
Gazpacho – mix 1 large peeled and chopped tomato with 25 g/1 oz chopped cucumber, 25 g/1 oz chopped green pepper, 25 g/1 oz chopped onion, 2 teaspoons vinegar, 75 ml/3 fl oz tomato juice and 5 tablespoons water. Purée until smooth then season to taste with salt and pepper.	130
1 portion Leanline Mediterranean Hot-Pot (see p. 204)	330
green salad (without dressing)	
100 g/4 oz black grapes	55
TOTAL	1075

BOSTON BEAN BAKE

15 g/½ oz low fat spread
1 onion, peeled and chopped
225 g/8 oz lean ham, chopped
1 × 425 g (15 oz) can baked beans in tomato sauce
100 g/4 oz mushrooms, sliced
1 teaspoon Worcestershire sauce
1 tablespoon pickle
1½ teaspoons cornflour
1 tablespoon water

Place the low fat spread and onion in a large bowl. Cover and cook for 3 minutes, stirring once.

Add the ham, beans, mushrooms, Worcestershire sauce and pickle, blending well. Cook for 10 minutes, stirring twice.

Mix the cornflour with the water and stir into the bean mixture. Cook for 3 minutes, stirring twice. Serve hot.

Serves: 4
Power setting: FULL
Preparation time: 20 minutes
Cooking time: 16 minutes

Calories per portion: 190

COUNTRY CASSEROLE

2 large leeks, washed and
    cut into 1 cm/½ inch
    slices
1 turnip, peeled and
    chopped
1 carrot, peeled and sliced
1 stick celery, scrubbed
    and chopped
450 g/1 lb lean minced
    beef
1 teaspoon dried mixed
    herbs
1 tablespoon tomato
    purée
300 ml/½ pint hot beef
    stock
salt and black pepper

Place the leeks, turnip, carrot and celery in a casserole dish. Cover and cook for 10 minutes, stirring once.

Stir in the beef, herbs, tomato purée, stock and salt and pepper to taste, blending well. Cover and cook for 7 minutes, stirring once. Serve hot.

To freeze

Cool quickly and place in a rigid container. Cover, seal, label and freeze for up to 3 months.

Serves: 4
Power setting: FULL
Preparation time: 20 minutes
Cooking time: 17 minutes
Suitable for freezing

Calories per portion: 300

SLIMMER'S CHILLI CON CARNE

75 g/3 oz lean minced
    beef
1 small onion, peeled and
    chopped
½ green pepper, cored,
    seeded and chopped
100 g/4 oz canned
    tomatoes with their
    juice
5 tablespoons tomato
    juice
½-1 teaspoon chilli
    powder
¾ teaspoon vinegar
2 teaspoons tomato purée
salt and pepper to taste
75 g/3 oz cooked red
    kidney beans
2 bran crispbreads

Place the beef, onion and pepper in a small casserole dish. Cover and cook for 5 minutes, stirring twice to break up the meat.

Add the tomatoes, tomato juice, chilli powder, vinegar, tomato purée and salt and pepper to taste, blending well. Cover and cook for 5 minutes, stirring once.

Stir in the kidney beans and leave to stand, covered, for 5 minutes before serving. Serve hot with the crispbreads.

To freeze

Cool quickly and place in a rigid container. Cover, seal, label and freeze for up to 2 months.

Serves: 1
Power setting: FULL
Preparation time: 10-15 minutes
Cooking time: 15 minutes
Suitable for freezing

**Calories per portion: 400
(including crispbreads)**

SPICED LAMB

3 tablespoons oil
1 onion, peeled and finely
    chopped
1 green pepper, cored,
    seeded and finely
    chopped
1 green chilli, seeded and
    finely chopped (cont.)

Place the oil, onion, pepper, chilli and garlic in a casserole dish. Cover and cook on FULL POWER for 4 minutes, stirring once.

Add the lamb, blending well. Cover and cook on FULL POWER for 4 minutes, stirring once.

Add the tomatoes with their juice, cumin, coriander, turmeric, cayenne

pepper, salt and water, blending well. Cook on DEFROST POWER for 12 minutes. Leave to stand, covered, for 3 minutes before serving.

If the lamb is not tender, cook on DEFROST POWER for a further 5-10 minutes.

3 garlic cloves, peeled and
 finely chopped
450 g / 1 lb lean lamb,
 cubed
1 × 397 g (14 oz) can
 peeled tomatoes,
 chopped
2 teaspoons ground
 cumin
1 teaspoon ground
 coriander
½ teaspoon ground
 turmeric
½ teaspoon cayenne
 pepper
1 teaspoon salt
150 ml / ¼ pint water

To freeze
Cool quickly and place in a rigid container.
Cover, seal, label and freeze for up to 1
month.

Serves: 4
Power settings: FULL, DEFROST
Preparation time: 20-25 minutes
Cooking time: 23-33 minutes
Suitable for freezing

Calories per portion: 350

LEAFY TROUT

3 large lettuce or spinach
 leaves, de-stemmed and
 washed
3 mushrooms, chopped
2 teaspoons chopped
 onion
2-3 tablespoons low fat
 plain yogurt
salt and black pepper
1 × 225 g (8 oz) trout,
 boned and prepared
 for cooking
1 leek, washed and sliced
2 tablespoons water

Place the lettuce or spinach leaves in a bowl
and cook for 1 minute to soften.

Mix the mushrooms with the onion,
yogurt and salt and pepper to taste, blending well. Use to stuff the trout then wrap in
the spinach or lettuce leaves.

Place the leek and water in a cooking
dish. Cover and cook for 2 minutes. Top
with the stuffed trout and cook for 4
minutes, turning the dish once. Leave to
stand for 2 minutes before serving.

Serves: 1
Power setting: FULL
Preparation time: 10 minutes
Cooking time: 9 minutes

Calories per portion: 275

CHICKEN ITALIAN STYLE

50 ml / 2 fl oz dry
 vermouth
1 × 397 g (14 oz) can
 plum tomatoes,
 drained and chopped
4 tablespoons tomato
 purée
1 garlic clove, peeled and
 crushed
1 onion, peeled and
 thinly sliced
1 teaspoon dried oregano
salt and black pepper
4 × 175 g (6 oz) boneless
 chicken breasts,
 skinned

Place the vermouth, tomatoes, tomato
purée, garlic, onion, oregano and salt and
pepper to taste in a cooking dish. Cover and
cook for 5 minutes, stirring once.

Arrange the chicken breasts, spoke
fashion, on top of the sauce, spooning a
little over the chicken. Cover and cook for
10 minutes, turning the dish once.

Leave to stand, covered, for 5 minutes.
Serve garnished with a few black olives.

To freeze
Cool quickly, cover, seal, label and freeze
for up to 3 months.

Serves: 4
Power setting: FULL
Preparation time: 15 minutes
Cooking time: 20 minutes
Suitable for freezing

Calories per portion: 350

GREEN BEANS WITH TOMATO DRESSING

1 × 283 (10 oz) packet
  frozen whole green
  beans
1 onion, peeled and
  thinly sliced
4 tablespoons water
2 tablespoons oil
1 garlic clove, peeled and
  crushed
225 g/8 oz tomatoes,
  peeled and chopped
2 tablespoons chopped
  fresh mixed herbs
3 tablespoons red wine
  vinegar
1 tablespoon soft brown
  sugar
salt and black pepper

Place the beans in a dish and top with the onion. Pour over the water, cover and cook for 6 minutes. Drain thoroughly.

Place the oil, garlic, tomatoes, herbs, vinegar, sugar and salt and pepper to taste in a bowl. Cover and cook for 5 minutes, stirring once.

Pour over the bean mixture, cover and leave to cool. Chill thoroughly before serving with cold meals or with hot garlic bread as a starter.

Serves: 4
Power setting: FULL
Preparation time: 16 minutes plus cooling
Cooking time: 11 minutes

Calories per portion: 115

FRUIT SORBET

4 tablespoons granulated
  sugar
5 tablespoons water
2 tablespoons lemon juice
200 ml/7 fl oz thick fruit
  purée (raspberry,
  strawberry or
  gooseberry, for
  example)
2 egg whites

Place the sugar, water and lemon juice in a jug. Cook for 4 minutes, stirring twice. Leave to cool.

Add the fruit purée to the syrup, blending well. Pour into a freezer tray and freeze until half frozen.

Remove the half frozen sorbet to a bowl and whisk until smooth. Whisk the egg whites until they stand in stiff peaks. Fold into the fruit purée with a metal spoon. Return to the freezer tray and freeze until firm.

Serve scooped into chilled glasses.

To freeze
Cover, seal, label and freeze for up to 1 year.

Serves: 4
Power setting: FULL
Preparation time: 20 minutes, plus cooling and freezing
Cooking time: 4 minutes
Suitable for freezing

Calories per portion: 125

JAMAICAN BANANA, PINEAPPLE AND FIGS

1 × 150 g (5 oz) banana,
  peeled and thickly
  sliced
1 × 50 g (2 oz) slice fresh
  pineapple, chopped
15 g/½ oz dried figs,
  chopped
7 g/¼ oz low fat spread
¼ teaspoon mixed spice
1 tablespoon dark rum

Place the banana, pineapple and figs in a small serving dish. Dot with the spread, sprinkle with the spice and pour over the rum.

Cover and cook for 1½ minutes. Serve at once.

Serves: 1
Power setting: FULL
Preparation time: 10 minutes
Cooking time: 1½ minutes

Calories per portion: 155

FRUIT CONDÉ

50 g/2 oz pudding or round-grain rice
600 ml/1 pint skimmed milk
25 g/1 oz sugar
450 g/1 lb fresh fruit (kiwi, mandarins, grapes, bananas and apples for example), peeled and segmented

Place the rice and milk in a large deep dish. Cover and cook on FULL POWER for 10 minutes, stirring once.

Stir in the sugar, blending well. Cover and cook on DEFROST POWER for 20 minutes, stirring four times. Leave to stand, covered, for 5 minutes.

Spoon the rice into four sundae glasses in alternate layers with the mixed fruit. Finish with a decoration of fruit. Serve warm or cold.

Serves: 4
Power setting: FULL and DEFROST
Preparation time: 20 minutes
Cooking time: 35 minutes

Calories per portion: 165

Illustrated on p. 206

APRICOT CHIFFON

1 × 135 g (4¾ oz) packet lemon jelly tablet
100 ml/4 fl oz water
2 × 220 g (7¾ oz) cans apricots in water or low-calorie syrup
300 ml/½ pint low fat plain yogurt

Place the jelly in a jug with the water. Cook for 2-3 minutes until the jelly has dissolved.

Drain the water or syrup from the apricots and add to the jelly to make up to 300 ml/½ pint. Chill until just beginning to set.

Reserve 5 apricot halves and chop the remainder into quarters.

Whisk the setting jelly until foamy, then whisk in the yogurt. Fold in the chopped apricots and turn into a 450 g (1 lb) loaf tin. Chill until set.

To serve, immerse the loaf tin briefly into hot water then invert on to a serving dish. Decorate with the reserved apricot halves.

Serves: 4
Power setting: FULL
Preparation time: 20 minutes, plus chilling
Cooking time: 2-3 minutes

Calories per portion: 120

SEVEN-DAY DIET PLAN

This seven-day meal plan has been prepared as a guideline for healthy cooking by microwave. It provides a 1000-calories-a-day diet for some-one fully aware of the advantages of microwave cooking and who wants to eat nutritionally – and well.

In addition to the foods listed, half a pint of low fat milk is allowed each day to be taken in tea or coffee. Synthetic sweeteners may be used in these beverages, though not ordinary sugar.

The menus have been kept calorie-conscious and deliberately simple, as longer and more involved recipes are less conducive to successful slimming.

The meals contain plenty of vegetables, salads, fruit and some wholemeal cereals in keeping with the modern view of the benefits of a high fibre diet. Slimmers find a high fibre-diet more satisfying and effective for weight control.

Foods recommended for the lunches could easily be taken as packed meals, and the main meals suggested for either Friday or Wednesday could be served at informal parties, especially if guests are also calorie-conscious.

In the recipes themselves, quantities are given for four people, though the calorific values stated are for just one quarter of the total amount of food so prepared. Slimmers catering only for one are recommended to make the four-portion amounts and freeze three of them for other days ahead.

Calorific values for certain vegetables and salads are not given when these values are very low.

Low fat spreads are recommended in this 1000-calorie meal plan, and should be used very sparingly. If ordinary margarines or butter are used instead, the calorific value of the day's meals will be nearer 1200 than 1000 calories. The calorific value will also be increased if full cream milk is used in place of the recommended skimmed milk, which may be fresh pasteurised skimmed milk, or reconstituted low fat powdered milk.

By following this diet, the average woman can expect to lose between 1½ to 2 pounds of weight a week. However, actual weight lost will depend on an individual's own energy requirement, which can vary quite a lot even between two people of the same age and body size who appear to be equally active.

Weight loss may not always be the same each week even though the daily calorie intake is kept to 1000 calories. This may be because the body takes time to adjust to the changes in quantity and types of foods consumed.

When the required weight loss has been achieved, the calorie intake can be gradually increased. For example, butter and full cream milk can be taken in place of the low fat alternatives recommended for slimmers. The daily amount of bread, potatoes, rice and so on may be increased and slightly larger portions of meat, fish and cheese may be eaten. To stop regaining the weight lost, it is strongly recommended that slimmers continue to avoid high calorie sweet foods and restrict their intake of alcoholic drinks.

Sunday

BREAKFAST	CALORIES
25 g/1 oz Special K (or similar 'slimmers' cornflake cereal)	100
fresh fruit	50
150 ml/¼ pint skimmed milk	50

LUNCH	
100 g/4 oz roast chicken	215
1 small baked potato	50
100 g/4 oz Brussels sprouts	
75 g/3 oz braised leeks	
1 recipe Peaches and Curaçao (see p. 226)	100

SUPPER	
75 g/3 oz canned salmon	115
cucumber, celery and watercress salad	
wholemeal roll with low fat spread	100
banana	50

Monday

BREAKFAST	
glass of tomato juice	25
1 slice wholemeal bread topped with 40 g/1½ oz grated Cheddar cheese and slices of tomato (cook on FULL POWER for ¾ minute)	150

LUNCH	
Oriental chicken salad – mix 50 g/2 oz beansprouts with 25 g/1 oz chopped mushrooms,	220

1 sliced leek, a few radishes, 75 g/3 oz cooked chopped chicken. For dressing, mix 1 tablespoon lemon juice, few drops of Worcestershire sauce, 1 teaspoon olive oil and salt and pepper to taste. Garnish with watercress sprigs.

50 g/2 oz black grapes	35

DINNER	
1 portion Country Casserole (see p. 210)	300
1 tablespoon mashed potatoes	50
spring greens	
1 baked apple stuffed with mincemeat	150

Tuesday

BREAKFAST	
½ grapefruit	30
100 g/4 oz finnan haddock (cover and cook on FULL POWER for 2 minutes. Leave to stand for 1 minute)	
wholemeal roll with low fat spread	100

LUNCH	
1 × 25 g/1 oz slice lean ham wrapped around 50 g/2 oz cottage cheese, 2 sticks chopped celery	120
1 crispbread	25
1 pear	50

DINNER
1 portion Kidney Casserole (see p. 208) 300
broccoli
50 g/2 oz boiled rice
1 recipe Rhubarb and Orange Compôte (see p. 226) 75

Wednesday

BREAKFAST
1 small glass unsweetened orange juice 50
1 scrambled egg 100
1 slice wholemeal toast with low fat spread 100

LUNCH
50 g/2 oz Edam cheese, chopped and mixed with a coleslaw of shredded cabbage, grated carrot and apple, chopped celery and 2 tablespoons low fat plain yogurt 230
1 crispbread 25

DINNER
1 portion Spiced Lamb (see p. 210) 350
cucumber raita – chop 50 g/2 oz cucumber and mix with 1 tablespoon plain yogurt. Season with salt and pepper and sprinkle with chopped mint 50

carrot and onion Salad – mix 1 small sliced and blanched carrot (see p. 106) with a few onion rings, a little lemon juice and salt and pepper to taste. Sprinkle with ground ginger.
1 chapati or ½ small pitta bread 50
small portion Apricot Chiffon (see p. 213) 120

Thursday

BREAKFAST
1 small glass unsweetened orange juice 50
40 g/1½ oz lean bacon, cooked 150
grilled tomatoes
1 slice wholemeal toast 75

LUNCH
40 g/1½ oz liver sausage 150
2 crispbreads 50

tomato and cucumber
1 apple 50

DINNER
1 recipe Cod Steak with Herbs (see p. 219) 120
1 tablespoon mashed potato 50
1 tablespoon peas 25
French beans
1 recipe Orange and Apple Fool (see p. 226) 125

Friday

BREAKFAST
½ grapefruit 30
1 boiled egg 100
1 slice wholemeal bread with low fat spread 100

LUNCH
75 g/3 oz cottage cheese 100
carrot and celery sticks
1 crispbread 25
1 orange 50

DINNER
grapefruit and prawn cocktail 100
1 recipe Beef Kebab (see p. 218) 345
1 portion Fruit Sorbet (see p. 212) 125

Saturday

BREAKFAST
1 small glass unsweetened orange juice 50
sliced mushrooms and sliced tomatoes on 1 slice wholemeal toast with low fat spread (cook on FULL POWER for 1 minute) 150

LUNCH
1 small jacket potato, cooked then stuffed with 25 g/1 oz grated Edam cheese and 1 tablespoon plain yogurt 190
mixed green salad
1 tablespoon low-calorie salad dressing 50

DINNER
1 × 100 g (4 oz) pork chop 300
apple slices with cloves (cook on FULL POWER for 3 minutes)
cauliflower and carrots 25
small portion of ice cream 100

Cooking for One

Whether you regularly eat alone, eat at a different time from the rest of the family or simply want a hearty snack, there are many times when you need to cook for one. In this respect, the microwave will prove speedy, effortless and, moreover, economical.

SEVILLE DUCK WITH NUT STUFFING

1 × 400 g (14 oz)
   duckling breast
   portion, boned
2 tablespoons thick cut
   marmalade
salt and freshly ground
   black pepper
Stuffing:
1 stick celery, scrubbed
   and chopped
4 tablespoons fresh white
   breadcrumbs
2 teaspoons orange
   marmalade
1 teaspoon chopped fresh
   rosemary
25 g/1 oz chopped nuts
beaten egg to bind

Remove any excess fat from under the skin of the duck.

To make the stuffing, mix the celery with the breadcrumbs, orange marmalade, rosemary and nuts. Bind together with the beaten egg. Use to stuff the wing of the boned duck. Lay the duck on its breast, spread with more stuffing, roll up and secure with string or wooden cocktail sticks.

Meanwhile, preheat a small browning dish for 4 minutes (or according to the manufacturer's instructions). Add the duck and turn until brown on all sides. Cook on FULL POWER for 2 minutes.

Brush with marmalade and season with salt and pepper to taste. Cook on DEFROST POWER for 18 minutes, turning twice.

Leave to stand for 5 minutes, brush with any remaining marmalade and serve. Crisp under a preheated hot grill if liked.

Serves: 1
Power settings: FULL, DEFROST
Preparation time: 30 minutes
Cooking time: 29 minutes

BARBECUED BEANS

2 teaspoons oil
1 small onion, peeled and
   chopped
½ garlic clove, peeled
   and crushed
1 small tomato, peeled
   and chopped
1 teaspoon brown sugar
pinch of mustard powder
pinch of chilli powder
1 teaspoon tomato
   ketchup
100 g/4 oz canned butter
   beans, drained
salt and freshly ground
   black pepper

Place the oil, onion and garlic in a bowl. Cover and cook for 2 minutes.

Add the tomato, sugar, mustard, chilli powder and ketchup, blending well. Cook for 1 minute.

Add the beans and salt and pepper to taste. Cover and cook for 3 minutes, stirring once. Serve hot.

Serves: 1
Power setting: FULL
Preparation time: 5 minutes
Cooking time: 6 minutes

DEVILLED TROUT

1 teaspoon mustard
    powder
pinch of salt
pinch of sugar
Worcestershire sauce
1 × 225 g (8 oz) frozen
    trout, prepared for
    cooking
25 g/1 oz butter

Mix the mustard powder with the salt, sugar and a little Worcestershire sauce to make a stiff paste.

Slash the trout in several places with a sharp knife and spread the devilled mixture on both sides. Place in a small cooking dish and dot with the butter.

Cook for 6 minutes, turning the dish twice. Leave to stand for 2 minutes before serving.

Serves: 1
Power setting: FULL
Preparation time: 5 minutes
Cooking time: 8 minutes

BOMBAY TROUT

3 tablespoons extra thick
    plain yogurt
1 teaspoon mild curry
    paste
1 tablespoon mango
    chutney
chilli sauce
1 × 225 g (8 oz) trout,
    boned
salt and freshly ground
    black pepper
1 banana, peeled and
    sliced
desiccated coconut to
    garnish

Mix the yogurt with the curry paste, mango chutney and chilli sauce to taste, blending well.

Season the trout, inside and out, with salt and pepper to taste. Stuff with the banana and place in a small cooking dish. Coat with the curry mixture and cook for 4 minutes, turning the dish once.

Leave to stand for 2 minutes before serving garnished with desiccated coconut. Serve with boiled rice and chutney.

Serves: 1
Power setting: FULL
Preparation time: 5-10 minutes
Cooking time: 6 minutes

PORK, APPLE AND WHISKY SAUTÉ

175 g/6 oz pork fillet
salt and freshly ground
    black pepper
15 g/½ oz butter
1 small dessert apple,
    peeled, cored and
    sliced
1 tablespoon whisky
50 ml/2 fl oz double
    cream
chopped parsley to
    garnish

Preheat a small browning dish for 7 minutes (or according to the manufacturer's instructions).

Cut the pork into long thin strips and season generously with salt and pepper to taste.

Add the butter to the browning dish and swirl quickly to coat. Add the pork and turn quickly on all sides to brown evenly. Cook for 1½ minutes.

Add the apple slices and cook for 2 minutes, stirring once.

Add the whisky and cream, blending well. Cook for ½-1 minute but do not allow to boil.

Serve at once garnished with chopped parsley. To make the sauté a complete meal, serve it with a portion of freshly cooked noodles.

Serves: 1
Power setting: FULL
Preparation time: 10 minutes
Cooking time: 11-11½ minutes

KIWI TROUT

1 × 225 g (8 oz) trout,
  boned
1 kiwi fruit, peeled and
  sliced into rounds
salt and freshly ground
  black pepper
3 slices Parma ham

Stuff the trout with the kiwi fruit slices and season to taste with salt and pepper. Wrap in the slices of Parma ham and place in a small cooking dish.

Cook for 3 minutes, turning the dish once.

Leave to stand for 2 minutes before serving hot with a soured cream, mayonnaise or mustard sauce.

Serves: 1
Power setting: FULL
Preparation time: 10 minutes
Cooking time: 5 minutes

BEEF KEBAB

100 g/4 oz rump steak,
  cut into 2.5 cm (1 inch)
  cubes
100 g/4 oz mushrooms,
  wiped
2 tablespoons lemon juice
1 tablespoon chopped
  fresh parsley
1 small clove garlic,
  peeled and crushed
  (optional)
ground black pepper
2 small tomatoes
½ green pepper, cored,
  seeded and cut into
  large pieces
sunflower oil

Place the steak, mushrooms, lemon juice, parsley, garlic if used and pepper to taste in a bowl. Mix well, cover and leave to marinate for 2 hours.

Thread the meat and mushrooms on to a long wooden skewer with the tomatoes and green pepper. Brush very lightly with sunflower oil.

Preheat a small browning dish for 4 minutes (or according to the manufacturer's instructions). Add the kebab and cook for 1 minute. Turn over and cook for a further ½ minute. Serve at once with a green salad.

Serves: 1
Power setting: FULL
Preparation time: 10 minutes, plus marinating
Cooking time: 5½ minutes

LIVER STROGANOFF

15 g/½ oz butter
100 g/4 oz lamb's liver,
  cut into short narrow
  strips
½ small onion, peeled
  and thinly sliced
¼ green pepper, cored,
  seeded and chopped
25 g/1 oz mushrooms,
  wiped and sliced
1 teaspoon plain flour
50 ml/2 fl oz beef stock
1 teaspoon tomato purée
pinch of sugar
salt and freshly ground
  black pepper
1 tablespoon double or
  soured cream

Preheat a small browning dish for 6 minutes (or according to the manufacturer's instructions). Add the butter and swirl to coat. Cook for a further 1 minute.

Add the liver and turn quickly on all sides to brown. Cook for 2 minutes, stirring once. Remove from the dish with a slotted spoon and set aside.

Add the onion, pepper and mushrooms to the dish. Cover and cook for 3 minutes, stirring once. Stir in the flour, blending well.

Gradually add the stock, tomato purée, sugar and salt and pepper to taste. Cook for 1½ minutes, stirring once.

Return the liver to the dish and cook for 1 minute, stirring once. Stir in the cream and serve at once with noodles or rice.

Serves: 1
Power setting: FULL
Preparation time: 10 minutes
Cooking time: 14½ minutes

COD STEAK WITH HERBS

1 × 175 g (6 oz) cod steak
salt and freshly ground
  black pepper
1 tomato, peeled and
  sliced
½ teaspoon dried basil
1 teaspoon chopped fresh
  parsley
2 teaspoons lemon juice

Place the fish in a small cooking dish and season with salt and pepper to taste.

Top with the sliced tomato. Sprinkle with the basil, parsley and lemon juice.

Cover and cook for 3 minutes. Leave to stand, covered, for 2 minutes before serving.

Serves: 1
Power setting: FULL
Preparation time: 5 minutes
Cooking time: 5 minutes

STEAK WITH GREEN PEPPERCORNS

1 × 225 g (8 oz) rump or
  fillet steak
1 teaspoon coarsely
  crushed green
  peppercorns
knob of butter
1 teaspoon oil
1 teaspoon lemon juice
1½ teaspoons brandy

Trim away any fat from the steak. Press the peppercorns into both sides of the steak, cover and leave to stand for 30 minutes.

Preheat a small browning dish for 6 minutes (or according to the manufacturer's instructions). Add the butter and oil and swirl quickly to coat. Cook for a further 1 minute.

Add the steak, pressing down on to the dish firmly. Cook for 1 minute. Turn over and cook for a further ½-1 minute.

Transfer to a warmed serving plate. Add the lemon juice and brandy to the pan juices and stir well to blend. Pour over the steak and serve at once.

Serves: 1
Power setting: FULL
Preparation time: 5 minutes, plus standing
Cooking time: 8½-9 minutes

CHICKEN AND MACARONI SALAD

50 g/2 oz short-cut
  macaroni
300 ml/½ pint boiling
  water
1 teaspoon oil
salt and black pepper
50 g/2 oz cooked chicken,
  chopped
1 small stick celery,
  scrubbed and chopped
25 g/1 oz cooked
  sweetcorn kernels
50 g/2 oz fresh or canned
  pineapple, cubed
1 teaspoon flaked
  almonds
¼ green pepper, cored,
  seeded and chopped
1 teaspoon mayonnaise
2 teaspoons lemon juice

Place the macaroni in a bowl with the water, oil and a pinch of salt. Cover and cook for 10 minutes. Leave to stand for 3 minutes then drain thoroughly. Allow to cool

Mix the macaroni with the chicken, celery, sweetcorn, pineapple, almonds and pepper, blending well.

Beat the mayonnaise with the lemon juice and salt and pepper to taste. Fold into the salad. Serve lightly chilled.

Serves: 1
Power setting: FULL
Preparation time: 15 minutes, plus cooling and chilling
Cooking time: 13 minutes

ONE-POT CASSOULET

25 g/1 oz streaky bacon,
  rinded and chopped
50 g/2 oz garlic sausage,
  cubed
2 small tomatoes, peeled,
  seeded and chopped
100 g/4 oz baked beans in
  tomato sauce
salt and freshly ground
  black pepper
pinch of mixed dried
  herbs
25 g/1 oz fresh wholemeal
  breadcrumbs

Place the bacon and garlic sausage in a small heatproof serving dish. Cook for 2 minutes, stirring once.

Add the tomatoes, beans, salt and pepper to taste and herbs, blending well.

Cover and cook for 3 minutes, stirring once.

Sprinkle with the breadcrumbs and brown under a preheated hot grill until bubbly if liked. Serve hot.

Serves: 1
Power setting: FULL
Preparation time: 10 minutes
Cooking time: 5 minutes

RICE SALAD

50 g/2 oz long-grain rice
300 ml/½ pint boiling
  water
salt and freshly ground
  black pepper
15 g/½ oz raisins
15 g/½ oz salted peanuts
1 tomato, peeled and
  chopped
¼ green pepper, cored,
  seeded and chopped
50 g/2 oz cooked
  sweetcorn kernels
2 tablespoons French
  dressing

Place the rice, water and a pinch of salt in a bowl. Cover and cook for 12 minutes, stirring once. Leave to stand, covered, for 5 minutes. Drain thoroughly and allow to cool.

Add the raisins, peanuts, tomato, pepper and sweetcorn to the rice and mix well to blend.

Add the French dressing and salt and pepper to taste and toss well to mix. Chill lightly before serving.

Serves: 1
Power setting: FULL
Preparation time: 10 minutes, plus
cooling and chilling
Cooking time: 17 minutes

SAUSAGES WITH HORSERADISH SAUCE

3 pork sausages
2 tablespoons French
  dressing
Sauce:
75 ml/3 fl oz mayonnaise
2 tablespoons whipped
  cream
1 teaspoon creamed
  horseradish
1 small stick celery,
  scrubbed and chopped
½ dessert apple, cored
  and chopped
1 small dill pickle,
  chopped

Prick the sausages thoroughly and arrange on a grill rack or plate. Cover with absorbent kitchen paper and cook for 1½ minutes. Turn over and cook for a further 1 minute. Place in a shallow dish, pour over the French dressing and chill for 2 hours.

Meanwhile, to make the sauce, mix the mayonnaise with the cream, horseradish, celery, apple and dill pickle. Chill lightly.

Serve the sausages with the sauce.

Serves: 1
Power setting: FULL
Preparation time: 10 minutes, plus
chilling
Cooking time: 2½ minutes

STUFFED MACKEREL

25 g/1 oz cottage cheese
½ teaspoon grated lemon rind
2 teaspoons lemon juice
25 g/1 oz fresh white or brown breadcrumbs
pinch of mixed dried herbs
salt and freshly ground black pepper
beaten egg to bind
1 × 225 g (8 oz) mackerel, cleaned and backbone removed

Mix the cottage cheese with the lemon rind, lemon juice, breadcrumbs, herbs and salt and pepper to taste, blending well. Bind together with beaten egg. Use to stuff the mackerel and place in a small cooking dish.

Shield the head and tail of the mackerel with a little foil and slash the skin in 2 or 3 places to prevent bursting. Cook for 3-3½ minutes. Allow to stand for 5 minutes before serving.

Serves: 1
Power setting: FULL
Preparation time: 10 minutes
Cooking time: 8-8½ minutes

STIR-FRIED BEEF WITH GREEN PEPPERS

75 g/3 oz rump steak, thinly sliced
½ teaspoon salt
½ teaspoon caster sugar
1 teaspoon dry sherry
1 teaspoon cornflour
dash of chilli sauce
freshly ground black pepper
1 tablespoon oil
1 small green pepper, cored, seeded and thinly sliced
1 small tomato, cut into wedges
1 spring onion, chopped
pinch of ground ginger
1 teaspoon soy sauce

Place the steak in a bowl with half of the salt, the sugar, sherry, cornflour, chilli sauce and pepper to taste. Mix well and leave to marinate for about 20 minutes.

Preheat a small browning dish for 8 minutes (or according to the manufacturer's instructions). Add the oil and cook for a further 1 minute. Add the green pepper, tomato, spring onion, ginger and remaining salt. Cook for 1 minute, stirring once. Remove from the dish with a slotted spoon.

Add the steak mixture and cook for 1½ minutes, stirring once. Add the green pepper mixture and soy sauce. Cook for 1 minute, stirring once.

Serve at once straight from the dish.

Serves: 1
Power setting: FULL
Preparation time: 10 minutes, plus marinating
Cooking time: 12½ minutes

LEMON LAMB CHOPS

1 or 2 medium lamb chump chops
1 tablespoon oil
grated rind of ½ lemon
1 tablespoon lemon juice
1 teaspoon brown sugar
½ teaspoon ground ginger
salt and freshly ground black pepper

Place the chops in a shallow dish. Mix the oil with the lemon rind, lemon juice, sugar, ginger and salt and pepper to taste. Pour over the chops, cover and leave to marinate for 3 hours, turning the chops occasionally.

Preheat a small browning dish for 6 minutes (or according to the manufacturer's instructions). Add the chops and cook for 5-6 minutes, turning over once. Baste with a little of the marinade halfway through the cooking time.

Serve hot with vegetables or salads.

Serves: 1
Power setting: FULL
Preparation time: 5 minutes, plus marinating
Cooking time: 11-12 minutes

221

RYE STROGANOFF SLICE

100 g/4 oz roast beef or
  pastrami
salt and freshly ground
  black pepper
1 tablespoon finely
  chopped onion
40 g/1½ oz button
  mushrooms, sliced
2 tablespoons horseradish
  and apple salad relish
1 tablespoon soured
  cream
cayenne pepper
1 large slice rye bread,
  toasted

Cut the roast beef or pastrami into strips. Place in a bowl and season to taste with salt and freshly ground black pepper. Add the onion, mushrooms, relish and soured cream, blending well. Cook for 1-2 minutes until hot and bubbly, stirring once.

Add lemon juice and cayenne pepper to taste, blending well. Spoon over the toasted rye bread and serve at once.

Serves: 1
Power setting: FULL
Preparation time: 5 minutes
Cooking time: 1-2 minutes

CHEESY CHIVE AND GARLIC JACKET POTATO

1 × 225 g (8 oz) potato,
  scrubbed
25 g/1 oz Brie, rind
  removed and chopped
1½ tablespoons garlic
  and chive salad relish
salt and freshly ground
  black pepper
snipped chives to garnish

Prick the potato and place on a double thickness sheet of absorbent kitchen paper. Cook for 6 minutes, turning over once. Leave to stand for 3 minutes.

Halve the potato and scoop out the flesh into a bowl. Add the Brie, relish and salt and pepper to taste. Mix well to blend then spoon the mixture back into the potato cases. Return to the oven and cook for 1-2 minutes to reheat.

Serve hot sprinkled with snipped chives.

Serves: 1
Power setting: FULL
Preparation time: 5 minutes
Cooking time: 10-11 minutes

CHOCOLATE MOUSSE WITH ROSE LEAVES

25 g/1 oz plain chocolate
small knob of butter
1 egg, separated
15 g/½ oz white
  chocolate
rose leaves for decoration

Place the plain chocolate in a bowl and cook for ½-1 minute until melted. Stir in the butter, blending well.

Add the egg yolk and mix well to blend. Whisk the egg white until it stands in stiff peaks. Fold through the chocolate mixture with a metal spoon. Pour into a small serving dish and chill to set, which should take about 2-4 hours.

Meanwhile place the white chocolate in a bowl and cook for ½ minute to melt. Very lightly oil the underside of a few washed rose leaves. Dip the underside in the white chocolate to coat. Leave to harden and set then carefully peel away the leaf from the chocolate.

Serve the chocolate mousse prettily decorated with the rose leaf-shaped white chocolate leaves.

Serves: 1
Power setting: FULL
Preparation time: 15 minutes, plus
chilling
Cooking time: 1-1½ minutes

VEGETABLE CURRY (p.233)

QUICHE LORRAINE (p.250)

ORANGE AND APPLE FOOL

1 apple, peeled, cored and
    sliced
grated rind and juice of 1
    small orange
sugar or artificial
    sweetener to taste
1 egg white
1 teaspoon plain yogurt
½ teaspoon soft brown
    sugar

Place the apple, orange rind and juice in a bowl. Cover and cook for 3 minutes.

Allow to cool then purée in a blender or pass through a fine sieve. Sweeten to taste with sugar or artificial sweetener.

Whisk the egg white, until it stands in stiff peaks. Fold into the apple mixture with a metal spoon. Spoon into a serving dish and chill thoroughly.

Just before serving, top with the yogurt and sprinkle with the brown sugar.

Serves: 1
Power setting: FULL
Preparation time: 15 minutes, plus chilling
Cooking time: 3 minutes

MARMALADE SUNDAE

25 g/1 oz marmalade
25 ml/1 fl oz water
1 tablespoon brandy
2 scoops vanilla ice cream

Place the marmalade, water and brandy in a dish. Cook for 1-1½ minutes until very hot and bubbly, stirring once. Allow to cool slightly.

Place the ice cream in a serving dish and spoon over the still warm marmalade sauce. Serve at once.

Serves: 1
Power setting: FULL
Preparation time: 5 minutes, plus cooling
Cooking time: 1-1½ minutes

CHOCOLATE FUDGE SUNDAE

50 g/2 oz plain chocolate
50 ml/2 fl oz sweetened
    condensed milk
2 tablespoons water
knob of butter
1 scoop vanilla ice cream
1 scoop chocolate ice
    cream
Topping:
whipped cream
chopped nuts

Place the chocolate, broken into pieces, in a bowl with the condensed milk. Cook for 2-2½ minutes until the chocolate has melted, stirring once. Add the water and butter and stir well to mix.

Place the ice cream in a sundae glass. Spoon over the chocolate fudge sauce. Top with a swirl of whipped cream. Sprinkle with the nuts and serve at once.

Serves: 1
Power setting: FULL
Preparation time: 5 minutes
Cooking time: 2-2½ minutes

QUICK CHOCOLATE CUSTARD

50 g/2 oz plain chocolate,
    broken into pieces
100 ml/4 fl oz milk
½ teaspoon instant coffee
    powder
½ teaspoon powdered
    gelatine
1 small egg (sizes 4, 5 or
    6), beaten
¼ teaspoon vanilla
    essence

Place the chocolate in a bowl and cook for 1-1½ minutes to melt. Stir in the milk, blending well. Cook for a further 1-1½ minutes until very hot but not boiling.

Stir in the coffee and gelatine, whisking well to blend. Add the egg and vanilla essence, blending well.

Strain into a serving dish and chill until set. Serve with whipped cream if liked.

Serves: 1
Power setting: FULL
Preparation time: 5 minutes, plus chilling
Cooking time: 2-3 minutes

RHUBARB AND ORANGE COMPÔTE

1 stick rhubarb, cut into
  2.5 cm (1 inch) pieces
1 orange, peeled, pith
  removed and cut into
  segments
2 tablespoons orange
  juice
liquid sweetener
  (optional)

Place the rhubarb, orange and orange juice in a serving dish. Cover and cook for 1½-2 minutes until cooked.

Sweeten to taste with liquid sweetener if liked. Serve at once.

Serves: 1
Power setting: FULL
Preparation time: 6 minutes
Cooking time: 1½-2 minutes

FRUIT COMPÔTE

100 g/4 oz mixed dried
  fruit
150 ml/¼ pint water
50 ml/2 fl oz orange
  syrup
1 teaspoon Cointreau
  liqueur
1 teaspoon toasted flaked
  almonds

Place the fruit in a cooking dish with the water. Cover and cook for 2 minutes. Leave to stand for 5 minutes.

Add the orange syrup, cover loosely and cook for 3½-4 minutes, stirring once. Leave to stand, covered, for 15 minutes.

Stir in the Cointreau, cool then chill.

Serve lightly chilled sprinkled with the almonds.

Serves: 1
Power setting: FULL
Preparation time: 5 minutes
Cooking time: 25½-26 minutes

Illustrated on p. 206

PEACHES AND CURAÇAO

2 fresh peaches, skinned,
  stoned and sliced
1 tablespoon Curaçao
  liqueur

Place the peach slices in a serving dish. Cover and cook for 1 minute.

Add the Curaçao, blending well. Serve at once while the peaches are still hot.

Serves: 1
Power setting: FULL
Preparation time: 5 minutes
Cooking time: 1 minute

GINGER SPONGE WITH GRENADINE SAUCE

25 g/1 oz butter
25 g/1 oz caster sugar
½ egg, beaten
25 g/1 oz self-raising
  flour
½ teaspoon ground
  ginger
40 ml/1½ fl oz
  Grenadine syrup
½ teaspoon arrowroot
  powder
40 ml/1½ fl oz water

Cream the butter with the sugar until light and fluffy. Gradually beat in the egg, blending well. Fold in the flour and ginger with a metal spoon. Stir in 2 teaspoons of the Grenadine syrup.

Lightly grease a small individual pudding bowl or measuring jug and add the sponge mixture. Cover loosely with cling film and cook for 1½-2 minutes until well risen and cooked. Allow to stand for 2 minutes.

Meanwhile, mix the arrowroot with the water in a small jug. Stir in the remaining Grenadine syrup. Cook for ½-1 minute, stirring twice until the sauce is clear and thickened.

Turn the pudding out on to a serving plate and spoon over the sauce.

Serves: 1
Power setting: FULL
Preparation time: 10-15 minutes
Cooking time: 4-5 minutes

Vegetarian Cooking

Vegetarian cooking is nutritious healthy cooking without meat and it is gaining in popularity. Many people, for health, social or economic reasons, are turning to vegetarian 'meatless' meals as a total replacement for, or as a partial alternative to, the traditional meat and two vegetable family meal. Converted vegetarians and 'meatless' meal fans will find plenty of inspiration in this chapter for meals using pasta, rice, vegetables, fruit, nuts, cheese and eggs.

COUNTRY VEGETABLE SOUP

50 g/2 oz butter
1 onion, peeled and chopped
450 g/1 lb frozen mixed chopped vegetables
300 ml/½ pint hot vegetable stock
1 bay leaf
½ teaspoon dried rosemary
¼ teaspoon dried sage
600 ml/1 pint milk
salt and freshly ground black pepper

Place the butter, onion and frozen mixed vegetables in a large bowl. Cover and cook for 5 minutes, stirring once. Add the stock, bay leaf, rosemary and sage, blending well. Cover and cook for 9 minutes.

Remove and discard the bay leaf. Purée the soup in a blender then return to the bowl.

Stir in the milk and salt and pepper to taste, blending well. Cook for 4-6 minutes until hot.

Serve with chunks of crusty bread.

To freeze
Cool quickly and place in a rigid container, allowing 2.5 cm/1 inch headspace. Cover, seal, label and freeze for up to 3 months.

Serves: 4
Power setting: FULL
Preparation time: 10 minutes
Cooking time: 18-20 minutes
Suitable for freezing

CURRIED APPLE BISQUE

25 g/1 oz butter
1 onion, peeled and chopped
2 dessert apples, peeled, cored and chopped
1 teaspoon curry powder (medium strength)
450 ml/¾ pint hot vegetable stock
salt and freshly ground black pepper
150 ml/¼ pint double cream
toasted flaked almonds to garnish (see p. 180)

Place the butter, onion and apples in a bowl. Cover and cook for 5 minutes, stirring once. Add the curry powder, blending well and cook for 1 minute.

Gradually add the stock. Purée in a blender and return to the bowl.

Season to taste with salt and pepper and cook for 3-4 minutes. Stir in the cream, blending well. Cook for 1 minute to reheat.

Serve hot, sprinkled with the toasted flaked almonds.

Serves: 4
Power setting: FULL
Preparation time: 15 minutes
Cooking time: 10-11 minutes

QUICK SWEETCORN SOUP

1 × 481 g (1 lb 1 oz) can
  cream-style sweetcorn
75 g/3 oz curd cheese
450 ml/¾ pint milk
½ teaspoon ground
  nutmeg
salt and freshly ground
  black pepper
chopped crispy bacon and
  parsley to garnish

Place the sweetcorn and cheese in a large bowl. Cover and cook for 5 minutes, stirring twice.

Gradually add the milk, nutmeg and salt and pepper to taste, blending well. Cover and cook for 8 minutes, stirring twice.

Serve hot garnished with chopped crispy bacon and parsley.

Serves: 4
Power setting: FULL
Preparation time: 5-10 minutes
Cooking time: 13 minutes

LEMONY SALAD APPETIZER

2 tablespoons oil
1 garlic clove, peeled and
  crushed
1 small onion, peeled
finely grated rind and
  juice of 1 large lemon
150 ml/¼ pint dry
  vermouth
2 tablespoons soft brown
  sugar
3 tablespoons chopped
  parsley
salt and freshly ground
  black pepper
225 g/8 oz young carrots,
  cut into matchsticks
225 g/8 oz shelled broad
  beans

Place the oil, garlic and onion in a bowl. Cook for 2 minutes, stirring once.

Add the lemon rind and juice, vermouth, sugar, parsley and salt and pepper to taste, blending well. Add the vegetables and stir well to coat in the marinade. Cover and cook for 5 minutes, stirring once.

Allow to cool then chill thoroughly. Serve chilled as part of a salad.

Serves: 4
Power setting: FULL
Preparation time: 15 minutes, plus
  chilling
Cooking time: 7 minutes

NOODLES AU GRATIN

225 g/8 oz egg noodles
600 ml/1 pint boiling
  water
1 tablespoon oil
450 g/1 lb leeks, washed
  and sliced
4 tablespoons cold water
salt and freshly ground
  black pepper
2 hard-boiled eggs, shelled
  and chopped
6 eggs, beaten
150 ml/¼ pint single
  cream
100 g/4 oz Emmenthal
  cheese, grated

Place the noodles, boiling water and oil in a bowl. Cover and cook for 6 minutes. Leave to stand while cooking the leeks.

Place the leeks in a bowl with the cold water and a pinch of salt. Cover and cook for 8 minutes, stirring once.

Drain the noodles and leeks and place in a greased serving dish with the chopped hard-boiled eggs.

Mix the 6 eggs with the cream and salt and pepper to taste and pour over the noodle mixture. Top with the grated cheese.

Cook for 10-12 minutes, turning the dish twice. Serve hot.

Serves: 4
Power setting: FULL
Preparation time: 20 minutes
Cooking time: 24-26 minutes

SPAGHETTI WITH NEAPOLITAN SAUCE

350 g/12 oz spaghetti
1.4 litres/2½ pints boiling
    water
1 tablespoon vegetable oil
Sauce:
2 tablespoons olive oil
1 large onion, peeled and
    chopped
1 garlic clove, peeled and
    crushed
450 g/1 lb tomatoes,
    peeled, seeded and
    chopped
1 tablespoon chopped
    mixed fresh herbs
    (thyme, oregano,
    parsley, for instance)
salt and freshly ground
    black pepper
15 g/½ oz butter
grated Parmesan cheese
    to sprinkle

Hold the spaghetti in a deep bowl with the water and vegetable oil to soften, then submerge. Cover and cook for 10 minutes. Leave to stand, covered, while preparing the sauce.

Place the olive oil, onion and garlic in a bowl. Cover and cook for 3 minutes.

Add the tomatoes, blending well. Cover and cook for 3 minutes.

Add the herbs and salt and pepper to taste, blending well. Cover and cook for a further 2 minutes.

Drain the spaghetti and toss with the butter. Arrange around the outside of a heated serving dish.

Pour the sauce into the centre and serve at once, sprinkled with Parmesan cheese.

Serves: 4
Power setting: FULL
Preparation time: 15-20 minutes
Cooking time: 18 minutes

SPAGHETTI AND MUSHROOM SALAD

350 g/12 oz spaghetti,
    broken into short
    lengths
1.4 litres/2½ pints boiling
    water
1 teaspoon oil
salt and freshly ground
    black pepper
4 spring onions, trimmed
    and chopped
2 celery sticks, scrubbed
    and chopped
175 g/6 oz mushrooms,
    wiped and sliced
1 tablespoon chopped
    fresh parsley
lettuce leaves
Dressing:
6 tablespoons oil
2 tablespoons wine
    vinegar
2 teaspoons curry powder
2 tablespoons tomato
    purée
1 teaspoon soft brown
    sugar

Place the spaghetti, water, oil and a pinch of salt in a bowl. Cover an cook for 10 minutes, stirring once. Leave to stand, covered, for 5 minutes then drain and cool.

Add the spring onions, celery, mushrooms and parsley to the spaghetti and mix well.

Blend the oil with the vinegar, curry powder, tomato purée, sugar and salt and pepper to taste. Pour into the spaghetti mixture and toss well to mix.

Line a serving dish with lettuce leaves and pile the salad mixture on top. Serve at once.

Serves: 4-6
Power setting: FULL
Preparation time: 10-15 minutes, plus
    cooling time
Cooking time: 15 minutes

VEGETABLES VINAIGRETTE

100 g/4 oz young green
   beans, topped and
   tailed
3 tablespoons cold water
salt and freshly ground
   black pepper
100 g/4 oz courgettes,
   thickly sliced
100 g/4 oz button
   mushrooms, wiped
2 hard-boiled eggs, shelled
   and quartered
2 tablespoons olive oil
juice of ½ lemon
chopped fresh herbs
   (parsley, chives,
   marjoram, oregano,
   for example)
1 lemon, quartered, to
   garnish

Place the beans in a bowl with 2 table-spoons of the water and a pinch of salt. Cover and cook for 2 minutes. Drain and refresh under cold running water. Drain well and pat dry.

Place the courgettes in a bowl. Cover and cook for 2 minutes. Refresh under cold running water. Drain well and pat dry.

Place the mushrooms in a bowl with the remaining water. Cover and cook for 1½-2 minutes, stirring once. Drain and refresh under cold running water. Drain well and pat dry.

Arrange the vegetables on a plate with the eggs. Combine the oil and lemon juice, season with salt and pepper to taste and beat with a whisk or fork until thick and creamy.

Spoon over the vegetables and sprinkle with herbs to taste. Garnish with lemon wedges and serve at room temperature.

Serves: 2
Power setting: FULL
Preparation time: 20-25 minutes
Cooking time: 5½-6 minutes

NOODLES WITH CHEESY LEEKS

350 g/12 oz egg noodles
900 ml/1½ pints boiling
   water
1 tablespoon oil
675 g/1½ lb leeks, washed
   and sliced
4 tablespoons cold water
salt and freshly ground
   black pepper
25 g/1 oz butter
25 g/1 oz plain flour
450 ml/¾ pint milk
1 teaspoon made
   mustard
100 g/4 oz cheese, grated

Place the noodles, boiling water and oil in a bowl. Cover and cook for 6 minutes. Leave to stand while cooking the leeks.

Place the leeks in a bowl with the water and a pinch of salt. Cover and cook for 12 minutes, stirring once.

Place the butter in a bowl and cook for ½ minute to melt. Stir in the flour then gradually add the milk, blending well. Cook for 4 minutes, stirring every 1 minute until smooth and thickened. Add the mustard, salt and pepper to taste and half of the cheese, blending well.

Drain the noodles and place in a serving dish. Drain the leeks and place on top of the

noodles. Pour over the cheese sauce and sprinkle with the remaining cheese. Serve at once.

To freeze
Cool quickly, cover with foil, seal, label and store for up to 3 months.

Serves: 4
Power setting: FULL
Preparation time: 20 minutes
Cooking time: 22½ minutes
Suitable for freezing

GREEK CASSEROLE

225 g/8 oz long-grain
   rice
600 ml/1 pint boiling
   water
2 × 283 g (10 oz) packets
   frozen casserole
   vegetables
6 tablespoons cold water

Place the rice and boiling water in a bowl. Cover and cook for 10 minutes. Leave to stand, covered, while preparing the vegetables.

Place the frozen casserole vegetables in a bowl with the cold water. Cover and cook for 10 minutes, stirring once. Drain well then stir in the herbs and tomato purée,

blending well.

Place the spinach in a bowl. Cover and cook for 8 minutes. Drain well and stir into the rice.

Place the vegetable mixture in the base of a serving dish. Spoon the rice mixture over the top in an even layer.

Mix the yogurt with the egg yolks, corn-

1 tablespoon chopped
    fresh herbs
4 tablespoons tomato
    purée
1 × 283 g (10 oz) packet
    frozen cut leaf spinach
250 ml/8 fl oz plain
    yogurt
2 egg yolks
1 tablespoon cornflour
1 tablespoon French
    mustard
200 g/7 oz feta or white
    Cheshire cheese, cubed
salt and black pepper

flour and mustard, blending well. Fold in the cheese and season with salt and pepper to taste. Spoon over the rice and cook for 8 minutes, or until the egg mixture is just set around the edges. Leave to stand for 5 minutes then serve.

Serves: 4-6
Power setting: FULL
Preparation time: 20-25 minutes
Cooking time: 41 minutes

PASTA WITH AVOCADO DRESSING

350 g/12 oz pasta shells
1.4 litres/2½ pints boiling
    water
1 teaspoon oil
salt and freshly ground
    black pepper
4 spring onions, trimmed
    and chopped
2 tablespoons chopped
    parsley
Dressing:
1 ripe avocado, halved
    and stoned
juice of 1 lemon
1 garlic clove, peeled and
    crushed
1 teaspoon caster sugar
150 ml/¼ pint single
    cream

Place the pasta, water, oil and a pinch of salt in a bowl. Cover and cook for 12 minutes, stirring once. Leave to stand for 5 minutes then drain and allow to cool.

To make the dressing, scoop the avocado flesh out of the skins and place in a blender with the lemon juice, garlic, sugar and cream. Purée until smooth then season to taste with salt and pepper.

Add the avocado dressing to the pasta shells with the spring onions and parsley. Toss well to mix. Serve lightly chilled.

Serves: 4
Power setting: FULL
Preparation time: 10 minutes, plus cooling and chilling
Cooking time: 17 minutes

SUMMER GARDEN VEGETABLES

1 small marrow, peeled
    and chopped
1 medium courgette,
    sliced
1 small onion, peeled and
    sliced
1 tomato, sliced
2 tablespoons grated
    Parmesan cheese
salt and freshly ground
    black pepper
½ teaspoon dried basil
½ teaspoon dried thyme

Place the marrow, courgette, onion, tomato, cheese, salt and pepper to taste, basil and thyme in a small casserole dish, tossing well to blend.

Cover and cook for 8-10 minutes, stirring once. Serve hot with chunks of crusty bread.

Serves: 2
Power setting: FULL
Preparation time: 10 minutes
Cooking time: 8-10 minutes

SWISS TOMATO CASSEROLE

40 g/1½ oz butter
40 g/1½ oz plain flour
450 ml/¾ pint milk
salt and freshly ground
    black pepper
100 g/4 oz Gruyère
    cheese, grated
4 tablespoons single
    cream
675 g/1½ lb ripe, firm
    tomatoes, peeled and
    sliced
½ teaspoon dried basil
2 teaspoons caster sugar
25 g/1 oz grated
    Parmesan cheese

Place the butter, flour and milk in a bowl. Cook for 5-6 minutes, stirring every 1 minute until smooth and thickened.

Add salt and pepper to taste, the cheese and cream, blending well.

Arrange a layer of sliced tomatoes in the bottom of a casserole dish. Sprinkle with salt and pepper to taste, a little basil and sugar. Cover with a little sauce. Continue layering, finishing with a layer of sauce.

Sprinkle with the Parmesan cheese, cover and cook for 10-12 minutes, turning the dish twice. Serve hot.

Serves: 4
Power setting: FULL
Preparation time: 20 minutes
Cooking time: 15-18 minutes

SPAGHETTI WITH CREAM AND ONION

350 g/12 oz wholewheat
    spaghetti
1.5 litres/2¾ pints boiling
    water
1 tablespoon oil
salt and freshly ground
    black pepper
50 g/2 oz butter
1 small onion, peeled and
    finely chopped
1 tablespoon plain flour
150 ml/¼ pint double
    cream
pinch of ground nutmeg
1 tablespoon fresh parsley
grated Parmesan cheese
    to serve

Hold the spaghetti in a bowl with the water, oil and a pinch of salt to soften, then submerge. Cover and cook for 12 minutes. Leave to stand, covered, while preparing the sauce.

Place half of the butter in a bowl with the onion. Cover and cook for 2 minutes. Stir in the flour, blending well. Cook for 1 minute, stirring once.

Gradually add the cream, nutmeg, salt and pepper to taste and parsley. Cook for 1 minute, stirring twice.

Drain the spaghetti and toss in the remaining butter and salt and pepper to taste. Add the cream mixture and toss well to mix.

Serve at once sprinkled with grated Parmesan cheese.

Serves: 4
Power setting: FULL
Preparation time: 10 minutes
Cooking time: 16 minutes

MUSHROOMS IN GARLIC BUTTER

100 g/4 oz butter
2 garlic cloves, peeled and
    crushed
1 tablespoon lemon juice
freshly ground black
    pepper
450 g/1 lb button
    mushrooms, wiped

Place the butter in a bowl and cook for 1 minute to melt. Add the garlic, lemon juice and pepper to taste, blending well. Cook for 1 minute.

Add the mushrooms, stirring well to coat in the butter. Cover and leave to marinate for 1-2 hours.

Cook, covered, for 5-6 minutes, stirring the dish once.

Serve the mushrooms hot with chunks of wholemeal bread.

Serves: 4
Power setting: FULL
Preparation time: 10 minutes, plus
    marinating
Cooking time: 7-8 minutes

GARDEN VEGETABLE CASSEROLE

40 g/1½ oz butter
1 onion, peeled and
    thinly sliced
3 tablespoons plain flour
1 teaspoon ground
    nutmeg
300 ml/½ pint milk
300 ml/½ pint hot
    chicken stock
salt and freshly ground
    black pepper
175 g/6 oz Cheddar
    cheese with ham and
    mustard, grated
450 g/1 lb peeled and
    thinly sliced potatoes
2 × 283 g (10 oz) packets
    frozen sweetcorn, peas
    and carrots
sliced tomatoes (optional)

Place the butter in a large bowl and cook for ½ minute. Add the onion and cook for 2 minutes.

Stir in the flour, nutmeg, milk, stock and salt and pepper to taste, blending well. Cook for 4 minutes, stirring every 1 minute until smooth and thickened. Add the cheese, blending well.

Layer one-third of the potatoes in a cooking dish. Top with one-third of the vegetables then one-third of the sauce. Repeat the layering twice, finishing with a layer of sauce.

Top with the tomato slices if used. Cook for 30 minutes, turning the dish twice, or until the potato is cooked in the centre of the dish.

Serve hot with a seasonal salad.

Serves: 4
Power setting: FULL
Preparation time: 20-25 minutes
Cooking time: 36½ minutes

VEGETABLE CURRY

50 g/2 oz butter
1 large onion, peeled and
    chopped
2 garlic cloves, peeled and
    chopped
1 apple, peeled, cored and
    chopped
2 tablespoons curry
    powder
2 tablespoons plain flour
1 teaspoon ground
    allspice
salt and black pepper
1 × 425 g (15 oz) can
    tomatoes
1 × 425 g (15 oz) can
    butter beans
1 vegetable stock cube
boiling water
675 g-800 g/1½-1¾ lb
    prepared mixed
    vegetables (celery,
    cauliflower, carrots,
    aubergine and
    courgettes, for
    example)
2 tablespoons chutney
50 g/2 oz sultanas

Place the butter in a large casserole and cook on FULL POWER for 1½ minutes. Add the onion, garlic and apple, blending well. Cook on FULL POWER for 3 minutes, stirring once.

Add the curry powder, flour, allspice and salt and pepper to taste, blending well. Cook on FULL POWER for 1 minute.

Meanwhile, drain the juice from the tomatoes and butter beans into a measuring jug. Add the crumbled stock cube and make up to 600 ml/1 pint with boiling water.

Gradually add the stock to the curry base, blending well. Cook on FULL POWER for 6 minutes, stirring three times.

Add the prepared vegetables, chutney and sultanas, blending well. Cover and cook on FULL POWER for 5 minutes.

Reduce the power setting and cook on MEDIUM POWER for 30 minutes, stirring twice.

Add the tomatoes and butter beans, blending well. Cook on FULL POWER for 5 minutes. Serve hot with boiled rice.

To freeze
Cool quickly and place in a rigid container. Cover, seal, label and freeze for 1 month.

Serves: 6-8
Power settings: FULL, MEDIUM
Preparation time: 30-40 minutes
Cooking time: 51½ minutes
Suitable for freezing

Illustrated on p. 223

VEGETARIAN DINNER PARTY

Lemony Salad Appetizer (see p. 228)
Vegetable Curry (see p. 233)
Boiled rice (see p. 128)
Accompaniments – choose from poppa-
dums, mango chutney, naan bread,
tomato and onion salad, cucumber raita
etc.
Plums with Port (see p. 161)

Timetable
Start cooking about 1¼ hours before re-
quired (or 15 minutes if the Vegetable
Curry has been prepared in advance).

1. Prepare Lemony Salad Appetizer up to
24 hours in advance and chill.
2. Prepare Vegetable Curry up to 12 hours
in advance or before serving starter.
3. Before serving starter cook the boiled
rice and leave to stand covered.
4. Serve Lemony Salad Appetiser.
5. Reheat Vegetable Curry on FULL
POWER for 6-8 minutes, stirring twice.
Serve with rice and accompaniments.
6. Cook Plums with Port after main course
and serve at once.

SWEETCORN PUDDING

2×283 g (10 oz) packets
    frozen sweetcorn
    kernels
50 g/2 oz butter, diced
150 ml/5 fl oz plain
    yogurt
1 egg
salt and freshly ground
    black pepper
75 g/3 oz fresh white
    breadcrumbs
100 g/4 oz Emmenthal or
    Gouda cheese, finely
    grated
25 g/1 oz toasted flaked
    almonds (see p. 180)

Place the sweetcorn in a medium casserole
dish. Dot with the butter, cover and cook for
6 minutes.

Meanwhile, beat the yogurt with the
egg, salt and pepper to taste, breadcrumbs
and 75 g/3 oz of the cheese.

Pour over the sweetcorn and gently stir
to mix. Cook, uncovered, for 10 minutes,
turning the dish once.

Sprinkle with the remaining cheese and
almonds and cook, uncovered, for a further
2 minutes. Serve hot.

Serves: 4
Power setting: FULL
Preparation time: 15 minutes
Cooking time: 18 minutes

MUSHROOM RISOTTO

75 g/3 oz butter
1 onion, peeled and sliced
225 g/8 oz brown rice
150 ml/¼ pint dry white
    wine
600 ml/1 pint boiling
    vegetable stock
225 g/8 oz mushrooms,
    wiped and sliced
1½ teaspoons dried basil
salt and freshly ground
    black pepper
3 tablespoons grated
    Parmesan cheese

Place the butter, onion and rice in a large
bowl. Cook for 5 minutes, stirring once.

Add the wine, stock, mushrooms, basil
and salt and pepper to taste. Cover and cook
for 20 minutes, stirring twice. Leave to
stand, covered, for 5 minutes.

Sprinkle with the Parmesan cheese and
serve while still hot.

Serves: 4
Power settings: FULL
Preparation time: 5 minutes
Cooking time: 30 minutes

VEGETABLES À LA GRECQUE

2 tablespoons oil
1 garlic clove, peeled and
    crushed
1 small onion, peeled and
    thinly sliced
2 tablespoons white wine
    vinegar
150 ml/¼ pint dry white
    vermouth
3 tablespoons tomato
    purée
2 tablespoons soft brown
    sugar
3 tablespoons chopped
    fresh marjoram or
    parsley
salt and freshly ground
    black pepper
225 g/8 oz button
    mushrooms, wiped and
    trimmed
225 g/8 oz cauliflower,
    broken into small
    florets

Place the oil, garlic and onion in a bowl. Cook for 2 minutes, stirring once.

Add the vinegar, vermouth, tomato purée, sugar, herbs and salt and pepper to taste, blending well. Add the vegetables and stir well to coat in the marinade. Cover and cook for 5 minutes, stirring once.

Allow to cool then chill thoroughly. Serve chilled with crusty bread as a starter.

Serves: 4
Power setting: FULL
Preparation time: 15 minutes, plus chilling time
Cooking time: 7 minutes

SPICED FRUIT AND VEGETABLES

1 tablespoon oil
1 onion, peeled and
    chopped
4 sticks celery, scrubbed
    and chopped
1 tablespoon plain flour
1 tablespoon curry
    powder
200 ml/7 fl oz hot
    vegetable stock
1 teaspoon ground
    ginger
grated rind and juice of 1
    lemon
1 × 400 g (14 oz) can
    apricot halves, drained
2 bananas, peeled and
    thickly sliced
450 g/1 lb cooking apples,
    peeled, cored and
    quartered
100 g/4 oz raisins
150 ml/¼ pint soured
    cream

Place the oil, onion and celery in a large casserole dish. Cover and cook for 5 minutes, stirring once.

Add the flour and curry powder, blending well. Cook for 1 minute.

Gradually add the stock, ginger, lemon rind and lemon juice, blending well. Cook for 3 minutes, stirring every 1 minute until smooth and thickened.

Add the apricots, bananas, apples and raisins. Cover and cook for 8 minutes, stirring once, or until the apples are tender.

Stir in the soured cream and serve at once.

Serves: 4-6
Power setting: FULL
Preparation time: 15-20 minutes
Cooking time: 17 minutes

Microwave and Conventional Cooking

Though not intended to be a replacement for the conventional cooker, the microwave proves a wonderful ally for the freezer, conventional grill, hob and oven, and can be used in tandem with them for quickly cooked but beautifully crisp and brown cakes, breads, biscuits, gratin dishes, soufflés and pastry tarts — all cooked doubly fast, doubly economically and doubly deliciously.

SAVOURY HOT POT

1 onion, peeled and chopped
15 g/½ oz butter
½ cucumber, peeled and sliced
salt and black pepper
100 g/4 oz cooked sliced ham
2 hard-boiled eggs, shelled and sliced
1 recipe Basic White Pouring Sauce (see p. 140)
50 g/2 oz Gouda cheese, grated

Place the onion and butter in a cooking dish. Cover and cook on FULL POWER for 3 minutes, stirring once. Top with the cucumber and season with salt and pepper to taste.

Cover with alternate layers of ham and eggs. Spoon over the sauce and sprinkle with the cheese. Cook on FULL POWER for 3 minutes, turning the dish once.

Place under a preheated hot grill and cook until golden, about 3-5 minutes.

Serves: 4
Power setting: FULL
Conventional oven setting: GRILL
Preparation time: 20 minutes
Cooking time: 9-11 minutes

COURGETTES PROVENÇALE

4 courgettes, about 15 cm (6 inches) long, topped and tailed
2 tablespoons water
1 × 215 g (7½ oz) can tomatoes, chopped
1 tablespoon finely chopped onion
1 garlic clove, peeled and crushed
salt and freshly ground black pepper
50 g/2 oz cheese, grated

Place the courgettes in a bowl with the water. Cover and cook on FULL POWER for 5-6 minutes or until soft. Drain thoroughly.

Cut each courgette in half lengthways and scoop out the flesh with a teaspoon. Coarsely chop the flesh and mix with the tomatoes, onion, garlic and salt and pepper to taste.

Place the courgettes in a greased ovenproof dish. Spoon the tomato mixture into the courgettes and sprinkle with the cheese. Cook in a preheated hot oven for 10-15 minutes until hot and bubbly. Serve at once.

Serves: 4
Power setting: FULL
Conventional oven setting: 220°C, 425°F, Gas Mark 7
Preparation time: 15-20 minutes
Cooking time: 15-21 minutes

THE BEST OF BOTH WORLDS

Get the best of both worlds by using the speed and efficiency of the microwave with the browning and flavour-enhancing powers of the conventional cooker:

- Casseroles: cook in the microwave on FULL POWER for 10-15 minutes to get a good start and then in the conventional oven at 180°C, 350°F, Gas Mark 5 for 45-60 minutes to achieve a flavour that can only be developed over time.

  Alternatively, pre-brown meat on the hob and then cook in the microwave on MEDIUM POWER until tender.
- Quiches, tarts and flans: bake the pastry case conventionally then add the filling and cook in the microwave for speed.
- Pancakes and crêpes: make them conventionally then stuff and cook in the microwave.
- Bread and yeast doughs: prove the dough in the microwave for double-quick results then bake conventionally for a crusty brown finish.
- Double-crust pies: bake conventionally then reheat when required in the microwave.
- Cakes and biscuits made by the melted method: melt the butter, syrup or honey mixtures in the microwave then bake conventionally.

SAUSAGE AND TOMATO QUICHE

Pastry:
175 g/6 oz plain flour
pinch of salt
75 g/3 oz butter
about 2 tablespoons iced water
Filling:
225 g/8 oz chipolata sausages, pricked
75 g/3 oz Cheddar cheese, grated
2 tomatoes, peeled and sliced
2 eggs, beaten
200 ml/7 fl oz milk
½ teaspoon dried basil
salt and freshly ground black pepper

To make the pastry case sift the flour and salt into a bowl. Rub in the butter until the mixture resembles fine breadcrumbs. Bind together with the water to make a pliable dough.

Roll out on a lightly floured surface to a round large enough to line a 23 cm (9 inch) flan dish. Bake 'blind' in a preheated moderately hot oven for 15 minutes. Remove baking beans and cook for a further 10-12 minutes until golden and cooked.

Meanwhile, place the sausages on a roasting rack and cook on FULL POWER for 3-3½ minutes, turning once.

Sprinkle the cheese over the base of the cooked flan. Arrange the cooked sausages spoke fashion on the base, arranging tomato slices between each. Blend the eggs with the milk, basil and salt and pepper to taste. Pour evenly over the filling.

Cook on DEFROST POWER for 14-16 minutes, giving the dish a quarter turn every 3 minutes. Leave to stand for 15-20 minutes – the flan should set completely during this time. Serve warm or cold cut into wedges.

To freeze
Cool quickly and place in a rigid container. Cover, seal, label and freeze for up to 3 months.

Serves: 4
Power settings: FULL, DEFROST
Conventional oven setting: 200°C, 400°F, Gas Mark 6
Preparation time: 30 minutes
Cooking time: 57-66½ minutes
Suitable for freezing

237

VEGETABLE MEDLEY AU GRATIN

350 g/12 oz cauliflower
   florets
2 tablespoons water
25 g/1 oz butter
1 large onion, peeled and
   sliced
1 large green pepper,
   cored, seeded and
   sliced into rings
2 medium cooked
   beetroot, peeled and
   chopped
salt and freshly ground
   black pepper
150 ml/¼ pint double
   cream
½ teaspoon lemon juice
1 garlic clove, peeled and
   crushed
100 g/4 oz cheese, grated
50 g/2 oz brown
   breadcrumbs
2 hard-boiled eggs, shelled
   and chopped
1 tablespoon chopped
   parsley

Place the cauliflower and water in a bowl. Cover and cook on FULL POWER for 5 minutes, stirring once. Drain thoroughly.

Place the butter in a bowl with the onion and pepper. Cover and cook on FULL POWER for 6 minutes, stirring once.

Place the beetroot in the base of a large heatproof dish. Top with the onion and pepper mixture and the cauliflower florets. Season to taste with salt and pepper.

Mix the cream with the lemon juice and garlic. Spoon over the vegetables. Mix the cheese with the breadcrumbs, blending well. Sprinkle over the top of the dish. Cook on FULL POWER for 4-6 minutes, turning the dish twice.

Place under a preheated hot grill and cook until golden and crisp, about 3-5 minutes.

Mix the hard-boiled eggs and parsley together and spoon down the centre of the dish. Serve hot or cold.

Serves: 4-6
Power setting: FULL
Conventional oven setting: GRILL
Preparation time: 25-30 minutes
Cooking time: 18-22 minutes

FISH COBBLER

240 g/1½ oz butter
40 g/1½ oz plain flour
450 ml/¾ pint milk
350 g/12 oz haddock
   fillets, skinned and cut
   into 4 cm (1½ inch)
   pieces
50 g/2 oz peeled prawns
100 g/4 oz frozen peas
1 tablespoon chopped
   parsley
salt and freshly ground
   black pepper
Cobbler topping:
225 g/8 oz self-raising
   flour
50 g/2 oz butter
50 g/2 oz cheese, grated
about 6 tablespoons milk
milk or beaten egg to
   glaze

Place the butter in a bowl and cook on FULL POWER for 1 minute to melt. Add the flour, blending well. Gradually add the milk and cook on FULL POWER for 5 minutes, stirring every 1 minute until smooth and thickened.

Add the haddock, prawns, peas, parsley and salt and pepper to taste. Spoon into four individual or one large pie dish.

To make the cobbler topping, sift the flour and a pinch of salt into a bowl. Rub in the butter until the mixture resembles fine breadcrumbs. Stir in the cheese and mix to a soft but manageable dough with the milk. Roll out the dough on a lightly floured surface to about 2 cm (¾ inch) thick and cut into rounds, using a 5 cm (2 inch) plain or fluted scone cutter.

Arrange the cobbler rounds on top of the fish mixture, overlapping slightly. Brush with milk or beaten egg to glaze. Cook in a preheated hot oven for 25-30 minutes until well-risen, golden and cooked through.

Serves: 4
Power setting: FULL
Conventional oven setting: 230°C, 450°F, Gas Mark 8
Preparation time: 25-30 minutes
Cooking time: 31-36 minutes

LEMONY FISH PANCAKES

Pancake batter:
100 g/4 oz plain flour
pinch of salt
1 egg
300 ml/½ pint milk
oil to cook
Filling:
450 g/1 lb smoked cod or
*   haddock fillets*
300 ml/½ pint milk
25 g/1 oz butter
175 g/6 oz button
*   mushrooms, wiped and*
*   sliced*
3 tablespoons plain flour
2 tablespoons lemon juice
3 tablespoons chopped
*   parsley*
freshly ground black
*   pepper*

Sift the flour and salt into a bowl. Make a well in the centre and add the egg. Whisk in the milk, a little at a time, for a smooth batter.

Heat a 20 cm (8 inch) diameter frying pan and add a few drops of oil. Pour in a quarter of the batter and tilt the pan to coat the bottom evenly. Cook until the underside is brown, then turn over and cook for 10 seconds. Remove and repeat with the remaining batter to make four pancakes, stacking the pancakes between greaseproof paper as they are cooked. Keep warm.

Meanwhile, place the fish in a shallow dish with the milk. Cover and cook on FULL POWER for 7-8 minutes. Drain and reserve the milk. Skin and flake the fish, removing and discarding any bones.

Place the butter in a bowl and cook on FULL POWER for ½ minute to melt. Add the mushrooms, cover and cook on FULL POWER for 2 minutes. Stir in the flour, blending well. Gradually add the reserved milk, lemon juice, parsley and pepper to taste. Cook on FULL POWER for 3 minutes, stirring every 1 minute until smooth and thickened. Fold in the fish and cook on FULL POWER for 1 minute.

Fill the pancakes with the savoury filling. Roll up and serve at once.

To freeze
Cool quickly, put in a rigid container, cover, seal, label and freeze for up to 2 months.
Serves: 4
Power setting: FULL
Conventional oven setting: HOB
Preparation time: 20 minutes
Cooking time: about 25-30 minutes
Suitable for freezing

SMOKED HADDOCK SOUFFLÉ

40 g/1½ oz butter
25 g/1 oz plain flour
200 ml/7 fl oz milk
4 tablespoons double
*   cream*
4 eggs, separated
1 egg white
225 g/8 oz cooked
*   smoked haddock fillets,*
*   flaked*
salt and black pepper

Place the butter in a bowl and cook on FULL POWER for 1 minute to melt. Stir in the flour, blending well. Gradually add the milk and cream and cook on FULL POWER for 3½-4 minutes, stirring every 1 minute until smooth and thickened.

Add the egg yolks, blending well. Fold in the fish and salt and pepper to taste.

Whisk the egg whites until they stand in stiff peaks. Fold into the fish mixture with a metal spoon.

Spoon into a buttered 18 cm (7 inch) diameter soufflé dish. Bake in a preheated moderately hot oven until well-risen, firm and golden, about 35 minutes.

Serves: 4
Power setting: FULL
Conventional oven setting: 190°C,
375°F, Gas Mark 5
Preparation time: 20 minutes
Cooking time: 39½-40 minutes

EXOTIC CHICKEN

4 × 225 g (8 oz) chicken
*   joints*
salt and black pepper
1 small orange, peeled,
*   pith removed and sliced*
4 canned pineapple rings
1 small banana, peeled
*   and sliced*
4 maraschino cherries
2 tablespoons brown rum
pinch of ground paprika
pinch of ground ginger
pinch of curry powder

Season the chicken with salt and pepper to taste. Place the orange slices and pineapple in the base of a lightly greased flameproof dish. Top with the chicken quarters and cook on FULL POWER for 14 minutes, rearranging the chicken pieces once.

Add the banana, cherries and rum. Sprinkle over the paprika, ginger and curry powder. Cook under a preheated hot grill until golden and bubbly, about 3-5 minutes. Serve hot.

Serves: 4
Power setting: FULL
Conventional oven setting: GRILL
Preparation time: 15 minutes
Cooking time: 17-19 minutes

CHEESE SOUFFLÉS AND PROVENÇALE SAUCE

Sauce:
1 tablespoon oil
1 small onion, peeled and finely chopped
1 garlic clove, peeled and crushed
1 × 425 g (15 oz) can tomatoes
2 teaspoons tomato purée
1 bay leaf
pinch of sugar
pinch of dried basil
pinch of dried mixed herbs
1 teaspoon lemon juice
salt and freshly ground black pepper
Soufflés:
25 g/1 oz butter
15 g/½ oz plain flour
150 ml/¼ pint milk
½ teaspoon mustard powder
2 eggs, separated
100 g/4 oz cheese, grated

To prepare the sauce, place the oil, onion and garlic in a bowl. Cover and cook on FULL POWER for 3 minutes, stirring once. Add the tomatoes and their juice, tomato purée, bay leaf, sugar, basil, mixed herbs, lemon juice and salt and pepper to taste, blending well. Cover and cook on FULL POWER for 6 minutes, stirring once. Reduce the power setting and cook on MEDIUM POWER for 10 minutes. Remove and discard the bay leaf.

To make the soufflés, place the butter in a bowl and cook on FULL POWER for 1 minute. Add the flour, blending well. Gradually add the milk and cook on FULL POWER for 2-3 minutes, stirring twice to keep smooth. Add the mustard, egg yolks and cheese, stirring well to blend.

Whisk the egg whites until they stand in stiff peaks. Fold into the cheese mixture with a metal spoon. Pour into 4 buttered individual soufflé or ramekin dishes. Bake in a preheated moderately hot oven for 15 minutes until cooked and golden.

Serve immediately, cutting a slit in the tops of the soufflés at the table so that the Provençale sauce can be poured in.

Serves: 4
Power settings: FULL, MEDIUM
Conventional oven setting: 200°C, 400°F, Gas Mark 6
Preparation time: 30 minutes
Cooking time: 37-38 minutes

HAM, EGG AND BEAN PIE

25 g/1 oz butter
1 small onion, peeled and finely chopped
2 sticks celery, scrubbed and chopped
1 tablespoon chopped fresh sage or 1 teaspoon dried sage
1 × 450 g (1 lb) can baked beans with pork sausages
175 g/6 oz cooked ham, chopped
2 hard-boiled eggs, shelled and quartered
salt and freshly ground black pepper
175 g/6 oz shortcrust pastry
175 g/6 oz puff pastry
beaten egg to glaze

Place the butter, onion, celery and sage in a bowl. Cover and cook for 4 minutes, stirring once. Add the baked beans with sausages, ham, eggs and salt and pepper to taste, blending lightly.

Roll out the shortcrust pastry on a lightly floured surface and use to line a 20 cm (8 inch) diameter pie dish. Spoon the prepared filling into the dish and brush the pastry rim with beaten egg.

Roll out the puff pastry on a lightly floured surface and use to cover the filling. Press the edges well to seal, then crimp the edges to give a decorative effect. Use any pastry trimmings to decorate the pie as liked. Brush with beaten egg to glaze.

Cook in a preheated moderately hot oven for 20 minutes then reduce the heat to moderate and cook for a further 30-35 minutes.

Serve the pie hot or cold.

Serves: 4
Power setting: FULL
Conventional oven setting: 200°C, 400°F, Gas Mark 6; then: 180°C, 350°F, Gas Mark 4
Preparation time: 20-40 minutes
Cooking time: 54-59 minutes

GAMMON EN CROÛTE

1 × 1.4 kg (3 lb) gammon
    joint
450 g/1 lb puff pastry
Stuffing:
25 g/1 oz butter
1 small onion, peeled and
    chopped
25 g/1 oz walnuts,
    chopped
25 g/1 oz parsley,
    chopped
100 g/4 oz fresh white
    breadcrumbs
freshly ground black
    pepper
grated rind and juice of
    ½ orange
1 small egg, beaten

Place the gammon on a roasting rack and cook on MEDIUM POWER for 33-36 minutes, turning over once. Leave to cool completely.

Meanwhile, place the butter and onion in a bowl. Cover and cook on FULL POWER for 2 minutes, stirring once. Add the walnuts, parsley, breadcrumbs, pepper to taste, orange rind and orange juice, blending well. Bind together with the beaten egg. Leave to cool completely.

Slice the gammon joint diagonally into 3 pieces. Sandwich back together again with the stuffing.

Roll out the pastry on a lightly floured surface so that it is large enough to enclose the joint. Brush the edges with beaten egg and fold around the joint to enclose. Place, seam-sides down, on a baking sheet. Make a slit in the pastry crust to allow any steam to escape.

Glaze with beaten egg and decorate with any pastry trimyings. Cover with cling film and chilx for 30 minutes.

Remove the cling film and cook in a preheated hot oven for 40 minutes until golden and cooked through. Cover the pastry with foil for the latter part of the cooking time if it appears to be browning too much.

Serves: 5-6
Power settings: MEDIUM, FULL
Conventional oven setting: 220°C,
425°F, Gas Mark 7
Preparation time: about 40 minutes
plus cooling and chilling
Cooking time: 1 hour 15 minutes-1 hour
18 minutes

SPICY SHEPHERD'S PIE

25 g/1 oz butter
1 onion, peeled and finely
    chopped
25 g/1 oz plain flour
200 ml/7 fl oz light stock
450 g/1 lb cooked minced
    lamb
1 tablespoon
    Worcestershire sauce
pinch of ground nutmeg
large pinch of mild curry
    powder
salt and freshly ground
    black pepper
1 × 225 g (8 oz) can
    baked beans
1 recipe Creamy Mashed
    Potatoes (see p. 106)

Place the butter and onion in a bowl. Cover and cook on FULL POWER for 3 minutes, stirring once. Add the flour, blending well. Gradually add the stock, lamb, Worcestershire sauce, nutmeg, curry powder and salt and pepper to taste, blending well. Cook on FULL POWER for 10 minutes, stirring twice.

Add the baked beans and stir well to blend. Spoon into a serving dish and cover with the creamed potatoes. Cook on FULL POWER for 4 minutes.

Place under a preheated hot grill and cook until golden, about 5-8 minutes. Serve hot.

To freeze
Cool quickly, cover, seal, label and freeze for up to 3 months.

Serves: 4
Power setting: FULL
Conventional oven setting: GRILL
Preparation time: 20-25 minutes
Cooking time: 22-25 minutes
Suitable for freezing

TURKEY AND BACON PIE

25 g/1 oz butter
100 g/4 oz mushrooms, wiped and sliced
1 bunch spring onions, trimmed and chopped
25 g/1 oz plain flour
300 ml/½ pint chicken stock or milk
3 tablespoons sage and onion mustard
225 g/8 oz cold roast turkey, chopped
salt and freshly ground black pepper
4 rashers middle or back bacon, rinded
225 g/8 oz puff pastry
beaten egg or milk to glaze

Place the butter in a bowl and cook on FULL POWER for ½ minute to melt. Add the mushrooms and spring onions, blending well. Cook for 3 minutes, stirring once.

Add the flour, blending well. Gradually add the stock or milk and cook for 3½-4 minutes, stirring every 1 minute until smooth and thickened. Add the mustard, turkey and salt and pepper to taste, blending well. Leave to cool.

Line a 900 ml (1½ pint) pie dish with the bacon. Spoon over the turkey filling.

Roll out the pastry on a lightly floured surface and use to cover the filling. Press the edges well to seal, then crimp to give a decorative effect. Use any trimmings to decorate the pie as liked. Make 2 slashes in the centre of the pie crust to allow any steam to escape. Brush with beaten egg or milk to glaze.

Cook in a preheated hot oven for about 30 minutes until crisp and golden. Serve at once.

To freeze
Cool quickly, wrap in foil, seal, label and freeze for up to 3 months.

Serves: 4
Power setting: FULL
Conventional oven setting: 220°C, 425°F, Gas Mark 7
Preparation time: 25-30 minutes
Cooking time: 37-37½ minutes
Suitable for freezing

CHICKEN WITH CAMEMBERT

1 × 1.4 kg (3 lb) oven-ready chicken, prepared for cooking
2 small Camembert cheese portions, sliced
25 g/1 oz butter
salt and freshly ground black pepper

Carefully loosen the skin from the breast of the chicken and stuff with the cheese slices. Secure the skin back in place with wooden cocktail sticks.

Place on a roasting rack or upturned saucer in a cooking dish and dot with the butter. Season with salt and pepper to taste and cook on FULL POWER for 18 minutes, turning the dish twice.

Remove and place in a roasting tin, basting with the juices. Cook in a preheated hot oven for 15-20 minutes until crisp and golden.

Serve hot or cold with a salad.

Serves: 4
Power setting: FULL
Conventional oven setting: 220°C, 425°F, Gas Mark 7
Preparation time: 15 minutes
Cooking time: 33-38 minutes

CRUNCHY APPLE CRISP

3 cooking apples, peeled, cored and sliced
4 tablespoons frozen concentrated orange juice, thawed
75 g/3 oz butter, softened
75 g/3 oz brown sugar
175 g/6 oz sweet biscuits, crushed
orange slices to decorate

Place the apples in a flan dish and spoon over the orange juice.

Lightly mix the butter with the sugar and biscuit crumbs. Spoon over the apples and cook on FULL POWER for 6 minutes, turning the dish once.

Place under a preheated hot grill and cook until golden and crips, about 3-5 minutes.

Decorate with orange slices and serve hot with cream.

Serves: 4
Power setting: FULL
Conventional oven setting: GRILL
Preparation time: 15 minutes
Cooking time: 9-11 minutes

CUSTARD TART

1 × 20 cm (8 inch) cooked
  flan case (see p. 237)
1 egg
1 egg yolk
25 g/1 oz sugar
250 ml/8 fl oz milk
ground nutmeg

Place the flan on a serving dish. Beat the egg with the egg yolk, sugar and milk. Strain through a sieve into the flan case. Sprinkle with ground nutmeg.

Cook for 15-18 minutes on DEFROST POWER until the custard is almost set, turning the dish three times. Leave to cool – the custard will set upon standing.

Cut into wedges to serve.

Serves: 4
Power setting: DEFROST
Conventional oven setting: 200°C,
400°F, Gas Mark 6
Preparation time: 30 minutes
Cooking time: 40-45 minutes

FRENCH APPLE TART

1 × 20 cm (8 inch) cooked
  flan case (see p. 237)
350 g/12 oz cooking
  apples, peeled, cored
  and chopped
caster sugar
pinch of ground allspice
3 sweet dessert apples,
  peeled, cored and
  finely sliced
4 tablespoons sieved
  apricot jam
4 tablespoons water
2 teaspoons lemon juice
1 teaspoon arrowroot
  powder

Place the flan on a serving dish. Place the cooking apples in a dish, cover and cook for 4 minutes, stirring once. Purée in a blender or press through a fine nylon sieve. Sweeten to taste with the sugar and add the allspice, blending well. Spread on to the base of the flan.

Cover with the sliced dessert apples, arranged in an attractive design.

Place half the apricot jam, half the water and the lemon juice in a bowl. Cook for 1 minute, stirring once. Spread over the apples and cook for 4 minutes.

Mix the remaining jam with the remaining water and arrowroot. Cook for 1-2 minutes until clear and thickened, stirring twice. Spread over the apples and leave until cool.

Serve cut into wedges with whipped cream.

Serves: 6
Power setting: FULL
Conventional oven setting: 200°C,
400°F, Gas Mark 6
Preparation time: 30 minutes
Cooking time: 35-38 minutes

BROWN BETTY

6 cooking apples, peeled,
  cored and thinly sliced
6 tablespoons brown
  sugar
4 tablespoons soft fresh
  breadcrumbs
finely grated rind and
  juice of 1 lemon
2 tablespoons water
2 tablespoons dry
  breadcrumbs
25 g/1 oz butter

Place half of the apples in a layer in the base of a heatproof dish. Mix 4 tablespoons of the sugar and the soft breadcrumbs together. Spoon over the apples. Top with the remaining apples.

Mix the lemon rind and juice with the water and pour over the fruit. Mix the dry breadcrumbs with the remaining sugar, blending well. Sprinkle over the fruit and dot with the butter.

Cover and cook on FULL POWER for 8-10 minutes, turning the dish twice.

Place under a hot grill and cook until golden and crisp, about 5 minutes. Serve hot with ice cream or whipped cream.

Serves: 4-6
Power setting: FULL
Conventional oven setting: GRILL
Preparation time: 15 minutes
Cooking time: 13-15 minutes

Microwave and Convection Cooking

Microwave and convection ovens are the latest and most sophisticated kinds of microwave oven to be marketed. They enable food to be cooked by microwave or convection means alone, together or in tandem. Some new models also allow the cook to microwave and grill food at the same time.

This means that it is now possible to achieve speedily cooked dishes that have all the flavour and appearance of conventionally cooked foods, but in a fraction of the usual time.

Most manufacturers of gas or electric microwave-and-convection combination ovens recommend a preheating time, usually 10 minutes, and you should follow your handbook instructions when using the recipes in this section.

LOIN OF PORK CAROLINA

1 × 1.4 kg (3 lb) loin of
  pork, boned
Stuffing:
25 g/1 oz butter
1 onion, peeled and
  chopped
100 g/4 oz sausagemeat
50 g/2 oz fresh
  breadcrumbs
50 g/2 oz prunes, chopped
1 × 50 g (2 oz) packet nuts
  and raisins
salt and black pepper
beaten egg to bind

Place the butter in a bowl with the onion and cook for 3 minutes, stirring once. Add the sausagemeat, breadcrumbs, prunes, nuts and raisins and salt and pepper to taste, blending well. Bind together with a little beaten egg.

Spread the loin of pork with the stuffing, roll up and tie securely with string.

Weigh then place in a roasting dish. Combination cook at 160°C (Gas Mark 3) and MEDIUM POWER together for 18 minutes per 450 g/1 lb. Allow to stand for 10 minutes, covered with foil, before carving to serve.

Serves: 6
Power setting: MEDIUM
Convection setting: 160°C (Gas Mark 3)
Preparation time: 20 minutes
Cooking time: about 1 hour

POTATO ROASTIES

450 g/1 lb potatoes,
  peeled and cut into
  pieces
4 tablespoons water
3 tablespoons cooking fat,
  oil or drippings

Place the potatoes in a bowl with the water. Cover and cook on FULL POWER for 12 minutes. Drain thoroughly.

Place the cooking fat, oil or drippings in a roasting dish. Cook in the convection oven at 230°C (Gas Mark 8) for 10 minutes.

Add the potatoes and turn over in the hot fat. Cook in the convection oven for 30 minutes turning over once.

Serves: 3-4
Power setting: FULL
Convection setting: 230°C (Gas Mark 8)
Preparation time: 10 minutes
Cooking time: 52 minutes

CHICKEN WITH HAM SKIRLIE STUFFING

1 × 1.8 kg (4 lb) oven-
ready chicken
25 g/1 oz butter
Skirlie stuffing:
100 g/4 oz medium or
coarse oatmeal
1 onion, peeled and
grated
50 g/2 oz cooked ham,
finely chopped
1 celery stick, scrubbed
and finely chopped
50 g/2 oz butter, melted
¼ teaspoon ground
nutmeg
½ teaspoon dried mixed
herbs
salt and freshly ground
black pepper
3 tablespoons whisky

Prepare the stuffing by mixing the oatmeal with the onion, ham, celery and butter, blending well. Add the nutmeg and herbs with salt and pepper to taste. Bind together with the whisky, mixing well.

Spoon the stuffing into the neck cavity of the chicken and secure with a skewer trussing needle and string.

Shape the remaining stuffing into small balls, to be added to the cooking juices for the last 30 minutes cooking time.

Lightly grease a roasting dish and rub the chicken breast, legs and wings with the butter. Season generously with salt and pepper.

Cook in the convection oven at 190°C (Gas Mark 5) for 40 minutes then at MEDIUM POWER for 25 minutes, turning and basting three times.

Remove from the oven, cover with foil, shiny side inside, and leave to stand for 10-15 minutes before carving. Use the juices to make a gravy (see p. 142).

Serves: 4-6
Power setting: MEDIUM
Convection setting: 190°C (Gas Mark 5)
Preparation time: 25 minutes
Cooking time: 1 hour 15 minutes-1 hour 20 minutes

SAVOURY CHEESE COBBLER

25 g/1 oz butter
1 onion, peeled and
chopped
½ green pepper, cored,
seeded and chopped
25 g/1 oz plain flour
1 × 213 g (7½ oz) can
butter beans
1 × 213 g (7½ oz) can
peeled tomatoes
chicken stock
225 g/8 oz cooked
chicken, turkey or
lamb, diced
1 teaspoon mixed dried
herbs
salt and freshly ground
black pepper
Topping:
100 g/4 oz self-raising
flour
pinch of salt
50 g/2 oz butter
50 g/2 oz cheese, grated
milk to mix

Place the butter in a bowl and cook on FULL POWER for 1 minute. Add the onion and pepper, cover and cook on FULL POWER for 3 minutes, stirring once. Stir in the flour, blending well.

Drain the juices from the beans and tomatoes into a jug and make up to 300 ml/½ pint with chicken stock. Add to the onion mixture, blending well. Cook on FULL POWER for 2 minutes, stirring once.

Add the beans, tomatoes, meat, herbs and salt and pepper to taste, blending well. Spoon into a 750 ml (1½ pint) pie dish.

To make the topping, sift the flour and salt into a bowl. Rub in the butter and stir in half of the cheese. Add sufficient milk to make a soft dough. Knead lightly on a lightly floured surface and form into a round. Cut into 8 wedges.

Arrange the wedges in a circle on top of the meat with the pointed ends to the centre of the dish. Brush the cobbler topping lightly with milk and sprinkle with the remaining cheese. Cook at 220°C (Gas Mark 7) for 20 minutes. Serve hot.

Serves: 3-4
Power setting: FULL
Convection setting: 220°C (Gas Mark 7)
Preparation time: 20-25 minutes
Cooking time: 26 minutes

CROWN OF LAMB

1 × 1.25 kg (3 lb) crown
  roast
Stuffing:
175 g/6 oz fresh white
  breadcrumbs
3 tablespoons chopped
  parsley
100 g/4 oz raisins
grated rind and juice of 2
  oranges
salt and freshly ground
  black pepper
25 g/1 oz butter
1 onion, peeled and finely
  chopped
1 egg, beaten
2 tablespoons chopped
  walnuts

Wash and dry the crown roast with absorbent kitchen paper.

To make the stuffing, place the breadcrumbs, parsley, raisins, orange rind and salt and pepper to taste in a bowl.

Place the butter in a small bowl and cook on FULL POWER for ½ minute to melt. Add the onion, cover and cook for 2 minutes. Add to the stuffing mixture with the orange juice and beaten egg. Bind well to make a stuffing. Fold in the walnuts.

Place the crown in a roasting dish and fill the centre with the stuffing mixture.

Preheat the oven to 190°C (Gas Mark 5) and cook for 35 minutes, then on MEDIUM POWER alone for 25 minutes.

Remove from the oven, wrap in foil and stand for 15 minutes before serving.

Serves: 4-6
Power settings: FULL, MEDIUM
Convection setting: 190°C (Gas Mark 5)
Preparation time: 15 minutes
Cooking time: 1 hour 27½ minutes

COMBINATION ROASTING CHART

Meat	Cut	Cooking Time	Internal Temperature After Standing
Beef	Best Cuts	10 minutes per 450 g/1 lb at 190°C (Gas Mark 5) then 7½ minutes per 450 g/1 lb on MEDIUM POWER	55°C Rare
		10 minutes per 450 g/1 lb at 190°C (Gas Mark 5) then 8½ minutes per 450 g/1 lb on MEDIUM POWER	65°C Medium
		10 minutes per 450 g/1 lb at 190°C (Gas Mark 5) then 10 minutes per 450 g/1 lb on MEDIUM POWER	77°C Well Done
Lamb	Leg, Shoulder, Fillet and Breast	11 minutes per 450 g/1 lb at 190°C (Gas Mark 5) then 10 minutes per 450 g/1 lb on MEDIUM POWER	82°C Medium to Well Done
Pork	Joints – boned or bone left in	10 minutes per 450 g/1 lb at 190°C (Gas Mark 5) then 10 minutes per 450 g/1 lb on MEDIUM POWER	77°C Well Done
Veal	Joint – boned and rolled	10 minutes per 450 g/1 lb at 190°C (Gas Mark 5) then 15 minutes per 450 g/1 lb on MEDIUM POWER	77°C Well Done
	Stuffed Breast	10 minutes per 450 g/1 lb at 190°C (Gas Mark 5) then 10 minutes per 450 g/1 lb on MEDIUM POWER	77°C Well Done
Poultry	Chicken – up to 2 kg/4½ lb	10 minutes per 450 g/1 lb at 190°C (Gas Mark 5) then 6 minutes per 450 g/1 lb on MEDIUM POWER	82°C Well Done
	– larger than 2 kg/4½ lb	10 minutes per 450 g/1 lb at 190°C (Gas Mark 5) then 4 minutes per 450 g/1 lb on FULL POWER	82°C Well Done
	Duck	10 minute per 450 g/1 lb at 190°C (Gas Mark 5) then 4 minutes per 450 g/1 lb on MEDIUM POWER	85°C Well Done
	Turkey	8 minutes per 450 g/1 lb at 190°C (Gas Mark 5) then 3 minutes per 450 g/1 lb on MEDIUM POWER	82°C Well Done

CONVECTION ROASTING/GRILLING CHART

Meat	Cut	Weight/Temperature	Timing
Beef	Fillet	4 cm/1½ inches at 230°C	10-13 minutes Rare
	Rump	2.5-4 cm/1-1½ inches at 230°C	14-16 minutes Medium
	Sirloin	2.5-4 cm/1-1½ inches at 230°C	17-20 minutes Well Done
	Hamburger	225 g/8 oz (frozen) at 230°C	10-15 minutes
	Sirloin or Rib joint	per 450 g/1 lb at 190°C	20-30 minutes per 450 g/1 lb plus 20 minutes
Lamb	Chump, Loin chops or cutlets	2 cm/¾ inch at 230°C	15-17 minutes Medium 18-20 minutes Well Done
	Shoulder or Leg joint	per 450 g/1 lb at 190°C	20-25 minutes per 450 g/1 lb plus 25 minutes
Pork	Chops	2 cm/¾ inch at 230°C	18-20 minutes Well Done
	Bacon	225 g/8 oz rashers at 230°C	12-15 minutes
	Sausages	450 g/1 lb thick at 230°C	15-16 minutes
	Gammon slice	2 cm/¾ inch at 230°C	10-12 minutes
	Loin or Leg joint	per 450 g/1 lb at 190°C	25-35 minutes per 450 g/1 lb plus 30 minutes

BOBOTIE

450 g/1 lb minced lamb
1 onion, peeled and chopped
juice of 1 lemon
50 g/2 oz blanched almonds
25 g/1 oz raisins
2 teaspoons curry powder
salt and freshly ground black pepper
4 eggs
1 teaspoon sugar
300 ml/½ pint milk

Mix the lamb with the onion and lemon juice. Chop half of the almonds and add with the raisins, curry powder and salt and pepper to taste. Spoon into a medium-sized ovenproof dish.

Beat one of the eggs with the sugar and stir into the meat mixture, blending well.

Beat the remaining eggs with the milk and pour over the meat. Sprinkle with the remaining whole almonds.

Combination bake at 180°C (Gas Mark 4) and FULL POWER together for 15-20 minutes. Serve with a tomato sauce if liked.

Serves: 4
Power setting: FULL
Convection setting: 180°C (Gas Mark 4)
Preparation time: 20 minutes
Cooking time: 15-20 minutes

BLACK PUDDING IN BATTER

1 tablespoon oil
1 onion, peeled and finely sliced
75 g/3 oz mushrooms, wiped and sliced
675 g/1½ lb black pudding, cut into large chunks
100 g/4 oz plain flour
pinch of salt
1 egg
1 egg yolk
300 ml/½ pint milk

Preheat the oven to 230°C (Gas Mark 8).

Place the oil, onion, mushrooms and black pudding in a medium-sized heatproof dish. Cook in the convection oven for 10 minutes.

Sift the flour and salt into a bowl. Make a well in the centre and add the egg and egg yolk. Mix, gradually drawing the flour into the egg, to make a thick paste. Gradually add the milk, beating to make a smooth batter.

Pour the prepared batter over the black pudding mixture, return to the oven and cook at 230°C, Gas Mark 8, for 25 minutes then on FULL POWER for 5 minutes. Serve at once.

Serves: 4
Power setting: FULL
Convection setting: 230°C (Gas Mark 8)
Preparation time: 10-15 minutes
Cooking time: 50 minutes (including preheating)

GAMMON AND APRICOT PIE

225 g/8 oz dried apricots
water
2 large gammon rashers,
    cut about 2.5 cm (1
    inch) thick
25 g/1 oz sultanas
salt and freshly ground
    black pepper
3 large potatoes, peeled
    and thinly sliced
300 ml/½ pint hot
    chicken stock
50 g/2 oz melted butter

Place the apricots in a bowl and cover with water. Cook on FULL POWER for 3½ minutes.

Remove the rind from the gammon and snip the edges evenly to prevent curling during cooking.

Place the gammon rashers in a large shallow dish and top with the drained apricots. Sprinkle with the sultanas and salt and pepper to taste.

Place the potatoes on top of the gammon in overlapping slices and cover with the chicken stock. Brush with the melted butter.

Combination bake at 190°C (Gas Mark 5) and FULL POWER together for 30 minutes. Serve hot.

Serves: 4
Power setting: FULL
Convection setting: 190°C (Gas Mark 5)
Preparation time: 20 minutes
Cooking time: 33½ minutes

SMOKED HADDOCK PARCELS

Pastry:
175 g/6 oz plain flour
75 g/3 oz butter
50 g/2 oz cheese, grated
beaten egg to bind
Filling:
100 g/4 oz cooked
    smoked haddock,
    skinned, boned and
    flaked
50 g/2 oz cheese, grated
2-3 tablespoons tartare
    sauce
1 egg yolk, beaten
salt and freshly ground
    black pepper
15 g/½ oz butter, melted

Preheat the convection or combination oven to 200°C (Gas Mark 6).

To prepare the pastry, sift the flour into a bowl. Rub in the butter until the mixture resembles fine breadcrumbs. Stir in the cheese and sufficient egg to bind to a pliable dough.

Roll out on a lightly floured surface and cut out 4×15 cm (6 inch) rounds.

Mix all the filling ingredients together. Divide into four equal portions and place each portion in the middle of each pastry round.

Moisten the edges with water and draw up to make triangular-shaped envelopes, pressing firmly to seal. Glaze with beaten egg and place on a baking tray.

Combination bake at 200°C (Gas Mark 6) and MEDIUM POWER together for 10 minutes.

Allow to cool on a wire rack. Serve warm or cold.

Serves: 4
Power setting: MEDIUM
Convection setting: 200°C (Gas Mark 6)
Preparation time: 30 minutes
Cooking time: 20 minutes (including preheating)

PÂTÉ EN CROÛTE

1 recipe hot crust pastry
    (see p. 250)
100 g/4 oz lamb's liver,
    finely chopped
225 g/8 oz pork
    sausagemeat
225 g/8 oz lean pork,
    minced
1 small onion, peeled and
    finely chopped   (cont.)

Line a 450 g (1 lb) loaf dish with grease-proof paper, leaving the paper high enough around the edge so that the pâté can be lifted out for cooking.

Prepare the pastry as on p. 250. Use two-thirds to line the base and sides of the loaf dish.

Prepare the filling by mixing the liver with the sausagemeat, pork, onion, garlic, sage, sherry and salt and pepper to taste,

blending the mixture well.

Spoon into the pastry-lined loaf dish. Roll out the remaining pastry to make a lid for the pâté. Brush the top edge of the pâté with beaten egg and position the lid. Crimp the edges to seal firmly. Make a small vent in the top of the pâté crust and decorate with any pastry trimmings as liked. Brush the pastry and decoration with beaten egg to make a glaze.

1 garlic clove, peeled
and crushed
½ teaspoon dried sage
1 tablespoon sherry
salt and freshly ground
black pepper
beaten egg to glaze

Carefully lift the pâté out of the dish and place on a baking tray.

Combination bake at 180°C (Gas Mark 4) and MEDIUM POWER for 18 minutes.

Allow to cool and serve cold with a Cumberland sauce if liked.

Serves: 6
Power settings: FULL, MEDIUM
Convection setting: 180°C (Gas Mark 4)
Preparation time: 30 minutes
Cooking time: 18 minutes

CHICKEN AND MUSHROOM PIE

900 g/2 lb raw chicken,
chopped
1 tablespoon seasoned
flour
100 g/4 oz mushrooms,
wiped and sliced
25 g/1 oz canned
sweetcorn kernels
1 small onion, peeled and
chopped
pinch of dried mixed
herbs
150 ml/¼ pint chicken
stock
salt and freshly ground
black pepper
1 × 213 g (7½ oz) packet
frozen puff pastry
beaten egg to glaze

Preheat the convection oven to 220°C (Gas Mark 7).

Toss the chicken in the seasoned flour. Place the chicken, mushrooms, sweetcorn, onion and herbs in a medium-sized pie dish. Pour over the hot stock and season to taste with salt and pepper.

Roll out the thawed pastry on a lightly floured surface and use to make a top crust for the pie. Glaze with beaten egg.

Combination bake at 220°C (Gas Mark 7) and FULL POWER together for 13 minutes.

Serve hot straight from the dish.

Serves: 4
Power setting: FULL
Convection setting: 220°C (Gas Mark 7)
Preparation time: 25-30 minutes
Cooking time: 23 minutes (including preheating)

SAUSAGE PLAIT

1 × 215 g (7½ oz) packet
frozen puff pastry,
thawed
225 g/8 oz pork
sausagemeat
1 onion, peeled and
chopped
175 g/6 oz Gouda cheese,
grated
50 g/2 oz mushrooms,
wiped and sliced
3 tablespoons tomato
chutney
1 tablespoon
Worcestershire sauce
pinch of dried mixed
herbs
salt and freshly ground
black pepper
1 egg, beaten

Preheat the convection oven to 190°C (Gas Mark 5).

Roll out the pastry on a lightly floured surface to an oblong measuring 35×30 cm (14×12 inches). Mix the sausagemeat with the onion, cheese, mushrooms, tomato chutney, Worcestershire sauce, herbs, salt and pepper to taste and half the egg.

Spoon the filling down the centre third of the pastry, leaving a 2.5 cm (1 inch) border around the edges. Brush the edges with the remaining beaten egg. Fold the top and bottom borders over the filling. Cut the side borders with a sharp knife at 1 cm (½ inch) intervals to make diagonal slits. Fold and plait these over the filling to completely enclose. Lift on to a baking tray and glaze with the remaining beaten egg.

Combination cook at 190°C (Gas Mark 5) and LOW POWER together for 15 minutes. Serve hot or cold.

Serves: 4
Power setting: LOW
Convection setting: 190°C (Gas Mark 5)
Preparation time: 25-30 minutes
Cooking time: 25 minutes (including preheating)

QUICHE LORRAINE

Pastry:

175 g/6 oz plain flour
pinch of salt
50 g/2 oz lard
50 g/2 oz butter
2-3 tablespoons cold
    water

Filling:

15 g/½ oz butter
1 small onion, peeled and
    chopped
100 g/4 oz bacon, rinded
    and chopped
100 g/4 oz cheese, grated
2 eggs, beaten
2 tablespoons single
    cream
150 ml/¼ pint milk
salt and freshly ground
    black pepper

Preheat the convection oven to 180°C (Gas Mark 4).

To make the pastry, sift the flour and salt into a bowl. Rub in the lard and butter until the mixture resembles fine breadcrumbs. Add the water and bind to a smooth pliable dough. Knead lightly then roll out, on a lightly floured surface, to a round large enough to line a 20 cm (8 inch) flan dish. Prick the base with a fork.

Place the butter for the filling in a bowl and cook on FULL POWER for 1 minute. Add the onion and bacon and cook on FULL POWER for 3 minutes, stirring once. Drain away any fat and spoon into the base of the flan. Sprinkle with the cheese.

Mix the eggs with the cream and milk and pour over the filling. Combination bake at 180°C (Gas Mark 4) and LOW POWER together for 20 minutes.

Serve hot or cold cut into wedges.

Serves: 4-6
Power settings: FULL, LOW
Convection setting: 180°C (Gas Mark 4)
Preparation time: 25-30 minutes
Cooking time: 34 minutes (including preheating)

Illustrated on p. 224

VEAL AND HAM PIE

Pastry:

25 g/1 oz lard
150 ml/¼ pint milk
175 g/6 oz plain flour

Filling:

225 g/8 oz veal, finely
    chopped
100 g/4 oz gammon,
    finely chopped
pinch of dried mixed
    herbs
salt and freshly ground
    black pepper
beaten egg to glaze

Jellied stock:

1 teaspoon powdered
    gelatine
65 ml/2½ fl oz stock

Preheat the convection oven to 180°C (Gas Mark 4).

To make the pastry, place the lard and milk in a bowl and cook on FULL POWER for 2½ minutes. Place the flour in a mixing bowl and stir in the lard mixture. Mix well and knead to a smooth dough.

Cut off one-third of the pastry and reserve for the lid. Roll the remaining pastry into a ball and place underneath a floured jar about 12.5 cm (5 inches) in diameter. Gently mould the pastry up and around the jar. When the pastry reaches about 7.5 cm (3 inches) high around the jar cut away and neaten the top edge. Allow to cool and set before removing the jar.

Meanwhile, mix the veal with the gammon, herbs and salt and pepper to taste, blending well. Spoon into the pastry shell.

Roll out the reserved pastry to make a lid for the pie, reserving any pastry trimmings.

Brush the top edge of the pie with beaten egg and position the lid. Seal and crimp the edges. Cut a small vent in the top and decorate with any pastry trimmings as liked. Glaze the top and sides with egg.

Combination bake at 180°C (Gas Mark 4) and MEDIUM POWER together for 18-20 minutes. Allow to cool.

When cool, dissolve the gelatine in the hot stock and pour through the vent to fill. Chill to set.

Serves: 4
Power settings: FULL, MEDIUM
Convection setting: 180°C (Gas Mark 4)
Preparation time: 30-40 minutes
Cooking time: 30½-32½ minutes
(including preheating)

EVE'S PUDDING

450 g/1 lb cooking apples,
   peeled, cored and
   sliced
50 g/2 oz demerara sugar
1 tablespoon water
50 g/2 oz butter
50 g/2 oz sugar
1 egg, beaten
50 g/2 oz plain flour
¼ teaspoon baking
   powder
milk to mix

Place the apples and sugar in a 1.4 litre (2 pint) ovenproof dish with the water.

Cream the butter and sugar until light and fluffy. Gradually add the egg, beating well to blend. Add the flour, baking powder and sufficient milk to mix to a soft consistency. Spread the mixture evenly over the apples.

Preheat the convection oven to 200°C (Gas Mark 6) and cook for 30 minutes. Cook on MEDIUM POWER alone for a further 4 minutes.

Serve hot straight from the dish.

Serves: 4
Power setting: MEDIUM
Convection setting: 200°C (Gas Mark 6)
Preparation time: 20 minutes
Cooking time: 44 minutes (including preheating)

LEMON MERINGUE PIE

1 × 20 cm (8 inch) pre-
   baked flan case
Filling:
3 tablespoons cornflour
150 ml/¼ pint water
finely grated rind and
   juice of 2 lemons
75 g/3 oz caster sugar
2 egg yolks
Topping:
2 egg whites
100 g/4 oz caster sugar

Mix the cornflour and water in a bowl. Add the lemon rind and juice, blending well. Cook on FULL POWER for 5 minutes, stirring twice until the mixture is smooth and thickened. Add the sugar, blending well. Allow to cool slightly then beat in the egg yolks. Pour into the pre-baked flan case.

Whisk the egg whites until they stand in stiff peaks. Whisk in half the sugar until shiny and glossy. Fold in the remaining sugar with a metal spoon. Spoon or pipe the meringue over the lemon mixture.

Bake at 140°C (Gas Mark 1) for 35-40 minutes until cooked and the meringue is tinged golden.

Serves: 6
Power setting: FULL
Convection setting: 190°C (Gas Mark 5)
then 140°C (Gas Mark 1)
Preparation time: 20 minutes
Cooking time: 55-60 minutes

Illustrated on p. 4

APPLE AND RAISIN STRUDEL

1 × 215 g (7½ oz) packet
   frozen puff pastry,
   thawed
50 g/2 oz butter
25 g/1 oz digestive
   biscuits, crushed
675 g/1½ lb cooking
   apples, peeled, cored
   and sliced
25 g/1 oz raisins
1 teaspoon ground
   cinnamon
2 tablespoons sugar

Preheat the convection oven to 200°C (Gas Mark 6).

Roll out the pastry on a lightly floured surface as thinly as possible to make a large square. Place on a clean tea towel.

Place the butter in a bowl and cook on LOW POWER for 2 minutes to melt. Brush the pastry with the melted butter then sprinkle with the digestive biscuits. Cover with the apples, raisins, cinnamon and sugar.

Using the tea towel as a guide, carefully roll up the pastry like a Swiss roll and tuck under the ends.

Place on a baking tray and brush with the remaining melted butter.

Combination bake at 200°C (Gas Mark 6) and LOW POWER together for 20 minutes.

Serve hot or cold sprinkled with icing sugar if liked.

Serves: 6
Power setting: LOW
Convection setting: 200°C (Gas Mark 6)
Preparation time: 25 minutes
Cooking time: 32 minutes (including preheating)

ACKNOWLEDGMENTS

The author and publisher thank the following microwave oven and food manufacturers for providing recipes included in this book:

A.E.G. Telefunken (UK) Ltd: Baked Egg Custard (p.118), Brunch (p.27), Cabbage with Bacon (p.108), Calf's Liver Helvetia (p.80), Cauliflower with Tomato Sauce (p.104), Chicory with Tomatoes (p.107), Chocolate Lemon Cake (p.182), Fennel with Ham and Cheese Sauce (p.102), Golden Autumn Pudding (p.166), Haddock with Dill Sauce (p.49), Mushrooms with Bacon (p.108), Noodle and Ham Bake (p.136), Peaches with Chocolate Sauce (p.162), Pheasant with Walnuts and Grapes (p.91), Piperanda (p.122), Roquefort Canapes (p.27), Russian Chocolate (p.190), Semolina Pudding (p.160), Tipsy Tea (p.193), Welsh Rarebit (p.27).
Anchor Foods: Bearnaise Sauce (p.141), Cauliflower Soup with Croûtes (p.31), Cheesy Mushrooms and Prawns (p.120), Curry Sauce (p.142), Fruit Compôte (p.226), Ginger Sponge with Grenadine Sauce (p.226), Hollandaise Sauce (p.141), Mulled Wine (p.191), Potted Turkey (p.32), Rich Hot Chocolate (p.190), Stuffed Jacket Potatoes (p.33).
Anchor Hocking Corporation: Asparagus and Herbed Butter Sauce (p.92), Casserol Rice with Spinach (p.129), Chicken Galantine (p.42), Chicken Italian Style (p.211), Garden Vegetable Casserole (p.233), Herbed Rice Salad (p.127), Lemony Salad Appetizer (p.228), Mincemeat Tartlets Noël (p.155), Plaice and Asparagus (p.47), Poached Fruits with Crunchy Topping (p.167), Poussins au Printanier (p.85), Prawn and Watercress Soup (p.35), Raspberry Mousse Cake (p.158), Seafood Pasta Salad (p.132), Smoked Ham Flan (p.30), Smoked Seafood Pâté (p.202), Stuffed Cabbage Rolls (p.207), Stuffed Tomatoes (p.107), Supreme Chocolate Cake (p.180), Vegetables à la Grecque (p.235).
Apple and Pear Development Council: Mock Goose Stuffing (p.146).
Belling and Company Ltd: Apple and Coconut Charlotte (p.163), Blackcurrant Baked Cheesecake (p.160), Butterscotch Sauce (p.145), Carbonnade of Beef (p.67), Chelsea Buns (p.171), Chocolate Refrigerator Cake (p.163), Chocolate Yogurt Cake (p.176), Country-Style Pork (p.72), Devonshire Cod (p.46), Frosted Coconut Cake (p.186), Ginger Cake (p.177), Highland Prawns (p.44), Hot Spicy Grapefruit (p.45), Mediterranean Chutney (p.197), Pâté Maison (p.43), Raspberry Jam (p.195), Rich Fruit Cake (p.175), Spaghetti Milanese (p.135), Tropical-Style Macaroni (p.136).
Birds Eye/Anchor Hocking: Broad Beans with Ham and Cream (p.92), Brussels Sprouts with Horseradish (p.103), Cauliflower in Stilton Sauce (p.105), Creamy Broccoli Spears (p.107), Creole Salad (p.204), Garden Casserole (p.122), Greek Casserole (p.230), Green Bean with Tomato Dressing (p.212), Green Beans in nangy Tomato Sauce (p.95), Herbed Sprouts (p.106), Herby Baby Carrots (p.92), Lamb Fricassée (p.78), Noodles with Pea and Bacon Sauce (p.131), Savoury Pancakes (p.63), Stir-Fry Salad (p.111), Sweetcorn Pudding (p.234), Turkey Divan (p.89).
Bosch Ltd: Apple and Raisin Strudel (p.251), Aubergine Dip (p.26), Cheese Soufflés with Provençale Sauce (p.240), Chestnut Stuffing (p.146), Courgettes Provençale (p.236), Cumberland Sauce (p.143), Fish Cobbler (p.238), Pâté en Croute (p.248), Potato Casserole (p.94), Quiche Lorraine (p.250), Roast Turkey and Cranberry Stuffing (p.89), Roast Veal with Mandarins (p.83), Sausage Plait (p.249), Sole Veronique (p.65), Veal and Ham Pie (p.250).
British Chicken Information Service: Chicken and Coconut Curry (p.84), Chicken Bourguignon (p.87), Chicken Goulash (p.85), Chilli con Pollo (p.86), Mediterranean Meatballs (p.88), Prawn and Chicken Pie (p.83).
British Trout Association: Barbecue Bacon Trout (p.55), Bombay Trout (p.217), Cheesy Trout Burgers (p.55), Cox's Trout (p.202). Devilled Trout

(p.217), Garlic Trout (p.54), Kiwi Trout (p.218), Leafy Trout (p.211), Trout Niçoise (p.63).
Campbells Soups Ltd: Beef Olives Provençale (p.66), Cheesy Baked Potatoes (p.94), Chicken Blanquette (p.86), Chicken Breasts with Asparagus Sauce (p.82).
Cannon Industries Ltd: Apple Crunch Cake (p.181), Bobotie (p.247), Chicken and Mushroom Pie (p.249), Chicken Risotto (p.32), Country-Style Terrine (p.31), Creamed Mushrooms (p.32), Exotic Kipper Pâté (p.33), Fresh Apricot Jam (p.195), Gammon and Apricot Pie (p.248), Loin of Pork Carolina (p.244), Oriental Chicken Soup (p.33), Smoked Haddock Parcels (p.248), Swiss Fondue (p.124), Three-Fruit Marmalade (p.194), Tomato Chutney (p.198).
Colmans Ltd: Provençale Vegetables (p.103), Turkey and Bacon Pie (p.242).
Corning Ltd: Beef Kebab (p.218), Chocolate and Coffee Crown Cake (p.179), Chocolate-Topped Sponge Ring (p.179), Cod Steak and Herbs (p.219), Country Casserole (p.210), Fruit Sorbet (p.212), Kidney Casserole (p.208), Lemon Almond Cheesecake (p.156), Lightning Coffee Cake (p.179), Orange and Apple Fool (p.223), Orange Tipsy Cake (p.178), Peaches and Curaçao (p.226), Pineapple Rice Pudding (p.149), Pork and Beansprout Stir-Fry (p.71), Rhubarb and Orange Compôte (p.226), Savoury Spinach, Ham and Tomato (p.44), Spiced Lamb (p.210), Storecupboard Pizza (p.123), Upside-Down Peach Cake (p.176).
Danish Agricultural Producers: Gammon en Croûte (p.241).
Davis Gelatine: Bavarian Rum Pie (p.161), Easy Chocolate Mousse (p.164), Orange Jelly (p.157), Pineapple Roll (p.159), Raspberry Mousse (p.160).
Duck Advisory Bureau: Duck with Apple Sauce (p.90), Duck with Damson Sauce (p.90), Duck with Grapefruit (p.90).
Findus Foods: Corn on the Cob with Garlic Butter (p.99), Crunchy Green Beans (p.103), Golden Carrot Soup (p.41), Hot Fudge Sauce (p.195), Stuffed Jacket Potatoes (p.99), Tangy Baked Bananas (p.161).
General Foods: Festive Pudding (p.150), Flapjacks (p.184), Hot Swiss Trifle (p.149), Microwave Mint Jelly (p.196), Microwave Strawberry Jam (p.194), Orange and Redcurrant Jelly (p.196), Peach Flakes (p.157), Quick Custard Sauce (p.195), Steamed Golden Syrup Pudding (p.148).
H.J. Heinz Company Ltd: Ham, Egg and Bean Pie (p.240).
Jif Lemon Bureau: Lemony Fish Pancakes (p.239).
Kraft Foods Ltd: Cheeseburgers (p.124), Fruity Sponge Pudding (p.153), 'Philly' Onion Soup (p.41).
Milk Marketing Board: After Eight Coffee (p.191), Foaming Mocha (p.190), Hot Peppermint Chocolate (p.190), Oriental Liver (p.82), Quick Sweetcorn Soup (p.228), Raspberry Cream (p.164), Sausage Goulash (p.29), Seafood Lasagne (p.132), Seafood Scallops (p.64), Sole Bonne Femme (p.59).
Moulinex Ltd: Christmas Pudding (p.166), Cream of Mushroom Soup (p.41), Marble Cake (p.174), Plaice Curry (p.54), Tomato Soup (p.34).
National Dairy Council: Seafood Supper (p.54), Speedy Fudge (p.201).
New Zealand Lamb: Chilli con Carne (p.80).
Outline Slimming Bureau: Boston Bean Bake (p.209), Fruit Condé (p.213), Potato and Carrot Soup (p.207), Sesame Jelly (p.207), Slimmer's Jacket Potatoes (p.203).
Philips Microwave: almond and Ginger Clusters (p.200), Apricot Upside-Down Pudding (p.148), Chilli Macaroni Beef (p.131), Marinated Mushrooms (p.45), Meatloaf with Mushroom Topping (p.70), Pasta Salad Italienne (p.109), Peppermint Meringue with Pears (p.155).
Sea Fish Industry Authority: Bedford Prawns and Scallops (p.53), Bouillabaise (p.55), Cider-Soused Mackerel (p.60), Coley Mediterranean Style (p.52), Crispy Whiting (p.52), Haddock with Prawns (p.50), Herring with Mustard (p.52), St

Clements Plaice (p.50), Stir-Fry Monkfish (p.53).
Sharp Electronics (UK) Ltd: Beef Hot-Pot with Dumplings (p.67), Bortsch (p.35), Bramble Syllabub (p.164), Chicken Breasts Parmesan (p.88), Chicken Chantilly (p.84), Chicken Liver Pâté (p.44), Chocolate Mint Sauce (p.146), Country Rabbit Casserole (p.72-3), Crab Mousse (p.46), Date and Walnut Loaf (p.252), Gammon Steaks Hawaiian (p.81), Halibut with Tomatoes and Cream (p.61), Hungarian Goulash (p.67), Lemon Meringue Pie (p.251), Potato Roasties (p.244), Raspberry and Rhubarb Tart (p.184), Ratatouille (p.99), Savoury Cheese Cobbler (p.245), Soft Treacle Toffee (p.201), Spicy Sausages (p.80-1), Sticky Orange Pudding (p.252), Stroganoff Superb (p.66), Tom and Jerry's (p.191), Yorkshire Tart (p.252).
Siemens Domestic Appliances Ltd: Exotic Chicken (p.239), Ham and Cheese Pudding (p.125), Hot Dogs (p.29), Meatloaf with Cheese (p.121), Mushrooms in Garlic Butter (p.232), Noodles au Gratin (p.228), Quick Vienna Sponge (p.183).
Toshiba (UK) Ltd: Apple Fool (p.158), Barbecued Spareribs (p.72), Braised Pheasant in Cream Sauce (p.91), Brown Rice Salad (p.129), Cheese and Onion Bake (p.125), Chop Suey (p.93), Cider and Sage Jelly (p.196), Cococnut Ice (p.200), Crème Caramel (p.165), Dried Fruit and Banana Loaf (p.177), Egg and Bacon Rolls (p.113), Florentines (p.185), French Apple Tart (p.243), Glazed Beetroot (p.93), Japanese Punch (p.192), Peanut Stuffing (p.147), Red Mullet with Tomatoes (p.60), Ruby Pears (p.162), Seville Duck with Nut Stuffing (p.216), Spicy Almonds (p.27), Steak au Poivre (p.71), Walnut Cake (p.178).
Tricity/THORN EMI Domestic Appliances Ltd: Bread and Butter Pudding (p.153), Chocolate Oaties (p.183), Crab Gratinée Diable (p.45), Devil's Dip (p.26), Malt Loaf (p.172), Mixed Fish Curry (p.59), Moussaka (p.73), Mulligatawny Soup (p.42), Mussel Chowder (p.36), Savarin (p.172), Scampi Provençale (p.56), Skate with Caper Butter (p.61), Spicy Apple Juice (p.192), Streusel Cake (p.179), Sweetcorn Relish (p.197), Swiss Tomato Casserole (p.232), Vegetable Curry (p.233), White Wine Sauce (p.144).
U.S. Rice Council: Devilled Kidneys and Sausage with Rice (p.81), Festive Chicken with Rice (p.130-1), Glazed Ham and Apricot Rice (p.82-3), Haddock with Mushroom Rice (p.56), Kedgeree (p.126), Lamb Pilaf (p.79), Orange-Stuffed Loin of Pork (p.71), Quick Seafood Paella (p.203), Rice-Stuffed Breast of Lamb (p.73), Rice-Stuffed Trout (p.51), Rice Wholemeal Muffins (p.168), Roast Beef with Onion Rice (p.126), Sardine and Rice Snack (p.28), Savoury Rice Ring (p.127), Spanish Omelette (p.112), Spiced Eggs and Cauliflower on Rice (p.121), Spicy Sausage Risotto (p.129), Stuffed Shoulder of Lamb Valencia (p.74), Sweet and Sour Chicken over Rice (p.87), Veal Continental with Rice (p.130), Vegetable Rice Salad (p.110), Vegetable Risotto (p.128).
John West Foods Ltd: Beef and Apricot Curry (p.70), Mackerel Dolmades Style (p.60), Pineapple Streusel (p.159).

The publisher also thanks Toshiba (UK) Ltd, Home Appliances Division for providing the microwave oven and David Mellor, Covent Garden, London, for providing cookware, dishes and cutlery used in photography.

The photographs on pp 75, 77, 97, 205 and 206 were taken by Jay Ladva. The photograph on p.58 was provided by the Sea Fish Industry Authority, that on p.78 by the Milk Marketing Board, and that on p.152 by John West Foods Ltd. All other photographs are from the Octopus Publishing Group picture library.

Line drawings by Linda Broad.

INDEX